A Theory of Modernity

To Gyuri and Marysia

A Theory of Modernity

Agnes Heller

First published 1999

2 4 6 8 10 9 7 5 3 1

Blackwell Publishers Inc.
350 Main Street
Malden, Massachusetts 02148
USA

Blackwell Publishers Ltd
108 Cowley Road
Oxford OX4 1JF
UK

Library of Congress Cataloging-in-Publication Data
Heller, Agnes.
A theory of modernity / Agnes Heller.
p.   cm.
Includes bibliographical references and index.
ISBN 0-631-21612-X (hc: alk. paper)—ISBN 0-631-21613-8 (pbk: alk. paper)
1. Postmodernism—Social aspects.
2. Civilization, Modern—Philosophy.   I. Title.
HM449.H38   1999   306'.01—dc21   99–19776   CIP

British Library Cataloging in Publication Data
A CIP Catalogue record for this book is available from the British Library.

Typeset in 10 on 12 pt Sabon
by Kolam Information Services Pvt., Ltd, Pondicherry, India
Printed in Great Britain by MPG Books, Bodmin, Cornwall

This book is printed on acid-free paper.

Contents

Preface

In this book I present *a* theory of modernity, *one* theory of modernity among all possible theories, including those already in existence. It is hardly an exaggeration to say that all political and social theories and philosophies conceived *in* modernity are also theories or philosophies *of* modernity. They all differ from one another. It is also possible that the self-same author will devise two or more different theories of modernity in his or her lifetime. But these theories will not differ in the same way that philosophical systems conceived by the same author would – as, for example, Wittgenstein's *Philosophical Investigations* differs from his earlier *Tractatus.*

One of the two main sources of theories of modernity are the life experiences of the author (experiences that he or she shares with many others), and the philosophical description of and reflection upon those experiences which encompass the modern tradition and which the author shares with all others involved in understanding modernity. The life experiences will also be filtered through some of those (inherited) descriptions and reflections. As a result, when it comes to theories of modernity, "authorship" will be more blurred than in the case of other philosophical enterprises. There is a common referent in modernity; namely, shared life experiences and the descriptions of and the reflection upon the common elements of these experiences – what we normally call "social reality." But since each life experience is also idiosyncratic, the referent, the so-called "social reality" of modernity, will appear in a very different light if presented from different perspectives. This is why I did not choose *The Philosophy of Modernity* as the title of this book, but *A Theory of Modernity.* The word "theory" is most appropriate to describe two of my preconceptions. Firstly, I want to suggest that each theory somehow *sees* modernity and develops a *view* of modernity – that there is a very strong visual element here. If there exists a capacity of an "intellectual intuition," it is here that one can reckon with it. Empirical observations are at first not ordered by a theory but by a personal intuition into the "essence" of modernity, a kind of *Wesenschau* insofar as modernity shows itself to the person who sees it as a vision of the true *essence* of modernity. This vision which grows out from experiences has to refer back to common experiences. Moreover, it needs to prove that the vision of the essence of modernity is reasonable or rational insofar as it can be made plausible. Although one can make one's theory plausible in different ways, this cannot be accomplished by demonstrations and arguments alone, because certain facts need to be presented. These facts are, of course, always interpreted facts, but they need to be presented in their capacity of being facts – that is, of "what is the case." This kind of presentation is beautifully exemplified by Foucault. Foucault offers an authorial intuition into the essence of modernity with and through the interpreted presentations of modern texts, writings, or institutions. No theory of modernity can avoid a reference to knowledge – common, shared knowledge – however perspectivistic the *theoria* of the author may be. In order to think about something, one needs to present that something about which one thinks, just as Heidegger had to refer to commonly known and almost self-evidently representative technological devices and other "things," such as the atom bomb (although he radically severed thinking and knowing). One thinks about things one knows; one can think *with* other people only about things everyone knows, without being aware of the significance and real essence of the things known.

More often than not, theories of history assume the form of the social and political sciences, or at least use the content of those sciences as the raw material and springboard from which to think – as a trampoline for thinking, if you will. The question of how far and to what extent social sciences are sciences, and what "being a science" means when it comes to theories of modernity, cannot be answered in general terms.[1] For example, "science" means something entirely different for Hegel and Weber, Nietzsche and Luhmann, and Durkheim and Barthes. I cannot replace the word "theory" (in *A Theory of Modernity*) with "philosophy," for even if many theories of modernity are philosophical in part of their presentation, only a few of them could have been described as a philosophy of modernity, and even fewer now in the midst of the deconstruction of metaphysics.

To sum up: what I present here is my intuition into the essence of modernity, founded on my own life experiences. Some of those experiences are idiosyncratic; some of them I share with all those who lived through the Holocaust and totalitarian dictatorships; some again I think I share with all the men and women (and not just with theorists) who –

nowadays – reflect upon their own experiences with modernity and attempt to understand modern life in general. To express myself in old philosophical jargon: I fuse the perspectives of the one, the few, and the many. All of these could have resulted in writing a historical novel rather than a theory of modernity, but I also refer to many traditional texts, which – either directly or indirectly, with or without having this purpose – present a philosophy or theory of modernity. I incorporate their perspectives into my idiosyncratic intuition to the extent that it is possible.

There are entire libraries filled with books written on the different theories of modernity. I could have jumped onto this respectable bandwagon, but I decided against that option. If before presenting one's own intuition one first presents all the representative positions/intuitions about the same thing, one then writes a handbook, a compendium, a textbook on the theories of modernity, but not a theory of modernity. Such a book addresses first and foremost the people who want to collect information (who is who, who said what) instead of thinking about the things of most concern to oneself. I wanted to address people who ponder our shared world. Of course, I do not want to superimpose my theory of modernity onto my readers. But I also do not want them to pick one theory of their own from among the rich supply. Rather, I want them to give their own intuition a chance to grasp the essence of modernity, to see modernity through their own life experiences with the help of the crutch of tradition that they can either use or throw away.

I present, at the beginning, three representative theories of modernity: those of Hegel, Marx, and Weber. They are "classical" theories, and all-encompassing, or at least they can serve as the fundaments of all-encompassing theories. The first two are typical modernistic philosophies/ theories which initiated "isms," whereas the third has undercut its own possibility to initiate an "ism." Although Weber has encompassed more essential elements of modernity than Hegel and Marx, he can also be regarded as the first swallow of the postmodern trend that became prominent one half-century later. In all of the following chapters, I present my own perspective on the "essence of modernity." I refer to other philosophies and theories, even to the most significant ones, but generally only in the footnotes and not in the main text. I present quotations mainly in the footnotes. Moreover, I do not even refer to the representative authors on all occasions and in all contexts where they have something significant to say, but limit and concentrate my references to their works in the discussion of issues to which they contributed most, or where the centerpoint of their perspectives, their central idea about the essence of modernity, can be best located. For example, Nietzsche is discussed first in the chapter on modernity's dynamics,

Heidegger eminently in the chapter about technology, Adorno in the chapter on culture, Habermas in the chapter on democracy, Foucault in the chapter on the civilizing process, and so on. I wanted to write a readable book, a relatively slim book, and this was the only way to do it.

A Theory of Modernity can also be read as the last part of a trilogy which I started with *A Theory of History* and continued with *A Philosophy of History in Fragments*.[2] Yet it was not originally intended to be the last volume of such a trilogy. The destiny of modernity became a matter of central theoretical concern in my discussions with my late husband, Ferenc Fehér, beginning in 1978. We wrote a few studies together, as well as separately, on various aspects of modernity. The first account of our common concept of modernity was the study "Modernity's Pendulum," which we planned to publish together with a few other papers written on Eastern Europe in the period of transition. The death of Ferenc Fehér put an end to these plans, and for a while I gave up the project of a theory of modernity altogether.[3] In May 1995 I was invited to give a graduate course in Caracas, and I chose the theory of modernity as my lecture topic. The main structure of this book is based on the "Caracas lectures." In the following year, in May 1996, I gave a course on the same topic in Pisa, and during the fall of the same year at the Graduate Faculty of the New School. In Pisa I added the main section of the first chapter, and in New York the "historical" chapter, to the Caracas lectures. After having elaborated my theory of modernity for the third time, I realized that I must put an end to it. And the proper end to a project is to write it down.

Yet in Pisa, I already became aware of the continuity between my two former books on a theory (philosophy) of history and my theory of modernity in the making. This is a theory of modernity from a postmodern perspective, and the postmodern perspective was elaborated in the two books on history, particularly in *Philosophy of History in Fragments*. The philosophical presuppositions of my theory of modernity are simply taken over from the two books on history/historicity. I will sum up those presuppositions without elaborating them, just enough to clarify my philosophical hypotheses about the essence of modernity. These hypotheses can be proven, but being proven is not the warranty of being true. One can also prove that they are wrong. The hypothetical character of the presupposition must be emphasized, for they will be presented in a categorical manner. I could have introduced all my sentences with the preamble, "I think so," "in my mind," "this is only my opinion," and so on. Yet, irrespective of the waste of space and energy, this would have been lacking in sincerity. Of course, everything that I am going to write about modernity, my philosophical suppositions included, serves as the foundations of my own perspective, of my own *theoria*. But if I were not convinced that my theory is at least one of the possible true theories of modernity – further, if I were not almost certain that my presuppositions are not just opinions but also true opinions (in Plato's sense), if I were not ready to take philosophical responsibility for them – I would hardly have put pen to paper. Without a firm theoretical foundation one cannot elaborate any relatively consistent theory of philosophy (not even in fragments). But it is also the matter of responsibility to make *the choice of the foundation transparent* first and foremost to ourselves, then also to the readers. Some foundations are better than others, yet even the most solid foundations are chosen by the man or woman whose philosophy rests on it. They cannot be taken for granted; they are not absolutely firm. They remain unproved, yet they are the only crutches upon which an authentic philosophy can rely.[4]

Agnes Heller
Budapest, May 1999

Acknowledgments

Many ideas developed in this book have grown out from lengthy and passionate discussions with my late husband, Ferenc Fehér.

I also received inspiration from discussions with my students in several classes held on the questions of modernity at the New School University from 1986 until 1996.

I thank György Markus, Maria Markus, and Mihaly Vajda for reading the book in manuscript and helping to correct it by making valuable comments.

I am grateful to Marcia Morgan for editing the book with friendly care and patience and for preparing the index. Thanks are also due to Aaron Vlasak for his editing assistance.

Agnes Heller

1

Modernity from a Postmodern Perspective:

The Philosophical Presuppositions

These days, "postmodern" is both a household expression and a slogan. The so-called postmoderns are either celebrated or abused. It seems as if this description (or self-description), postmodern, cannot be introduced into a serious conversation because the principle of contradiction (or identity) does not apply to it whatsoever. The same can be asserted and negated about the postmodern simultaneously in the same relation. One must first clarify what it means to be postmodern before introducing the term into a discourse – this time into the discourse on modernity. Yet employment of the term seems important, and not only in this theory of modernity. If one decides to use it, one needs to circumscribe its employment.[1]

I will not speak of postmodernists unless I refer to certain styles and tendencies in art, particularly in architecture. I will not use the term "postmodernism," for I circumscribe the postmodern perspective as being alien to all "isms." Finally, I will not identify the postmodern with post-*histoire*, insofar as this identification presupposes the juxtaposition of the postmodern with the modern.

There are two uses of the term postmodern which are not necessarily connected to postmodernism, postmodernists, and post-*histoire*. I term the first use the "unreflected concept of postmodernity" and the second use the "reflected concept of postmodernity." This is not a distinction of contents but of attitudes. The unreflected concept of postmodernity is naive. Unaware, it carries on the attitude of the grand narrative and the correspondence theory of truth, attitudes which it otherwise – and consciously – rejects. Everything is relative, there is no truth, all cultures are equal – such and similar statements are uttered with certainty and with an air of superiority. Reflected postmodernity is self-reflective, for it also constantly questions itself. It is not only ironical[2] but it treats irony also ironically, or rather with humor. Romantic irony is related to pathos, humor rather to seriousness and a kind of weak skepticism. It is true that both naive and reflected postmodernity are offspring of the Enlightenment. They are related and therefore can inbreed. But my perspective will be the perspective of reflected (self-reflected) postmodernity.

There are different versions of reflected postmodernity. Mine is but one version among many. Yet there are a few common features in their perspectives, attitudes, and what they share: this is why they belong to the family of the "reflected postmoderns."[3]

I understand the several versions of reflected postmodernity as manifestations of the "postmodern historical consciousness."[4] What do I mean by "historical consciousness"? The term does not express a commitment to a paradigm of consciousness. If one wishes, one can think of it along with a paradigm of language, of communication. It also makes sense in a philosophy which rejects all paradigms. The term "historical" stands for the German *geschichtlich*, and not for *historisch*. There is no human life without historical (*geschichtliches*) consciousness, whereas what we call *historisch* is modern.

Historicity is the constituent of the human condition. Men are mortal, for they are conscious of their finitude. Men are also creatures with (at least) two identities. They are identical with themselves and they are identical with at least one group, the so-called "social *a priori*" into which their "genetic *a priori*" had been thrown, and with which it needs to be dovetailed in the process of becoming a certain kind of person. Identity is not formal identity; it means sameness through difference and differentiations.[5] Identity (in the above sense) is also temporal and spatial. It includes identity with a place (or with a few representative places) and identity through time. Identity in place and identity through time is the geography and narrative of a people's, or group of people's, life. The meanings that a group of people attribute to its way of life – its language, rules, and norms, beliefs, ceremonies, and so on – are homogenized – although not entirely – into one meaning; that is, into a world which includes the geography and the narrative of this people. The famous questions of Gaugin's Tahiti painting – "Where did we come from? What are we? Where are we going?" – are constantly raised and answered.[6] I call the answer to these questions the "historical consciousness." It is the historical consciousness that presents a world. Again, it consists of the geography and the narrative(s) of a people or of a culture.

I distinguish below between six stages of historical consciousness. They are philosophical and not empirical concepts, but they are also ideal types:[7]

1   Consciousness of unreflected generality. *The myth.* One people thinks about itself as humans, as generality. Others are excluded. The birth of the world is tantamount to, or leads toward, the coming into being of this people. There is no future tense, but the repetition of the same.
2   Consciousness of generality reflected in particularity. *The histories.* Consciousness reflects upon the state, city (citizens), about the political institutions coming into being. Yet the human condition as such is reflected in the histories (be they mythical and historiographical). There is no future other than repetition of the *telos.*
3   Consciousness of unreflected universality. *The universal myth.* The human condition itself appears in its universality, albeit unreflected (there are no legitimate alternative stories). Historical consciousness as temporality (narrative) becomes three-dimensional (for example, creation).
4   Consciousness of particularity reflected in generality. *The foundational stories of modernity.* Generality is reflected (humanism, the contract) as resulting in the modern condition. The modern condition is thus reflected as if it were the human condition (generality). Histories include all the known past cultures and presuppose a future as an element of the unknown.
5   Consciousness of reflected universality. *The universal history (grand narrative).* There is one single history, written with a capital H – namely, the world history of the human race as such. The present is thought of as the result of the whole historical development, whether it is conceived as progressive or as regressive. The future can be known, predicted, and conceived. It is a total (totalized) future.
6   Consciousness of reflected generality. *The postmodern consciousness.* I will give an account of the constituents of the postmodern consciousness as I see them. In the main, I will stick to features which are shared by several variants of the reflected postmodern consciousness. But first I need to briefly give my story concerning the stages (the *Gestalten*) of the historical consciousness sensible.

My story resembles a grand narrative, for it gives an account of the changes in historical consciousness in sequences that form a kind of a spiral. The last stage returns to the first stage (both are consciousnesses of generality), except that the last stage is the reflected form of the first. Whether the changes I describe here can be termed "progressive" or "regressive," or neither, varies with the eye of the beholder. On my part I do not evaluate this, at least not directly. Instead of raising the question of whether it is progressive or regressive, I raise a different one: For what are we (the denizens of the present age) responsible? The denizens of the present are first and foremost responsible for the present or, rather, for people and for things of the present. Responsibility implies at least an implicit evaluation; one is responsible for something eminently important. The present world is eminently important for the denizens of this world, not because it is better or worse than other worlds, but because this is the world in which we are in charge of certain people and things. The sense of *being in charge* is incipient in the reflected postmodern consciousness.

Why "consciousness of generality," unreflected and reflected? Because, contrary to the other kinds and forms of historical consciousness, all of which contained a normative concept of either a human group or of humankind, or at least of the human condition (whether the human condition had been described in terms of dignity or sin does not matter in this context), the empirical humankind – that is, all people who live on our globe at a certain time, irrespective of their culture – shares the consciousness of generality and reflected generality alone. There is no human group or human culture without a myth. They are entirely different, they do not know about one another, they do not even regard each other as humans; yet they share one thing, namely the stage of historical consciousness. In all other levels of the historical consciousness, the stage is unshared. Some peoples or cultures enter one stage, yet others do not. It is not only temporality and spatiality that is de-synchronized, but the understanding of spatiality and of temporality itself.

The consciousness of reflected generality has already gained momentum. Modernity is general; it steamrolls over the entire Earth. Now, once again, the whole world with all of its people shares the same stage; and if it shared nothing else, it still would share historical consciousness. Generality has become reflected, for the idea of the common fate of what is *contemporaneous* has already appeared on the common horizon.

––––––

Postmodernity is not a stage that comes after modernity, it is not the retrieval of modernity – it *is* modern. More precisely, the postmodern perspective could perhaps best be described as the self-reflective consciousness of modernity itself. It is a kind of modernity that knows itself in a Socratic way. For it (also) knows that it knows very little, if anything at all.[8]

I speak about the modernists in the past tense not because their position is in fact in the past, but because the modernist consciousness preceded the postmodern one. It is true here, as usual, that one seeks in vain for a linear temporal sequence. For example, at the turn of the century postmodern consciousness – the reflected kind included – had already made its appearance, and it was a strong showing.[9] For a long while afterwards, mainly due to the vicissitudes of European history, many versions of high modernism gathered momentum.[10] In the past 20–30 years the postmodern perspective has turned back with a vengeance and become dominant. Yet the modernist perspective is not entirely gone, and might yet make a comeback. Why is this so? A modernist view which comes after the strong showing of the postmodern perspective will be part and parcel of the postmodern condition. Once one option or view among many, modernist modernity cannot regain its absolute self-confidence. It needs to take its adversaries seriously, and if it does it will no longer be the same.[11]

The modernist moderns have claimed a privileged position in history for themselves. They assumed that because of the present stage of historical development, they are the first to understand what history is about. None of the answers to the questions "Where did we come from?," "What are we?," and "Where are we going?" have ever been true or correct. Only the moderns can answer those questions correctly and truly. None of our predecessors had an insight into the future. Only the moderns know mainly what the future is going to bring, even if they do not know all of the details. None of our predecessors could consciously create history, prepare the future, or plan it. Only the moderns are able to do these things. The answers to the question "What warrants the privilege of the moderns?" varied. Yet knowledge played a pivotal role in all of the answers. Science is a modern invention. Modern science, scientific knowledge as such, gives modern men an insight into the laws or regularities of historical development and allows for extrapolation, just as much as the knowledge of the laws of nature makes possible extrapolation with almost total certitude. Many variations have been composed on this main theme. The dominant version – variation – was the progressivist one. According to the creed of this version, science guarantees not only an insight into the future, but also the constant improvement of everything, such as technology, the economy, art, well-being, and the like.[12] Yet the pessimistic predictions also claimed scientific exactitude. Spengler's famous *Decline of the West* drew from the comparative study of "all" representative cultures whose alleged regularity analogously made the scientific prediction about the decline of the West plausible.

The postmoderns do not claim a privileged position in history; firstly, because they do not think in terms of so-called "historical laws." Historical laws are just schemes of understanding, abstractions of understanding (*Verstand*) which do not grasp historical phenomena by their roots, and simplify them precisely to the degree at which their essence and meaning will be lost.[13] Many postmoderns will not deny that regularities can be observed in histories, and that to establish such regularities may serve as the vehicle of orientation in the past. Bringing forth certain regularities from the past is the procedure whereby different things or events are identified (and identity of difference is created) from a particular point of view. From this point of view, there is regularity; from another, there is none. If one envisages the entirety of a historical phenomenon or event, it is a *tode ti*, a *such-ness*, an *ipseity*, incomparable and incommensurable. Since comparison requires a yardstick with which to compare, comparison always fall short of the grasping of the event.[14] Every historical event is unique and contingent.

The thought that historical facts and events are contingent is certainly not a postmodern discovery.[15] But the postmodern mind does not presuppose a necessity that realizes itself through those contingencies, since history has no "tendency." This is not to say merely that this tendency is yet unknown, or remains undiscovered or undiscoverable for the human mind. It could be said or believed that since we do not know whether there exists "a" history as such, whether it develops toward something, following a plan (for example, a divine plan) or a tendency (a natural tendency), it is entirely indifferent as to whether or not such a plan exists. For, as far as human creatures and actors are concerned, there is no aim, no goal, no general direction, no necessity in the events which we normally sum up with the term "history." Postmodern men and women think and act as if everything (every historical event) were entirely contingent in the strongest sense of the word (without plan, necessity, tendency, and so on), but do not speak of contingency in onto-metaphysical terms. A contingent person simply acts and lives with the consciousness of contingency.

There is an essential difference in the existential status of high modernist and postmodern thinking, although they share (or at least may share) the awareness of personal contingency, both in the form of cosmic and of social contingency.[16] The threat of cosmic contingency is coeval with the emergence of the modern mechanistic view of the universe, with the substitution of the infinite matter of the immense necropolis for the living and ensouled divine Cosmos, and of the brave new world where the single person is just a Zero, where he or she does not count, and where God is dead, for the Eternal Governance is lost.[17] The certitude that science promised to offer, the belief in the Power of Reason that allows man to *make* a world of his own design and liking, dressed the wound of the consciousness of contingency but did not heal it. The postmoderns, denying that necessity is marching toward its *telos* through historical contingencies, lay the wound bare. The (reflected) postmodern consciousness is, among other things, a gesture of exposing this wound. Understanding the future as being-open – that is, keeping the wound of contingency bare without applying the medicines that knowledge and/or faith offer – and taking responsibility for the present and the future, are difficult positions to assume. Allow me here to advance one of my suggestions. Because the position of reflected postmodernity is tremendously difficult, unreflected postmodern thinking accompanies reflected postmodern thinking as its shadow. I would say, employing a bad metaphor, that reflected postmodern thinking is accompanied by two shadows. One version of unreflected postmodern thinking becomes fundamentalist. The other becomes cynical, as I will discuss later. Fundamentalism is a postmodern position for those who cannot live with an open wound, who need the drogues of future certainties. Cynicism is a postmodern position for those who do not mind the wound and reject, or fail to take, responsibility. In order to take responsibility in the consciousness of contingency, one needs to think in terms of an "absolute present tense."

I will exemplify the absolute present tense with the metaphor of the railway station. Roughly from the second half of the 19th century onward, at least in Europe but also in the New World to a certain extent, the modernist conception of modernity dominated the institutions of imagination.[18] Modernism experiences "being in the present" as living in a *transitory* state, stage, or world, compressed between the past and the future. The past, which was normally seen as "necessary" (for the reason that it cannot be changed) was supposed to have lead up to the present – the present on its part as a limit, as a "just now," an insignificant moment which always transcends toward an infinite future, being conceived as the territory of freedom. In the modernist view, the present is like a railway station where we denizens of the modern world need to catch one of the fast trains that run through, or stop in this location only for a few moments. Those trains will carry us to the future. Settling in the railway station would have meant stagnation – for them.[19]

Modernist imagination marginalized the present through the historical recollection of the past (as necessity) and through the project and projection of an infinite future (freedom) which is the territory of human experiment and creation, which can be devised – moreover, forced – to obey the human will. There are two alternative mental packages: the liberal kind and the Marxist kind (the latter both in its social democratic and radical versions). The liberal kind envisioned the future in the model of infinite progression toward the best possible world. The Marxian and socialist kinds envisioned it as a development with a turning-point, where the best possible world appears at a stroke. The conflicts between those two images appeared in the juxtaposition of "reform/revolution" or "evolution/revolution." Revolution was then understood in an entirely

future-oriented way.[20] Both versions, however, shared the faith in progression; both based their faith on scientific knowledge, and both claimed
absolute certainty for their predictions. Both said four things at once.
Firstly, the future is free – we (men) create it. Secondly, we can expect not
just a betterment in the future, but a qualitatively better world and way
of life. Thirdly, we can predict with certainty (scientifically) that we are
going (freely) to create and achieve things in the future under certain
conditions (evolution or revolution) which, however, can already be
extrapolated. Fourthly, the constant development of technology is pivotal
for progression. Although technology may develop nonteleologically, it
opens up, wittingly or unwittingly, the *telos* for "mankind" in (future)
history.[21] Actually, the progressivist–liberal view and its many versions,
and the Marxian/socialist view and its many versions, both harbored a
hidden teleology.[22]

Modernity drew legitimacy from both versions of "progressivism."
The railway station of the present was legitimated by the fast trains
running through the station, which can be caught by the denizens of
the present to carry them to new railway stations, all the more comfortable than the previous ones, *ad infinitum*. Even the classical Marxian
view which promised "the end of alienation," that is, Paradise on Earth,
has not entirely abandoned thinking in terms of *ad infinitum*. On the
contrary, the end of alienation is supposed to put an end only to "pre-
history"; from then onward will the "real history" of mankind, in fact,
begin.

To sum up, "high modernism" *legitimated modernity with the future*,
not with the future of the present but with a distant future which is
allegedly incipient in modernity itself from its gestation onward.[23] By
now, the legitimation of modernity with the future has broken down:
whereas the revolutionary paradigm collapsed catastrophically, the evo-
lutionary paradigm slowly eroded.

The legitimating philosophy of modernity was realized; yet, instead of
Heaven descending upon Earth, Earth was transformed into Hell. Indeed,
the fast trains ran toward their final destination – and the names of the
terminal railway stations were Auschwitz and the Gulag – the stations of
extermination.

My remark that the legitimating philosophy of modernity was realized
in the exterminating camps of the totalitarian states is not a figure of
speech. For this was what actually happened: the idea that the present is
just a transitory stage before the opening up of the grandiose future; and
the idea that it is man and modern man alone who is free to create this
future according to his plans; and finally the idea that the absolutely
free future will be ushered in by a shock, an extraordinary event, a

catastrophe, in one. Briefly, a modernized version of the Jewish–Christian *Apocalypse* and the modernized version of the Greek idea of *Kairos*, two entirely different conceptions of time, were merged into one. It is a modern idea in general that Greek and Jewish–Christian traditions should be united. They can be united in different ways. This combination, the unification of apocalypse with *Kairos*, proved to be lethal. The apocalyptic imagination promises the end of all times, but it is God who ushers in this end – men have no part in it. On the other hand, the Greek idea of *Kairos*[24] as time-for-something makes time human-(decision-) dependent. It is the actor who needs to do things at the proper time, who has to grasp the proper time-for-something. But what the actor can do at the proper time is an action, a political decision, or at most a decisive move in war – but it can never be a decision in which the actors usher in the absolute future, if for no other reason than the fact that the Greeks did not even have such a concept of "future." It was Apocalypse and *Kairos* united in one forceful mythological image that prepared the moral/ontological/metaphysical transgression that we know by the names of Auschwitz and the Gulag. Men have played God here; they prepared the Apocalypse. They were seeking for the right time and the right place to "make" the Apocalypse happen, as if it were just an event, one historical action among many.[25] In this sense, the moral/ontological/metaphysical transgressions[26] of the 20th century were the realization of ideas that had been concocted in the innocent-looking witch kitchens of the 19th century, during the grand period of high modernism.

The progressivist legitimation of modernity has not collapsed. Rather, it eroded – it is still in the process of erosion. No spectacular catastrophes shook their faith in their legitimating power, not even the weight of "facts." As far as the "facts" are concerned, it is no more difficult to verify the theory of universal progression today than it was a century ago. But there is less willingness to do it, or to neglect "facts" which move toward the opposite direction. The slow change in the historical consciousness – from the modernist to a postmodern one – can be observed everywhere, yet it would be difficult (and possibly of no importance) to make a catalog of the single motives (such as pollution of the rivers and the forests) or symptoms of the change.[27] The disbelief in linear progression, even in the case of natural sciences, makes all models of "infinite progression" suspect.

The postmoderns accept life on the railway station. That is, they accept living in an absolute present. They do not wait for the fast trains so that they should be rushed to their final destination. All final destinations are unmasked as harboring disaster. Thus the postmoderns claim ignorance in the matters of final destination; they accept the "provisory state," the here and now, as the final stage – for them. The future is unknown.

The present is absolutely present because the future which is beyond our horizon is unknown. The postmoderns do not claim to have a special, privileged position in history. They do not believe that they know the future better than their ancestors ever did. (Maybe, they know it less.) They do not claim that science offers them the key to open up the future, because they are aware of the fragility of science. They think in terms of contingency; not just the contingency of the single individual (both cosmic and social), but also the contingency of historical times and ages – the contingency of their present.

The absolute present includes the future – the future of the present. And it includes the past – the past of the present. The denizens of the absolute present behave in a backward way, out from the future of the present toward the past, as much as they think forward. The present is understood, as far it can be understood, if illuminated by the light of tradition (the past). In this sense, the postmoderns return to Hegel. Hegel writes, in the Preface to the *Philosophy of Right*, "here is Rhodus, here you jump. One cannot jump over Rhodus." "Here is the rose, here you dance." The postmodern thinkers do not try to jump over Rhodus. The present is Rhodus. They dance where the rose is. They pick the rose from the Cross of the present, just like Hegel. But, unlike Hegel, they fall short of offering a full and direct proof of legitimacy for the present age.

In Hegel, world history – or, better, the grand narrative that constituted world history as the march of the world spirit – has legitimated the modern age. The modern age appeared as the result of the vicissitudes of the world spirit, and in this sense (if not in any other sense) also as the end of history. The postmodern conception of radical contingency does not allow for this figure of legitimation.

I cannot emphasize enough that to admit that one is living on the railway station of the present allows for a heightened kind of *responsibility*. A responsible person is in charge (takes responsibility). But one cannot be in charge of an unknown and unknowable future.[28] One carries responsibility for the present (the future of the present and the past of the present). This means roughly that one is in charge of one's contemporaries, of one's Togetherness. This is the only promise that, when given, will probably be kept. All other promises are empty.

In Hegel's system, world history legitimates the present as its outcome.[29] In the "infinite" "progressivist" story, it is the future that legitimates the present and its conflicts and sufferings. Neither of these options is open to the postmoderns. Yet the present cannot legitimate itself by itself. Contingency does not legitimate contingency. It seems as if nothing else remains but to say that modernity legitimates itself through sheer facticity. It exists; its very existence legitimates it. Moreover, it exists in a Hegelian sense as essential existence, as actuality. Nothing has a stronger claim on men than actuality.[30] But this is a meager kind of legitimacy and it will not really work.

A postmodern conception, one must admit, does not find strong legitimating claims for modernity. I must repeat, for I think that it is essential, that postmoderns can still stand for modernity in taking responsibility for it. They can say with Luther, "Here I stand and cannot do otherwise."[31] By taking responsibility, they can accept the contingency of modernity as their destiny and as the destiny of the present age – not in the sense of the present being predestined, but in the other sense that it could be transformed into the destiny of its denizens, who take responsibility for the railway station of the present.[32] *One can legitimate modernity (the present) only practically.*

The future of the present is the present. It does not transcend the present. One cannot act from the position of something (an end, idea, value, and so on) of which one knows nothing. But from this it does not follow that nothing can exist, that nothing will come into being from which we now know nothing. To think that we cannot see or know anything beyond our horizon and that we cannot take responsibility for something we do not know, and to think that things will never change, that nothing will be different from what it is now, that the present is the last wisdom and that there is nothing beyond our horizon, are two entirely different propositions.

I will illuminate the difference between those two thoughts again, metaphorically. We are sitting around the table of modernity. One can see all chairs occupied by the things of the present (and the future of the present), the things we know or we can extrapolate. But one can also leave one chair unoccupied. This chair waits for the Messiah. The Messiah might come or He might not come. Yet, we will never know when He arrives or whether He arrives.[33]

Unreflected postmodern consciousness does not leave an unoccupied chair – there is no place here for the Messiah to come. In contrast, the traditional grand narratives believe in the false Messiah because they claim to know who (what) the Messiah is or, even worse, they claim to know what makes the Messiah arrive. Whatever the content of this kind of promise, it is a false promise. If someone comes and declares "This will be the historical redeemer of mankind, I know its name" – then we might easily identify him as the prophet of the false Messiah. The prophet of the true Messiah remains silent. He does not know. But he knows one thing – *that one should not say that the Messiah will never come.* One should never let the empty chair be occupied by a pretender (and every occupant is a pretender), but it is better if one does not remove the empty chair. My conviction, or rather my feelings, suggest that I leave the chair there, in the middle of the room at the head of the table, where it remains all the time exposed in its emptiness. The chair speaks to the denizens of the absolute present honestly only in its emptiness. My intuition suggests that only emptiness is fullness for the moderns, that there is no other kind of "hope beyond hope,"[34] at least not for those who assume the position of reflected postmodernity.

————

Aristotle remarked in his *Politics*[35] that, contrary to the well-bred Asians, uncultivated Europeans developed the love of freedom. This makes up, so Aristotle said, the European half of the Greeks (the Asian half is refinement). Speaking of freedom, here Aristotle meant political freedom, independence, and the disgust of despotism. This theme returns in all significant and representative European narratives.

Europe's autobiography begins with the love of freedom. The people of Europe, so the story runs, have been kept continuously oppressed, exploited, and enslaved, and frequently tyranny reigned. But the desire for freedom has burst out again and again in the great acts and events of liberation and the constitution of liberties throughout European history. Even long before the age of grand narratives, simultaneously with the emergence of historical thinking, Machiavelli in his *Discorsi* presented the European political mind as the inventor of the Republic's model, as the creator of free spaces for the constitution of liberties.[36] Even the stories of the other traditions of Europeans, particularly the Jewish, were now recounted in an early version of liberation theology.[37] The salvation story as the miraculous liberation from Egyptian slavery, and the story of revelation as "the constitution of liberties" (laws) by Moses, became reconfigured in the spirit of the awakening modern thinking. The European autobiography culminates in the grand narratives, ranging from Rousseau, through Condorcet and Fourier, to Hegel and Marx.[38] The story always goes on about the expansion, the deepening, of the possibility of realizing freedom through alienation, through the vicissitudes of slavery, oppression, "superstitions," and other such things. Yet, in the end, freedom conquers.

Freedom conquered indeed, and it did not only conquer in a few ways, but conquered totally. *Freedom became the foundation of the modern world. It is the foundation that grounds nothing.*[39]

A building stands on its foundation – on the soil, the rock, or the cellar. It is safe, steady, and reliable only if it is well founded. If the foundation is shaken (for example, in an earthquake) the building collapses. No building stands forever, but a well-founded building survives several generations; one can rely upon its existence.

A state, a city, a religion, an institution is founded. They are founded by the founding fathers, the great legislators, the settlers. The world so founded also survives many generations. The institutions can be changed, yet it is always possible to return to the foundation. In earlier times, revolution meant exactly this; to return to the foundation.

True statements, arguments, beliefs, and convictions are grounded. If someone asks the question "Why is this so, and not otherwise?" one can have recourse to the grounding of the thing. There are final grounds that cannot be further grounded, but that ground all of the other statements, arguments, and beliefs. If such final grounds are shaken, the arguments, beliefs – truth itself – become ungrounded. Thinking is ungrounded if there is no resting point in grounding. An abyss opens up; one cannot set one's feet firmly anywhere.[40]

The way a world is founded is analogous to the way a philosophy is grounded, and conversely. No wonder, then, that the deconstruction of the pre-modern "natural artifice"[41] and the deconstruction of metaphysics are coeval.[42]

In discussing the principle of identity,[43] as in several other contexts, Aristotle speaks of demonstrations. In a demonstration one has to make recourse to sentences which are for their part nondemonstrable, and which are in no need of demonstration. A principle such as this is a final, ultimate principle, an *archē*. Without presupposing such principles, demonstrations would go on *ad infinitum* and nothing could have a grounding. Unless one presupposes certainties, one cannot have science or one cannot conduct an argument, nor even a conversation. Actually, the principles of identity, contradiction, and the excluded third are taken for granted as certainly valid and true, because we actually do conduct conversations and have arguments – all that would be entirely impossible had we not presupposed their absolute certainty. This is a transcendental argument. In philosophy (metaphysics) one needs transcendental arguments – and other arguments[44] – to establish a firm ground for further arguments. The "edifice" of metaphysics is grounded on self-evident principles which are, however, frequently reflected upon.[45]

The main institutions of imagination of a pre-modern world also contain self-evident principles, as well as self-evident stories, descriptions which are not necessarily followed down to their foundations. For example, God is an absolute foundation of the Jewish and Christian world. He is the absolute certainty; the absolute Existence, Justice, Goodness, Truth, and so on. It is also a self-evident truth, however, that one person is born noble, whereas another is born into serfdom. There is no need to connect those two certainties with demonstrations, and even less of a need to deduce one from the other. It is enough to refer to God's will: it was God's will that the world looks the way it does. This is not metaphysical grounding but legitimation of the authority.[46]

The worldly foundation of metaphysics is also metaphysical, as much as metaphysics grounds the metaphysical structure of the world. Men live in two worlds, and they are aware of the difference between the two. One world is the legitimating; the other is the legitimated.[47] The stories of the legitimating world (myths, histories) justify the institutions of the socio-political (legitimated) world together with their institutions and arrangements. The foundation of the House (home, *haza, Heimat*) is in Heaven (in the ideas, God). Tradition exhales and inhales the "spirit of a people," to employ Hegel's expression, which is taken for granted, repeatable and constantly repeated.

I made the bold statement that Freedom is the foundation of the moderns, which means that every demonstration needs to have recourse to freedom, which on its part warrants the truth and the goodness of the *demonstrandum*. Freedom is then taken for granted and constantly repeated as all traditions are, the *archē* at which all arguments stop, the limit that sets order and warrants certainty. Similarly, then, Freedom is the foundation of the house, a solid ground: everything built upon it will stand on it from generation to generation – only an earthquake can shake it.

The problem is, however, that Freedom as the ultimate principle, as the *archē* of modernity, cannot perform one single task that an *archē* is supposed to perform and has performed in previous histories. This is why the building "goes to the ground," is destroyed (*zu Grunde gehen*) in a nondialectical way.

That freedom grounds *means*, namely, that everything is ungrounded. It means – and this amounts to the same thing – that grounding starts anew every time. Every political act grounds itself; every life grounds itself; every philosophy is self-grounding.

For example, modern political philosophy begins with the theory of *contract*. Contract grounds a political arrangement. Yet if freedom is the ultimate foundation, all contracts can also be annulled. Everything that is legitimated can be de-legitimated. Morality (in Kant) is grounded (where else?) in transcendental freedom. Yet transcendental freedom cannot be transcendentally deduced. It is "the fact of reason" – bluntly, it is ungrounded. Wittgenstein's *Tractatus* begins with "facts." Facts are descriptions of a world, for the world is the totality of facts. There must be a world where there are facts,[48] but the world does not ground the facts. This is a transcendental argument, which remains equally ungrounded. One can start a new philosophy with entirely different presuppositions. One can freely choose any starting-point, any kind of ground for building one's world (one world among many possible ones). *The moderns are sitting on a paradox.* This is the constellation of the modern world: it is grounded by a principle which, in principle, does not ground anything; it is founded on a universal value or idea, which, in principle, negates foundation. Reflected postmodern consciousness *thinks this paradox*; it does not lose it from sight, it lives with it. The fundamental paradox of modernity is the paradox of freedom. All other paradoxes of modernity – the other fundamental paradoxes, the paradox of truth included – are grounded by the paradox of freedom.

Perhaps I was wrong when I said that Freedom does not ground anything. For if one thinks through Freedom as nonfounding ground, one thinks the paradox. And if one thinks this paradox through, the paradox begets other paradoxes. Aristotle says that everything begets the same. Man begets man. So does the paradox of freedom beget other paradoxes, among them the chief, and saddest one, the paradox of truth. Alas, if the paradox begets other paradoxes, this amounts to the same as a non-founding foundation. Truth becomes paradoxical because its foundation is paradoxical, because it is a foundation that does not found, a grounding that does not ground. This is, again, what postmodern thinking needs to think through.[49]

I have distinguished in the previous section between unreflected and reflected postmodern thinking. This might have sounded odd after I had identified postmodern consciousness with stage (6) of the development of historical consciousness, as the consciousness of *reflected generality*. If postmodern consciousness as such is described as "reflected generality," how can I still distinguish between unreflected and reflected postmodern thinking?

Postmodern thinking, all kinds of postmodern thinking, reflects on generality.[50] But not all kinds of postmodern thinking reflect upon themselves. The self-reflection of postmodern thinking implies thinking through the paradox of freedom (and of truth), carrying it out, never losing it from sight.

Postmoderns sit on the paradox(es), but they do not need to think them as paradoxes. All the paradoxes of modernity (not just that of Freedom and Truth) can be temporalized. They are normally temporalized. For example, in modernity, universality/difference (particularity) assumed a paradoxical character. As long as the normative idea or concept of humankind (man is a political animal) has had nothing, or very little, to do with empirical humankind (all cultures with which we share the globe), the categories of universality/difference have not assumed a paradoxical character. For the paradoxical character of universality/difference comes into relief only if it is thought together with the set of normative/empirical statements, where both the normative and the empirical aspects can be thought together, with equal right and equal justification, with universality, as with particularity (difference).[51]

What do I mean by temporalization of the paradox? At time X one is absolutely certain that universality is oppressive and that the promotion and protection of difference is the only right thing to do, that the statement, "every culture is as good as the others," is absolutely true, and that if the wrong ideas of universalism – together with their institutions – were only removed, all of the problems of the world (wars, oppression, economic disasters, and so on) would be solved. A few years later, at time Y, one may be sure that the opposite is the case, or that there is no truth at all.

Unreflected postmodern thinking can be self-righteous or cynical (depending on the character or the mood of the thinker) or both, but it is never ironical and has no sense of humor. Reflected postmodern thinking, that faces the paradox, can excel in irony and in a sense of humor; it can also be laden with *pathos* or despair, and occasionally also cold and detached (depending on the character of the thinker). But it is neither self-righteous nor cynical (given that it is self-reflective).

But unreflected postmodern thinking is postmodern to the same extent as the reflected kind, and it is no less founded on freedom. Freedom is totalizing in the sense that it is holistic. It can be interpreted in all possible ways, and interpretations often contradict one another not just theoretically but also practically – in judgment and in action. Freedom as ground and as *telos*, a European invention, can also be turned against Europe; it can also be turned against modernity. Modernity, grounded on freedom which does not ground, is left not only without certainties but also becomes unable to resist certainties, whatever their source. Those who live without fundaments are ready to embrace certainties without foundation, to embrace all kinds of fundaments.

Postmoderns must learn to live without Truth. But one can live without Truth in different ways. It sounds odd to say that postmoderns must learn to live without truth. After all, the modern concept of truth as presented in the correspondence theory of truth has already occupied the place of other concepts of truth, primarily by marginalizing truth in the sense of revelation. Truth is then identified with "true knowledge" of facts and with correct deduction. Hegel said that this concept falls short of being the determination of truth; rather, we should speak of "correctness," and in my mind he was right. The correspondence theory of truth trivializes truth and transforms the search for truth into a technological matter.[52] But even if the correspondence theory of truth is trivial, it works – at least it works in its own territory. There is no hidden paradox here. Or, rather, one can do without the paradox. The paradox of truth appears only in and through reflection.

"This is true" or "That is untrue" are *not* the answers to the question "What is truth?" but to the question "Is this true?" It is *not* the answer to the quest for truth (as in "I want to know the truth"). The question "What is truth?" and the quest "I want to know the truth" – that is, *thinking about truth* and *desiring truth* – are *existential* and not just cognitive (epistemological) positions. The person who positions himself or herself as the person who asks such questions and desires truth is not satisfied with answers that refer to true/false knowledge, because it is not this that they think about and that they desire. What they think about and desire is meaning. It is certainty, it is an absolute – it is an *absolute foundation*. This is what modernity cannot offer.[53] However, the quest for the absolute and the way one thinks about it is not incomprehensible, yet it cannot be eradicated from man's mind (*Gemüt*). This is what Kant called the unquenchable need for metaphysics.

But, why paradox? – one may ask again. Why not the theory of dual truth? In science one accepts the correspondence theory of truth because it works well pragmatically, whereas one satisfies one's quest for truth in religions. In one territory, one achieves true knowledge that is always approximative, and in the other territory one grasps one's Truth with the gesture of faith. But it does not work that way. Why not?

Truth is truth because the finite mind, the transient exister, is involved in it (for true knowledge in the spirit of the correspondence theory of truth as well). The transient exister can also be involved in one of the discoveries of physics but, with the exception of an exister who is a physicist, this is rarely the case. Yet transient existers are all involved in *historical truth*. Historical truth is not just approximative, but depends on the existential position from which the question "What is truth?" is raised. Historical truth is the truth in which one is involved. There is no common foundation from which moderns ask those questions. Rather, they are free to ask those questions from several positions. Truth will shine differently from each position, and since there is no common foundation for the moderns – except Freedom – each position will posit its own historical truth. "Ought" sentences cannot be deduced from "is" sentences, so the moderns are warned by the moderns. "Ought" sentences (value positions) cannot be true or false. But if you shift the issue and ask the question "Is it true that this is right?" or "Is it true that this is wrong?" you get back to the initial problem: it is true that *X* is right for *A*, it is true that *Y* is right for *B*. But no one will answer the question of what *is* right and what *is* wrong, or what is the truth about right or wrong.

But why is this paradoxical? After all, one can shrug one's shoulders – *X* is right for position *A*, and *Y* for position *B* – and there is no truth about those matters. However, truth (frequently also in cases of true knowledge) is also an existential involvement (historical truth). Without involvement (the absolute?), it means nothing to speak about truth. One cannot passionately defend anything without believing it to be true. And this is true even if one accepts that true knowledge is approximative, and that we moderns perhaps do not even understand the word "absolute" any more.

Truth became paradoxical because what I am now writing is true. I write it down because it is true. I am convinced that it is true. It is a historical truth because it can be verified by the speaker and never entirely falsified by the listener.[54] But many of my readers (you, perhaps?) will tell me that what I write is untrue, and you will confront me with your truth. You will try to falsify my truth (perhaps without success), yet you will verify yours (perhaps with success, just like I do). Truth confronts truth. We (You and I) are both speaking in the name of our respective truths. Although I believe that my truth is true, I also know that yours can be verified as well, and I will be unable to falsify it if it is a forceful kind of truth. This is the paradox.

Kierkegaard was the first to discover that modern thinking is paradoxical (after Kant, however, who believed in the solution of the antinomies). Kierkegaard described the absolute paradox from a Christian perspective (it is absurd and thus paradoxical that eternal truth came to the world historically). Yet he also made some suggestions about the possibility of carrying the paradox of freedom and of truth on our shoulders. Kierkegaard said that the exister, the existing thinker, "approximates,"[55] and in approximating true knowledge he leaps into truth, he embraces it as his absolute certitude. I say: this is my truth. This does not mean that I possess the truth, but rather the opposite – that my truth possesses me.[56] It means: I take responsibility for this truth. One lives up to the paradox of modernity if one takes responsibility for one's historical truth – that is, the truth in which one is involved absolutely as a transient, finite being, of finite knowledge and finite mind, as one who is aware of his or her fragility and the limits of his insights absolutely.

2

The Challenge of the Heritage:
Hegel, Marx, Weber[1]

In this chapter, I will speak about Hegel, Marx, and Weber only briefly, in order to bring their major and controversial contributions to the theory of modernity into relief. The reader should not expect a full but, rather, a concise presentation of these authors' theories of modernity. With regard to the neglected aspects of their respective philosophies, I will return to them in the footnotes of the forthcoming chapters.

Among the three major founding fathers of the theory of modernity, Marx is the typical child of the 19th century. The grand illusions of the age of progression mark his work more than that of Hegel or Max Weber. After all, Hegel's philosophy is closer to the 18th century than to the 19th century,[2] and Weber's work, particularly his later work, ushers in the 20th century. Precisely because Marx shared the grand illusions of the 19th century, particularly the illusions attached to the infinite and infinitely positive potentials of the development of technology and the mastery of nature, he could reject the present stage of modernity (capitalism) more radically than his great predecessor and his successor, and extend the grand narrative into the future.

Grand Narrative Without Presupposition

Hegel devised the first complete grand narrative, as he was the first to move radically into the deconstruction of metaphysics. Those two endeavors were but one.

The grand narrative was for Hegel the vehicle with which to deconstruct the pre-modern social arrangement and give legitimacy to the modern world. Deconstruction is not destruction.[3] Nothing can be deconstructed short of deciphering its genealogy or recounting its genesis.[4] Hegel's world history is the genesis of modernity. Modernity appears as the consummation of world history, as its hidden *telos*. All the worlds that are destroyed through negation lose their legitimacy. So does the world of alienation (to which, in the *Phenomenology*, the French Revolution still belongs). The modern world – where everyone is free – is self-legitimating, for it is not and cannot be destroyed by negation.[5]

Hegel is not responsible for the simplified notion of historical progression. He would be the last to deny that there are both gains and losses in history. Totalities (such as the spirit of a people) cannot be compared with other similar totalities as wholes. In order to compare, one needs a yardstick for comparison, and this yardstick needs to be a *quantity*. Two heterogeneous things can be compared only with a common thing that serves as the quantitative measure. Hegel legitimates the modern age by finding such a measure: the freedom of *all*. The extension of freedom (for one, for a few, for all) provides a yardstick for the comparison of different cultures. This yardstick is quantitative, yet it is also a quality; thus it fits the Hegelian bill of "measure" (that is, *Mass*, where quantity turns into qualitative difference). If measured by the extension of freedom, modernity is progressive compared to all the pre-modern ages. And qualitatively also, for where there is freedom for all (a quantitative expansion) an entirely new quality of life – life in equal freedom – comes into being. But this very strong legitimating underpinning of modernity does not prevent Hegel from recognizing losses. Where everyone is free there is no longer any heroism, any tragedy, any grandeur. Modernity is not just the end of history, but also the end of philosophy and art.[6] In the same passages where Hegel commits himself with utmost *pathos* to the modern island Rhodus, the absolute present age, to the rose of the present, he will speak of modern philosophy as the owl of Minerva, which begins its flight when darkness has already set in. Darkness. The modern age is darkness. This is the age in which we merely recollect the past and paint "gray in gray."[7] Hegel's is an enthusiastic commitment for a modernity without enthusiasm. He embraces modernity without cherishing any grand illusions; still, he does it with resolve. In this sense, he comes close to supporting the paradoxes of the modern age. Yet, he prevents himself from doing it.

One can understand the Hegelian project as a hidden *theodicea*. It is Reason (or the World Spirit as Reason) which comes – or returns – to itself in the modern world. History is a terrible slaughterhouse where purposes cross purposes, where guilt and evil reign. It is not the territory of happiness.[8] The individual and the particular are constantly sacrificed on the altar of the universal.[9] Still, it is God's walk in history to what the state is.[10] And the modern world, the outcome of the "cunning of

Reason," retroactively justifies all the guilt and suffering, the divine plan in history.

Yet the story can also be read as an anti-*theodicea*. After all, the divine plan is unknown – never declared or prophetized. The so-called *telos* of history can be detected only in retrospect. The pre-modern worlds, those of suffering, unhappiness and alienation, are justified in the act of de-legitimation, deconstruction. Their necessary doom (the standpoint of the absolute present) is the *only* justification of their existence. Teleology is constituted in recollection. The cunning of Reason is unintended. If it were intended, Reason would intentionally use men's suffering in order to achieve its goals. This God would be an evil demon, and not Hegel's Lutheran Godhead. One can state that History is rational because the modern world is, that History is the walk of Reason because it is only in modernity that we have acquired the ability to look at the world rationally – and it is now that it can look back upon us rationally. "Rationality" means, in the main, dialectical. A world – and a kind of thinking – is rational if negation is not destructive, but is inherent within the self-affirming motion of the world and the mind. Such is the modern world and mind. Negation can be intrinsic to the process of reaffirmation only in a mind and a world *in which there are no presuppositions*.

If the Hegelian grand narrative is meant to be the story of a divine plan, one attributes a presupposition to Hegel. If the Hegelian grand narrative is meant to grant absolute contingency which can be retrospectively recollected and ordered as a teleologically guided chain of processes and events that leads to the present, one also attributes a presupposition to the author. In my mind, Hegel was serious enough about doing philosophy without presuppositions to leave the interpretation of his philosophy of history open before different presuppositions. The interpretations of both Kojeve and Mittelstrass in this sense equally grasp the essence of the Hegelian story. The modern world has no presuppositions except the history which leads to it, and the way in which this history is told. The modern world is historical (*geschichtlich*) insofar as history is contained in it; it is its own history and nothing else. But if one smuggled presuppositions into this history and did not allow men and women to offer their own versions in recollecting the past, the story itself would fail to deconstruct the pre-modern edifice and would not legitimate modernity in full. Hegel's story is presuppositionless, just as modernity is.

Hegel thus deconstructs the pre-modern world through legitimating the modern one, and vice versa. He leaves wide open the question of whether there was or was not a divine plan working in history.

Reason is freedom for Hegel mainly in the sense in which I spoke about freedom: as the foundation of modernity which does not found. Moderns enjoy the freedom to negate, the freedom from all presuppositions (except their own tradition).

Hegel's famous, or infamous, claim that his system is without presupposition has solid grounds. Being without presupposition means only being without an *archē*, without an ultimate principle, without a foundation to which one can always return – without certainty. The Absolute in Hegel is not the starting-point but the result; the result of the *tradition*, of all the historically emerging categories (concepts, ideas). Totality, the Absolute, is all of the philosophical texts read together. The Absolute itself rejects presuppositions. For if all presuppositions are included in the Absolute (the result), if the Truth is the whole, no presupposition is truer than any other – all presuppositions are both true and untrue. From this, it follows that for modern men to choose one presupposition against all others – that is, to philosophize from the standpoint of one founding *archē*, – contradicts the "spirit of modernity." It is possible yet un-modern; it can be real but not actual. It can exist, or be done, but it will be like a mere letter from which the spirit has parted.

I think that Hegel's deepest understanding of modernity expresses itself in his insistence that philosophy needs to be without presuppositions, and that his deconstruction of metaphysics runs deeper than that of his successors, Marx included. What hides Hegel's radicalism before the postmodern age is – aside from misunderstanding – his clinging to the system. The misunderstanding is, briefly, the belief that Tradition as presupposition is a metaphysical presupposition. In my mind it is not what is presupposed in the language of philosophy without, however, giving preference to any concrete use of this language (none of them is fully true, but all of them are true together). History as presupposition is not a presupposition in a metaphysical sense,[11] for it simply declares the historicity (*Geschichtlichkeit*) of the modern age and the awareness of this historicity.

As I said, our problem with Hegel is – at least so I believe – that he presented the presuppositionless character of modernity with a presuppositionless system, that he avoided carrying the weight of the paradox of truth and freedom. The paradox (of truth and freedom) becomes explicit if someone chooses a presupposition and builds a (never completed) system on it, knowing that there are no absolute presuppositions and that the choice itself was contingent insofar as it was free. Only in this case does a modern philosopher carry responsibility on his shoulders. In Hegel's mind there was a choice between unreflected absolute presuppositions (which are indeed suspect) and absolutely no presupposition – he never considered the option of a nonfounded foundation.

If one identifies the absolute with the result of everything (all categories) that had been presented by the philosophical tradition as the truth, then indeed philosophy, as well as philosophical thinking, comes to an end. Neither philosophy nor philosophical thinking comes to an end because thinkers choose contingently (freely) only one (interpreted) tradition as they take responsibility for their choice, for their preference, love, or *Gunst*.

The modern world as Hegel sees it can survive soundly not because it has a foundation but because it can be kept in balance. It can be kept in balance because the conflicts of universality, particularity, and individuality can be carried out and resolved before being radicalized into self-destructive collisions. The universal, the particular, and the individual – all have enough room for development. They have enough insofar as they are not limitless – for there are boundaries, but the boundaries are elastic. In addition to this elasticity, there can frequently be a coalescence of the universal, particular, and the individual such that they are fused or fitted to one another, although always with a difference.

There are three spheres of activity in the modern world:[12] the family, civil society, and the state. Each embodies a special kind of human bonding. The family is a community with the bond of love. Civil society is society as such; competitive, interest-oriented, separating. But there are bonds here too: the bonds created by the division of labor, the bonds of belonging to the same profession or corporation, the bonds that are interest-induced yet not egotistic, identities and the bonds of solidarity. The state is the political society/community with the bond of citizenry, loyalty to the constitution.[13]

Every institution as a kind of bond is an ethical power. There are three ethical powers in modernity (*sittliche Mächte*): the ethical power of the family, that of the state, and of several institutions of civil society. But we must ask, what is ethical power?[14] Ethical power is yielded by an institution if men and women normally hold it dearer and higher than their own interests and pleasure, or if they – at least – are supposed to do so, or pretend that they are doing so irrespective of whether or not they are otherwise virtuous.[15] Although Hegel is not spelling this out, the modern world is endangered when the three ethical powers become steadily unbalanced, or one of them ceases to yield ethical power. Given that the modern world – as suppositionless as Hegel's system – has no foundation but the tradition that it entails, once the balance of the three powers which keep each other alive is seriously disturbed, the modern world, like Icarus bereft of his wings, falls onto the ground and into the abyss (*zugrunde geht*).

Hegel's description of the balance of (ethical) power in the modern world is one of his deepest insights. It seems that the balance of the three powers is not a necessary condition for the survival of the modern world. Yet after almost two centuries of experience with European modernity, it also seems as if modernity can reproduce itself without cataclysms and catastrophes only in those situations where the relative balance of the three ethical powers is maintained.

The nation–state has wielded an even more forceful ethical power than Hegel expected. The family has gained ethical power in all social strata and classes.[16] Finally, significant ethical powers have also emerged in civil society. Among them, trade unions, as the institutions of workers' solidarity, wielded an especially strong ethical power. In our times, simultaneous with the global expansion of modernity, the force of all those ethical powers has begun to weaken in the traditional centers of the modern world, and this might be a cause for concern, particularly for those who share Hegel's understanding of modernity (even if they have never heard the name of this obscure German philosopher).

In Hegel, among the three ethical powers, the power of the state is overarching. The center of this power resides in the constitution. The possibility of change in the constitution or the removal of the sovereign (which is always one person, and in this sense a monarch) is excluded from Hegel's model. This is not a mistake or a fault. Hegel is not interested in the history (political history) of modernity and the kind of history which may result in the change of sovereignty and the constitution. He does not believe in perpetual peace; his model states do wage wars. (Only in wars can the ethical power of the state be rejuvenated, for it is here that the sacrifice of life for the ethical power is imperative.) Still, for him there is one model of modernity, the one that works, the one with a proper balance of ethical powers. The eventuality of the emergence of regimes, such as the Bolshevik or Nazi totalitarian states, was absolutely alien to Hegel's imagination even after the experience with absolute freedom during the Jacobin dictatorship.[17]

This historical experience is not just an addendum to Hegel's conception of the three ethical powers, to his thought that since we can never jump over Rhodus we had better not try.

For Hegel, everything that is ethically relevant *is*; it exists, it is *embodied*. To tell the world what it "ought to be" or "should rather be" is foolish. Social and political utopias are useless and self-defeating. Moreover, morality in the sense of Kant has no place in modern life. A modern person stands in an individual moral relationship to the ethical powers, and everything else is just moralizing. Both the "ought to be" and "the ought to do" are empty and abstract imperatives; they have no content and prevent men from understanding what *is* and doing what *is* required from the ethical powers to be done.

I have dwelled on Hegel's criticism of the *attitudes* of utopian perspective and morality because these things become widespread in eras when modernity is accepted as an absolute present time, as the railway station where we are going to settle down among the others of our time. Hegel's rejection of all "oughts" fits well into the postmodern consciousness of modernity. The serious problem with such an attitude – and not just when it is formulated theoretically – is that it brings the "ought to be" and "the ought to do" under the same heading. The "ought to be" could always be replaced with sentences such as "I think it would be better if ..."[18] This is not the case with "ought to do," for the simple reason that the "ought to be" is expressed from the standpoint of the observer – even if it is a personal wish – whereas the "ought to do" addresses the actor – first and foremost myself.[19]

Although Hegel rejects morality in a Kantian sense, he speaks positively about morality both in the *Phenomenology* and in the *Philosophy of Right*, although in two different meanings. Both approaches are of utmost significance for a theory of modernity, yet neither is central to moral philosophy.[20]

That Hegel presented his theory of modernity under the title *Philosophy of Right* is in itself a significant philosophical statement. Among the three kinds of right (abstract right, morality, and the ethical life) the third, the ethical life, includes and also warrants the other two kinds of rights. The individual is involved in the ethical powers because he or she is an individual, a legal person endowed with legal rights – further, a moral subject endowed with moral rights and liberties. Ethical powers need to warrant those liberties: this is why they are termed rights and not permissions. In Hegel, rights are accordant with duties – otherwise he could not even discuss ethical powers.[21]

Hegel's conception is liberal, but his liberalism is not of a merely formal/procedural kind. Hegel gave substance to his liberalism – the *actuality* (*Wirklichkeit*) of the whole ethical world itself – as he refused formalism and proceduralism in general.

I will return briefly to the section on morality in the *Philosophy of Right*. Here Hegel is absolutely outspoken; he does not discuss morality in general, but the moral rights of a modern subject in particular. Moral rights are the rights which are due to the person as to a subject. The word "subject" has a double meaning. Moral rights as *rights* are due to the subjects of the state; they should be granted as permissions by the state (by the constitution) for the single individual. This means – among other things – that the other two ethical powers do not grant "rights" to the subject (he or she is in this sense not subjected to the family or the civil society); that is, moral rights are in those senses not enforceable. One does not exercise rights in the family, for the family is the bond of love, and love is beyond rights and duties.[22] The subject is a subject also, or primarily, in the sense that he or she is free to pursue *subjective* purposes and follow *subjective* desires.

Which are the three moral rights? The first is the right to subjecthood as such, the right to one's own purposes, motivations, and authorship. The second is the right to the pursuit of happiness – the right to satisfy one's needs and the right to self-realization. The third moral right is one's right to entertain and maintain one's own conception of the good. I have somewhat simplified Hegel's complex presentation; however, this is its essence. Also, I believe that Hegel was right. Those three rights are the moral rights, and there are no moral rights beyond those three. If the three moral rights are granted, the conditions for decent morality are more favorable than if they are not granted. But, I would add as a remark, *contra* Hegel, that one can be a morally existing individual without being a subject in the Hegelian double meaning, and one can be such under all possible circumstances.

Technology and Redemption

The philosophically significant radical thinking of the 19th century began – after Feuerbach's initiative – with Marx.

With the resolve to destroy the metaphysical systems and to unmask the world of the spirit as the distorted mirror image of reality, 19th-century radical thinking reversed Platonism, and engaged itself in inventing a new, other kind, of metaphysics. This novel metaphysics, however, never clicked, or at least it never clicked absolutely, irrespective of the intentions of its author. Marx wanted his conception to click, and so did Freud but, to offer a counter-example, Nietzsche did not. Here I have enumerated the three most influential radical thinkers of the 19th century. The theories, conceptions, ideas, and endeavors of the three men were entirely different. What brought them together in the minds of their contemporaries and successors is their enterprise of the reversal of metaphysics. Their conscious purpose was to dethrone and to unmask metaphysics in all of its forms (religion included), to fulfill and ridicule the promises of the Enlightenment. Yet men are living in two worlds. The deconstruction of metaphysics could be successful, but the empirical world could not be identified with the actual, true, essential world as such. The essence and the appearance had to be contrasted once again, in a new way, with a partially new vocabulary. The "real world" could not be located "up there" given that the Heaven was dethroned, but it could not be located "down here" either, because the difference between essence and appearance had to be maintained.[23] As a result, the "real world" was conceived as being hidden below the Earth, in the deep, in the cave, behind the walls. Science or philosophy had set the task of deciphering the essence of reality from its distorted appearance and, like good old metaphysics, the surface is not just hiding the essence but also distorting it. The thinker is to provide the key to the hidden essence, to help approach what is behind the seeming reality – from reality itself.

The new metaphysics, the reversal of the old, excels in digging deep into the essence and unmasking the illusions, appearances, and ideologies that distort it. This unconscious metaphysics can raise claims to be a "science."[24] Marx and Freud prided themselves in having discovered new sciences. Among those three radicals, Marx was the most metaphysical. Freud, after all, said in some places[25] that our main instincts are our mythology.[26] Nietzsche's metaphysical presuppositions were consciously and openly presented; moreover, they were recommended only for the few free spirits who were strong enough to stand the test of their acceptance.[27] Marx could devise a grandiose theory of modernity because he was convinced that his theory was scientific, absolutely true, and foolproof.

None of the three radical thinkers of the 19th century faced the paradoxes of modernity with utter resolve. But for Marx none existed; he – in Hegel's tradition – dissolved the paradoxes into dialectical motions. This makes him the most representative theorist of modernity in the century that has been stamped by the idea of progress. But he was also the most radical critic of the century of progress.

Marx formulated his grand narrative in two main texts, with several additional versions. All of them tell the story of the finally glorious march of freedom and reason. In the first version, elaborated in a fragmentary way in the unpublished *Paris Manuscripts*, Marx still resists the temptation of foundation. No ultimate principle or foundation (*archē*) is yet established here. The hidden purpose of history is incipient in the category (the idea) of man or, more precisely, in the idea of the human condition ("the generic essence"). Marx gives a phenomenological account of the main constituents of this generic essence (*Dasein*). There is an "if/then" teleological necessity here. If the human essence unfolds, it can only unfold its own categories.[28] The human essence was in fact unfolded (in history), and thus it unfolded its own categories.[29] The main categories of the generic essence are work (objectivation), sociality, universality, reason, and freedom.[30]

Marx makes his first essentialist move when he privileges one of the several constituents of *Dasein*, namely objectivation (as work), and when he identifies (in fact) all kinds of objectivation/subjectivation[31] with work (and labor) in the narrow sense of the word and, finally, when he narrows the analysis of work to the conditions of exploitation and the alienation of labor under capitalism.

There remained several breaks in the conception which were obviously noticed by the author. In order to come to an essentialist conclusion, Marx needed an essentialist starting-point. This he elaborated in the *German Ideology* (another unpublished manuscript), with the invention of "the materialist conception of history."[32] The grand narrative of the *German Ideology* is already based on the redemptive power of technology. When technology (as an *archē*) takes the place of creativity (as the main constituent of the generic essence), Marx plunges deeply into metaphysics,[33] although he believes that he has switched his perspective from philosophy to science, from idealist speculation into the territory of empirical observation.[34]

The forces of production now become the *archē*, the ultimate foundation; the development of the forces of production plays the role of the independent variable of historical development (progression). Contrary to Hegel, there is no ambiguity here: the *archē* is named. The line that leads up to us is identified as the constant development of technology (of know-how), as constant accumulation of pragmatic/instrumental knowledge.

Technology and its development is by definition rational, because it is through the development of technology that the metabolism between society and nature[35] leads in gradations to the domination and mastery of society (man) over nature. The borders of nature are constantly pushed back. It is the rational being, the reason of men, that pushes back those limits. Marx thinks in terms of an infinite process of progression, yet with a decisive *caesura*, the point from which nature would yield everything to satisfy all human needs.[36] Marx never conceived of the possible exhaustion of natural resources, nor did he conceive of the finitude and fragility of human reserves. After all, the borderlines of nature will be pushed back into the nature of the human race; men will become progressively more humanized.

As far as the internal and external human reserves were concerned, Marx saw only quantitative limits, never essential ones. At the beginning of historical development, technology could not satisfy human needs. As long as novel needs are produced without there being enough suppliers to meet everyone's demands, there must be a social division of labor (class society), alienation, and exploitation. Capitalism, in which the forces of production enjoy unprecedented growth, is the last class society, because it creates the conditions for the abolishment of scarcity. In the (near) future only one kind of scarcity will remain in force, and this is the scarcity of time. The day has only 24 hours, and man is mortal. But the species is immortal.[37]

The whole history of the human race is, for Marx, the history of mediation. Contrary to Hegel, for whom the absence of mediation brings doom to the world, in Marx mediation brings doom to each and every historical period and thereby opens up the possibility of a new mode of production. Economy is the name of mediation. Human relations, spirit, culture, and politics are just superstructures of the economic relations. Economic relations, the so-called relations of production, mediate between the forces of production and the totality of a given world (modes of production, which in a good Hegelian manner include both.) In the few but important hints that Marx offers us about his ideas of a communist future and of the end of alienation, the disappearance of all mediation, of everything particular, appears as the point from which to move forward. In the communist world there will be no market, no economy, no state, no family, no social classes, no stratification, no nations, no peoples, not even professions: only individuals and human-kind remain on the stage – the universal and the singular. They are directly related or, rather, united. Some will be astonished that in the texts of the great founding father of "scientific socialism," the word "individual" is the term that most frequently appears.

Marx's grand narrative begins with prehistoric times and expands into the distant future, the actualization of the unity of the *individuum* and the species, the end of alienation. He speaks about "the riddle of history solved,"[38] and this is not just a metaphor or figure of speech. The riddle of history is already solved if we do have prescience of the solution.

Until the birth of the 19th-century perspective, only God was supposed to be in possession of prescience; now men are expected to possess it. Even Hegel's witty remark that if you look at the world rationally, the world will look back upon you rationally, does not promise full transparency and is not applicable to the future, to the territory other than Rhodus. Marx says that man makes History (although under specific conditions), and that man can know what he makes.[39] The difference between the past and the future is known – for otherwise the future could not be known. This difference reduces to the newly acquired capacity of man to create all the conditions of his free actions freely.

History is the development of freedom. When the riddle of History is solved in praxis (in communism), Freedom will become absolute. The absence of mediations, of all the particularities in Marx's vision of communism, is the precondition of thinking Freedom as the Absolute. There are no external limits, then; neither nature nor society sets man's limits.[40] Only the individual can set limits for himself – this is tantamount to absolute autonomy. Man can develop all of his abilities; or, rather, only the development of one of his abilities can set a limit to the development of others. Let me repeat that mortality is the only thing that divides men – not mankind – from the gods.

Absolute freedom is absolutely rational. The final victory of freedom is, in Marx's story, also the final victory of Reason. Reason is almost always identified with mastery and creativity; that is, with domination of nature and with the exercise of human powers. Freedom means that the exercise of our own powers is only dependent upon our own selves. One of Marx's main accusations against the market is its irrationality. In the market, men cannot plan, they cannot exactly foresee the results of their action; things just happen behind their backs, frequently crossing their will and purpose. Marx was convinced that short of rational mastery there is a human waste – waste of labor time, waste of materials, and so on. Only in the case of a total mastery over nature and self-mastery of society is there a lack of waste. Marx contrasts the rationality of production with the irrationality of the relations of production. Within a factory, in the technical production process, there exist rational cooperation and a rational technical division of labor. Yet in the market, the territory of the social division of labor, of property relationships and valorization, everything is irrational. The abolition of private property, of the market, brings about freedom and rationality simultaneously, given that the relations of production will be brought into harmony with the forces of production; that is, with technology and the ability to use it.

I have recounted Marx's story briefly in order to sensitize why it was that both freedom and rationality were conceived so unproblematically in his dramatically optimistic version of the grand narrative. Although the history of mankind hitherto had been the history of class struggles, alienation, exploitation, and domination, it was still progressing toward the arrival of the last class society – capitalism. It is always the *archē* (the development of forces of production) that warrants the progressive tendency in world history. And, although Marx speaks about uneven development and has duly observed that everything is not always more developed in a higher mode of production than an earlier one,[41] he had no doubts that the future would be the world of total perfection. Marx believed, in the last instance, in gains without losses. He believed in the accumulation of all possible gains of history under the conditions of absolute freedom and rationality. The dream of gains without losses is seductive; it is a beautiful dream. But the theoretical foundation of this dream is fragile and its actual possibility absurd.

So far, I have discussed the Marxian grand narrative as a manifestation of modernist consciousness in the 19th century. His radical reversal of metaphysics; his unproblematic confidence in human reason, creativity, and freedom; his confidence in treating the present as a transitory stage, as the trampoline from which mankind will jump (in a revolution) into the future – all of these are symptoms of high modernity's perspective, yet do not amount to a theory of modernity. But Marx's self-description was in a way correct: this perspective was conducive to Marx's insight into the operation of modernity, an insight which exerted a tremendous – overt and covert – influence on the modernist perception of modernity for more than a century.

"All that is solid melts into air," declares Marx in the *Communist Manifesto*. Capitalism has destroyed all solidarities and loyalties, all firm beliefs and institutions of the pre-modern world. What was once the borderline beyond which men could not go will now become the limit that is constantly overcome.[42] Capitalism is for Marx the first (and transitory) stage of modernity. The modern *revolution* begins with capitalism. Capitalism revolutionized everything, and finally presents the already thoroughly modern world on a platter to the proletariat, which will destroy capitalism only to utilize the yields of the modern revolution for the benefit of humankind.[43] Sometimes, Marx distinguishes between more than just two stages of modernity (there is a transitory stage between capitalism and communism), but it is capitalism – the first and transitory stage of modernity – that he discusses with both vitriolic criticism and passionate enthusiasm.

I will sum up Marx's modernist conception of modernity (chiefly capitalism) in eight theses.[44]

Thesis 1. Modern society is dynamic and future-oriented: expansion and industrialization comprise its main features.

Marx is perhaps the first to constantly juxtapose the pre-modern and the modern (all pre-capitalist formations with the capitalist formation). All pre-capitalist societies are static and tradition-oriented, whereas capitalism is dynamic and future-oriented. (This is the reason why it removes all traditions from itself.) It is industrial capitalism that triggers the development of modernity – this is its "historical mission." Whether in the form of industrial capital or in other forms, capitalism expands throughout the whole world – it devours and homogenizes the world. The universality of modernity was one of Marx's major ideas, and it was confirmed by the actual historical development.[45]

Thesis 2. Modern society is rationalized.

As I have already mentioned, Marx described how the work process itself becomes wholly rationalized in capitalism.[46] Efficiency is no longer value-oriented but entirely goal-oriented. However, Marx's attitude toward this development remained ambivalent.[47] On one hand, he emphasized that production for production's sake (as an end in itself) is a major asset of modernity. Yet he could not accept that production should be related to any value other than itself.

But Marx restricted the discussion of the rationalization process to production (primarily to the work process) and did not extend it to other modern institutions.

Thesis 3. Modern society is functionalist

Marx described capitalism in terms of class relationships. But the main classes of capitalism differ from all previous classes insofar as they are so-called "socio-economic classes." The relationship of an individual to a socio-economic class is contingent, since he or she can move in between classes. Individuals can change classes, but the class relationship remains. Modern classes perform functions. The working class and the capitalist class can be described as Labor/Capital, respectively. The division of socio-economic functions is now identical to the social division of labor. The political dimension of modernity, however, cannot be described in a functionalist model, for political action and decision are socially transfunctional.[48] In Marx, however, politics was just an ideological superstructure.

Thesis 4. Science rather than religion becomes the basis of the accumulation of knowledge.

Religion was for Marx just the opiate of the people. His image of religion was deeply influenced by a high and mighty (and narrow-minded) rationalism. Still, Marx was not wrong: in modernity, knowledge is accumulated in science and not religion. It is in this sense that "God is dead."

Thesis 5. Traditional customs are dismantled and traditional virtues lost; certain values or norms become increasingly universalized.

Marx's concept of ideology, insofar as it describes the fact that particularistic interests contest one another by raising universalistic claims, grasps an important feature of the modern political life. This is precisely what Marxist movements themselves have done, even more so than other things.

Thesis 6. The canons of creation and interpretation are eroding.

In this matter, Marx's relation to capitalist modernity was ambivalent. He greeted commodity production insofar as the market destroyed all special canons with their special inherent norms (ethical canons included). But he also believed that great works of art cannot be created without a canon. Capitalism, given that it commodifies everything, is hostile to art, yet only capitalism gives birth to the fully independent individual, the creator of art. This is the issue where Marx came closest to detecting a paradox of modernity, but it appeared as the paradox of capitalism, which cannot be a real paradox since one is dealing with a transitory period. Communist society will abolish the market and let the individual genius freely develop.

Thesis 7. The concepts of "right" and "true" are pluralized.

The superstructure/model describes the pluralization of the concepts of "right" and "true." What is true from the position of one class or stratum is "untrue" from the position of the other. In addition, Marx has taken over the Hegelian position about historical truth, without subscribing to Hegel's idea that "the whole is the truth." Still, so Marx suggests, there are positions that offer a better approach to the essence of the world, and the truth formulated from this position is truer than other truths.[49]

Thesis 8. The inscrutability of the modern world and the contingency of human existence.

Capitalist relationships are inscrutable (unless one is in the possession of "science," of course), and modern men are exposed to contingency. The fetishism of commodities[50] (human relationships appear as if they were relationships among things) exemplifies the modern experience of disorientation, the modern ignorance of the consequences of one's actions and of the workings of the world. The rational (disenchanted) world is simultaneously enchanted.[51] Commodity exchange, the market, fills the world with ghostly appearances. The appearances remain ghostly as long as we do not decipher the secret. But is there a secret behind the appearances? And if there is, can it be deciphered? And what good is it, if it can be?

Reason Without Meaning

Weber, like Hegel, accepts the present not with subdued enthusiasm but with skepticism. Modernity is neither a progressive nor a regressive "stage" of world history in Weber, although his narratives can be, and frequently were, interpreted in both ways. He is interested – like those who speak of modernity from a postmodern perspective – chiefly in the specificity of modernity, in its difference and – like the modernist moderns – also in the transition from the pre-modern to the modern, in the "birth of modernity." But whether he concentrates on the specificity of the modern way of life or on the story of transition, he rejects all fundaments. There is no single independent variable for Weber in the historical development; sometimes there is one factor or another that is regarded as the most decisive. None of them can be singled out as the main cause, motivational force, or fundament of the modern way of life in general. For some readers, the famous book of Weber's youth, *Protestantism and the Spirit of Capitalism*, suggests that Protestantism (or, more generally, religion) triggered the victory of industrial capitalism. Others suggest, rather, that the rationalization of the legal system, or – similar to Marx – the rationalization of economy, was singled out by Weber as the major factor of capitalist development.

I think that all interpretations are both right and wrong, for Weber never wanted to give a final answer to the question of what has actually triggered capitalist development, since he never raised the question in this abstract manner. A historical phenomenon such as capitalism or modernity is not an objective fact; it can be approached by the subject, the individual researcher, understandingly, but not fully explained by causal laws or final causes, since thinking, imagination, attitude, and the mind itself is integral to what we are about to understand. Understanding is not just approximative knowledge, but the standpoint of approximation changes understanding itself.

Weber arrives at the stage of modern thinking at a time when the ancient social arrangement had already been destroyed. Thus he was no longer obliged to deconstruct the pre-modern social edifice with the help of a grand narrative. He did not need to deconstruct metaphysics like his great predecessors, for his thinking was already entirely post-metaphysical. When he claimed to be scientific, he thereby meant something entirely different from what Hegel or Marx meant. For Hegel "science" was the result, the sum total of historical knowledge, and this could be recognized as the logical system, whereas for Marx the task of science was to decipher the essence behind the appearances, to disclose the truth about capitalism and its doom. For Weber, science is characterized by falsifiability. Much before Popper, Weber spoke of scientific truth as fallible, temporal, transient, and falsifiable. Weber's reconstruction of the emergence of modernity is presented as tentative truth. The better, more reliable, the approximation, the more variegated are the perspectives of approximation. This is why the emergence of modernity had to be approximated from various perspectives. Weber has not chosen among them; he did not want to pick the "major cause." The modest endeavor of approximation – and for Weber science is characterized by modesty – requires *not* pointing hastily at major causes when the scientist is able to detect many. Let science discuss, analyze, and understand all of them; let it figure out and support with reliable evidence at least a few important correlations and leave the question concerning the "final cause" to non-scientific, biased, emotional narratives. Weber falls short of saying, "Leave this to philosophy." He never mentions philosophy among the value-spheres.[52] It seems as if he believed that what was once philosophy had become by now either science in its modest quest for tentative knowledge or religion in its quest for meaning. Weber rejects totalizing thinking; the different perspectives cannot be totalized unless the synthesizer occupies a hidden (and nonscientific) evaluative position.[53]

The modern arrangement is also to be contrasted with all pre-modern social arrangements in Weber's work. But his rejection of the evaluative/totalizing presentation of modernity also has a retroactive effect. Weber does not discuss pre-capitalist formations as such, or *Volksgeister* in their totality; he thinks that the past can best be described and recapitulated through histories in the plural, and not with one all-encompassing "History." There are histories told about this and that, about religions and legal systems, about the city and the agriculture; and one can follow up such histories in different periods and by different nations. Certain histories disappear for many centuries, only to reappear once again.[54] It is not only totality and universal tendencies that are suspect to Weber, but also continuity. Among other things,[55] this is why one can understand him as a reflective postmodern thinker.

The poetic character called Reason is transmuted by Weber into prosaic characters such as rationality and rationalization.

Reason was and is a polysemous word. One can distinguish between many kinds of reason, and philosophers normally do.[56] They normally put a higher value on one kind of reason than the other, but even if they do not give different values, they attribute different accomplishments to one kind of "reason" or another.[57]

Weber actually does not distinguish between different kinds of reason, but between different rationalities. He was not interested in human faculties, their essence and their exercise, but in human attitudes and ways of fighting, cooperating, and understanding. This was a great – philosophical – innovation by a so-called nonphilosopher. If one thinks of reason in terms of faculties, the whole discourse takes either an essentialist or an anthropological turn. On the contrary, one can speak of rationality without referring to generic essence or *Dasein*, without answering the question concerning the essence of man (What is man?) and without plunging into merely pseudo-empirical descriptions.[58] What was interesting for Weber was not whether the human being is more rational than emotional, but the typical motivations of human actions, and as a result the predictability and understandability of human actions. It is in this sense that he distinguishes between value rationality and purposive rationality (*Zweckrationalität*).[59] One understands a person's action (why he or she normally acts in a particular way) by understanding the values that he or she follows, or by the relationship between the means by which he or she chooses to achieve certain goals and the goals achieved.

As is well known, Weber insisted that in the modern world rational actions are less frequently guided by values and more frequently by the proper choice of means to a given end. Of course, he never proposed the stupidity[60] that there be no more values to guide modern attitudes. Rather, he proposed that for the moderns values do not overpower the rational means/goal pattern. End-realization is optimized, whether the goal is pragmatic, evaluated, or both.

Rationalization, as the expression suggests, is a kind of rationality, yet it is also the opposite of rationality. Institutions are rationalized. Actions can be rational without being rationalized. More precisely, actions are rationalized only within rationalized institutions. Yet in a rationalized institution the single action remains rational only as a part of the whole, but in itself its rationality can become truncated.[61] For example, I might obey the rules of my institution, but I am unable to set a goal, let alone to evaluate it or choose the means to realize it – for even the means are given up for me by the rationalized institution itself.[62]

In the demise of value rationality, the rationalization of institutions is the symptom as much as the condition of the disenchantment of the world. The word "disenchantment" refers to many connected yet not entirely identical phenomena – for example, the loss of myth, the end of philosophy, deficit in meaning, loss of beauty and color – yet also the abandonment of fanaticism, madness, and legitimation through charisma.[63]

Actually, Weber's description of modernity quite resembles that of Hegel: the modern world is prosaic, there is no place left for grandeur, there are no heroes, there is no poetry.[64] The difference is that in Hegel it is worthwhile to pay this price; for Weber this is at least very questionable. Weber's pessimism is closely related to his conception of value-spheres.

The concept of value-spheres does not only challenge the tradition of thinking in totalities; it also explodes Hegel's conception of modern *Sittlichkeit*. In Hegel, the common *ethos* of the modern world was warranted by the three ethical powers and by the overarching power of the state as the repository of everyone's *Sittlichkeit*. Nothing similar remains in Weber's understanding of modernity. Instead of being the unifying power and the carrier of *Sittlichkeit*, the modern – democratic – state is formalized and bureaucratized; its leaders are no longer statesmen, but at best shrewd politicians.[65] Resembling Tocqueville, Weber never allowed himself to admix sympathies with expectations. His sympathies were still with the modern legal state (*Rechtstaat*), yet his expectations of "plebiscitarian democracy" were low.

The state is, then, not the repository of highest *Sittlichkeit*, but is there a replacement? Weber does not believe in such a replacement. Rather, the absence of a common *ethos* marks the modern world. However, this does not result in the absence of all kinds of *ethos*. At least, Weber designs his understanding of the modern value-spheres as of *value-spheres*. This is not a world in which everyone is related to a greater or lesser extent to the same ethical powers. Rather, people are related to *their own ethical powers*. They can choose among the deities of the modern Olympus. Each modern social sphere is also a value-sphere. It is required of all those who belong to one of these spheres that they acquire the values of their own sphere, and abide by the rules of this sphere as to their own binding ethical power.

Science, politics, art, religion, law, economy – these are the major value-spheres.[66] Ethics or morals cannot be value-spheres, because each sphere has its own norms and rules, its own ethics, and the person must choose among them. He or she cannot join all of them, perhaps not even more than one authentically.[67] The choice of a value-sphere is, namely, an *existential choice.*[68] When one chooses a value-sphere, one chooses oneself as the man or woman who is committed to this sphere. Weber discussed all value-spheres, but only two were discussed from the vantage point of the existential choice: science and politics,[69] in his lectures "Science as a vocation" and "Politics as a vocation."

It is true that there exists an ethical commitment for Weber which transcends the borderlines or the validity limits of the single spheres. This is a negative obligation, an interdiction: there is to be no admixing of the spheres – the norms of one sphere are not to be applied to the other spheres. This was good advice. Europeans soon realized what disaster follows if politics becomes aestheticized, or if religion, art, or the economy become politicized. It turned out that Weber's interdiction is in fact an interdiction against the totalization of society and against fundamentalism.[70]

This brings us back to the main theme of the disenchantment of the world.

All spheres can be existentially chosen, but not all spheres are in an equally dominating position. In the (modern) times of rationality and ratonalization, the spheres that profit most from disenchantment of the world will occupy a dominating position. Rationalization became widespread, and religion and art also became increasingly rationalized.[71] But not everything profits from rationalization. Only the economy and science profit from it – for they (contrary to the values of other spheres) gain importance, and also progressively develop under the condition of rationalization. Although all spheres can be chosen existentially, science is the dominating spiritual sphere of modernity. But we know that science is fallible and falsifiable, that its true knowledge never amounts to "truth." Weber succinctly, although not outspokenly, distinguishes between the concept of truth and the concept of true knowledge. True knowledge is always temporary, it will be superseded. Truth is absolute; it is Meaning. If you embrace Truth, your life has a meaning. Scientific pursuits will never provide one's life with meaning, except for the life of the scientist for whom science is a vocation, a calling. Religion and art are the spheres that can disclose Truth and provide life with Meaning. But in the modern life – although they can always be existentially chosen – they will never dominate, for they do not profit but, rather, lose through rationalization. The expression "disenchantment with the world" means first and foremost that the dominating spheres of modern life do not provide life with meaning. As far as the dominating spheres (science, politics, the economy) are concerned, life has no meaning.

The dominating spheres (particularly science and the economy) are the spheres of accumulation (accumulation of knowledge and wealth). But progressive accumulation is an infinite process. There is never an end to it, neither in a single person's life nor in the lives of a generations. The absolute present time is the world of dissatisfaction. Modern society is a dissatisfied society, for the major needs are cumulative, quantified and quantifiable, whereas the needs that can be satisfied are provided by spheres that are neither progressive nor cumulative – by the spheres of religion and art.

This picture looks grave. It is grave but not entirely dark, for Weber believes in the vocation of science. In his mind, this is a great and challenging vocation. Perhaps this is a vocation that suits modern man more than all others, with the exception of politics. Only these two vocations make modern man face human finitude, transience, and fragility with honesty. Those who choose science as a vocation (and perhaps even politics as a vocation) also choose to face the thought and the experience of human finitude not with despair but with courage and pride. They willingly accept everything that transience offers and everything it takes away, and they do not seek solace or consolation in other places and other spheres. They understand themselves as visitors in a place and time of which they know little and where they can only do small things. But there is something that they can still grasp and something that they can still do. The true dignity of modern man, so Weber believes, rests with this unconscious and modest courage.

3

The Two Constituents of Modernity I:

The Dynamics of Modernity[1]

In what follows, I will distinguish between two constituents of modernity: the *dynamics of modernity* and the *modern social arrangement*. What I would term the "essence" of modernity is the correlation of the two. I will begin the discussion of the two constituents with the dynamics of modernity, because the dynamics appeared long before the birth of the modern social arrangement.[2] There is no modernity in existence before (or without) the appearance of the modern social arrangement, whereas the modern social arrangement without modernity's dynamic is a truncated version of modernity, constantly endangered in its very survival.

It is safe to say that the *dynamics of modernity* is a kind of dialectics. After all, the philosophical concept of dialectics – in its Platonian as well as in its Hegelian version – have employed the inherent motion of the dynamics of modernity while conceptualizing it. Yet since the dynamics of modernity – as I see it – is not modelled in the spirit of Plato and/or Hegel, I will refer to it as the *undialectical dialectics*. Undialectical dialectics can also be enlightenment, since it introduces, accompanies, and follows the process of enlightenment. It can possibly be understood in the sense of Horkheimer/Adorno, as the dialectics of enlightenment.

The story that I will briefly recapitulate is a European story. It belongs to the several representative autobiographies of Europe. This is a story that can be told exclusively from the standpoint of modernity and, more precisely, from the standpoint of the European Enlightenment, understood as the event that ushered in modernity. The position that one takes toward modern enlightenment directly affects the way in which one tells the story.

The dynamics of modernity first appear in the European autobiography in the city of Athens during the finest days of democracy. Socrates and the Sophists are the significant actors who embody the dynamics in both action and thought. The tradition is called into question. Convictions that had been held to be true, holy, and certain are now queried and tested. What was believed to be true can now be proven to be untrue; what has been accepted as right can now be proven wrong. "This is not true, but something else is," "this is not good, but something else is" – all assertions such as these result from negation. More precisely, all assertions presuppose that something that was hitherto asserted will now be negated, that what had been taken for granted is no longer a given. If the father's wisdom does not stand the test of reason, it will be refuted, ridiculed, annihilated.

If nothing is taken for granted, everyone can ask why. Why should I agree to do this and not that? Why should I believe in the truth of this rather than the truth of that? These are the questions that usher in the dynamics of modernity. These are the questions that will keep it alive.

It is not difficult to see that the deconstructive move of the dynamics of modernity cannot be stopped from within the dynamics itself. If the dynamics are stopped or required to be stopped, the stopping power must be external to the dynamics.

The dynamics cannot be stopped from within the dynamics because its logic is that of bad infinitude.[3] Everything is open to query and to testing; everything is subject to rational scrutiny and refuted by argument. Now, rational argument can come to a resting point only under the condition that it is backed by something final (an *archē* or axiom) that is taken for granted. Finally, the argument or the demonstration must have recourse to something that does not need to be demonstrated. If there is no such *archē*, there is no fixed point upon which to rely. Every argument begets new arguments, every truth becomes untruth, every truth can be proven untrue and vice versa. How can one stop the process of constant negation without an *archē*?

But why must one stop the process of constant negation if the negation is followed by a truer assertion? Why cannot one shake every conviction and belief constantly and continuously? And if the questioning needs to be stopped, what should limit the infinite dynamics, and how?

The dynamics of modernity first begin to shake traditions and convictions in a world of tradition and fixed convictions. They can be helpful in the delivery of a modern social arrangement. But they have successfully completed this task only once, 2,000 years after its first appearance on the so-called world stage. At the time of their first appearance, the dynamics of modernity encountered a very ambiguous reception.

Philosophy, at least beginning with Socrates, was the offspring of these dynamics. Socrates/Plato (as well as, in all probability, Parmenides and Heraclitus) introduced the motions of the dialectical procedure of delegitimation/legitimation (such as: the appearance, the opinion is false; the other world, the essence, is true) into a new language game. The second (legitimating) move has created a new measure of Goodness and Truth fit to replace the tradition. We now call this new language game metaphysics. Philosophies invented new fixed points to replace the traditional stories and beliefs, mainly those traditions and beliefs that philosophy has helped to destroy.[4] From then on, fixed points such as Being, Idea, or pure Form became the main characteristic from which one could negate opinions in a legitimate way. Philosophy made a double move: it has taken over the motion of negation, shaken the certainties of tradition, but invented an end-station, a limit to questioning, a nontraditional boundary of "truth," which was supposed to have been proven by the same kind of rational arguments or demonstrations that destroyed mere opinions and sheer beliefs.

The dynamics of modernity – once they go on unabated – destroy the life of the tradition. And if there is no new world to usher in, the work of dialectics becomes destructive. The transformation of dialectics into metaphysical philosophy was a way of rescuing the *polis* from destruction while maintaining enlightenment, *logos* (the dynamics of modernity as squeezed into a metaphysical straitjacket, such that further questioning becomes impossible). While helping Socrates, his master, to destroy the tradition of the fathers, Plato created a new tradition in which the dynamics of modernity are halted from above, by the Sun, by the *demiurge*, by the supreme Idea of Goodness, by the "higher world."[5]

Hegel is right when he accuses Plato of sacrificing the free personality (freedom itself) on the altar of Certainty. Yet, he is also confident that in the wake of modern enlightenment this sacrifice is no longer needed. It remains to be seen whether it is or is not.

Hegel's proposition is simple.[6] Since the modern world is pluralistic, the freedom of the personality is warranted; there are three (not just two) ethical powers, and as a result dialectics is, and will be, the *normal life process* of the world. Modernity will not just resist the destructive power of negation, for it is, rather, maintained and constantly rejuvenated by it. Without negation, the modern world would be fossilized. The main contrast between all pre-modern worlds and the modern one is that the traditional worlds were really destroyed through fatal and tragic conflicts, whereas the modern world is not destroyed but fuelled toward evolution by its own conflicts. The conflicts of the modern world will not take a tragic shape; this world will not go down because of insoluble contradictions. In the modern world, so Hegel thinks, all of the contradictions will be sublated. This is why the dynamics of modernity are constructive once the modern social arrangement has taken the place of the old. The question of whether the dynamics of modernity should be stopped, and by what power and how, cannot be raised. The dynamics must go on without being stopped. Yet something absolutely firm still remains in the modern world which cannot be destroyed by the modern dynamics, just as the sea cannot be destroyed by its waves. *This is the modern social arrangement itself.* The motions of the dynamics of modernity are the waves of the modern social arrangement.

Hegel's description fits well with the normative concept of modernity. It is true that modernity is not destroyed by negation, but flourishes through it.[7] This can be best exemplified by the role of dynamic justice in the life of a modern society or state.[8] The justice of the standing institution is constantly challenged. In a liberal political order it can be challenged by everyone. And once a new institution is in place, citizens begin to challenge the justice of this new institution immediately. Nothing remains stable, nothing is consensually accepted; there is dissent about everything everywhere. This is modern life. We can all cry out in indignation, whether we are right or wrong, that this institution is not just and other institutions should replace it because they would be far more just. It is true (and this is the internal aspect of the dynamics of modernity) that the challenge in the name of justice almost never comes from the same quarter. One party accuses the institution of injustice, whereas the other defends it and declares it to be fair and just. Two conceptions of justice then collide, yet both operate with the same concept of justice, namely dynamic justice.[9] They take dynamic justice itself for granted. The defenders of the institution under attack say: "It is just as it is, you are wrong," instead of saying "How dare you attack the sacred order?"

Not all versions and manifestations of the dynamics of modernity are as constructive as the institutionalization of dynamic justice. The dynamic of modernity is not confined to the limits of dynamic justice. As already mentioned, the dynamics cannot be stopped from the inside. With dynamic justice, it takes a relatively lengthy process to change an institution (an institution which, we should not forget, is defended as being just for a long time by many). This is the case whether it is social security, divorce law, the retirement age, the power of presidency, and so on, so that men and women can get used to the changes and can choose to modify their idea of justice. The ongoing reformation of institutions very rarely does harm, for example, if the institution is constantly changed to the basic law itself. To the contrary, it does much good, by keeping the spirit of citizenry alive in matters that concern a greater part of the constituencies. It is an exception when institutions are challenged absolutely, as in "There should not be institutions." Anarchism is as rare as it is idiosyncratic. This is why the idea that one needs to put limits on dynamic justice has occurred only in totalitarian, authoritarian, and fundamentalist societies. There is talk of nihilism even without there being any sign of nihilism. Yet nihilism is still not only the fancy of conservatives and traditionalists.

Marx said, and he meant it as praise for the greatness of capitalism: "Everything that is solid melts into air." But what if he were right, what if everything solid would just evaporate? Can men live without things to rely upon, without anything stable or solid? Is this what Enlightenment without limits is about?

Enlightenment is Janus-faced. The problem is that the two faces can rarely be seen simultaneously; enlightenment turns one of its faces to the spectators and another to the actors.

Hegel told a story about Enlightenment in which the new kind of rationalism, "pure insight," appeared as the negation of religion, as "pure faith." Yet it has turned out, so Hegel's story continues, that the essence of both is in the last instance the same. The essence of pure faith is Thought, whereas the essence of pure insight (enlightenment) is the Subject.[10] In Hegel's dialectics, both Faith and Insight sublate each other and, finally, Thought and Subject are united in the honeymoon bed. Enlightenment is preserved but superseded. Therefore, *not* everything solid melts into the air in Hegel's system.

But if the dynamics of modernity develop and reproduce as an *undialectical dialectics*, no sublation can be expected. Enlightenment is far from being superseded; it remains constantly at work. The spectator who sees only the young and beautiful face of the enlightenment is committed to the rationalistic enlightenment; the spectator who sees only the old and ugly face of enlightenment is committed to romantic enlightenment. I speak of enlightenment in both cases, for it is not only the rationalistic kind but also the romantic kind that is practicing the dynamics of modernity. Both represent the enlightenment.

Rationalistic enlightenment relies on technology as the *archē* of modernity, whether or not it makes this explicit.[11] One can be convinced that in technology and science, these two cumulative and progressively developing institutions, nothing solid will remain. New technology should constantly replace the old. Rationalization requires – among other things – the constant replacement of the old with the new. And the word "progression" also stands for the constant replacement of the old by the new. The human mind busies itself with inventing new models. If science and technology were to cease to develop, the modern world would collapse.

Rationalistic enlightenment applies the model of technology to all aspects and spheres of modernity;[12] for example, to the way in which new institutions replace the old ones. In rendering the model of the dynamics of modernity, Hegel was still thinking in the old dramatic scenes of politics, and employed theological concepts such as sin, hardened heart, forgiveness, and so on, to describe the model of the political circulation of rationality in modernity. Yet the victorious empirical model of the rationalistic enlightenment is not just undialectical – it is also prosaic. An old institution needs to be replaced by the new because it does not function well. The new is not an evil; it does not need to be forgiven. Rather, it must be compared with the old according to its effectiveness; it is through comparison, measuring, numbering, and calculating that superiority is granted.

Romanticism soon discovers the ugly face of enlightenment. Everything solid melts into air. For the men and women of romanticism, life is not a technological problem to be solved. It needs to be lived. The solid things are not machines, but beliefs, myths, customs, ceremonies – and truths. If all that is solid melts into air – and this is the world toward which modernity is heading – then all truths are melting into the air and nothing will remain sacred. If there will be no more gods, myths, faiths, truths, emotions, and intuitions left to destroy, because all of them have already been destroyed, enlightenment will turn against itself in a fit of destructive madness. This and similar gloomy predictions are not entirely unfounded. Modernity's dynamics – the undialectical dialectics – are both destructive and self-destructive.[13] After having destroyed everything around itself, after having transformed the world into a spiritual desert, it might destroy itself.[14]

Hegel knew what he was saying: infinite subjectivity will run amok if not united with or sublated into thought, into the totality of the truth of the philosophical cum religious tradition. The subject as subject negates all objectivities and destroys everything except itself, the destroyer. The modern subject is free. There is no limit to subjective freedom.

Yet, all things are limited. They are things because they are limited. Ideas and thoughts are in this sense also "things." One needs to distinguish them from other ideas and thoughts, as one distinguishes one thing from other things. The dynamics of modernity first turn against distinctions.

Distinctions are reformulated and limits made elastic. Traditional distinctions are lifted; for example, the distinction between men with titles and those without, the distinction between sacred and profane. What had been previously disallowed is now permitted. There remains, then, only one distinction – one that does not distinguish anything except itself: the Difference. The elimination of distinctions is *universalization*.

The issue of the limit poses itself again, for, as I have said many times, the dynamics of modernity cannot be stopped from within, and can turn and move in every direction. After the barriers that stood before the modern social arrangement had been removed by the dynamics of modernity and the universal categories had been created (such as "man," "art," "culture") the process of modernity's dynamics continued to draw distinctions between the permitted and nonpermitted, the good and bad. The certitudes of yesteryear are shaken – all certitudes are shaken. Yet, one needs to understand that there always remains a limit, a border, a barrier, as long as there are distinctions; for example, the distinction between within/without, or essential/unessential. The deconstruction reaches its limit if there is nothing left to deconstruct, for nothing remains outside. If there is nothing external, finitude as such becomes destroyed by the undialectical dialectics. Then one can no longer say "This idea is not true, it is a prejudice," but one will say "there is no truth." (In such a statement, all distinctions are lifted.) One no longer says "It is wrong to distinguish between cultivated and non-cultivated people, for all people have a kind of culture," but, rather, one says "All cultures are alike." (Here also, all distinctions are lifted.) One does not say "What you have regarded as good is not good, or it is not good in an unqualified way," but, rather, "There is no good." (Again, all distinctions are lifted.) The Janus-faced enlightenment tells us with one of its mouths that we had better be aware of our transience and finitude; yet its other mouth tells us that it makes no sense to distinguish between good and bad and the like, that there is no truth. It destroys all finitude, for it destroys the conditions of finitude: the possibility of *distinction and of identification*. Enlightenment thus becomes *nihilism*.

There is truth in the insight that the end of enlightenment is nihilism.[15] But if the end of enlightenment is nihilism, enlightenment as such is nihilism, for the tendency that leads to its fulfillment is "presencing" in every move of the dynamics of modernity as undialectical dialectics.

This seems to be a logical problem, but it is very real, and not only in the language game of philosophy or cultural discourse.[16] The end of enlightenment (nihilism) is achieved when it is fulfilled, and it is fulfilled when there is nothing left to destroy in the circle of finite things. When there is no tradition left to negate, the dynamics of modernity itself will be negated. If there are no more distinctions to be eliminated, the elimination of the distinctions will be negated. After the process of universalization, the dynamics of modernity turns against universality to establish new differences, differences which are neither traditional nor continuous, differences which are freely constituted through the negation of universality. One can say, for example, "Modernity as such is nihilistic, it arrives at the conclusion that nothing is true – and this is a true statement about enlightenment. As a result every discourse is futile and self-serving, and ought to be eliminated." The conclusion can also be modified: "All discourse has to be stopped, for the negation of the truth of nihilism needs to be enthroned." The latter argument is in fact the recapitulation of the chain of thoughts of a Lenin or a Mussolini. In their pragmatic – political formulation, only "the bourgeois intellectuals" continue to talk; yet one should act instead. Negation is to be absolutely first: action destroys the thing, and not just the mere thought (the idea) of the thing. However, after the new truth has been established, discourse should be eliminated (one should stop talking or criticizing). For the truth of the new truth cannot be doubted.

In fact, contemporary fundamentalism is the offspring of the nihilistic enlightenment. One absolute truth is articifially established on the ruins of the destroyed old truths, and their destroyers will be hailed as repositories of supreme wisdom.[17]

The absolute truths which are embraced through the negation of nihilism are, to repeat, also nihilistic in their essence. They are not traditional even if they appear in a traditional garment.[18] They are reinvented, reinterpreted, and re-institutionalizedin the mode of enlightenment discourse, through the motion of negation. Their certainties do not precede uncertainties, but are embraced as a reaction, as the "indeterminate" negation of uncertainties.[19] Undialectical dialectics negates destruction and becomes constructive. Needless to say, this construction comes into being through the simple (and undialectical) negation of nihilism as destruction, and becomes destructive overall.[20]

Long before the real enlightenment discourse arrived at the historical point of its own destruction in the European totalitarian regimes, Nietzsche put nihilism at the centerpoint of his philosophical reflection. For Nietzsche, enlightenment *is* nihilism. He offered the deepest and the most circumspect diagnosis of nihilism to this very day by analyzing its disturbing symptoms.[21]

Nietzsche begins his genealogy of nihilism at the point at which the dynamics of modernity was first launched, in the stories of Socrates and of the sophists. But, unlike the typical autobiographical European narratives which I sketchily presented at the beginning of this chapter,

Nietzsche's story detects continuity where others speak of discontinuity.[22] In his mind, Judaism and Christianity speak almost the same language as the sophists and Plato. Judaism and Christianity are speaking this nihilistic language not because they believe that nothing is true or good, but because they reverse the value hierarchy of the pre-modern social arrangement. In a pre-modern social arrangement the good men are the noble ones, the members of the aristocracy, whereas badness is associated with slavery, with being common, with dwelling on the lowest level of the pyramid. This is a very deep insight. Almost all of the variants[23] of the pre-modern social arrangement had pyramidal shapes.[24] In a "normal" genealogy the heroes of a pre-modern social order are presented as offspring of gods or demi-gods. This is the case in all Indo-Germanic myths. The Jewish genealogy is truly "abnormal." Instead of legitimating themselves with divine origins, the ancient Hebrews legitimate themselves as offspring of slaves (of slaves who had been elected by the only true God as his people). Christianity added its token to this reversal of values. It declared the superiority of the kind of love which spreads from bottom up: the lowliest creatures are loved by God the most. This is a blatant absurdity if one identifies oneself with the spirit of an old and aristocratic order.[25] Nietzsche intended to take an extremist position and provoke his times. But by now his description of the message of Jews and Christians seems to be a rather sound interpretation. The fundamental truths of the Christian religion contributed to the destruction of the old Roman order, and were later also frequently used as de-legitimating devices against the embodiment of Christianity on Earth. Heretics lived on this tension and contradiction.[26]

Nietzsche distinguishes between different kinds of nihilism and tells various stories about their manifestations.[27] The main constituents of nihilism are the reversal of values, asceticism, and denial of life, but also cognitive thinking, theoretical thinking, democracy, social thinking, "Alexandrinism," and decadence in general. In his most dramatic formulations, he points to two main kinds of nihilism: one is about willing nothing, the other is about willing The Nothing.[28] Negation is in principle the essential feature of all Nietzschean variants of the dynamics of modernity, but this negation is not always understood as the negation of tradition, truth, and so on, but also includes the move to construct truth,[29] to build another world – one negates life in both forms. It is interesting that sometimes Nietzsche also refers to himself as a nihilist, an absolute nihilist by virtue of negating all decadent (passive) nihilisms and opening up the perspective of a world beyond the modern (democratic and egalitarian) social arrangement. This was, indeed, a very modern idea.

In the 19th century, modernity's dynamics had not yet turned on itself. This happened only in the 20th century, and it continues to happen after WWII. This is the case (even though, for the present, in a less threatening and a less catastrophic form) just as in the era of European totalitarianism, during which – even though the various regimes had enlightenment – they were thinking and acting like the spiritually decayed children of "enlightenment as nihilism."[30]

Enlightenment as nihilism produces all of the paradoxes of modernity – the paradoxes of freedom and truth. There is nothing "objectively" paradoxical in the modern social arrangement. But since the modern social arrangement cannot come into being or survive without the help of modernity's dynamics, if one thinks the modern social arrangement, one must also think the dynamics of modernity and the paradoxes that it produces. The emphasis is on "if one thinks," for in pragmatic dealings the paradoxes are not thought through but are mostly pragmatically oriented and temporalized. For example, universality and difference compose a paradox for essential thinking. Yet in the course of pragmatic dealings there is first a tendency toward universalization. If there is nothing left to universalize (or for other contingent, sometimes political, reasons), then it will come to a *volte face*. The discourse will turn around and at this time, at least for a while, universality will be abandoned in favor of particularity. This is actually happening now. After a while, one can expect a new *volte face* to come about. Unreflected postmodernity jumps onto the last bandwagon and participates in the current temporalizing avoidance of the paradox. Reflected postmoderns, however, face the paradox.

4

The Two Constituents of Modernity II:

The Modern Social Arrangement

The midwife of the modern social arrangement is the dynamics of modernity. The modern social arrangement cannot come into being unless it is preceded by a process of enlightenment. Yet, just as modernity's dynamics can disappear into nought without having helped the birth of the modern social arrangement, once the modern social arrangement sets foot in one place in the world (and this happened in Western Europe), it will expand and be exported with or without the dynamics of modernity.

Let me first give a preliminary idea of my concept of the "modern social arrangement." What I call a "social arrangement" can be also described as the distribution of social positions, social division of labor, and the like. The dividing line between the pre-modern and the modern ways of social arrangement emerges from the *essentially* different ways in which social positions are distributed, or the "labor" (function) is socially divided. In Luhmann's terminology, the moderns switch from the model of stratification to a functionalist model.[1]

In the first approach I will distinguish between the pre-modern and the modern social arrangements in the following way.

In the pre-modern social arrangement, the social functions that men and women perform are mostly determined by the social position allocated to them in the hierarchy of social stratification at the time of their birth. Contrarily, in the modern social arrangement the position that men and women finally occupy in the hierarchy of stratification is acquired (in the main) by them, through their performance and the exercise of their abilities in fulfilling specific functions in specific institutions. In fact, there is no third possibility, of establishing a working empirical correlation between social functions performed and social position occupied.

There is, however, a third, logical possibility. One can at least imagine a society without a hierarchy of social positions and without a division of social functions. More precisely, those two need to be combined. Only if there is no division of social functions can one think a social arrangement without any hierarchy, given that a social arrangement with any hierarchy also presupposes the division of functions.[2,3] If one dismisses social utopias as models,[4] only two possible combinations remain – the pre-modern kinds and the modern kinds.

But the modern social arrangement is fossilized unless the most constructive function of modern dialectics – namely, dynamic justice – is constantly kept in motion. The more it is kept in motion and the more widely is it practiced, the more the destructive nihilism gathers momentum. This tendency, on its part, might again result in an innocuous or a dangerous *volte face*.[5]

Still, the modern social arrangement is a steamroller. Once established in one place in the world, it runs over all pre-modern cultures and arrangements.[6] It first ran over Europe, then the colonies, and by now modernity is the dominant social arrangement across the whole globe. What remains to be called pre-modern are insignificant remnants of the defunct world.

This is a preliminary statement, an hypothesis which I have not yet supported with theoretical (and empirical) evidence. There are two common elements in all objections.

The first common element originates in a too rosy picture of modernity, in the existent illusion of universal progression. Even after Auschwitz and the Gulag it seems, for some, difficult to abandon. In Asia or Africa men kill each other irrationally in local wars – must they be pre-moderns? What about the two world wars? What about Bosnia and Albania today? Are those people also pre-moderns, or are they more rational? Fundamentalism is pre-modern, they say. For example, Muslim fundamentalism is pre-modern absolutely! But why? Was the ideology of Nazism or Bolshevism less fundamentalist? Or are American biopolitics[7] less fundamentalist?

It is easy to identify modernity with its normative concept and denounce all states and societies which do not live up to this normative concept (rationality, universality, and so on) as pre-moderns.

The second element of the position which maintains that the so-called "Third World" has remained pre-modern stems from a specific interpretation of modernity as a steamroller. Since the liberal forms of life are the representative manifestations of freedom, and freedom is the grounding of modernity in the states or countries – so the argument runs – where there are no liberal forms of life, modernity has not yet set foot. Only the best functioning liberal democracies with their liberal ways of life are modern. Everything else is pre-modern.

There is some truth to this argument, for modernity has two constituents in my view, and if one of them is lacking (the dynamics of modernity) and only the social arrangement became modern, can one still speak reasonably of modernity? One cannot cut the essence of modernity into halves. If one half is absent, one could claim that the whole is also absent.

My objections to this counter-argument are as follows.

It is true that life is entirely different in different parts of the globe, and so are ideologies and political institutions. But if one only compares the countries of the so-called Third World with one another, the differences would be no less spectacular. Why stand China or Brazil closer to Papua New Guinea than to the United States or Australia? One can insist that Papua New Guinea is closer to Brazil than to Australia according to per capita production, the alleged main criterion of "development." But the idea of development, as well as the accepted yardsticks of development – of being developed, underdeveloped, developing, and so on – is itself modern. The current practice of comparing all cultures on the globe by the same yardstick and the general acceptance of a common scale for comparison indicates best that one works with the presupposition that the modern social arrangement has already been expanded across the whole globe, and what needs to be "measured" here and now is the distance of one or the other culture from the perfect model of the modern social arrangement.

I, on my part, do not think in terms of a "perfect modernity." All countries that have switched from the essence of the pre-modern arrangement into the essence of the modern arrangement are all modern. The very fact that they can be compared quantitatively (mainly by their per capita production) is just one indication of their modern character. Without being modern, they could not be compared quantitatively at all.[8] But they are moderns in their own way.

But – and here comes the most serious objection – it seems as if several cultures could not accommodate themselves to modernity at all. They are no longer pre-modern, but instead of reproducing modern forms of life, they simply perish. This can be true. After all, neither Australian aboriginals nor North American Indians could successfully adapt to modernity. They, indeed, perished or are now lingering on the social margins with the help of their conquerors. This is a loss. Yet this loss, instead of disproving my thesis about the irresistibility of the modern steamroller, confirms it. At the very present time, several African societies are plunging into constant tribal wars and chaos, showing their great difficulties in adapting to modern life. They might become able to adapt. Conversely, many cultures who seem at present well-adapted might lose this capacity. I continue to repeat that I do not know whether modernity is able to survive. But this uncertainty does not alter the description of the modern social arrangement. Also, it does not change the circumstance that modernity can survive only if it survives on the global scale, with or without heavy losses.

I will now turn to the second counter-argument. Indeed, different ways of life characterize different countries, states, and cultures. But this was true about pre-modern social arrangements as well. Even in the small archipelago of the Greek *polis* states, the ways of life in Athens, Sparta, Miletos, and Theba were essentially different.[9] This was also true of the territory in the Roman Empire. Why are we then astonished that neither the political institutions nor the ways of life are exactly the same within the modern social arrangement?

Obviously, it is because it was assumed (prematurely) that a steamroller such as modernity univeralizes, homogenizes, and thus obliterates differences. It has factually obliterated the pre-modern social arrangement and it is about to obliterate everything that is *incompatible* with the modern social arrangement. But it will not obliterate what is *compatible*. And very different ways of life – fundamentalist ways included – have turned out to be entirely compatible with the modern social arrangement.[10] One does not need to go as far as Chile or South Africa. There are tremendous differences between the dominant patterns or styles of life in Australia and the United States.[11] In Australia, religion plays a very marginal role. The United States, however, is the most religious of all countries. This is very important in matters of the way of life. Still, the United States is not only a modern state, but the state in which the dynamics of modernity and the modern social arrangement appeared from the beginning in concert.[12]

Half of the essence (of modernity) is no essence, the next objection runs. My question is, however, whether the dynamics of modernity is absent in autocratic or even totalitarian states, or whether it can take only liberal-democratic forms. I think that this belief expresses just another illusion concerning modern life.[13] Every "revolutionary" regime establishes its own institutions for the dynamics of modernity. For example, the communist and Nazi regimes constantly turned over the traditional ways of life. Although dynamic justice was outlawed, or at least strongly restricted, negation became a permanent feature of the totalitarian regimes. This was a kind of permanent revolution, always initiated from the top. The right to initiate negation rested with the absolute authority of the party. The denizens of the totalitarian regimes could have repeated with Marx more than anyone else that "Everything that is solid melts into air." Those who believe that anti-modernist fundamentalist regimes are entirely stagnant (Iran is here the only fixed example), that they do not negate, forget that modern fundamentalism comes into being through negation.[14]

Without the presence and employment of the dynamics of modernity, one cannot mobilize masses in a revolution to return to an alleged past.[15] Fundamentalism, once institutionalized, can make great use of the accumulation of technological and scientific knowledge.

One could object that modernity is founded by freedom. I, indeed, always say so. How can one then speak of societies as states, countries, and cultures as cases of the "*modern* social arrangement" if people living there are blatantly unfree?

Freedom is, first, not just political liberty. Freedom as the nonfounding foundation of modernity is the absence of limits and restrictions in general. This does not mean that there are no limits or restrictions in force for many or for the majority. In Hegel, modernity is about the freedom of all, and this also means that no single man can be absolutely free; actual individuals could be more free within pre-modern social arrangements. But this is just one modern interpretation of freedom, and it is perceived from the standpoint of a normative model.

To deny God and God's commandments, to conquer the whole world in the sign of a future-oriented ideology, to harness nature absolutely – these are all interpretations of freedom. There are almost infinite interpretations of freedom.

One is not necessarily free if one's world is founded on freedom. If nothing is sacred, some will be mightier than others. If there is no agreement about truth and good, one interpretation of true and good will still conquer and still oppress all other interpretations. And then, something might become sacred again, at least temporarily, in the form of an ideology. Modernity is not a paradise. It is just another social arrangement.[16]

My third counter-argument is empirical. The modern social arrangement is roughly 200 years old; it is a very new arrangement. Deconstruction of the pre-modern social arrangement takes time, although in historical terms not much time, and the deconstructive process is uneven. Some ways of life, some institutions, stubbornly yet temporarily resist, whereas others submit quickly.

Although economy is not the foundation on which all ideological and political superstructures are erected, as Marx suggested, Marx's intuition grasped major characteristics of the modern steamroller. If something can be exported quickly, this is technology; and if something can put heavy pressure on every way of life, this is the steamroller of economy.

Although modernity as a steamroller is far from being identical with capitalist economy, the conjunction of capitalist economy and the globalization of economy spreads quickly. Single cultures must sacrifice most of what became incompatible with this economy.[17]

At what point does a country stop being pre-modern and become modern? The question cannot be answered. From which perspective? In what? In which relationship? – one might ask. Marx says that within capitalism all of the pre-capitalist formations are still in place, but they are marginalized and atypical. This can hardly be said now about the United States, Germany, or the new democracies of Central/Eastern Europe,[18] but it can be said about many other countries, such as India, or certain regions of other countries, such as Sicily and the Eastern region of Brazil. The hybrids are empirically hybrid, but their time is limited.[19] We can refer to them as cases of the "modern social arrangement."

This is why nostalgia makes little sense. However much one dislikes the present, there is no way to return to the past. The traditional pre-modern arrangements are already dissolved or are in a state of dissolution. Re-establishment is a modern move. The cat bit his own tail. I would add to this a very simple consideration. Only the modern arrangement can sustain – feed and let live – those ten million people who now share our globe. In case of the restoration of pre-modern arrangements – even if this were within the range of our possibilities – at least half of the population of our Earth would be doomed (dying of hunger, epidemics, and war). It is not entirely impossible that this is what is going to happen – but desirable it is not.

———————

In what follows, I will briefly compare the pre-modern social arrangement with the modern one. I will approach the two major social arrangements twice: firstly as vehicles of socialization, and secondly as social structures.

1 I assume that a human being is genetically programmed for life in society. But he or she is programmed to live in any society and not in a concrete society. The new-born is accidentally thrown into one particular social world. I term the new-born's genetic endowment the "genetic *a priori*," whereas I term the concrete social world into which the single person is thrown the "social *a priori*."[20] Socialization is the process of dovetailing; the social and the genetic *a prioris* need to be dovetailed.[21]

In the pre-modern social arrangement (and this is true about all of them) the single person is thrown by accident of birth into a rank in a hierarchically ordered society. Every rank has an inherent *telos*. The new-born is thrown into one particular teleologically constructed world, and thereby generally acquires his or her destiny at the moment of his (or her) birth. A slave is destined to do this or that, to be this or that. If one was thrown into the world as a slave, one had to *become* what one was born to *be* – a good, perfect slave. Socialization means acquiring the abilities to function as a slave. These abilities are "total" abilities, including skills, patterns of behavior, language, use of objects – all the know-how necessary for *being* a slave. The man who was born a free citizen received a very promising lot (*telos*) in his cradle: to *be* what he was born to *become*, a good citizen and a virtuous man. In my favorite allegory, the genetic *a priori* is put into an envelope and the envelope is addressed to one of the caste of the hierarchically ordered society. Although every birth is an accident, for no one is destined by her genetic *a priori* to be born in a particular time, in a particular place, and in a particular estate, one receives one's fate simultaneously with one's life. This is how the accidental character of birth is covered up. Slaves are by nature slaves – so Aristotle expressed the conviction of his contemporaries.[22] The accident of birth is not just destiny, yet it also appears as necessity.

This is not an example, but an exemplified description of the pre-modern social arrangement. Since "the envelope" of the genetic code is thrown into a determined place in the social hierarchy, the function that a person performs (is about to perform, ought to perform) is inscribed into his social position as thus prescribed for him. Yet, I repeat, in this (pre-modern) arrangement function is all-encompassing, or almost all encompassing. For example, the circumstance in which a woman functions as a servant is not just "service" but encompasses her behavior toward her mistress and master, the way she is dressed, her virtues and vices, and her loyalties.[23]

A dramatic change comes about in the modern social arrangement.

Men and women are here – as previously – thrown by accident into the world. Now, as always, the genetic *a priori* and the social *a priori* need to be dovetailed.[24] As far as the genetic *a priori* is concerned, the old story continues. As far as the social *a priori* is concerned, an entirely new story needs to be told.[25] To return to my previous metaphor: the genetic *a priori* is still put into an envelope and thrown into a letterbox. But the envelope is not addressed – it remains blank. Men and women are thus accidentally thrown into a world in which they do not receive their destiny (their *telos*, their destination) at the time of their birth. This is what is meant by social contingency. Social contingency is not the fact that one is thrown into the world by accident, but it is the consciousness (the awareness) of having been thrown and of having been thrown into a world in which one's destiny cannot be received. If destiny, *telos*, virtues and vices do not await us at the time of our birth, there is only one remaining option to avoid being entirely lost in the chaos of contingency; namely, to address the envelope ourselves. Briefly, one transforms one's own contingency into one's own destiny.[26]

To be thrown into a world in which one does not receive one's destiny, for better or worse, means to be thrown into Freedom. To be thrown into freedom is at first approach a negativity. It means not to be born to become this or that, not to be "born to," but just to be born. To be thrown into Freedom can be described as to be thrown into Nothing. Whoever is thrown into Freedom is thrown into Nothing. To be thrown into Nothing – this is "the modern condition."[27]

Once thrown into freedom, one is still as much thrown into a concrete world of communicative networks, languages, and customs, as once thrown into one's destiny. The concrete network, although it performs the work of "dovetailing," is no longer binding. One no longer receives the *path* of life; rather, one receives a *trampoline* from which one can jump – forward, backward, up, down – or, incidentally, one could remain motionless on the trampoline. But everything becomes chosen because everything *can* be chosen.[28] No way of life is taken for granted. Men and women become "self-made."

2   The pre-modern social arrangement can be illustrated using a pyramid, where layer is put upon layer, the base is wide, and the top is narrow. The layers describe and prescribe the position of men and women; they are the "allotted places" for men and women in the social hierarchy.

"Social hierarchy" is not the best expression here, because this hierarchy is all-encompassing: social, political, ethical, aesthetic – all are included. At the top of the pyramid there normally stands a single male: the chieftain, the monarch, the pharoah, the emperor. Moreover, in all particular layers single males play the determining and ruling role: in the family, for example, – the *pater familias*, the master of the household, and so on. Even within families, hierarchy reigns. In many pre-modern cultures, first, second, and third sons perform different functions; they are born for different forms of life.

The pre-modern social arrangement is thus ruled by the principle of asymmetrical reciprocity. There must be reciprocity among the different layers of the pyramids and their denizens, and there is, but this relationship must also be – in principle – asymmetrical. Symmetrical reciprocity exists only among those men and/or women who are thrown into the self-same sociopolitical stratum (for example, between the members of the English gentry).

The modern social arrangement is, conversely, the system of symmetric reciprocity. At least according to the *fiction* of the modern social arrangement, symmetric reciprocity is the starting-point – the beginning, the trampoline, (equal opportunity) – although asymmetrical reciprocity will result from one's personal powers in the jump from the trampoline. Asymmetrical reciprocity results from the functions that men and women perform, and is not essential to their beings. For in the fiction (and imagination) of the modern social arrangement, function and being are not identical. The *function a person performs is not an organic aspect of the person's being*. It is only the social performance of a person. This is all the more so because the functions of a person may change; the same person can perform quite different functions at different times, as well as simultaneously. The function that a person performs is no longer representative in the traditional sense.[29] This also means that the performance of a social function is by definition above or below the imperatives of representation.

I have made the claim that the social *a priori* needs – as always – to be dovetailed to the genetic *a priori*, and that the modern social arrangement has to take care of socialization just as the pre-moderns do. Even here, the primary social *a priori* is the particular, and not the universal and individual in the sense of the genetic *a priori*. But if it is true that in the modern social arrangement it is not stratification that determines the functions that men and women perform but vice versa, then primary socialization cannot perform the work of dovetailing. It can only provide the conditions for dovetailing. It can socialize in the use of ordinary language, in the everyday use of man-made objects, in the understanding and the practice of everyday customs, as it can provide the newcomer with some abstract ideas about the dominant world explanation. But it cannot do much.

In the pre-modern social arrangement, the differentiation between everyday life and institutionalized life is blurred, or not yet fully developed. There is always a strict distinction between the everyday/noneveryday, the real world on the one hand, and the other truer world (the sacred, divine, legitimating, cosmic world order) on the other.[30] The noneveryday world legitimizes life in full. Here, everything men and women had to become could be learned, assimilated, and created in one single world that men and women shared with their environment, their equals and their unequals. They learned from experience, just as from stories and myths, what to know and what to be.

In the modern social arrangement, everyday life is truncated. It encompasses only the life within the family, among neighbors, and this is not considered to be a life at all. The common advice, "Wait until you get to know life," makes sense in the modern world and here alone. It reads: "Wait until you become the breadwinner, until you are on your own, until you must make your own way; until you are a homemaker – wait until you grow up and then you will be in the midst of life." Life begins when a person first occupies a place in an institution *outside* the family. Living means being on your own – it means to have left behind security, the network of everyday life, and to adjust to the functional division of labor. *Life means to perform a function necessary for survival, which opens up the territory for competition, success, and failure.*

In the modern world it is the network of institutions, and not everyday life, that establishes social hierarchy, the system of asymmetric (functional) reciprocity. One institution stands higher than the other, just as within one institution positions are hierarchically ordered. People who occupy different positions in an institutional hierarchy also perform different functions. This is the well-kept secret of the old hierarchical order's destruction. It now depends on the function that one performs within an institution – or more institutions – to which social stratum (class) the person belongs. In a factory one can perform the function of unskilled labor, of direction and management, or one can do office work or skilled labor – all of these are different functions performed in the self-same institution – and differing functions will allocate you to different social strata (classes). One can change one's function and climb to a higher social stratum (class) or fall to a lower one. This is how modernity constructs its asymmetric reciprocity (within the framework of the over-arching network of symmetric reciprocity.)

Thus the modern world is not a pyramid. The pyramid was destroyed. But how?

It was the dynamics of modernity that deconstructed the old social arrangement, the "natural artifice." In fact, the old "natural artifice" was destroyed with the slogan, "All men are born free." This creed became the dominating imaginary institution, the dominating fiction of modern life. The fundament of modern life (which, as we know, does not found) is a positing which is in fact a negation.[31] It is the absolute negation of all pre-modern social arrangements, because of the common feature of these arrangements that some people were born free (whereas, by definition, others were born unfree).

I speak about the deconstruction of the natural artifice. The term sounds odd. Something is either natural, or it is an artifice. But the deconstruction of the legitimating theories of the pre-modern arrangements were meant as negations of a natural artifice.

The pre-modern social arrangement was, in fact, regarded as the order of nature. Aristotle says[32] that we can call "natural" everything that is shared by all known political orders; for example, precisely that there are masters and slaves, and that there is the essential hierarchical difference between men and women. Although every other difference is not something against nature, neither is it entirely *by* nature (for example, the difference in concrete political constitutions), since it is also an artifice.[33]

The early moderns who deconstructed the pre-modern natural edifice unmasked it as an artifice. The pre-modern social arrangement became deconstructed to the extent that it was seen as an artifice (the natural thing one cannot deconstruct, only the artifice can be deconstructed), an artifice that was supposed to be natural. Since everyone is born free, the pre-modern presupposition was an artifice.

Thus, in order to transform the natural order into an artifice, one needed an alternative concept of *nature*. If one can assume that exactly the opposite of the pre-modern social arrangement is "by nature," the pre-modern "nature" becomes an artifice, and as an artifice it can be the object of a historical narrative instead of a mythological one. But the new edifice which is going to be erected on the ground of nature must be sincerely called an "artifice," an artifice, however, which is not randomly but *naturally* erected. This natural ground is called Freedom (or Reason). *Man is free by nature; man is rational by nature.* So are all men. Whether the "state of nature," the fictitious starting-point of the erection of a new artifice, is imagined as the state of constant wars or as the idyllic state of peace may be otherwise important, but both variants of the story participate equally in the deconstruction of the pre-modern natural artifice.

Nothing is more equally divided than *bon sense* – says Descartes. All men are born free, but they are everywhere in chains – cries out Rousseau.[34]

Many scholars interpret Descartes' dictum ironically. After all, what Descartes is about to tell us is that most people are foolish and few of them practice good sense. Yet, in my understanding, the sentence is far from being ironical. In a nontragic, skeptical manner, Descartes says the same thing as Rousseau. All men are born free, indeed, yet all of them are in chains. All people are equally endowed with *bon sense* – yet there are very few rational people. If not all men were born free, the fact that they are everywhere in chains could not be described as an anomaly, as a cause for outrage. Just as if *bon sense* were not equally divided among all human creatures, it would be really nonsensical to devise methods and rules for the proper use of reason. These two French authors succinctly formulated one of modern life's fundamental contradictions: the discrepancy between its normative concept[35] and its reality (empirical factuality).

This is a representative discrepancy, because this discrepancy opens up a wide territory to the nonnihilistic practices of the dynamics of modernity.[36] These are the practices which do not transcend – not even in thought, desire, or madness – the horizon of the absolute present time.

Seemingly, there is little in common between being born with good sense while failing to practice it, and being born free yet living everywhere in chains. But both "discrepancies" offer the above-mentioned territory for the dynamics of modernity, because they point to something that needs to be, and also can be, approximated. In practical philosophy (moral philosophy, political philosophy), practice needs to point to the center which needs to be approximated. Obviously, in a nihilistic discourse there is nothing to approximate. Political discourse avoids nihilism if the center to be approximated is pointed out and the distance from the center is indicated less dramatically, as in the case of Rousseau, and more dramatically, as in the case of Descartes.

Dynamic justice (as the dynamics of modernity in general) can well operate in this wide field. This is the territory in which the dynamics of modernity come to support the modern social arrangement and vice versa. The "discrepancy" is where the essence of modernity manifests itself in full.[37]

The Cartesian and the Rousseauian concepts of the discrepancy are equally decisive for the essence of modernity. In the first case, the Center to be approximated is Rationality. Everything that falls short of rationality – be it an institution, decision, or way of life – manifests the discrepancy between actuality and reality; that is, the distance from the center. Of course, one is aware of the impossibility of reaching the center; the discourse is not about reaching but approximating the center. However, this discourse itself soon bifurcates into secondary discourses. What is Reason? What is the Rationality that occupies the Center? What is to be approximated?[38] And what kind of rationality should rather *not* be approximated – for, on the contrary, a greater distance would be more desirable?

In the Rousseauian discourse it is equality in freedom that occupies the centerpoint; it is equality of freedom that needs to be approximated. "Every man is equally born free" is the foundational sentence of modernity, and this is why modernity does not reach its own essence if some men are more free than others. But what does freedom mean? How can one be "equally" free?

In order to avoid misunderstanding, I stated that the discrepancy between the actuality and reality of rationality and equal freedom and the dynamics of modernity that operates within this territory belong to the essence of modernity. From this, however, it does not follow that equal freedom or rationality is an unrealized utopia or dream of modernity – for it is *the reality*. There is equal freedom in modernity, in fact, as there is also rationality. The dynamics of modernity is not pushing toward the *"actualization of a norm,"* but toward *"the expansion of a reality."* For example, if everyone is equally endowed with reason and conscience, there is a discrepancy if women do not have access to the same kinds of labor or performance of the same functions as men. "Equality of freedom" is already reality in the qualified male suffrage. This is expanded in universal male suffrage, as well as in universal suffrage. At this point, in this case, the center is in fact hit. One cannot go further. The claim to equal freedom is then expanded to other spheres, for example, to create conditions of free choice or equal opportunity in the sphere of the economy.[39]

After these scattered remarks, the very centerpoint that needs to be approximated, that embodies the actuality of modernity in full, looks rather diffuse. But how can a centerpoint be diffuse?

Verily, it is less diffuse than all of my preliminary distinctions have suggested. For in the end all the concepts and mini-discourses about the actual center of modernity, about the concepts of rationality and equal freedom(s), are fused in the simple and pedestrian centerpoint of *equal opportunity* (or equal start). Finally, this is the gist of the matter, because "equal opportunity" is the essence of the modern social arrangement.[40]

If the role (the function) that a person performs in the division of social functions determines the place that the person will occupy in the ranks of social stratification (hierarchy) – that is, in the relationships of *command and obedience* – the rules can be adequate to the structure; they can be just only under the condition that the *initial position* of all men and women are alike.[41] The center of the circle would be hit if in fact the initial position of all men and women were alike – if they would start under equal conditions. Since it is impossible to guarantee an equal start,[42] theories of justice try to look for social compensations instead.

What does it mean that equal opportunity is at the heart of the model of the modern social arrangement, and that equal opportunity can never be the case? First of all, it means that the word "equal" is an essential modern *mana-word* (which can also be in the form of equal freedom, equal endowment with reason, conscience, and so on). "Equal" is a measure. It is quantitative, it equalizes and annuls differences, distinctions, and uniqueness. It measures; it makes us believe in measuring and that we ourselves are measurable. This is why I suggested that the Cartesian and the Rousseauian claims are fused in the model of "equal opportunity." It is an equal (quantifiable) opportunity to command or to obey, to dominate or to be dominated, to succeed or to fail. It is assumed that the more properly (functionally, not morally) one uses one's reason, and the more rational are the institutions that warrant initial equality or recompensate for initial inequality, the better one can make use of equal opportunity in order to finally arrive at the top of the inequality hierarchy. Everyone starts at the same starting line, and all – one, two, three – run! The stopwatch works and the laurel wreath awaits the winner at the finish. The others arrive late, or they just give up.

The claims for more justice seem variegated, however. Some do not claim distributive justice (that is, the kind of justice which is approximative of the modern social arrangement model through warranting the condition of equal opportunity or recompensations if it is, for the time being, not the case) but justice in terms of *caritas*, or in terms of equal need, satisfaction, or social equality in general. None of those latter claims is adequate to the model of the modern social arrangement. They are either demagogical or utopian, aesthetic or religious, in their inception, because "equality" is an empty word if it is employed without qualification. Equality in freedom is equality with qualification. The qualification is "of freedom," and this is modern. Yet equality in wealth, for example, is not a modern conception unless it is assumed in the concepts that men and women are going to choose it freely. This does not contradict human nature (that is, the universal genetic *a priori*), but the social arrangement as such (the particular social *a priori*). Or, equality before God is a religious idea (it belonged to the imaginary institution of the Christian world before the times of the Enlightenment).

I described the abstract model of the modern social arrangement *sine ira et studio*. This social arrangement is perhaps not very attractive, but it is ours. It also has a great advantage: nothing here fits perfectly with anything else. There are relatively separate spheres, many major discrepancies, several discourses, panels, fragments, and niches. And there is more than one "logic" of modernity. There exist relatively separate tendencies which can support, intersect, or eventually collide with one another. Moreover, the relationship between the modern social arrangement and the dynamics of modernity takes different shapes in the three logics of modernity.[43]

5

The Three Logics of Modernity I:

The Logic of Technology – Science as the Dominating World View of Modernity

In this chapter, I distinguish between the three logics of modernity: the logic of technology, the logic of the functional allocation of social positions, and the logic of political power (institutions of rule and domination).

The reader will immediately take notice of the third logic with suspicion. Philosophers of an older school will recall the Hegelian triad, whereas students of 20th-century philosophy will think of Hannah Arendt's distinction between political action, work, and labor. For better or worse, my distinction has nothing to do with Hegel and very little to do with Hannah Arendt.

I do not think of the three developmental logics in terms of sublation. None is more abstract or concrete than the others. However, when I speak of the developmental logic, in each case I am speaking about the process of socio-ontological concretization. After all, if a tendency is set into motion, it prevails for a while and will be concretized insofar as it develops the power to maintain its identity under different circumstances, in various contexts and milieus. In this process, new constituents make their appearance. Even if some of the previously significant constituents disappear or are relegated to the background, they are not deleted from historical memory. Insofar as they are preserved in historical memory, they are also preserved in the complex network of institutions, structures, and action types which carry one logic or another.

I cannot emphasize enough that I do not regard any of the three developmental logics as "primary" in comparison with the other two. I do not want to pick even a relatively independent logic of historical development in an age in which I have described "the absolute present tense" or "the railway station of the present."

To understand modernity in terms of three developmental logics is *my way* to make sense of modernity. More precisely, this is my perspective. But this time my perspective is a recommendation to take three different perspectives. I think that this perspective (to sporadically change perspectives) brings my message closer to the reader. This message is simple. Modernity is not to be seen as a homogenized or totalized whole, but as a fragmented world of some open but not unlimited possibilities. The "three logics" scheme – for it is a scheme – prevents me from taking one of the extreme positions.

One of the extreme positions entertains a belief in the infinite and open possibilities of the modern world. If one thinks in terms of the paradoxes of modernity, one cannot take this extreme position. Even if one begins to think modernity within the category of unlimitedness, limits will eventually appear and all things will reach their respective limits. One may say that in pre-modern societies men were aware of their limits and acted from within those limits, whereas modern man is at first confident that there are unlimited possibilities and progression, only to later discover the limits through a direct confrontation. When two or three logics of modern development or some constituents within these logics collide – an eventuality which is a constant draw within the cards of modernity – a limit will eventually be reached. Without such limits and the actors' awareness of the limits, modernity would soon destroy itself. All of modernity's major developmental tendencies can be both destructive and self-destructive.

Yet my theory of the three developmental logics also avoids another extreme position. It became fashionable to speak of modernity as a homogenized, totalizing world in which there are no ways "out," no alternatives, and if there are it is only by a miracle.[1] The conception of the three logics, of the three developmental tendencies, suggests that our world is heterogeneous and that the hope does not necessarily come from the source of the greatest danger. There are two reasons for this: firstly, the locus of the greatest danger cannot be identified; secondly, the mosaics of the modern world do not fit, and there are simultaneously several "imaginary institutions of signification" rather than a only one.

I speak about three tendencies, three logics (and about several tendencies within each of those three). But what is a tendency, and why do I speak of "logics" or even "developmental logic"? I mean here something very simple; in fact, it is so simple that it can be exemplified with everyday experience. If an institution is established or, to use Hegel's language, a new "category" comes into being, it has a tendency to develop its own possibilities. Whether the development of the possibilities which are latent within a category is called progression, regression, or just development depends on the evaluation of the category in question. When a love relationship comes into being, when a child is born, when a school is established, the Aristotelian *dynamis* as the potentiality of the things that it encloses *is* already present as reality. The three logics of modernity are logics in this sense. At the very conception of modernity they are present as *dynamei*, and they begin to develop what is slumbering within them from the beginning. However, it would be too strong a statement and too Aristotelian for my taste to think of the development from the *dynamis* to *entelecheia* as teleological. In the case of the three logics of modernity (as perhaps in most cases), there is more than one option in the *dynamis* stage. The development itself excludes certain options either temporarily or permanently. If it were only about one single logic, fewer potentialities would present themselves in time and the unfolding of the dynamics could become more narrow and progressively more unilinear. However, if there is not one logic but three, and if they are relatively although not entirely independent, then the selection from the possibilities of one logic is not just an internal business, because the environment is essential in the process of eliminating certain possibilities and letting others evolve more forcefully.[2] A category cannot develop other possibilities than the ones which slumber in it at the moment of its conception. In this respect, the development of each of the logics is self-propelling. Yet, the selection and the elimination of the possibilities is not written on the body of the category in its *dynamis* stage. Even if one of the constituent's evolutions is thwarted only for a historically insignificant time, its character will be different, and this may influence the other logics in a different manner.[3] This is why it would be foolish to think of the developmental logics in teleological terms. Of course, retrospectively, one can establish a teleological sequence, but this would only prove the one thing we already know; namely, that all categories can only develop into the realities that slumber in them in their coming into being.

I presume that the three logics – the logic of technology, that of the functional allocation of positions, and the logic of political power (and of the institutions of domination) – are not only supporting one another, but also mutually restricting each other, sometimes to the point of collision. The dynamics of modernity normally operate on all three levels; otherwise, functional difficulties or deficits will occur on one or more levels.[4]

The content and the structure of all three levels can also differ substantially. Until now, only the developmental logic of technology has in fact been (empirically) universal. There are social forces that offer models for one or more types of "alternative technologies." But so far they have remained models. The pluralization of the developmental tendencies in technology has not come about.[5] On the contrary, the developmental tendency of the social and the political sphere has been far from uniform or unilinear. And one can hardly expect that it will be so in the future.[6] It is true that liberal democracy has proved to have offered the best long-term opportunity for the other two logics to develop in directions in which their balance could be optimally maintained. But it is questionable whether the tendency can also be extrapolated.

There is an essential difference between the three developmental logics. The logics of modernity are not natural forces; they develop because they are developed by historical actors or agents. Yet their development requires different kinds of actions, as well as different kinds of thinking.[7]

However, specific kinds of actions and specific kinds of thinking do not appear in pairs.

The developmental logic of technology only seems to require cognition in the sense of problem-solving,[8] yet the conditions of the development of technology became increasingly dependent on the development of modern sciences.[9] Problem-solving or puzzle-solving suffices in "normal science" but not in "revolutionary science," and sciences do not develop without recurring episodes of scientific revolutions.[10] Even those who think in terms of Heideggerian "enframing"[11] cannot deny that revolutionary sciences require theoretical–philosophical thinking, the choice of ultimate principles (*nous* or *Vernunft*), and also creative, productive, and not just reproductive, imagination.[12] Yet, both the choice of principles and the operation of imagination stand in the service of *knowing*. Thinking and knowing are here not opposites. One thinks in order to know (*wissen*), not just to know more but also to know something else. This is innovative thinking, as innovative as thinking is related to political action. Yet although thinking itself gives *satisfaction*, there is no complete satisfaction without getting to know something else, without illumination, without "results."

At this point, it rather seems as if thinking types and action types could be "paired." After all, what is the difference here between the requirement of the logic of technology and that of the logic of politics (statecraft)? One could say that politics as administration, the daily operation of bureaucracies, is problem-solving, whereas it is the "revolutionary politics," the kind of politics that produces the change in the political action paradigm, that requires *Vernunft* (practical reason) and the choice of the fundamental principles (*archai*) for action.[13] This similarity is, however, restricted in scope and relevance. For, the action type that is constantly needed in politics is *not* problem-solving, but "taking initiative." In the democratic model everyone can (in principle) take the initiative. If I were to draw a parallel between "normal science" and "normal politics," I would rather stress that they are *opposites*. Thinking in normal politics is far from being a kind of problem-solving, for it is, rather, the combination of reflection and imagination. This is why Arendt said rightly that in totalitarian states, where everything becomes "politicized," there is in fact no politics at all. Politics as administration is close to problem-solving, yet this is not "normal politics" but "policy-making."[14] In administration as much as in technology, everything depends on the result. Yet this is not true about political action in general, or if it is, "result" means something entirely different than in technology or in sciences. It has very little to do with the accumulation of knowledge, if at all. The Hungarian revolution in 1956 is no less representative because it was defeated,[15] and the actions of the revolution's participants were not considered irrelevant because of the defeat. The "result" above and beyond the defeat – if one can speak of a result at all – is the historical vindication of the revolution's cause. Yet even without the retroactive vindication of a cause, a political action proper does not lose its inherent significance. The significance is present in the action itself, in the enthusiasm of the actors and their faith in the meaning of their cause, in the pleasure of the action, and in the narrative recollection of the action. Political action is an end in itself, which, however, does not mean that political actors seek only to act. They seek also the realization of their ideas, of changing their world, of attaining liberty or constituting new liberties. That an action is an end in itself means that even if those goals are not attained, or only partially attained (which is almost always the case), political action does not lose its significance and its beauty. It *aims* at results, yet it is *not dependent* on them. This is just like making love. For this reason the accumulation of know-how is neither aimed at, nor resultant from, political action. Administration as problem-solving does not aim at constant accumulation of know-how to solve (social or political) problems, as is required in technology or in natural sciences.[16]

These were only preliminary polemical fragments to stress the heterogeneous character of the modern world and to look skeptically at all suggestions to the contrary. Contrary to Weber, I doubt that within one sphere (for example, the political) there is *one* ethics (for example, the "ethics of responsibility") and *one* set of norms and rules to guide the activities of all those who enter this sphere. Contrary to Heideggerian thought, I doubt that all activities of our modern world are "enframed"

by the same metaphysical thinking, subject/object relation, and technological imagination. Contrary to the Habermas school, I doubt the relevance of the consensus theory of truth. Although I do not question that
there is a dominant world explanation, I do see the modern world as
fragmented, conflicting, and sometimes even chaotic on all levels and in
all counts.[17]

"The essence of technology is not technological," says Heidegger[18] and
this sentence, polemically directed against the Marxian and liberal
aggrandizement as well as against the romantic diabolization of technology, can serve as a good starting-point.

But what is the essence of technology? It is not the definition of
technology. After all, technology can be defined in different ways; for
example, that it is "a means to an end." This definition is not incorrect,
yet it does not touch the essence of technology. It is the instrument. But
what is an instrument? And what does it mean to be instrumental? It is a
way of revealing.[19] Revealing is bringing forth. What is brought forth is
true.[20] Technology, therefore, has a relation to the way in which things
are revealed, in the way truth is thought. Technology does not bring forth
as *poiesis* but challenges (*herausfordern*), it makes nature an energy
supply, a standing reserve. Man itself is transformed into a standing
reserve.[21] Heidegger calls the challenging claim that gathers man to
order self-revealing as a standing reserve *Ge-stell* (enframing).[22] It is
not the development of technology that brought about *Ge-stell*, but the
converse. "Lange bevor gegen Ende des 18. Jahrhunderts in England die
erste Kraftmaschine erfunden und in Gang gesetzt wurde, war schon das
Ge-stell, das Wesen der Technik, verborgenerweise in seinem Gang. Das
besagt: Das Wesen der Technik waltete vordem schon, so zwar, dass es
allererst den Bereich lichtete, innerhalb dessen sich überhaupt derglei-
chen wie ein Erfinden von Kraftzeugungmaschine auf die Suche machen
und es mit sich versuchen konnte."[23]

The essence of technology is verily not technological. It does not reside
in the machine, the thing. It resides in the way modern men think. To
simplify Heidegger: modern men are thinking in terms of subject/object.
The world is the object, men are the subjects. The subject treats the world
(nature as *natura* and not as *physis*) as the arsenal of things for human
use. Men themselves are objects for use. The whole universe is instru-
mentalized or is in waiting as a "standing reserve" for subsequent instrumentalization. Truth is understood in terms of the correspondence theory
of truth – it is identified with true knowledge (about things of possible
use). The question of why modern men are thinking and imagining the

world as a standing reserve, why their world actually became a standing reserve, cannot be answered. Although it sometimes seems as if Heidegger would pin down the source of *Ge-stell* in the structure of metaphysics (metaphysical thinking), metaphysical thinking is not identified as "the cause" of the *Ge-stell* but, rather, as one of its conditions.[24]

In Heidegger's version, technology's logic is pre-coded as the *Ge-stell*. I generally accept this version without necessarily employing Heidegger's terminology. One can employ other terminologies and still maintain that the essence of technology is not technological, that it resides in man's way of thinking, perceiving, imagining, and understanding, so that we are enframed by the knowledge and self-knowledge of our own conception of truth (and reason). Instead of *Ge-stell*, one can speak of "the language" of the moderns as well as the "imaginary institutions of modernity."

I subscribe without hesitation to Heidegger's thesis that the essence of technology is not technological. But I do not subscribe to his suggestion that *Ge-stell* "enframes" *the whole world* of the moderns, our world, our *Weltbild* in its entirety.[25] Several authors (dead or alive) would unhesitatingly accept that the essence of technology is not technological without identifying the essence of technology with the essence of modernity.

Max Weber's rationalization thesis comes closest to Heidegger at this point, since in Weber all spheres of the modern world are rationalized. Moreover, their rationalizations are said to be evolving on a total scale, where religious imagination has a lion's share.[26, 27] Still, Weber's world is pluralistic, fragmented, and heterogeneous. One can also interpret Luhmann's idea about the constant reduction of system complexity in Heideggerian terms, yet in Luhmann's world the single person is an independent system of his or her own and is far from being "part" of the standing reserve.[28] In Castoriadis, autonomy is the major imaginary institution of modernity.[29] One could say that autonomy is also a constituent of the essence of technology, yet Castoriadis sees it exclusively as the constituent of democracy.[30]

Let me state my position succinctly.

In my mind there is one single dominant imaginary institution (or world explanation) in modernity, and this is science. Technological imagination and thinking elevated the correspondence theory of truth to the sole dominant concept of truth, and thus science to the position of the dominant world explanation. Thus our modern "vision of the world" as a whole is shaped by science as ideology.[31] Yet there is more than one imaginary institution in the modern world. Moreover, I think that science as the dominant world explanation of modernity is put into effect by an alternative imaginary institution, and vice versa.

I could first mention the division of value-spheres as described by Weber, which offers the opportunity to criticize the rules of one sphere from the standpoint of another sphere (for example, to criticize the sphere of economy from the position of the sphere of politics or art or religion, or economics as a science). This is in fact a common practice in our times, and as such indicates the fragmentation of the frames of world explanation. But this in itself does not support a forceful argument against the Heideggerian conception. One could say that all those spheres, both the sphere being criticized and the sphere from which one is criticizing it, are equally manifestations of *Ge-stell*; they are equally enframed, even if not in the same way. None of them offers a way "out"; they share the same concept of truth and their mutual critique resembles a family quarrel.

I could mention, secondly, the constant presence of an anti-technological drive in modern thinking. I could refer to romanticism or go back to Rousseau; I could enumerate phenomena such as anti-modernistic nostalgia, ecology, anti-rationalism, doomsday images, and so on. After all, the mass media are full of doomsday images and prophecies, and they are far more popular than scientific explanations. But these and similar examples do not speak against Heidegger. Heidegger's own concept of being enframed could be used as an argument against Heidegger. He insists that we are enframed (and this is the essence of technology) and he practices originary thinking,[32] which is presumably not metaphysical. That is, he himself proves with his thinking that his interpretation of modernity as *Ge-stell* is not correct, given that his own acting/thinking must be located somehow outside the frame. This argument is lame firstly because all critiques of technology and technological imagination are by definition enframed, by the simple fact that they continue to think in terms of technology. Believing that science and technology are devils, as far as thinking is concerned, is essentially no different from believing that technology is the savior, because for both situations technology is the essence. Furthermore, Heidegger never says that he can think outside of the frame. He bangs at the door without being able to get out from enframing. On my part, I accept this position.[33] What I do not accept are Heidegger's finishing lines where he refers to *poiesis* as the Savior (the saving power, *rettende*) in the sense that the saving power comes from the place where the greatest danger is. I do, however, think that this "saving power" is not something that *has been*, and not something *that is to come*.

I think, namely, that the moderns are enframed in a double way, and that the their two major imaginary institutions do not fit together. This is why the dominating imaginary institution of technology cannot entirely dominate the sphere of politics or of the social–functional. At least until now, the political logics and the logics of the functional division of social position have not been entirely dominated by science or by technological imagination in general. *Poiesis* has never died. If we are still poetically dwelling on Earth, this has little to do with technology and far more to do with (modern) historical consciousness itself.[34, 35]

Both historical imagination[36] and technological imagination were incipient at the birth of modernity. The two imaginary institutions of modernity lived side by side in a constant interplay. If we are enframed, we are enframed by two different frames, which do not entirely fit.

Perhaps action has been invaded by technological imagination, yet recollection was not. Thinking insofar as action is concerned can be described as having been patterned by *problem-solving*, yet recollection is certainly not. Recollection is, rather, imprinted by thinking as *interpretation*. The age of technology is also the age of hermeneutics.[37]

Technological imagination is characterized by the accumulation of knowledge. The recollection of the past can also follow this model. This was recognized by Nietzsche and later also by Heidegger.[38] But living historical hermeneutics has nothing to do with a positivist rendering of history. It is rooted in the self-understanding of the moderns, self-understanding as being historical. The self-understanding of being historical implies the consciousness of limit, fragility, and finitude, the consciousness that one "cannot jump over Rhodus." This is also the self-understanding of the repeated movement of turning to face the past in order to decipher it, entering into a conversation with the past, cherishing the past, *making the past constantly present*. Nostalgia is a part of this game. It is because of the historical imagination that there are always many alternative ways to the self-understanding and self-interpretation of the moderns. Since the past is not "given" by the dominating world view, the dominating world view (science) itself sets the past free, lets the past be interpreted by single individuals, by men and women who share life experiences rather than knowledge.[39] The different past interpretations move in the direction of a variety of present interpretations (and vice versa). Men step back from the act of making – step into the attitude of contemplation which is just the opposite of the attitude required in technological imagination – for this act of contemplation is not a respite that precedes action. It is not the attitude of observation which needs to be transformed into doing something; it is not a means to an end. It is a meaning-rendering activity, an end in itself, and in the same sense it is also *poiesis*. It is the creative act of the spectator, the creative act of creating nothing but meaning, nothing but beauty, all the useless things.

It is only in the world of universal utility that historical imagination with its interpretative zeal can entirely abstract from utility.[40] The idea that beauty is without interest is a modern idea.[41] As beauty is without interest, so are the interpretations of past beauties, poems, heroic acts, statues, actions, and other such things. These stories cannot be usefully employed;[42] they do not directly (but, rather, indirectly) refer back to life. What is the use of poetry? What is the use of philosophy? What is the use of an interpretation of Hamlet? What is the use of looking at an African statuette? Nothing, absolutely nothing. Never in pre-modern times was so much premium placed on being of no use as in the world of universal utility, as in the modern world.

Let me exemplify this with the modern's relation to nature. It is indeed a modern thing to relate to nature, including human nature, as to a standing reserve. Yet it is also a modern thing to adore the beauty of a landscape, a tree, or a face only for its own sake.[43, 44] The more nature is regarded a mere object, a standing reserve for use, the more beautiful it becomes in the eye of the beholder *who lets nature be*, untouched as it is.

Although I think that the historical imagination puts a premium on a noninstrumental attitude in substituting meaning-rendering for knowledge and interpretation for problem-solving, I would not deny that technological imagination can and does invade the territory of historicity. I have already mentioned cumulative positivist history writing, but there is more to it. The expansion of the territory of the *interpretanda* for hermeneutical practices follows in some way the logic of technology, for although the old is deciphered and absorbed, new *interpretanda* are always sought after. In some way, one *interpretandum* can be exhausted and new *interpretanda* can only keep in motion the hermeneutical practice itself. This phenomenon cannot be attributed, however, to historical imagination itself, for it belongs to the story of the *distribution* of cultural goods.[45] To this, I would add that the contacts between the two separate imaginary institutions of modernity are not one-sided. Historicity and historical thinking have invaded science, and continue to invade it.[46]

Although every serious thinker discusses the logic of technology as having been triggered by and embedded in technological imagination, certain concrete technological discoveries or implementations of discoveries are still regarded as the crucial "stations" of this developmental logic. On this count, there is little difference between the typical thinkers of the 19th century (such as Marx) and those of the 20th century. Marx said in *Capital* I [47] that it is not the employment of the steam but the replacement of hands by machines that is the real launching moment of the industrial

revolution. It is this which finally leads to the liberation of mankind from
the yoke of labor. Heidegger mentions the use of the typewriter for the
same reason (it changes the original, unmediated use of human hands
into an instrumental use), as the significant event in the development of
technology in the direction of modern catastrophes such as war, Nazism
and Bolshevism. For Hannah Arendt there were – among other things –
two decisive technological events: the use of atomic energy[48] and the
launching of the first satellite (the Sputnik) to circle the Earth. She
actually says that although the *modern age* started at the time of the
Enlightenment, the modern *world* began with the explosion of the first
atomic bomb.[49] She adds that the so-called Earth-alienation of modern
man has culminated – so far – in the launching of the satellite, an event
that makes it possible from now on for men to leave their natural
habitat.[50]

I do not doubt that it makes sense to reflect on the developmental
logics of technology in terms of events. All of the events enumerated thus
far were significant insofar as they changed man's imagination. But
I think that to pick up spectacular technological events[51] from the (relative) continuum of the development of technology is contingent. From
this, I do not conclude that it is wrong. I only conclude that there are
other, less spectacular, technological events (for example, the mechanization of the household or the network of telecommunications) which are
far more significant for men's and women's everyday life than the Sputnik
and the atomic power plant, and change their imagination in a more
significant way.

My point is that historical imagination selects those specific events
among the many significant events of technological development which
can be regarded as watersheds from a given philosophical perspective.
What constitutes a watershed is a matter of interpretation. A technological event is not necessarily "objectively" a significant watershed, but
becomes one in the interpretative code of a philosophy. This is one of
the "feedbacks" of the historical self-understanding of our age into the
interpretation of the imaginary institutions of technological development.

What do I mean by "dominant world explanation"? What does it mean
that science became the dominant world explanation in modernity?

"Where do we come from? What are we? Where are we going?" The
fundamental questions of historicity are an essential constituent of the
human condition. One understands one's world as historicity, yet historicity is not identical with understanding one's world.

Aristotle introduces his metaphysics with a generalized sentence: "Every man desires to know," and this is a simple truth. Moreover, no man can survive without knowing, and mostly he desires to acquire more knowledge than is necessary for survival. One needs to know the things one is expected to do, yet one also needs to know the things that one is expected to believe in.[52] One needs to know why things are what they are, and why they are the way they are and not otherwise. One also needs to know who or what the ultimate authority may be, from what or whom one can expect the answers (if there is such). Tradition, customs, priests, parents, elders – they are the authorities. Yet they, too, point at higher, superhuman authorities. The "dominant world explanation" is the highest authority – or, more precisely, the highest authorities draw legitimacy from a dominant world explanation.

In the spiritual realm that Hegel termed "the absolute spirit," neither art nor philosophy qualify for the role of dominating world explanation. Only religion (in a broad sense of the word) and science can provide the basic services of the superhuman authority to turn to for answers to the questions concerning what is, how, and why.[53]

Modernity is a social arrangement in which science, and not religion, provides the service of the basic world explanation. This is one of the major differences between the essence of the pre-modern social arrangements and the essence of modernity. I would add that technological imagination could not dominate modern fantasy without science becoming the dominant world explanation.

Science as the dominant world explanation is also dependent on freedom as the nonfounding foundation of modernity. Religion put limits on scientific inquiry; where religion is the dominant world explanation, the infinite progression/regression of science (without limits) is *hybris* or sin, and thus is impossible. The dynamics of modern scientific development (science as we now know it) cannot be launched without freedom as the nonfoundational quasi-*archē*. Freedom has set scientific inquiry free, and science has since expressed its gratitude. For its part, it has set all the answers concerning *the meaning of life* free, and with them also all the religious questions, by declaring its ignorance and neutrality in matters of ultimate existence, truth as revelation. Religion, losing its position of dominating world explanation, is now one of the languages of historical imagination. The discrepancy between facts and norms (values), this famous logical/epistemological question in modern thinking,[54] resulted from the emergence of science as the dominating world explanation, from the mutual loosening of bonds between the good and the true.

As the essence of technology is not technological, so the essence of science as the dominant world explanation of modernity is not "scientific."

Moreover, it can hardly be identified with "the spirit of science." The "spirit of science," the desire to know and to know more, is perhaps losing momentum at a time when science succeeds in becoming the dominant world explanation, although great scientists remain committed to this spirit. The significant scientists are – even now – skeptical. They do not entertain grand illusions in the capacity and force of their science. They know that their results will be regarded as childish in the next generation, that they ask questions they cannot answer. In short, they are far from entertaining illusions about their science, and this is how they are committed – in a Weberian sense – to science as a vocation. Furthermore, they are well aware that scientific inquiry requires fantasy, intuition, and speculation, as they are also aware of the fragility of scientific inquiry. Perhaps they will enter the Olympus of modern science (like a Madame Curie); perhaps not. Yet whether they do or not, they will wittingly/unwittingly enforce the dominant world explanation in providing a myth for the mythology of science.

Since science is the dominant world explanation of modernity, it permeates all spheres and aspects of life. A dominant world explanation serves as (1) the authoritative point of reference (production of truth), (2) the network of dominating institutions (for the production and distribution of truth), and (3) an authoritative model.

(1)   That science is the dominant point of reference means that "true" and "scientific" (or "proven by science") are employed synonymously; the three statements (true, scientific, and proven by science) may be interchanged without changing the content of a sentence. Similarly, in the era when (Christian) religion was the dominant world explanation, if someone said "it is written (in the Book)" this meant "it is true," for whatever was written (in the Bible) was by definition true. Thus, if something is acclaimed as being "scientifically proven," it is legitimated as true knowledge. As a result, every truth claim employs "scientific" legitimation. The Nazi race ideology boasted of having been "scientifically proven"; Marxism/Leninism declared itself the "sole true science of society." Nowadays, there is a science called "ufology" (doing research on the UFO phenomenon); there is a religion called "scientology."

"Is this so?" asks someone, and the other answers "I have read it in the science pages" – which means that it is certainly true. Human credulity, blamed by the men of enlightenment as being responsible for the longevity of religious "prejudices," became increasingly more vested in sciences. "Scientific" is a mana-word which inspires faith and belief of a new kind; namely, a kind of faith or belief which denies being what it actually is and claims to be entirely free from its own essence.[55]

Faith and belief are needed now as always. One has to accept many things as being true without being able to independently verify them, without having considered counter-arguments, and so on. Religious faith which is also religious knowledge does not have to be well-versed in theology, just as little as the knowledge of scientific facts today requires being able to know the science of which it is a fact. However, the gap between knowing about something, and knowing (being able) how to use the language of something (of a specific science) with learning and skill, has been increased throughout the modern age.

Credulity is not just naiveté. It is also an attempt to jump over the widening gap, the manifestation of the desire to know, to understand things beyond the scope of phenomena and the tools ready at hand. Already shaken in his values and traditional customs, modern man resists the loss of his dearly acquired belief in science. There must be something fixed, something that carries the mantle of authority. And there must be something that is "holistic" in the sense that it embraces many territories of human life. "Science" is not just chemistry and physics, it is not biology or meteorology, it is SCIENCE as such, science with capital letters. From the postmodern perspective, History with a capital H has departed, yet Science with a capital S is continuing to hold its sway over minds.[56]

(2) Science is not the spirit of science; it is the spirit of the institution(s) of science. As in the medieval world, when religious faith was also faith in the Church, so is the blind acceptance of science also the legitimation of the institutions of science. It is in the institutions of science that science is produced, or precisely where scientific truth is produced. In Foucault's expression, it is scientific discourse that manufactures truth.[57]

This means that the naive concept of truth (truth as being there with the need to discover it, to let it be seen) is replaced with another concept which describes (and interprets) the modern knowledge-seeking procedure more adequately. A scientific discourse is conducted in all branches of sciences. To enter this discourse one needs a certificate that qualifies one to participate, and one also needs to be accepted as a member of an institution of scientific discourse. Truth is the product of such a discourse. Since the discourse continues, for it is never-ending (and switches from one paradigm to the other), old truths will become untruths and new truths will be constantly produced. Still, this magic works because it is not without reason that one kind of knowledge is accepted (or produced) by a community of scientists as true (for the time being).[58] Not everything could be produced as true. Yet there are always alternatives waiting to be produced as truth. In this sense, there is a "territory" (a force field) within which the discourse produces its truth. Outside of this territory there is untruth; within this territory there can be both truth and untruth, depending on the community that produces knowledge as truth. It is an illusion that the best argument will always win (And what makes an argument the best anyway?), but it is very unlikely that a very bad argument could.[59]

When Foucault described how modern scientific discourse produces truth, he actually employed the language of technology. Before Foucault, the traditional ontological language was still in use (one discovers the hidden truth). Heidegger employs a kind of meta-discourse here when he insists that the essence of technology – that is, the pragmatic concept of truth – is itself in the last instance a kind of revealing (*aletheia*). He then uses the ontological language to make us understand the instrumental/pragmatic use of the modern concept of scientific truth and the modern method of scientific inquiry.[60]

(3)   But the increasing domination of science as the world explanation is to be seen first from its expansion. "Science" escalates. Firstly, the so-called "social sciences" come into being. They try to imitate hard sciences; they claim to be not just "as scientific" as the former, but scientific in the same manner. The *science of man* follows. This is no longer an ontological/existentialinquiry into the essence of man or *conditio humana*, but the way to learn to treat men as one treats external nature, as a "standing reserve." "Man" becomes the playground of science, medicine, experimental psychology, and pedagogy.[61]

Foucault takes the notion of science as force seriously. A world explanation is not dominating only insofar as it is overwhelming, overarching, and legitimating, but also because it dominates in the sense of exercising power. Even if a world explanation exercises its power exclusively through the imagination of man, it is a force – not just one force among many forces but a force that dominates a force field. Yet science as the dominant world explanation dominates a broad force field through both the imagination of men and its institutions – institutions which institutionalize science and its employment, and institutions which shape themselves on the modern sciences, including institutions of discourses. It is through rationalization, and through modelling social and other institutions on the idea of optimization, that science becomes not only a force but an oppressive force. Every force is oppressive which does not meet sufficient counter-force, which is not counter-balanced in a foreign territory. One could say that science as the dominant world explanation is on its own territory when pragmatic success justifies its procedures. For example, scientific rationalization in psychology or in education, or optimization in political institutions or penitentiaries,[62] have almost no accountable pragmatic success rates. What is considered as success for one is seen as catastrophe by another. Imitating hard sciences does not open the way to further "progression," whatever that means, but to the oppression of the victims of the scientific practices. Prisoners will not become honest citizens if scientific methods are applied in the penitentiaries, and mental patients will not be men and women of healthy constitution if they are "normalized."[63] To this, I would add that science as the dominant world explanation has not been diminished in power since the "normalizing" practices have given way to other, sometimes opposite, practices – such as anti-psychiatry, permissive education, and the like. For the procedure remains the same. One changes practices because, so the legitimation runs, "science" has now discovered that the previous practices were incorrect and now it produces the correct ones.[64]

When science is serving as the "model" for practices, institutions, and actions where neither the institution nor the action is guided by a dominating (or possible) paradigm of science, one is already facing the interplay between the logic of technology and the logic of the distribution of positions in modern society. In the stories of Foucault, the two logics were not necessarily and absolutely supporting one another. Rather, one was serving the other.

The ideology of science can support the dominant social division of positions (the second logic of the modern social arrangement.) Since it is an ideology, it is also a Jolly Joker. The switch from "scientific" disciplining to "scientific" permissive education is a good example of the usual case, when the changing practices of one logic leave their mark on another. Conflicts between the two logics present themselves (among other cases) when technology's logic is followed far beyond the requirements of society's logic, or vice versa.[65]

6

The Three Logics of Modernity II:

The Logic of the Division of Social Positions, Functions, and Wealth

The description of the second developmental logic as "the logic of the division of social position, functions and wealth" sounds too complicated. I could have described it more simply, as "the logic of civil society" or "the logic of the modern social arrangement." These descriptions, however, do not overlap. The concept of civil society is itself malleable. It refers to capitalistic economy just as, also, to a great variety of civil institutions. Only in the Western type of liberal democracy will the term "logic of civil society" roughly cover the logic of division of social positions, functions, and wealth. The "modern social arrangement" is a broader concept than the "logic of civil society," but it is too broad, since all the three logics of modern society are aspects of the modern social arrangement, and so can also be the dynamics of modernity. In one essential way, however, the second logic of modern society is the carrier of the *essential difference* between all pre-modern arrangements and the modern one, for the main *institutions* of the social hierarchy constitution are located here. If "equal start" or "equal opportunity" is the virtual beginning of modern man's life, and if the institutional positions are unequal and hierarchically ordered, then the allocation of social positions, functions, and wealth should be such as to ensure "initial equality" as much as the *just inequality* of the results. The "idea" of modernity is, however, not attained. I also think that it cannot be attained, because of the tension between static and dynamic justice. Briefly: a modern society is just if all denizens, all those concerned by the operation and the application of its norms and rules, agree that it is just. Yet if all agree, dynamic justice is eliminated along with the dynamics of modernity (no one will then say that "This is not just. Something else would be better").

Yet a modern society cannot survive without the constant presence of the dynamics of modernity. As a result, modern society cannot be fully just.[1] The idea of social and political justice is the constant (and constantly valid and validated) idea of modern life under the condition that the content of the idea is never to be fulfilled. The contestation of justice is constantly going on.

The developmental tendency of the second logic of modernity is also, but not entirely, dependent on the contestation of justice. Different social strata contest justice. What is just for one is unjust for the other. What is more just for one is less so for another. Therefore, under the conditions of political freedom the contestation of justice not only pushes the social and political arrangements for change in one single direction, but after having been pushed in one direction, in all probability they will be pushed in another direction.[2] This immediately shows that the second logic of modernity differs essentially from the first. A constant accumulation of knowledge continues in the first logic, in addition to an increase in rationalization and functionalization. This cannot be said, however, about the second logic. The development moves in one direction for some time, only to return to another, different, or at times opposite, direction. What is more or less rational greatly depends on the evaluations of all those concerned; here there are many kinds of rationality and irrationality. An institution or a measure that functions well in one respect appears as a dysfunction in another respect. Experiences can be accumulated, but usually are not.[3] Here we can observe a constant pendulum movement in which the prevalence of certain unilinear tendencies is not prevented, but there are only a few of these cases. One can hardly say, for example, that the institutions that allocate positions or resources are now more rational than, say, in England at the end of the 19th century.[4] Or, if they are more rational, it is because the term "rationality" itself has since assumed additional meanings.[5]

I continue to return to the question of rationality, because it is a springboard from which we can move. "Rationality" is not an inherent quality of an act or an institution. Institutions are rational if they are taken for granted or if one can justify them argumentatively, and they can be rational from one perspective, and for one purpose, while they are nonrational from another perspective and for another purpose.[6] The judgment concerning the rationality of an institution or action is not free of evaluation.[7] One can claim that the best education is the most rational investment in a country, just as one can also claim this not to be the case. One can support a means to an end as rational (for example, the best means to achieve an overall system of good education), whereas others will tell you that the recommendation is entirely irrational, because the recommended means will not result in the required end (education will worsen as a result). The contestation concerning rationality goes on simultaneously with the contestation of justice.

Frequently or typically, the second logic is hindered by the third logic (the logic of political institutions). However, the third logic itself is not self-propelling but is, rather, pushed toward intervention into the second logic, by the actors or by certain institutions of the second logic itself (for example, trade unions). Furthermore, the institutions of the second logic of modernity are themselves heterogeneous, and they do push or pull the institutions (systems) that allocate positions, functions, resources, and wealth in different directions; this is how the contestation of justice and of rationality works.

The relative independence of the second logic is decisive for modernity's survival, because this is the logic where the two major aspects of modernity (the modern social arrangement and the dynamics of modernity) are concentrated. On paper, one can make modernity's dynamics of technology develop in the absence of the two other logics. This was, for example, Marx's utopian design. And it does not only happen on a piece of paper, but in pre-modern social arrangements too, that political institutions of rule and domination (such as tyranny, democracy, republic, monarchy, and so on) replace one another and are constantly contested in the absence of relatively independent first and second logics.[8] Yet the second logic is the heart of modernity as we know it, and it is modernity's heart first and foremost because of its heterogeneity. When the relative independence of the second logic is thwarted in modernity, dysfunctions appear at all levels, even if the function of the second logic is properly fulfilled.

It makes sense at this point to cast a glance toward the totalitarian states/societies. As I have mentioned previously, they were (and are) modern societies, but they are modern societies in which the second logic was limited in its independent development. In the Soviet Union, for example,[9] the allocation of social positions, functions, and wealth was entirely modern, insofar as the fundamental model of the modern social arrangement was put in its place. Traditional estates and classes were abolished, society atomized, and men and women were regarded and actually functioned as contingent persons. There was, at least in principle, an equal opportunity (except for the "class aliens") to compete for positions in various institutions. The functions that men and women performed, and the wages and salaries allocated to them, depended on the positions that they finally succeeded in achieving in the social hierarchy. Yet, this modern allocation of men and women to specific institutional positions did not develop in a relatively independent way, but was superimposed on society by a dictatorial state power, with the intention of totalizing society. Moreover, the communist party allocated a fixed position for the institutions in an institutional hierarchy. The institution, the Party, gained absolute supremacy over all other institutions. The position that someone acquired in the Party predetermined the position that the same person would occupy (if obedient!) in all other institutions (for example, political power, wealth, access to education, hospitals, shops, and so on). As a result, society was homogenized, the differences among the possibilities offered by those institutions and the competition among the institutions being, at least officially, annulled. It became impossible for the second logic to develop on its own, to exhibit its own contradictions; the contestation of justice and the contestation of rationality were outlawed. Yet in the absence of such contestation the pendulum is not free to swing, or its swinging will be entirely arbitrary.[10] Society is put under pressure by the state – that is, the Party – to behave as if it were an institution of technology, to follow a cumulative technological dynamism, a development alien from the "normal" logic of the modern system of allocations and transactions. As a result, the three logics of modernity which were in fact present in Soviet societies behaved not just differently, but differed essentially from the three logics under liberal democracies.

If one still wants a proof of the problematic character of an abstract/ unified concept of rationality, the Soviet example presents one. The Party raises a goal, namely to overcome the per capita production of the capitalist world, and it chooses the means to realize this goal. Yet instead of closing the gap, the totalitarian closure widens it – society develops in the opposite direction than planned. Finally, it turns out that the relatively independent logic of society (and technology) cannot be entirely blocked; yet it can still be thwarted.

It turned out – if this were not already presupposed – that liberal democracy is the best political institution to grant the relative independence of the second logic. I want to emphasize that the independence is still relative. It must remain relative, given that there are three logics and that the three mutually limit one another. I have already mentioned state intervention as one way of limiting the logics of society. Yet the second logic also depends on the first.[11] This is so obvious that it hardly needs to be mentioned. We need only speak of the simplest correlation: the development of technology increases the productivity of the institutions of production. Yet there are many things beyond the obvious. The development of technology has deeply influenced the structure of the personal household, family relationships, required skills, professions, and education; not to mention perception of time and the perception of spatial distances, which permeate all institutions of the second logic.

From this point on, I will discuss only "Western" modernity, for this is the kind of modernity which, for the time being, shows the greatest capacity for survival. The basic institutions of the second logic (in Western modernity) are the *market* – more precisely, the universalization and the generalization of the market relationship – *personal–private property, private law,* and *human rights.*[12] No concrete, simple institution of modernity is external to, or undetermined by, at least one of the basic institutions. When one speaks of modern *life,* or the modern form of life, one needs to scrutinize the second logic.

There is a gap between the life of the moderns and the world of the moderns. "Life" simply means the way in which men and women produce and reproduce. Reproduction includes giving birth to children and raising them (within the familial institution and other institutions which replace the family). It also means education, the manners of advancement, the ways to adjust to the world, and "making oneself," being an "adult" from the time one enters the social division of labor until old age. Reproduction is pragmatic; it means survival or even success, but not the "good life" or happiness. In order to live a good life one needs to have a world above and beyond pragmatic demands – a world of imagination, of unnecessary activities and useless ideas.

The subject of life (reproduction in a broad sense) is *historicity* (a person in his or her own historical quality, as *ipseity*). However, historical consciousness is not a necessary precondition of life, of historicity; for the former (but not necessarily the latter) includes reflection. Reflective historical consciousness asks questions and creates distances. It may even make adjustments, and make pragmatically devised life problematic, dangerous, and more difficult or even impossible.[13]

Modern life is the life of the single person, for the singularity of the person is an essential aspect of the second logic of modernity.[14] There is no market or private law if there are no human rights, with the singular person as the elementary building block of society.[15] Conformity exists only where life presupposes the singularity of persons; without singularity there is no "mass," neither "mass society" nor "mass democracy."[16]

The market is the center around which the second logic revolves.[17] It is in the emergence of the labor market in the broadest sense that the essence of the second logic – and of the modern social arrangement in general – appears. The "labor market" (in the broader sense) means that it is in the market that men and women allocate themselves by choosing a place in a hierarchically structured institution. Freedom and equality are presupposed in the market.[18] The person presents his or her capacities and sells the use of these capacities in exchange for a certain position and for the wage (salary) allocated to this position. The new social arrangement operates through market transactions, for it is in market transactions that men and women become allocated to certain positions in order to use their capacities. Even if one presupposed that capacities simply enter into transactions, even if one were to abstract entirely from the conditions of the build-up of such capacities prior to their entering the market (inherited money, family education, and so on), even if one were to discuss the ideal type of the modern social arrangement alone, one would come to the conclusion that equal transactions will result in a hierarchy of men (and women) due to the differentiation of functions, income (wealth), and power.

The fundamental differentiation of the functions performed in an institution is concordant with the differentiation between the levels of access to control and management of the institutions themselves. This is one major characteristic of capitalism. In "classical" capitalism the differentiation is between the access to control and management of the economic – social institutions developed roughly, although not entirely, alongside the simple functional opposition between Capital and Labor. Capital was in control and Labor was being controlled. Capital has managed; Labor has been managed. In the 20th century, particularly after WWII and in the "First World," the differentiation of skills, of learning, and many other factors resulted in a modified scheme of continuity rather than of strict opposition in the hierarchical relationships, both in management and in control (and not only in wages and salaries). The combination of private property and market relations can still be termed "capitalism" even if there is no "capitalist society." The latter description first became problematic because of the heterogeneity of the second logic itself, but mainly because the two other logics are not determined but only influenced by the second one. In a pure capitalist society, there could be no pendulum movement and modernity could not survive.

Monetarization has chiefly contributed to the deconstruction of the pre-modern social arrangement, for qualitative distinctions are annulled by monetarization. The question to ask is no longer "what" or "who" (What do you own? Who were your ancestors? Who are you?) but "how much" (How much do you earn? How much have you inherited?) The difference between men (and women) can finally be reduced to differences in quantities.

The monetarization of the value of social positions can also result in the monetarization of the value of a person, the occupant of the position, and the monetarization of human relations in general. The second logic points in this direction. This is one of the unilinear tendencies, among the few that one can detect in the second logic. Whether the pendulum swings in one direction or another, the value of a man who occupies one position and exercises one function remains quantified. The more capitalism develops, the more this will be the case. In areas of strong pre-capitalist traditions – Europe for – example, the tendency toward the monetarization of social–human relations develops only slowly and reluctantly,[19] whereas in the United States it is regarded as if it were "natural."

Modernity's tendency toward the monetarization of social relations was discovered in the early stage of modern development; it was abused, yet it was also welcomed.

Romantics abused monetarization on many counts. Their arguments are well known. For example, it is no longer what you *are* but what you *have* that counts; personal qualities and virtues do not matter, only wealth and income are respected and recognized. The romantic description (and criticism) of modernity hits the nail on the head. Yet, it also entertains the illusion that men and women were ever, in any society whatsoever, respected according to their quality and merit alone! In the pre-modern world, all merits, qualities, and personal values were originally allocated to the position that a person occupied at birth. A slave could develop only the qualities of a slave, and thus the questions of the romantics could not have even been raised.[20]

Yet the romantics did not juxtapose the old world to the new, but juxtaposed the model (the ideal or the "actuality" of the new) to its own reality. Given that "to each according to their merit" and "to each according to their excellence" became universal ideas of justice only in modernity, for it was only in modernity that merit and excellence ceased to be dependent on the overarching idea of justice of "to each according to their rank," the essentialist interpretation of these ideas seemed well founded. What do I mean by the "essentialist" inter-pretation?

If I say, "to each according to their merit," I am only recapitulating the essence of the modern social arrangement. That is, a person will receive remuneration according to the position that he or she has acquired by his or her own efforts in the social division of labor. That he (or she) would be respected because they earn a certain amount, because they occupy a place of a certain magnitude on the ladder of advancement, does not contradict the original claim that they merited the position by their excellence, that they are a self-made man or woman. In fact, the tendency to monetarize social relations increases with the possibility of becoming a self-made man or woman.

The romantic position might also be termed "essentialist," because it defines "merit" or "excellence" in a traditional manner, as personality, refinement, strength of character, or the practicing virtues. But one can also excel in the capacity of climbing, and have merit in seeking good and useful contacts, or bringing a great deal of money in to an enterprise. In the ideas of justice the content (substance) of "merit" and "excellence" is not defined; the romantics, however, define it. Only if one subscribes to the romantic and substantionalist definitions will monetarization appear as the betrayal of the modern idea of justice – which is, in fact, not the case.

The monetarization of human relations also has its defenders. Monetarization frees men and women from personal dependency. The relations of subordination and superordination have traditionally been embedded in the relations of personal dependency.[21] It is through the monetarization of social relations that the relations of subordination and superordination cease being also relations of personal dependency.[22] In addition, monetarization is a grand equalizer. If you have money, your birth and your education do not count. You can become equal with men who were superior to your parents; you can even become the superior. Finally, monetarization is friendly to good luck, adventure, and risk-taking. To put it simply: monetarization may not be very dignified, but it does offer greater freedom.

The romantic and the anti-romantic stories can also be synthesized. Kant performed such a synthesis. He distinguished between the person and personality (the moral individual). The person has a market price, but the personality does not; he is priceless, he has dignity.[23]

Yet, even without much philosophical clout one has the intuition that the romantic position is somewhat exaggerated. Based only on empirical observation, it does not ring absolutely true that by now everything can be bought and sold without limits, that wealth makes everyone beautiful, clever, erotically attractive, and morally good. It also does not ring true that personalities who do not climb very high on the ladder of wealth and power will never receive respect and recognition, that decent (good) people are never loved for their own sake, and that no one marries strictly for love. The Timons of Athens are not the best judges. Perhaps the monetarization of social relations carries the tendency toward the monetarization of all human relations, but does not fully succeed. Or perhaps, in this case, the pendulum is pushed in the other direction. I am not talking about the monetarization of social relations, for this tendency is unilinear, but about the expansion of the spirit of monetarization over all human relations. Cultural discourse and historical imagination in general limits the tendency toward a full monetarization of human relationships and the sheer monetarization of the value of person(ality).[24] The relationship between *apeiron* and *peras* manifests itself in the relationship between the tendency toward total monetarization and the constant limitation of this tendency to the sphere of economic/social relationships. This is a combat, and even if monetarization here seems to get the upper hand and the fears of the romantics are thereby reconfirmed, one can never be sure.[25]

———————

Monetarization has resulted in a dramatic change in the system of need allocation and need satisfaction.

In pre-modern societies, different qualitatively determined needs are allocated to each and every separate estate, political class, man and woman, and age group, and frequently also to subgroups of classes (estates).[26] These qualitatively determined needs are not allocated separately, but in "bundles." They are also allocated with their satisfiers. A free Athenian citizen needs moderate wealth, a piece of land, free education, exercise, and participation in political decision-making and warfare. These needs already include some primary satisfiers (for example, moderate wealth is a need and a satisfier simultaneously) but not all of them (for example, democracy or polity satisfies the need for political participation, yet tyranny does not). The qualitative allocation of satisfiers in principle includes the limit (*peras*).[27] Lack or excess does not properly satisfy a need. Furthermore, needs which are not allocated to the members of the group (because they are of different quality) are disapproved of, censured, and therefore not satisfied. There are needs which are below the dignity of a group of people, and there are needs which are beyond the permitted limit for a group of people. In both cases it is *hybris* to covet satisfiers of such needs.[28]

Modern need allocation is entirely different.

Needs are not allocated in qualitative bundles, but in a homogeneous quantity (money). Money is both the need and the satisfier. Yet neither qualitative needs nor qualitative satisfiers are allocated to any one individual.[29] Equalization means exactly this: everyone gets the same quality (money), although not the same quantity. Moreover, everyone can – in principle – buy with his or her money whatever he or she wants. In principle, this means that the satisfiers are linked to personal choice. Freedom is granted insofar as the concrete qualitative satisfiers can be chosen from among the many that are offered.

Furthermore, everyone is free to re-translate quantity into qualities by his or her own choice. Individuality as an individual hierarchy of needs and satisfiers is thereby warranted. Everyone will be the master of his or her structure (system) of needs. This is the "idea" of the consumer market.

This is how the market circuit is closed. Firstly, as discussed previously, the person appears on the market and becomes allocated to certain social positions, where he or she performs his or her function and is remunerated accordingly. Then, he or she arrives at the market as a consumer, and re-translates the quantitatively allocated bundle of homogenized satisfiers into qualitative satisfiers – and does it, in principle, according his or her own system of needs. The starting-point is quality (skills, professional abilities, capacities), and their mobilization is remunerated in quantity (money); ultimately, this quantity will be retranslated into qualities (consumption, satisfiers of consumption).[30]

Yet the quantitative satisfiers cannot be re-translated into approximations of the traditional need structures. This is not just because the old need structures were allocated to estates, whereas the new structure permits and even furthers personal choice. There is another difference. The traditional need structures moved within certain limits, but now the limits to the scope and to the substance of the qualitative need structures have also been removed. They are removed through the logics of technology on the one hand, and through the internal dynamics (the unilinear tendency toward full monetarization of social–human relationships) inherent in the second logic on the other hand.

The development of technology creates new needs and new satisfiers for old needs. Capitalist production can only be maintained through the constant production of new satisfiers.[31] Apart from the strata living in dire poverty, it is the satisfiers that create needs and not vice versa.[32]

Technological development plays a pivotal role, not just on the side of production but also on the side of consumption. Firstly, technological imagination embraces the imagination of the consumer (for example, the newest is always the best). Secondly, the personal character of the re-translation of quantitative satisfiers into qualitative ones also becomes more and more fictitious, since imagination itself will be more and more technologically engineered.[33] It is through technological devices (the manipulation of imagination) that certain bundles of qualitative satisfiers are offered, so to speak, "ready-made" for the re-translation of quantities into qualities. In this sense, it is not single qualitative satisfiers that are offered in exchange for money, but certain ways of life, whole ways of life.[34] Technology now makes the function of the systematization of satisfiers, a function that was performed in earlier times by the then existent traditions (for example, religious traditions, local traditions working-class traditions, clubs, and so on), into a way of life and sells it on a large scale, often a global scale. Yet, it is not just technology that pushes the second logic in the direction of infinite expansion toward the abandonment of all limits, but also the tendency to monetarize all social relations. Since money is pure quantity, if one allocates money as the sole satisfier, one thereby allocates infinitude. Money cannot ever be enough – there can always be more of it. The monetarization of satisfiers results from, or is accompanied by, the homogenization of need structures into "alienated" needs.

I use the Marxian expression of "alienated" needs because I find it fitting. Needs are alienated if they are superimposed on men and women who then become obsessive, working as a kind of compulsion. Systems of needs sold by the media as forms of life are also superimposed on the single person; they become effective through imitation.

Kant enumerated the three homogenized (alienated) needs: the hunger of having, the hunger of power, and the hunger of fame. Men have always coveted wealth, power, and fame. Yet in a pre-modern world, wealth, power, and fame were all qualitatively allocated and defined. One coveted wealth of something, power for something, fame in something – but not power, wealth, and fame as such. Many kinds of wealth, fame, and power were below the dignity of a free or noble man. In modern times, however, the qualification of power, wealth, and fame is of no importance. One can become a famous politician, a writer, an actor, a strip-tease girl, a mafioso, a religious leader, a war hero, or something else – it does not matter. What matters is just being famous. One can wield power in everything; one can acquire wealth in anything. As far as wealth, fame, and power are concerned, the slogan "anything goes" rings true.[35] Needs are unlimited, for power, wealth, and fame know no limits.

But Kant makes another interesting and telling observation. He speaks of man's "unsociable sociability" (*ungesellige Geselligkeit*). Men do all the wrong things. They hurt their fellow creatures; they kill them because they want to be respected and loved, and for no other reason. This is the paradox of homogenized/alienated needs. They are infinite; man, however, is finite. Why the obsession to covet infinite satisfiers if you are but a finite being?

The satisfiers of homogenized/alienated needs (wealth, power, and fame) are coveted in order to satisfy nonalienable, merely qualitative needs, such as friendship, love, and respect. Finitude is vanquished through fame. The famous are "immortal."[36] Yet men of wealth, fame, and power will always suspect that they are not loved, befriended, and respected for their personalities, but for their money, power, and fame;

and they will envy the poor, the powerless, and the humble for the authenticity of friendship, love, and respect that they receive.

Let me return here to the essence of the second logic from a different perspective. Men and women are allocated to positions in the hierarchically ordered institutions, where they are supposed to perform certain functions. There is a third unilinear tendency of the second logic (besides monetarization and the constant emergence of new needs); namely, specialization. It is the first logic (the logic of technology) that pushes toward increasing specialization, yet both specialization and professionalization are also inherent within the second logic.

The more the pre-modern arrangement is left behind, the more the "idea" of the modern social arrangement will gather momentum. According to this idea exclusively, the position that one occupies in the hierarchy of society must determine the function that one performs. In order to live up to this idea, however, positions need to be allocated to men and women according to their "merit" and "excellence"; that is, according to their skill and education. As a result, education and the institutions of education will "forge" the person so that he or she is able to occupy a place in the division of positions. No universal education is needed, but specialized education is needed to fit men and women to positions as precisely as possible, or to fit them to a bundle of functionally similar but hierarchically sub- and superordinated positions. One can no longer be educated in useless things such as music, poetry, and philosophy just for pleasure's sake. The aim is not to enjoy something, but to do something for use, personal and social use, something in social demand. One supplies abilities and capacities for social demand. What is not in demand cannot be used and is of no value. The description thus far belongs to the internal tendency of the second logic of modernity. The logic of technology results first in the concrete character of the skills and professions, and second in the rationalization of the institutions, whether or not they have any direct correlation with technology, production, and so on. Increasing specialization of skills in a factory may enhance productivity, whereas it was Max Weber's illusion that modern bureaucracy becomes more effective through increasing specialization.

Romanticism has launched several attacks against specialization.[37] But even nonromantics are ill at ease at the sight of modern specialization. Hegel called modern society a "spiritual animal kingdom."[38] Animals are specialized in one thing and are incapable of doing anything else. Contrary to animals, man as a spiritual being is by essence universal. Yet, in the modern spiritual animal kingdom, men become specialized just as animals are – and this is against their essence.

Yet, what we call "culture" (or general culture) was born simultaneously with the specialization of skills and professions. Even the concept of CULTURE (and the German concept of *Bildung*) was first coined and employed in the present sense by thinkers who became aware of the unavoidability of specialization. *Kultur* is meant as a weapon against specialization, not insofar as it annuls specialization (which it does not do), but insofar as it is available to all those who become aware of the crippling effects of specialization and do not want to succumb to it. On the one hand, one is a specialized being and participates in the division of labor with one's specialized skill; on the other hand, one also acquires general culture, knowledge, and ability, the capacity to do things for enjoyment's sake or for the sake of sociability.[39]

Here, the difference between simple *modern life* and the *modern world* reappears. One can live in modernity; one can reproduce oneself successfully with skill and without culture. But it is culture that offers modern men a world, and it is culture that carries and mediates historical consciousness which points beyond technological imagination.

Equality plays a triple role in the modern social arrangement: as equality before the law, as equality in rights, and as equal opportunity. In an optimal situation, the political institutions (the third logic) warrant equal rights and equality before the law. These are the kinds of equality that carry historical imagination, rather than enframement by technological imagination. They are historical not because they are in the past, but because they are present (the past is inhering in the present). They are historical as "here and now" – in stories, ceremonies, collective and individual remembrance, genealogy, and so on. The third kind of equality (equal opportunity) which is enhanced by technological imagination can also become a playground for historical imagination.[40] But there is mostly a double-bind here, a double-bind in the social field as well as in the life of the individual.

It is not just that different skills or professional abilities are allocated to a hierarchically ordered space, yet the hierarchically placed positions also constitute bonds of command and obedience. The constitution can warrant equality before the law and equal rights of individuals as individuals, yet it cannot warrant equal treatment of persons who occupy different places in an institution. The more freely the second logic develops, the more will the weight of oppression and domination shift from the political to the social sphere.[41]

In the pure model of modernity, domination, oppression, and violence are concentrated solely in the institutions of society. These include productive institutions (from shops to banks), reproductive institutions (marriage and family), institutions of education, health, commerce, and administration, as well as penitentiaries and so on. Domination is not solely practiced on the "body"[42] of the superordinated person within the hierarchy of its own institution (director/clerk, chair/untenured faculty, manager/worker), but on the body of men and women *upon whom* the different functions are practiced (the sick, the child, the madman, the deviant, the prostitute). It is not only marginals or members of the underclass who are victims of institutional domination for, incidentally, everyone can be treated as such. Foucault is right when he places emphasis on the functioning of micro-power. Micro-power is hardly noticed. It is mostly based on the inequality of knowledge, skill, insight, and somatic propensities. The oppressed suffers a constant deficit of information, a feeling of inferiority and contempt. Things are done to him or her for reasons that he or she is not aware of. If reasons are disclosed, the disclosed reasons do not fit into the world understanding of the victim.

Yet even if the members of the underclasses are not the only ones to carry the weight of social domination and micro-oppression, the underclasses carry the greatest weight. Their presence is not due to the malfunctioning of modernity, which can be easily corrected. The existence of an underclass is past of the functioning of modernity.[43] If social functions are practiced according to the position that one occupies, and if one can occupy a relatively higher-standing position by acquiring certain skills or professional capacities in the institutions of education, then if someone lacks the ability or the social and personal conditions to become educated, or can only acquire the crudest skills through learning, he or she will be disqualified even before the competition starts.

The modern social arrangement is a pluralistic human universe – but not in everything. As far as the essence of the second logic is concerned, it is far from being pluralistic. In all pre-modern societies, there were different channels of advancement. In the pluralistic modern society there is but one: getting education, surviving one's time in the institution of education. Progressively fewer alternative channels of advancement remain, and even their days are numbered. Men and women who are not fit for the classroom will not fare well, and will be degraded into social trash unless they have one very special skill which does not require education (for example, raw musical talent). But such exceptions are becoming more rare.

The exercise of power within the chain of hierarchy, or the practice of power on the body of men and women who feed the hierarchy and give it purpose, becomes increasingly more enframed by technological imagination. It is science that offers the ideas, the methods, and the procedures for practicing power. Foucault speaks mostly of the power of "normalization," yet this is the extreme case. The unemployed who petition for their dwindling benefits in front of the bureaus, and the refugees waiting for visas or work permits, are not bodies to be "normalized." They are "normal" only in that their situation does not allow them to function in the way in which they are able to function. Both are typical examples for modernity. Both belong to the functioning of the modern social arrangement. But wherever they are, whatever they await, men and women are classified and typified, they are marked, they serve as statistical figures. They are raw material for "scientific" practices, incidental objects of science as the dominating world view of modernity.

Men and women of higher learning are placed high on the social hierarchy and perform their functions accordingly. They have the skills of, for example, a doctor, a lawyer, a biochemist, or an economist. They can compete with people of similar skills for higher positions. Their "imaginary institution" is mostly technological. But what about the double-bind?

The double-bind means that one is bound both by technological imagination and by historical imagination. One leads a life successfully, and one also has a world (and incidentally also a good life). What does it mean to "have" a double-bind? Is this double-bind not just an illusion? Or is it possible to be bound by historical imagination alone without being bound by technological imagination at all, and vice versa?

The first and second logics in modernity – as logic – do not require a historical imagination. Or, if they do, they do not require it *as* historical imagination, but as a *skill*[44] among other skills (for example, teaching history). In principle, one can survive here and even become successful without historical imagination. But single persons can develop historical imagination. These are the individuals who do something well, but also keep a distance from the very thing that they are doing. They can do it well, but they attribute only relative significance to it in comparison with things of equal or perhaps even greater significance, to useless things. It is through such individuals that historical consciousness invades the functionally divided institutional hierarchies. Men and women of double-bind can be anarchists, rebels, skeptics, or ironists; but usually they are just men and women, for whom absolute spirit – that is, art, religion, and philosophy – matters most. They can become personalities.[45]

To be a personality presupposes a double-bind. For if the technological imagination does not bind a person at all, he or she will be unfit for social (and not necessarily for private) survival.

The role of the so-called intellectuals has been debated since the times of Mannheim.[46] He vested hope in the scientific objectivity, in the unbiased minds of the "free-floating intellectuals." From a postmodern perspective this model does not ring true, nor does it appear attractive. Nowadays, one does not believe in the "objectivity" of the so-called "social sciences."[47] Nor does one believe in intellectuals as "bearers of universal values."[48] They are people who occupy specific positions, whose specificity is linked to the working "of the general apparatus of truth." This is the description of one of the binds. As far as technological imagination (and the second logic) is concerned, intellectuals can be characterized just in this way. Yet there are intellectuals – just as there are also nonintellectuals – who are subject to the double-bind. There are intellectuals who practice the same skills as the other intellectuals (this is what makes them intellectuals). They are lawyers, history teachers, philosophy teachers, banking managers, or art historians; yet they practice their professions also with a historical imagination, with some distance. They can love their professions without having great confidence in their professional "ultimates" or in their skill's authority, and – most importantly – without claiming authority in matters of Truth. More precisely, they keep a distance from the kind of truth that is produced in their own discourse.

A person who is subject to the double-bind has a world, yet this the world is never transparent. It cannot be transparent because of the double-bind. From the position of historical consciousness (the position of the world), technological imagination will be intransparent, although it is included in the world. From the standpoint of technological imagination (for those men and women who have a world), the world as such will become entirely intransparent. The double-bind is freedom insofar as one is not bound by one exclusive imaginary institution of signification alone, insofar as one keeps a distance from both, and can abandon oneself to both. This is freedom as autonomy, yet this freedom is a lack of freedom insofar as it is the free acceptance of the double-bind. It is through the double-bind that the paradoxes of freedom manifest themselves, as the truth about the paradoxicality of the freedom of the moderns.

7

The Three Logics of Modernity III:

The Logic of Political Power (Domination)

It was not just the idiosyncratic view of Karl Marx to describe the third logic, the political one, as the tendency to become a mere superstructure on the so-called "economic base;" that is, on capitalist society.[1] It seemed for a while as if the state would remain just the executive committee of the dominating economic class, or – in a liberal version of the same story – the warranty of the unhampered development of benevolent market forces. A similar view has recurred since then and remains at the present moment. The only function of the state is to warrant law and order on the necessary scale. The "minimal state" is either just an option polemically posed against the "caretaker state" of a social-democratic sort, or it is meant as the description of the main current tendencies, at least in the First World.[2]

But whether socialist or liberal, social-democratic, or something else, all of these concepts think of the state only, and exclusively, from the standpoint of society – particularly of the economy. The state either should or should not intervene in the economy. The political logic has to limit itself and be at the service of the second logic or, conversely, it should interfere with the second logic so as to limit it, but not in a dictatorial way. Moreover, it should limit the second logic relatively, not absolutely. All of these concepts of the "political" think of the political as the handmaiden of the economic/social.

The swing of modernity's pendulum results, indeed, from the clash of these two options in the interplay between state and economy. If – within this interplay – state intervention becomes "minimal," the danger of popular unrest appears, the social balance becomes deeply disturbed, and at times dictators can replace democratic governments. On the other hand, the intervention of the state can become forceful and endanger the relative independence of the second logic, and social stagnation will be the outcome even if the intervening state remains liberal and democratic.[3] The "crisis of the welfare state" in the 1980s meant that welfare policies arrived at a limit at which signs of exhaustion and stagnation became visible not just for the ideological enemies of the system, but also for their beneficiaries. Then came the "monetarist" counter-strike which, in the immediate present, seems to have arrived at its limits.

Obviously, the pendulum of modernity will be pushed back once again to a certain extent. And the story begins anew.

Seen from the description of the pendulum of modernity, the interplay between the second and third logics seems to be entirely enframed by technological imagination, even if the first logic, the logic of technology, was in no way involved in the development of the interplay. But for the most part, it is.[4] For simplicity's sake, I will abstract from the direct push coming from the first logic, which can be exercised on the state and society alike. I will speak only about "enframing," about technological imagination, insofar as it devours the sphere or the concept of the political.

The interplay between society (economy, distribution) and state intervention (redistribution) is a kind of problem-solving. The problem itself (for example, of reallocation or redistribution) is not quantitative, yet the solution to the problem reduces to quantitative measures. Due to the monetarization of need allocation, the process of redistribution and the surveying of the available resources become a matter of calculation. The question is, how much should be redistributed from the available resources to a certain number of people? Even the conditions that make redistribution mandatory, or which manditorily put an end to a kind of redistribution, can be described in technological terms. "Disturbances," or the risk of "disturbances," are malfunctions similar to the malfunctions of a machine. They have to be put right through the implementation of new policies. "Stagnation" is also a malfunction, provided that the machine, society/economy, is not supposed to stagnate. One has to accelerate the speed of such a machine. In each and every swing of the pendulum, new methods are added to old ones to cope with malfunctions or stagnation. Some methods are taken over in the next swing, and they are also improved; there is a kind of "accumulation" of experience.[5]

Sometimes it looks as if the constant vacillation between society and economy (and law and order) would be the state's sole function in the modern world. If this were so, historical imagination would not characterize the political logic, and none of the logics of modernity would need historical imagination. If this were so, historical imagination would be only a "remnant" of the times when modernity was still *in statu nascendi*. If this were so, the whole theory of "double-bind" would prove untrue or irrelevant. If this were true, modern men would just need life and not a world. Or, alternatively, if this were so, no distinction would remain between life and world in "adult" modernity.[6]

But is that so?

There are certain, continuously present and frequently occurring, events in modern life which at least permit a negative answer to this question. One could, perhaps, also give a positive answer. I could argue for both the positive and the negative answers. Yet, I will only indulge in taking care of the negative answer, thereby following Kant's spirit (if not his words). If I could demonstrate (and not necessarily prove) the possibility that there can be no political logic without the constant presence of historical consciousness in modernity, this would be enough for me to make my case.

But first I will elaborate a point which, at least initially, works against me.

Forging, drafting, and crafting a constitution was, in Aristotle's division of active life, a kind of *technē*, not a kind of *energeia*. Yet in the ancient world very few constitutions were drafted. In legendary times, they were invented by the great founders of states, such as Lycurgus or Numa Pompilius.[7] Political authority was wielded not by drafted constitutions, but by monarchs who ruled by the right of the first conqueror, or by biological ascendancy as legitimated by tradition.

The most obvious tendency in the third logic is to leave behind traditional legitimation as the main source of authority. Yet if traditional legitimation is no longer the source of political authority, what was once the exception must now become the rule. Constitutions need to be drafted.[8]

Every modern state borrows legitimacy from its constitution, and the constitution itself is man-made. Constitution-making as *techē* begins to occupy a pivotal role. The authority of a state is crafted; it is intentionally crafted in order to perform a function – to serve as the highest source of political authority, as the fundamental law.

In the Age of Reason, drafting constitutions became a national pastime in France. People drafted constitutions just as they composed poems or sonnets. In states where there are not yet constitutions in place, the drafting of constitutions is by now no longer a private enterprise (although only totalitarian governments prohibit it). It is done in parliamentary committees by "experts," first and foremost by constitutional lawyers.[9] All kinds of constitutions have been drafted, and only some of them have ever been implemented.

Yet, despite all the appearances, drafting constitutions is only rarely a mere technical procedure. The drafters can look for models nowadays – for example, the American or the postwar German constitutions – but they cannot copy those models. Constitutions must consider national traditions, and national traditions are historical traditions. A constitution needs to fit not only "society" or "the economic order," but the people who are living in a social and economic order. Irrespective of whether one person plays a decisive role in drafting the constitution (such as Croce in Italy) or whether it is done by teamwork, it will remain a constitution only under the condition that it is also historically rooted. Even something that is entirely new can be historically rooted. That which is entirely new is, for example, a democratic constitution in a state where there was never a democracy and a democratic constitution. But there is always a cultural background which wittingly or unwittingly has to lend traditional legitimacy even for a brand new constitution.

This may shed light on an interesting phenomenon. Although constitutions can be copied, a merely copied constitution does not gain legitimacy. It will not function as a constitution, for in order to function as a constitution it needs to have authority and legitimacy. The funny thing that pertains to this situation can be described as follows: for a constitution to perform its task (to be recognized and felt as an authority for the people), the constitution cannot be drafted with an eye on the performance of this task alone. A constitution drafted in the sense of pure functionalist technicalities will not perform its function; that is, to be the carrier of legitimacy. Historical imagination needs to be embedded in it in order to summon authority. This is why the Weberian distinction between legitimation by law and legitimation by tradition does not need to be understood as a distinction between two opposites. This is not only because legitimation by law can also become a tradition, as happened in the United States, but because the law, and particularly the supreme law itself, carries an aspect of tradition.

The universality of modern political institutions (first and foremost, the constitution) expresses itself in an entirely different way than the universality of technology, of technological imagination, or the universality of economy and economic institutions. If a new technological device is discovered in Germany and enters the world market, the same technological device (whether fabricated in Germany, Japan, or Thailand) will be used everywhere, and will everywhere perform the same function. People speak the same language in mathematics or astrophysics everywhere in the world. Traditional economies can prevail within the global economy, yet only if they fit into the global economy. Economy, just as technology, became an empirical universal. This is to say that enframing (*Ge-stell*) technological imagination became, in fact, universal.[10]

Yet political institutions cannot be exported. America can easily export television sets and television programs, Coca-Cola and McDonald's. Yet the American constitution belongs to the American people, and to them alone. It cannot be exported, for it would need to be exported along with the legal spirit of the American population, because without it the American constitution is null and void. It is the American "people" ("we the People") who authorize the constitution. Without citizens – specific citizens with specific pasts, and political instinct – there is no constitution. I reassert that constitutions cannot be exported, and this is why their universality – provided that they are in any sense universal – must be sought in different quarters.

If the models of state intervention cannot be entirely imitated and exported in the same manner from state to state as can economic policies (Keynesianism or monetarism), the reason does not lie in the function of the state intervention policies, but in the perception of the state, politics, and the constitution by the population – a culture, briefly, in historical imagination.

Moreover, even if the crafting/drafting of constitutions is seemingly a kind of *technē*, it is less so in the modern world as it was in the Aristotelian world. The modern world is characterized by a future-oriented imagination. One could object that a future-oriented imagination is more technological than any other kind of imagination, for it is in the spirit of technology always to invent something else, something new, a new model or prototype. So far, this can be admitted, except that the essence of imagination which guides the crafters of new constitutions is itself not technological but historical.

A shortlist of the political inventions of the moderns can be devised. They have invented liberalism, parliamentary democracy, universal suffrage and the secret ballot, constitutional monarchy, the federal republic, and the federal state in general. They have invented totalitarianism, the political spectrum that extends between right and left, human rights, universal rights and the rights of citizens, the supra-state political institutions (from the League of the Nations to the United Nations and its branches), the nation – state, nationalism, internationalism, and international institutions – and the shortlist could be easily amended.

This list seems to contradict my thesis that political constitutions cannot be exported. Almost all of the enumerated new institutions of the modern age had been discovered in one place on the globe and taken over later in other countries. They also seem to contradict my thesis about the importance of free-floating political imagination in the modern age. After all, many of the institutions mentioned here grew almost organically out from the old, replacing the old ones step by step – as, for example, the secret ballot (and the discovery of the ballot box) slowly replaced the open ballot in England.[11]

Yet, what can be exported is just the technology appropriate to all modern democracies (for example, the ballot box is convenient for a secret ballot), and what cannot be exported is everything else (for example, even the character of the ballot sheet, whether it contains names of individuals, of parties, or of both). Furthermore, even if certain institutions established in one country after a long process of trial and error can serve as a crutch for other countries (which has not gone through a trial-and-error period), the political institution will live and guide in another way – it will be qualitatively different.

In this respect, it is fruitful to compare the New World and the Old World, particularly America and Europe and their mutual misunderstanding of each other's political institutions and imagination.[12]

Historical recollection and the cherishing of past memories plays the most significant role in Europe and the great Eastern civilizations (China, India, Japan). Historical memory is kept in stories, legends, and symbols. Here, heroic events, great contests, and extraordinary trials all play an immense part. Historical memory recounts the stories of actions, of the genesis of institutions and their demise.[13] The internal structures of institutions past are not preserved in the deep chambers of historical consciousness,[14] but through the acts of men and women. This is how historical imagination preserves worlds, or at least fragments of worlds which are assembled by memory and imagination[15] for the sake of new actions and new initiatives. The fragments of past worlds are presenced in imagination.

The presencing of past memories as *worlding*[16] is sometimes referred to with much contempt, ideology, or false consciousness. The concept of ideology and its critique presents three different, although connected, ideas of enlightenment: the idea of rationality, the idea of reality, and the idea of universality.

A style of imagination and belief is called (or abused) as ideology because of its lack of rationality. All historical ideas are directly or indirectly rooted in value-rationality. After all, the experience that for a people its own genesis is valuable, that a heritage is valuable, that memories of real or imaginary communities are cherishable, cannot be supported with goal-rational arguments. There is no pragmatic reason behind teaching children history, myths, and legends; the mobilization of those myths or legends in the perception of the present world is then abused as irrational.

What is called reality is the world of needs and interest, particularly of interests. What is not directly related to interest is then "unreal" or "nonreal," and as such is believed to be not only useless but harmful. Ideologies are then "unmasked": behind the legends, myths, moral lessons, and stories, one has to detect the "reason" or "reality" – the interests. The anti-ideological drive is the drive to unmask, for nothing else is supposedly real but our interests, and nothing else is supposedly rational but the pragmatic pursuit of those interests. Everything else is a cover-up, a veil to be removed – like the veil of Maya, which must be eliminated for the real woman, the *naked* one, to appear. The phrase "naked interest" is telling, for interests are associated with nakedness, with the real thing behind the artificial costume of a fraudulent historical consciousness.

The third idea of enlightnment (after rationality and reality) – namely, the idea of universality – is a more complex aspect of the critique of ideology. Firstly, national, tribal stories, memories, are unmasked as hostile forces that block the acceptance of universality. Everything is particularistic and tribal except "humankind" or "man" as such. Yet, as it is, "humankind" and "man" have no representative stories.[17] Thus, the universalistic criticism of "ideology" selects among the tradition and accepts only the great (classic) works of art. For the classic works of art have universal significance; they speak of "men" even if they portray particular histories and particular men. The particularistic use of great works of art is thus frequently ascribed to illegitimate abuse.[18]

Yet, the universalists also "unmask" ideologies as stories which make a false claim to reality, rationality, and truth.[19] It is foolish to unmask nationalism as a mere "cover-up" for interest, yet if stories of a nation or an ethnic group are used to legitimize the current claims of the people or the group for the territory, the treasures, and the lifespace of another group, the claim can be false, and the story alone *does not prove* either the truth or the rightness of the current claim.

There is no modern world without "ideology." Ideology is neither a religion, nor a philosophy, nor the interpretations of folk stories or works of art. Yet it can draw from all these – and other – sources. Ideologies are collective beliefs that center around one of the ethical powers,[20] reinforcing it and protecting it. The modern state needs ideologies as collective images (enthusiasm for causes, re-living of the past), even if the second and the first logics could do without them. The modern state also needs the critique of ideologies, not because the rationalism or realism argument would hold ground, but because ideologies are sometimes not simply nonrational and nonreal (which suits them well), but can isolate their world of imagination from the other logics, a phantom world that severs all relationships with rationality and "reality."[21] By reality, I mean (in modernity) the image of the world that holds out under critical scrutiny or even requires critical scrutiny – as long as it does.[22] The closure of chauvinistic, and even more so of totalitarian, ideologies is widely discussed.

And what about the New World, particularly America? There are no old memories here, no old stories to tell, no mythologies, no indigenous fairy tales. No great or heroic acts of remote predecessors can be related, and the possibility of raising fraudulent claims on mythological grounds is also limited.[23]

Tocqueville writes that it is useful to get to know the origins of a people, yet Americans are the only people whose origin is really open to observation.[24] There are stories of the War of Independence as also of the Civil War, but those stories hardly form a living memory of a collective consciousness. American nationalism is strong, yet not historically grounded.[25] There is only one historically rooted story (and memory) which is especially American and this is slavery. Race and the language of race is the only quasi-historical language which can mediate the past and present in the public mind. Yet "race" itself is not historical.[26]

But Americans created two brand new myths, and they do work. I mean the American ideology of the "Wild West" and the American court drama. Both are linked to the major ethical power of North Americans – the constitution. The myth of the Wild West and the court drama are both centered around justice. They are also marginally around distributive justice but, first and foremost, around retributive justice.[27] Although the concrete stories of retributive justice in the myths of the Wild West and the court drama are typically modern American, they draw from the treasure-house of ancient myths. For there is a universal feature in the myths of all people that, besides the stories of justice or injustice in war, the stories of retributive justice or injustice (revenge) play the most significant role.[28]

The more "historical" an ideology is, the deeper its historical roots are, the greater part the acts of war and conquests (sometimes also peace or tragic defeat) will play in it. Modern wars are waged no less with ideologies than ancient ones. And the justification of war requires recourse to old stories today just as it did in the remote past. It could even be said that modern wars (if we assume that the first "modern" war was the Thirty Years War) are more "ideological" than ancient ones. I do not have the means to compare them.[29] The hope that modernity will eliminate wars has not yet been fulfilled.[30]

I am still discussing the third logic of modernity, the political sphere and its tendencies. It has become evident – at least, I hope so – that this third logic requires historical imagination, historical memory, and that this imagination, this memory, cannot be deduced from so-called Reality. It can not be explained by Rationality either, nor with University, for this is a kind of imagination which works only as long as it is not determined or "enframed" by technological imagination. This is why no reductionist attempt to explain "ideologies" from hidden interests could give an account of their power and might. Their power can be beneficial and destructive, but a power it is in its own right. This once again confirms the fact that men of modernity are caught in a double-bind, along with the modern world itself.

Among the several institutions and so-called "state forms"[31] that the moderns have invented, only a few can be discussed in some length in a general theory of modernity. I choose what are to me the most significant: the totalitarian state, liberalism (liberal rights included), and, finally, modern democracy.

The totalitarian state is as modern an invention as democracy.[32]

The totalitarian state is not identical with totalitarianism; firstly, because a state can acquire totalitarian potentials even if the government is elected by the majority,[33] and, secondly, because the most representative totalitarian states (foremost, Russian Bolshevism) also totalize society, whereas other totalitarian states (for example, Mussolini's Italy) do not.

A totalitarian state is always also a dictatorship. Yet it is not a military dictatorship.[34] Military dictatorships are traditional, as authoritarian governments are, yet the totalitarian dictatorship is anti-traditional. It defines itself mostly as being revolutionary, introducing a brand new order. Totalitarian dictatorships do not pretend to restore law and order but, conversely, declare to pursue permanent revolution. That is, the dictator of a totalitarian state is the originator of the dynamics of modernity. He says "no" to tradition; he says "yes" to the revolutionary innovations that take the place of tradition.[35]

The model of a modern totalitarian state was laid down by the Bolshevik regime, by the dictator Lenin, and by the despot Stalin. The secret of the modern totalitarian state is the totalitarian party – this was Lenin's political invention. The term "party" is on the one hand misleading, for a party is supposed to represent a "part" and not a "whole." However, "party," in the sense of the totalitarian parties, is not a token word. Totalitarian parties were first organized in a multi-party environment, yet they had "totalized themselves" already within this environment, forming a totalitarian mini-state within a democratic or an autocratic state. After having seized power, they immediately began to shape the state in the image of a totalitarian party, and after having accomplished political totalization, they also totalized the whole society, with all of its institutions.[36] A totalized society is a society in which pluralism is outlawed. In fact, pluralism exists but has no right to exist; at any time it can be punishable by law. Whether it is or is not will be determined by the political authority; that is, by the totalitarian party and its dictator. What is outlawed is sometimes entirely dependent on the whim and mood of the great dictator (for example, in the era of Stalin or Hitler).

Totalitarian dictatorship is possibly, but not necessarily, terroristic. In the terroristic phase terror reigns supreme, both in the sense of mass murder and in the sense of fear. This was the case during Stalin's reign. The regime maintains itself in continuous warfare, either through waging war against its own population, through waging a war against a selected group (the Jews), or through waging a war for world supremacy. Whatever methods of war and propaganda are used, totalitarian states are universalistic in their project even if not necessarily in their ideology, for they aim to conquer the whole globe.[37]

That the totalitarian party/state rule was originally fully implemented in the Eastern regions of the European continent does not speak against its modern character. The ideas that formed the center of the communist ideology were of modern Western origin, and Karl Marx was a modern German philosopher. From Bolshevism (and from Mussolinism), Nazism learned organization and the way to spread ideology and propaganda (although not the ideological content of the ideology and propaganda). After the defeat of Nazi Germany in WWII, the Soviet model was taken over into, or forced upon, a considerable part of the globe, including China, North Vietnam, North Korea, and the Soviet sphere of influence in Central/Eastern Europe.

Totalitarianism can serve for many as the counter-example of my idea presented in this chapter; namely, that constitutions cannot be exported. Now it seems as if totalitarian state "forms" can be exported.

It is true that totalitarian types of political institutions can seemingly be exported to a far greater extent than democratic institutions, for the implementation of a totalitarian regime hardly, if at all, depends on the people on which the totalitarian regime is superimposed. This is why the import of totalitarian institutions has not really been successful. If the regime has already been established, people cannot get rid of the totalitarian party without an indigenous revolutionary change or a change in the international balance of powers, or both. Meanwhile, however, the traditions of a country, a selectively mobilized or at least tolerated historical memory, infiltrates the forms of totalitarian institutions. In all Central/Eastern European countries, the same regime essentially existed. Yet this regime could assume (at least after the death of Stalin) special features stemming from the traditions of a country, and from the subsequent political choices of their people. Although the basic political institutions had actually been imported, they were slowly invaded by the differences of various "spirits of nations."

Among all the political forms of modernity, it is totalitarianism that shows the most extreme forms of the double-bind. Its emergence, its functioning, and its ideology manifest technological imagination at its pitch. Yet the mythologization of history, the abandonment of enlightenment "reality" and rationality, the absolutization of historical imagination and fantasy, in a highly reflective way, is here also the most exorbitant.

It was often pointed out that the extermination of the European Jews by Nazi Germany was possible only with the means of modern technology.[38] To a lesser extent, this is also true of the extermination of whole social, political, and ethnic groups in Stalin's camps.

Even if one abstracts from technological imagination, the sheer employment of the available modern technological resources (for example, gas chambers, trains) is significant. We speak of "death factories," and this is not a figure of speech. It is not just murder on the grand scale, but also the observation and persecution of political enemies which employs modern technology, such as telephone-tapping and the like. In the latter case, technology breaks through the walls of secrecy and silence. One can never be alone, and even if one trusts friends or partners, one cannot trust one's own house.

Yet, it is not the factual employment of technological devices but the mobilization of technological imagination that essentially matters.[39] Gas chambers are not employed because they are available just like guns, but because their employment appears as a case of problem-solving. The problem is: How can one murder with minimal effort and with the greatest effect? How can one apply the *maximini* principle to the extermination of people? The question is the productivity of mass murder, the per capita expenditure (in money and effort) of the task of murder. What they decided upon was "the final solution of the Jewish problem."[40]

Still, to attribute the totalitarian (and particularly the Nazi) extermination machinery to technological imagination alone is misleading, and it results in the one-sided acceptance of Heidegger's concept of "enframing."[41] For something has set the "task" of eliminating a group of people, or solving the "Jewish question," and this task was not set by technological imagination. The problem here becomes a technological "problem" as a result of the translation of an ideological system, an ideologically construed world of historical imagination, into a technological problem. Technological imagination alone can only become lethal indirectly, to the degree that men who are supposed to solve certain problems – for example, the production of nuclear energy – do not take into consideration the possible effects of their technological solution.[42] This is, I repeat, not just a moral problem. One can also speak of moral responsibility in cases where pure technological imagination is at work; if, for example, one fails to consider the foreseeable negative consequences of the use of nuclear energy, or if one neglects precaution for the sake of personal interest. Historical imagination, which mobilizes past memories and places them in the holistic frame of an ideology, is *directly* lethal, for it reinforces technological imagination while employing it in the service of a *closed world* of historical imagination. The question of "foreseeable consequences" cannot then be raised, for all consequences are already legitimized by the ideology itself. Even if the consequences turn out to be dangerous for the group whose ideology has set the goal for the problem which is to be "solved" by murder, it does not matter. The ideologically superimposed models of problem-solving might become irrational in all pragmatic aspects.[43] The pragmatic aspects of reality are annulled, given that reality is itself, in the sense used above, outlawed.

Thus, the double-bind characterizes the world of the moderns: problem-solving and interpretation, planning and recollection, calculation and reflection. The double-bind needs to be "double;" it needs to bind modern men and women to different historical places and spaces, to different activities, different evaluations. The danger of totalitarianism looms large whenever the two binds act in concert and pull in the same direction. Liberalism and democracy are invented to protect modernity from this danger. Whether they do it, or do it entirely, remains to be seen.

Modern democracy is the combination of majority rule and representation.[44] The systems of representation may be very different, but its principle may not be. Men (and later also women) cast their vote and thereby elect their representatives with the majority of votes. This is how majority rule is secured. Among the three powers which are to be divided (legislative, judicial, and executive), the legislative branch always consists of the elected representatives.[45] Mostly, the executive branch of power is also elected, but the judicial branch rarely is.[46] Through this arrangement, the essence of democracy is established: people only obey self-created laws. This essence has several typical manifestations. One is the possibility, for every member of the body politic, to actively participate in the business of politics and directly in the business of the state. They have the right to be elected, not just to elect. The state consists of citizens. In the classical model of democracy, citizens are both active and passive. This is not *in fact* the case, but here I do not deal with empirical facts.

Among the liberties of the moderns, democracy employs and mobilizes one of the so-called positive liberties: the freedom of the citizen to participate in the business of politics.[47] Negative liberties are not guaranteed by the democratic institutions but by the institutions of liberalism.[48] Sometimes liberalism and democracy support one another, but at other times they collide.

Since democracy is the rule of majority, democratic liberty is the liberty of the majority. It is possible that whenever the wish, the interest, or the design of the majority is pursued, the minority will remain defenseless, and will have no other option but to accept the decision of the majority, even if it suffers discrimination, oppression, or repression. This is why democracy can show totalitarian tendencies or become, as Tocqueville expressed himself, "tyrannical." It is the tyranny of the majority.[49] Experience teaches that in the spirit of democracy the political judgment or the political will of the majority is normally accepted as correct by the political minority. In the United States, where democracy is *the* political tradition, men and women generally believe that the majority always has the right. Here it requires great civil courage to stand by a minority opinion, to dissent openly and radically from the majority opinion. In Europe, a world of a more aristocratic or at least more patrician tradition, one rather presupposes that the minority is right and that the judgment of a single person weighs more than the judgment of the whole "theater."[50]

The rights of citizens are constituents of democracy, but the rights of "man" are the constituents of liberalism.[51] In the tradition of the democratic institutions, the single individual is no bearer of rights, nor is any human group, with the exception of the politically organized body of citizens. There is, however, one liberty which is an exception: the *freedom of the press*. The freedom of the press is the warranty of democracy, for the newspaper is the single major power which can elevate, as much as destroy, all politicians, large or small. The freedom of conscience and speech are, however, liberal rights, for they also grant those rights to individuals and not to political institutions (such as the press). In America, the first democracy,[52] the liberal right of the freedom of speech became absolute and sacrosanct – in comparison to the most European countries – because it reinforced the already extant democratic tradition of the freedom of the press.[53]

The main value of democracy is equality; in the case of freedom, the equality of freedom. The freedom of the press, as I indicated, has a special status.

Liberalism warrants the rights of "man," the rights of the individual. Among them, the most important are the right to hold property, the coalition right,[54] freedom of conscience and speech, the right to privacy, and the right of the person as a member of a minority, as an immigrant and the like. The principles of liberalism protect the person from the tyranny of the political, the minority from the tyranny of the majority. The main value of liberalism is freedom, and not equality. There is only one branch of liberal rights where equality is central, equality before the law, to which several rights are related (such as the right of public defense, the right to be held innocent unless proven guilty, the right to a fair trial, and so on). Yet, as in all the other cases, here also the rights pertain to persons,[55] to individuals, and not to citizens or political institutions.

For democracy, I repeat, equality is the highest value. Civic liberties have already been constituted – this is what an extant democracy means; political freedom is taken for granted.[56] In fact, democracy is identified with freedom, whereas equality is the value that democratic citizens will pursue in the spirit of democracy.[57]

Fehér[58] distinguishes three concepts of equality in the realm of the political: the formal, the conditional, and the substantive. I will elaborate upon his idea as follows. Formal equality is the kind of equality which is also central to liberalism, such as equality before the law or equal rights (if rights mean liberties and not socio-economic rights). Conditional equality gives rise to the idea of state intervention, of the redistribution of goods and services by the state. Conditional equality is the kind of equality typical in social-democratic states and welfare states in general.[59] The state cannot warrant equal opportunity (no one and nothing can), but it might provide minimum (or maximum) conditions under which equal opportunity is in fact possible. Thus, in the case of conditional equality, "equality" is never achieved, for the equality of "conditions" is itself a blurred, intransparent idea. How do you know that at the present moment the conditions have become equal? Obviously, there is in fact equal opportunity if everyone concerned believes that their opportunities are equal. Only personal belief (and no quantity or yardstick) can "measure" something that is not measurable. All the worse for the claim to "equality," given that everything that is supposed to become "equal" needs to be measured and compared.[60] The concept of socio-economic rights is rightly criticized for having been blurred; still, it does not cease to be relevant as the fundamental concept of conditional equality.[61]

Yet the democratic *ethos* pushes toward substantive equality. Equality is substantive if it claims that all men, as individuals, as ipseities, are of equal merit and worth, and that to differentiate among them as among persons is unsuitable. The difference in wealth and income is far more easily accepted by the democratic *ethos* than the difference between single individuals as personalities. This is so because wealth is a quantity just like height or weight, whereas individuality or personality is a quality.

The constant trend toward equalization, toward noneconomic egalitarianism, is the common feature of all democracies, ancient democracies included. The single individual who has grown too large is regarded as a constant threat to the democratic spirit. If he grew large as a statesman, citizens resent his political power.[62] Yet even if the political threat of the concentration of powers in one man is absent, citizens resent grandeur. They suspect that there is something fishy in grandeur, that there is no merit behind it, but a certain kind of illicit sorcery.[63] "Cut the head off the tall poppies" or "Jack is as good as the master" are the well known slogans born out of the egalitarian spirit of democracy.[64]

Hegel complained about the lackey attitude; in the eyes of the lackey, every great man is petty. After all, all "great men" go to the toilet to urinate, and all of them shout or whine occasionally – they are just like all of us. Why respect them, then?

Hero worship is just the other side of the coin. There are select heroes or "cult figures" that one worships, not because they are different or better, but because they are like all of us, and yet were incidentally performing something extraordinary; for example, becoming a well-known pop singer or football star. It is unlikely for a Nobel prize winner in physics to attain the same kind of respectability, because people cannot seriously think that it was just sheer good luck that made this "poppy" grow that high.

Substantive equality manifests itself in *ressentiment*.[65] *Ressentiment* is not just a feeling, although it is also the feeling of resentment or envy. It is not a personal feeling, a personal blunder, a sign of a person's pettiness. *Ressentiment* inheres in the institutions of democracy, for it is the essential aspect of the spirit of substantive egalitarianism, which is the always recurring tendency in all democracies. If the *ethos* of the institution contains the belief that personal grandeur is just a trick and an infringement upon the *ethos* of equality, *ressentiment* is produced and reproduced by the democratic institutions themselves. It is the ugly face of democracy. But all institutions have ugly faces, and the question is: Ugly for whom?[66] Max Weber tells a story about his encounter with American workers. He asked them, "Why do you elect a president whom you despise?" They answered, "It is better if we despise him than if he despises us." The spirit of democracy was wisely juxtaposed here to the spirit of aristocracy, the American tradition to the European tradition.[67]

Modern liberal democracies are combinations of liberalism and democracy. The pendulum of modernity has begun its swing here too; at one time the liberal aspect gets the upper hand, at another time the democratic aspect pushes liberalism into the background. The optimal condition for the survival of modernity is the recurring temporal restoration of the balance between liberal and democratic aspects and institutions which happens in and through the dynamics of modernity.

Certainly – as has been frequently stated – in a modern constitution the institutions of liberalism limit democracy and the institutions of democracy limit liberalism. For example, the first amendment to the constitution of the United States warrants those rights. Even if the majority of the citizens would vote against them, those rights could not be abolished. This is a typical example of where liberalism limits the scope of democracy. However, during the Cold War, for example, they institutionalized the so-called anti-American committee – the institution (unquestionably democratic, for it enjoyed the support of the majority) was anti-liberal to the extent that it legalized even soul searching, it limited the freedom of conscience without touching the "right" to it.[68]

I mentioned the substantive trends in democracy. Yet democracy can also be entirely formal. Similarly, there can be a strong substantive strain within liberal institutions and practices, whereas liberalism as well as democracy can become entirely formal. Liberalism and democracy are not simply living together; they are intertwined, and they mutually interpret one another. In a merely democratic interpretation liberal aspects become entirely formal and, conversely, in a merely liberal interpretation democratic institutions assume just a formal character. It is the optimal state for the functioning of a modern liberal democracy for liberalism and democracy, as well as their substantive and formal features, to be "outbalanced."

Liberalism is substantive if one of the liberal rights, such as the right to own property or have personal freedom, does not allow for democratic interpretation. If most liberal rights do not allow any democratic interpretation, particularly the two mentioned above, democracy becomes formal; that is, it becomes limited to periodical free elections of the representatives by universal suffrage. Such was the case, for example, in the Weimar democracy at the time of its defeat.[69] It seems obvious that if democracy cannot interpret the liberal institutions and thus becomes sheerly formal, the proper balance between democracy and liberalism becomes strongly disturbed.

The opposite is the case if all, or almost all, liberal rights and values are exposed to democratic interpretation, and the substantive elements of liberal rights begin to wither. At this stage, liberalism becomes merely formal. Liberalism is formal if it is limited to the liberal procedure and the mere maintenance of a system of rights, and if it resigns the prerogative to interpret its own values. This happens nowadays, for example, in American liberalism and particularly in the liberal discourse, to the extent that the communitarian agenda is accepted.[70] Liberalism is in retreat. There are authors who call themselves liberals and who accept women's genital mutilation on the ground "that this is their custom," "their ethos." Liberalism is then restricted to fair procedure, to which all possible content can be given. No one dares to cry out with Voltaire, with the traditional European liberal "écraser l'infame!" ("crush the infamous!").

The modern state was defined by Max Weber as the institution which has the monopoly on the legal use of violence. One can accept this description to a certain extent. After all, there are no legal private armies in a modern state[71] and, with a few exceptions, wars are declared by the institutions of the state and they are fought by national armies.

Violent crimes are punishable by law, and there is only one set of laws for all and one legal practice. Criminal trials in America[72] are trials in which *the people* persecute the offender, in which the people (the jury) issue the verdict and frequently also the sentence. The state that executes the sentence is merely the arm of the people.

There is a constant war going on between the legal and the illegal use of violence. People want "law and order," an effective police force, and relative security in their houses;[73] that is, they want the state to exercise its legitimate power.[74] But, they do not want the state to interfere with their right, and with their right to hold arms.[75] The latter right supports the ideological claim that it is the people and not the state which in fact has the monopoly on the legitimate use of violence, and that the single citizen, if the situation so requires, can exercise violence legally (not just in self-defense or protection of others, but also in citizen's arrest). In the pioneer mythology, the main story is about justice/injustice, irrespective of the circumstances in which individuals and institutions are involved. Yet there is a far more pedestrian and realistic mythology, which is about the fight between the police force and the criminals.

However, the legitimate exercise of violence seems to be more diffuse and less monopolized in a modern world than the Weberian definition suggests.[76] It has frequently been pointed out that in modernity force and violence have become sublimated. Competition is, for example, a sublimated form of violence and force. Sublimation is a protection on the one hand, an aspect of the civilizing process;[77] yet on the other hand, it is a cover-up for violence. Force and violence go unnoticed if sublimated. Moreover, as Foucault pointed out many times,[78] science and its technologies enjoy the real monopoly of the legitimate use of violence and force in many institutions (for example, in mental asylums, in clinics, and sometimes in schools). Lately, the question has been raised as to whether majority cultures do not exercise violence or force against minority cultures whenever they push for assimilation. Moreover, the violation of nature by certain practices of modern technology has also become regarded as a kind of force, which at least indirectly threatens man's well-being or even survival.

Sometimes, the terms "force" and "violence" are too broadly used and thus misused as "big" words to give weight to a claim. Yet it still remains true that the "legitimate" use of violence and force is far more widespread and far more variegated in the modern world, as Weber's definition might have suggested. One could even experiment with the idea that the state-exercised violence and force can be controlled more easily than the many indirect political types of force and violence, which are difficult to scrutinize and present to the public.

What is scrutinized by the public eye are the political institutions and the political actions. The meaning of "political action" is, however, also very diffuse. Many theorists have tried to pin down "the concept of the political," but some decisive aspects of "the political" elude all definition.[79] I, on my part, have offered a vague description of the "political." I meant thereby every act, discussion, decision, and so on, concerning the determination of freedom if elevated to the public sphere. I still consider this description to be helpful, for it offers the understanding of the kind of politics that can be called "republican." In the modern world "republican politics" is essential politics because republicanism is about the "politicization" of the issues of freedom by carrying them into the public sphere. Republicanism is not identical with being "democratic" or "liberal," although republicanism uses the opportunities offered by democracy and liberalism. But what can be called "the republican moment" is the moment of liberation that precedes the "constitution of liberties," liberation from tyranny or liberation as the rejuvenation of the political body and, in this sense, returning to the beginnings. The republican moment is a political world in *statu nascendi*.[80] In the republican moment there are no standing political institutions. The power "lies" on the street; men and women are actively involved in exercising their freedom.[81] The republican moment is, however, rare and never long-lasting. After the constitution of liberties, certain freedoms are taken for granted and politics will be conducted – not exclusively, however – as the daily business of the political class.

But even if the republican moment is the exception, citizens can always open up a republican space where they can take initiative and do politics, not on a daily business, not even as a vocation, but as the activity of a politically acute citizen.[82] A republican space can be opened up everywhere, in all issues concerning the determination of freedom and in all spheres. Such republican dimensions or spaces do not replace the continuous processes of debates, discussions, and decisions, but cut across them, inspire them, criticize them, and sometimes also change their direction. Modern politics often becomes trivial, yet it has its nontrivial moments. Those nontrivial moments can be elevating, yet they can also be threatening and dangerous. Occasionally although infrequently, democratic politics, or rather politics in a democracy, can also show some grandeur.[83]

8

Culture and Civilization I:
The Three Concepts of Culture

Both "culture" and "civilization" are universal terms. More precisely, they have both assumed a universal content in modern times. True, the contents of the two terms cannot be precisely determined, all the less so because the English employs the term "civilization" to describe the same phenomena that the Germans encompass in the term "*Kultur,*" whereas the French, in referring to the "*civilization Française,*" in fact encompass the content of both the German *Kultur* and *Zivilisation.* In this chapter, I will employ these concepts more in the German (and also in the French) understanding, for this understanding has also recently become accepted by the English-speaking world; for example, in terms such as "multi-culturalism," or "cultural relativism."[1]

In order to avoid any misunderstanding, I want to state that culture is not a separate logic of modernity. The three concepts of culture, to which I presently turn, encompass, discuss, and describe – sometimes apologetically, sometimes critically – several interrelated phenomena that they define as being cultural. The referents (the discussed phenomena) can either be selected from all the three logics, from two of them, or from just one. The apologetic and/or critical discussion of the phenomena normally mobilizes one or the other of the two dominant kinds of modern imagination (technological or historical), sometimes in the awareness of the double-bind, sometimes unaware of it. Any one of the logics, or all taken together, can be blamed for the decay of "our" culture; for example, the market, democracy, technology, or the culture industry, to mention only the culprits in the most representative stories.[2] Just as much as this is possible, any of the logics can be hailed (or at least accepted) without further ado. The postmodern perspective can accommodate all variations.

I distinguish between three concepts of culture:[3] culture understood as "high culture," culture understood as "cultural discourse," and finally the anthropological concept of culture. The three concepts will be treated quasi-historically. In fact, a kind of concept of "high culture" preceded the appearance of the concept of culture as discourse, whereas the anthropological concept of culture is quite recent. Markus, who distinguishes between two concepts, has convincingly demonstrated that both the concept of high culture as well as the anthropological concept do result in paradoxes if taken seriously and carried to extremes. After having read the preceding chapters, this will not astonish anyone. Rather, what may be astonishing is the converse; namely, the discovery that the second concept of culture as cultural discourse offers a philosophical reading that avoids the paradox. This is so because there is at least one interpretation of the concept of cultural discourse that is intentionally paradoxical.[4]

The First Concept of Culture

The concept of culture as high culture has included the creations of the mind, of hands, and of imagination that were collectively termed by Hegel as the Absolute Spirit: the representative works of art, theology, philosophy, and – in the 19th century – also science. The term "high" indicated the space high above the surface of everyday life and thinking. It was assumed that one lifts oneself up if one enters the territory of high culture. High culture was in a sense understood as virtual reality, yet a virtual reality more real (more true) than everyday reality. "High" in the expression of high culture shows the affinity of art, so understood, with metaphysical imagination. The entry into this virtual reality was associated with ascension, although "high" culture was also said to be weighty and deep (and neither weight nor depth is easy to associate with motions such as "lifting" or "ascending").

How high art became deified,[5] and how the idea of the genius has occupied the position of the apostle,[6] have been frequently discussed. The deity "high art" needs a genius, not an apostle. The apostle is unfree in the sense that as a messenger he mediates the divine message; he is humble. On the contrary, the genius is supposed to be a free creator who creates – like God – *ex nihilo*. If one adores the works of high art, one bows before a human creator, before human powers, before human freedom itself. Humility is then the expression of its opposite of pride.

But a people is hardly one of high culture because some of its denizens have created great works of art or philosophy. It was sensible for Hannah

Arendt to say that the ancient Greeks had no "culture."[7] By now, we speak of the high culture of ancient Athens, but the high culture of ancient Athens was not constituted in Athens, but in other times and places in relationship to Athens. In Athens, *poeisis* and *technē* belonged to life, to religious and political life, and not to a (then) nonexistent cluster of culture or art. Arendt said that it was the Romans who invented "culture." Culture was what the Other (the Greek) had offered, the yardstick, the model "for us" (the Romans). Culture is canonic. The term and the concept of the canon had been forged in Greece, yet it was the measure of beauty and not the measure of high culture. Although the Romans still had not used terms such as "high culture" or "high art" in their modern understanding, they had already distinguished between men "of culture" (men who spoke Greek, who understood the Greek models and appreciated them, men who essentially had taste) and uncultured people, the rude ones who were illiterate and ignorant in the arts of the Greeks. This was a typical attitude in Hellenism and the first wave of cultural assimilation gathered momentum at this time. The elite of the conquered worlds discovered the differences between their own customs, myths, stories, architecture, and so on, on the one hand, as inferior in many senses, and the Hellenistic/Greek model, on the other, as superior. Successful assimilation demanded acquisition of ease in doing things the way the Greeks did, in appreciating Greek poetry and Greek manners. The distinction between culture and civilization was not made at this time. A Hellenistic "cultural center" consisted of the temple, the bath, and the theater (just as a later Christian cultural center consisted of the church, the baptistery, and the cemetery). It is true that it does not sound good to speak of a cultural center in the latter case, for the Christian way of life in the Middle Ages was not a culture in the same sense as the Greek way of life had been in the era of Hellenism.

When the idea of high culture (and of high art within high culture) appears, it becomes a task and an aspiration for men of uncultivated traditions to assimilate to high culture. I think the phenomenon of assimilation is primarily a cultural one, and if this is so, one could speak reasonably of assimilation for the first time in Hellenism. It was then that former "barbarians" became "uncultivated." To be uncultivated is a blemish, but a blemish that one can remove through assimilation. Firstly, one must assimilate to Roman customs, and then to Greek refinement. But soon a tendency in the opposite direction made itself known. Oriental religions regained their powers (which finally conquered the Western world through Christianity) and exercised them through dissimilation, which on its part resulted in a novel phenomenon of counter-assimilation, assimilation to the difference.[8] It was then and there, in the era of Hellenism (where the dynamics of modernity began its "second push" toward the breakthrough of the modern social arrangement, without success), that we first witnessed the conflict between assimilation to the universal (the general) as the main tendency and its reverse, dissimilation toward the difference.[9] Dissimilation, or assimilation to the difference, remained an undercurrent at its inception, until it later became universal (*catholic*), until the once dominant cultures began to assimilate to Christianity. But at the moment that it ceased to be the Other, Christianity also ceased to be a *culture* in the sense that Hellenistic Greek culture once was. For the young Augustine, both Christianity and Manicheanism were cultures to which he assimilated by dissimilating himself from the Roman/Greek way of life. But for the Bishop of Hippo there was only one true *spiritual life* – and no culture.

I have provided this sketchy story in order to illustrate two points: (a) one needs the dynamics of modernity to have "high culture," and (b) one needs the "other" as a relatively open model of a way of life to which one is *able* (allowed) to assimilate, in order to develop the readiness to enter into this other presumably higher, yet at first still alien, way of life. This is why one can safely say that Greece (Athens) had no high culture, that Christianity had no high culture, yet the Hellenistic world and the modern world do have high culture.[10]

There is no high culture without low culture. At first, low culture is not associated with the "primitive,"[11] but with the nonrefined, the alien, the rude. So as to avoid any misunderstanding, let me reiterate that *for us* there is Athenian culture, just as there is also medieval/Christian culture, but they were constituted not by the ancient Greek world, not by the medieval Christian world, but by the Others for whom *they* became the Others – models of refinement and high spirituality, for example, for the Renaissance world and imagination.

The distinction between high and low is not always also cultural; this topology can also establish the hierarchy of the steps on the ladder of ascension in a homogeneous spiritual universe. For example, the initiated ones can enter the virtual reality – or the higher, the deeper, the truer reality – but this is by no means a matter of choice. The access to entry is normally inherited by the members of a priestly cast, or acquired by divine frenzy.[12] In the case of a culture, however, where there is a high/low distinction, the access to the higher realm is neither inherited nor acquired by frenzy (not even by the poetical frenzy to create),[13] but by the capacity to form a cultured judgment. It is not the artist who "enters" high culture; he or she creates works of art. Rather, it is the person of refined tastes who appreciates great art. High, refined taste replaces traditional priesthood, initiation, or frenzy. There is a kind of freedom and openness for, in principle, it is not only men of extraordinary descent or extraordinary capacities who can develop good taste, but many different kinds of people. Frenzy and artistic creativity can harbor secrets, but there are no secrets to refinement in taste. High culture can is something that can be learned. If this were not so, assimilation to a "higher" way of life would be impossible and nonsensical.[14]

There remain a few essential differences between the criterion of entry into the realm of high culture in nonmodern times and in modern times. The differences are slowly developing, but they mark the beginning of a new epoch. This new epoch is first characterized by an uneasy relation between high and low art and by the paradox of the judgment of taste.

Here are some simplifications: in the nonmodern cultures (even if they were constituted only retrospectively by the succeeding cultures as representative Others, such as the Athenian ancient Greek and the medieval Christian), there were people who had taste and others who had none. Since there was still one central model, the model of refinement, of the high reality, and in comparison everything else was regarded as pedestrian, unrefined, stupid, and strange, men *had taste* if they developed the capacity to distinguish the already consensually accepted high from the low, the cultivated from the rude (the stupid, the barbarian). The ability to distinguish entailed the ability to practice; that is, to combine the "know-that" with "know-how." Men of taste are marked out by their ability to distinguish good poetry from primitive rhymes and elegant customs from inelegant ones. There was but one single taste (with certain variations), and judgments contrary this taste showed lack of taste.

In modern times, however, it is not "having taste" or "not having taste" that makes the difference but, rather, having "good" taste or having "bad" taste. This distinction between good and bad differs in many ways from the distinction between having and not having taste. Firstly, one begins to distinguish between good and bad taste where the standard of taste is no longer stable and fixed, but mobile, changing, and temporalized. A work of art that hits the highest standard today may fall into disrepute tomorrow. The dynamics of modernity results in constant modification of the judgment of taste.[15] One can then say that this style is ugly whereas the other is more beautiful, even if "this style" is the current mainstream. One can say "This painting is not as beautiful as others believe it is ... In my view it is not beautiful at all." Men of good taste, contrary to men of taste, can disagree in their judgment of taste frequently.

The dynamics of modernity as the dynamics of taste requires a steady reorientation of the elite who want to assimilate the then relevant standard. Simultaneously, another question is also raised; namely, the question as to whether it is justifiable to raise a standard of taste at all, as to whether the distinction between high and low culture is relevant, or valid. And if the answer is yes, who is the repository of the standard of taste?[16]

It is at this point – from the emergence of the modern world in the era of the Renaissance until the 18th century – that the story of the sciences and the story of arts part company. It is true that science remains encompassed in the concept of high culture, and a verily cultivated man needs to know as many things about the constellations, natural history, and physical motions as about the works of art and philosophy. Still no one believed that the judgment concerning constellations or physical motions is a judgment of taste, and that in this way it is subjective. Knowledge was still believed to be firmly anchored in the Supreme Being, God or, alternatively, in the eternal laws of the natural universe. *Theodicea* bloomed, and not just due to Leibniz. The deconstruction of metaphysics and the Copernican turn begin to take shape first in matters of artistic taste and, in general, in questions concerning Beauty. In the trinity of Beauty, Truth, and Goodness, Beauty's place was shaken first and therefore immediately problematized.[17]

I have already mentioned the two first paradoxical-looking formulae in early modern philosophy.[18] Descartes says that every man is equally endowed with *bon sense*. But most men are foolish, for they do not take the proper path, the method which leads to true knowledge. Rousseau stated that all men are born free, yet everywhere they are in chains. Now, if every man is born free, endowed with equally good sense, every man is also born with the capacity to distinguish between the beautiful and the ugly. Moreover – and this is Hume's point – no one has the authority to tell one person what should please them and what should not. Things that please me are beautiful to me; things that displease me are ugly. No person is entitled to assume the role of an objective judge of taste. As we know, Hume ends his essay with a good empirical conclusion. The standard of taste is not based on a single objective criterion inhering in the work of art, but is constantly constituted by the cultural elite.

The cultural elite's taste determines what is good taste. But one becomes a member of the cultural elite insofar as one has good taste. There is a circularity here. Since it is no longer the social elite that offers the standard of taste, everyone can become a member of this (cultural) elite, at least in principle. But if everyone can become a member of the elite, the criterion to be a member of the elite is – I repeat – nothing other than having good taste. This circularity is, however, not a dangerous one. For, in fact, in "social reality" it was a cultural elite that emerged in

Europe as the bearer of the standard of taste. They were the ones who dictated taste, not because they agreed in their judgments, but because they disagreed on the same level of refinement. The others, confronting the men of good taste, were no longer the barbarians or the strangers, but the next-door neighbors with bad taste. The person of bad taste disqualified himself for candidacy to the cultural elite.

The Humean idea of the standard of taste is already paradoxical, but one can live with this paradox. Yet democratization makes the same paradox less and less liveable, and it will be more seriously challenged. Democracy centers around the idea of equality; again and again it displays a tendency toward substantive equality beyond political equality. The tendency toward claiming substantive equality cannot be stopped from the inside for, as I have tried to point out earlier, the dynamics of modernity goes to the extremes, until the point at which nothing more can be deconstructed, because everything already has been. If this is so, none of us can wonder whether democracy, once having been established, unfolds the tendency to realize substantive democracy. In a substantively determined democracy, the credo that all men are equal reads that no one is better than the other, neither more able nor more clever. And, as a matter of course, no one has taste better than that of anyone else. If one claims that his taste is better than the taste of the others, he is an elitist and disqualifies himself from being a good democrat. What is even worse, he cannot make a case for his claim. He cannot prove that his taste is better, because if the others say that it is not, he has no defense other than to make recourse to a substantivist definition of artistic quality. As a result, he must resign himself to referring to his own taste as the standard of taste. But how can one prove, using objective criteria, that Beethoven is more valuable than Elvis Presley, if not by reference to taste? The same thing holds true about argumentation in matters of art (beauty) as in matters of metaphysical or scientific truth: one needs an *archē*, something that is taken for granted, that everyone takes for granted, to prove the case. Yet, in science one normally shares this *archē*.[19] In art, one does not. This is why one keeps turning back to the issue of subjectivity, to taste as to the sole criterion of quality, and finally to the standard of taste – which is the starting-point that turned out to be shaky and without firm foundation.

But if there is no standard of taste, or at least one that cannot be established philosophically, then the differentiation between high and low art collapses. And since art (like culture)[20] is a binary concept, if there is no low art then there is no high art either. Finally, if this is the case, the whole first concept of culture collapses. This collapse is not just a theoretical one, but also a practical one. Cultural elites still need the process of assimilation to maintain themselves, even if in a more restricted understanding than in pre-modern cultures (for example, in Hellenism). Since the patterns of the standard of high culture and art were themselves pluralized, and different men – all with a high standard of taste – could possibly have different tastes, there still remained the ultimate confusion concerning the criteria of entry into the higher virtual reality. For if there is no higher virtual reality, there are no conditions of entry. Everyone enters in his or her own "other" world, and re-enters or exits from it occasionally by whim. For example, the condition to enter into the world of music as high art is to concentrate entirely on listening. If someone half listens to background music while simultaneously watching the television news, is he or she then entering the world of that music or not? Does he or she qualify for the conditions of entry? Does he or she re-enter (the world of music) every time he or she ceases watching TV and becomes aware of the sound of the background music? Does he or she exit this reality whenever he or she re-enters the world of the sporting news?

The paradox seems to be the following.[21] Those who draw the distinction between high and low art (or culture) can do so because they have inherited the first concept of culture; otherwise, this distinction does not make sense, since the negation (annihilation) of the distinction presupposes the distinction itself. However, the distinction between high and low art (or culture) is no longer self-evident. In a democratic world, everyone's convictions count. "Everyman (or woman)" will resent a distinction which presumably excludes him or her from the cluster of those who enter a world that he or she considers to be high. Anyone's taste counts as much as everyone else's. The cultural elite, if there is still one (as in France), will not find arguments against the manifestation of resentment, given that taste itself has become the criterion of the distinction between high and low. And what is constituted by taste can also be destroyed by taste. "Everyman" just resents the distinction, whereas the cultural elite for whom the distinction still counts will annihilate and destroy it in a sophisticated way – moreover, in such a sophisticated way that the negation of the distinction between low and high, the standard of nonstandard, will be less understandable for "Everyman (or woman)" than the distinction itself. The waves of self-hate of a cultural elite are combined with the waves of sophisticated self-justification.[22]

The first concept of culture is abused as undemocratic, given that everyone's taste counts equally. The same concept is also philosophically untenable and unjustifiable. Yet, the abolition of the first concept (of the distinction between high and low art or culture) is also philosophically untenable and unjustifiable. Since every taste counts, and in matters of taste the majority cannot decide (for if it could, not every taste would count), thus the taste of those who distinguish between high and low art counts as well – the taste of those who believe in a strict canon or standard of taste is an equally justified taste. One can put forward as many arguments in support of the first concept of culture (art) as against it. The ultimate judgment remains empirical: there are some for whom the distinction exists, and there are some for whom it does not. Among those who operate with the first concept of culture, some sing its praises, while others abuse it. But in both cases taste remains the authority of discrimination.[23]

The paradox that follows from the first concept of culture cannot be resolved or removed.[24] Yet, I would still make the attempt to provide a few philosophical propositions to avoid it. One can avoid (and not remove) the paradox if one rejects two decisive innovations of modern philosophy of art (or aesthetics); namely, the centrality of taste and the differentiation between good and bad taste. One can say that instead of differentiating between good and bad taste (where good taste is the sense for refinement and novelty, for grandeur and imagination in high art), one could reintroduce the old distinction between having taste and not having taste, the yardstick by which every product of culture, such as a chair, an "evergreen" melody, a piece of rock music, a sci-fi or a porno-graphic film, a piece of minimalist music, or an abstract painting – everything, in fact – can be judged regarding taste. Judgment is then the assessment of *perfection/imperfection* of a piece of artwork within its *own genre*. One can have taste or no taste in movies, in pop music, in classical music, in internal decoration, in Greek arts, and so on.

This kind of distinction by taste is not elitist, but it still operates with a standard and requires the practicing of some faculties as conditions of better judgment. Having taste or not having taste is then almost indis-tinguishable from the learned or unlearned assessment of a skill – the *technē* – of the creator or of the author. Here "perfection" stands for being well, properly, or skilfully made, where the spirit of the work of art does not count. Technological imagination guides the judgment.

My other recommendation will reintroduce historical imagination to the judgment, the second tie of the double-bind.

This second recommendation to avoid the paradox of the first concept of culture is to circumvent the concept of taste without returning to an objective or the absolute criterion of distinction. I recommend mobilizing two decisive characteristics of the modern social arrangement: firstly, its functionalist character; and, secondly, one of its imaginary institutions, namely, that of historical imagination, this time as hermeneutical imagi-nation.[25]

One can say that the differentiation between high art and low art in modernity follows the transformation of the social arrangement. To repeat briefly: as in the pre-modern social arrangement, the place that one occupied in the division of ranks determined the function that one performed. So, in the modern arrangement it happens the other way around: the function that one performs determines one's place in the division of ranks and social hierarchies. In a pre-modern arrangement – and this is still the case during the era of the deconstruction of the pre-modern natural artifice – the men of higher classes are the men of high culture. Their judgment – in matters of art – is also a function that they perform due to their place in the social hierarchy. This is not an obligatory but a contingent function. The taste of the Renaissance court or the taste of the early *Kulturbourgeois* was not the taste of the average nobleman or the average bourgeois. Yet it was a *function*, although an *optative* function, of the members of the above-mentioned classes.

The social stratum later termed "the lateiners" or "the intellectuals" was the stratum who *had* to perform the function of providing a standard for taste, including the standard controversies concerning taste, a function that was no longer prescribed for them by their social status at birth. This function is not optative, for it is prescribed in their *acquired* status. That is, in the case of the new cultural elite it is the function that they perform (being good at developing and employing the standard of good taste) that places them relatively high in prejudgment, although not necessarily also in income, in the social hierarchy.[26] The good taste is itself a function. But what kind of function is it? Does this function have any objective criteria? It is better to say: "Does this function have an objective criterion, other than making statements concerning the beautiful and ugly, high and low?"

It is a common observation that to provide the standard of taste is increasingly more related to the task of interpretation. It has become increasingly a hermeneutical exercise. Whatever the interpretation of the works of culture entails, the issue at stake – that is, the interpretandum – *ceases to be beauty, and becomes more and more meaning or sense*. The interpretation of high art and of high culture in general is about making sense and providing meaning. Since there are works of art (and culture) that are practically inexhaustible, those works of art (culture) will become the constant topics (objects) of interpretation. The high artwork is one that can be interpreted by every generation in a new way, which offers ever new readings, meanings, and revelation – through the act of interpretation – to those new generations. This is not a matter of taste; or, rather, a kind of shared taste is slowly developing though the acts of renewed interpretation. Interpretation deepens the texts, making them more meaningful. In addition, interpretation strengthens the aura of the work – be it a work of art or a work of philosophy or theology – where the aura has a force of attraction, for it evokes the feeling of nostalgia and/or recognition. Here is a work of a culture which is either different from ours or close to ours. Both difference and closeness can be attractive. To sum up, it is meaning, the appeal to nostalgia and/or the appeal to closeness, that places certain works of art "over time" at the top of the hierarchy. They are placed high because they have the potential to serve for infinite interpretability, and they have already been interpreted from various perspectives again and again. They perform a function – the function of rendering meaning and evoking the feelings of nostalgia and closeness. This conception presupposes that there is *something* in the first work of art that *cannot* be disciplined – its *secret*. The secret is beyond interpretation, but we do not know about the secret; rather, we *feel* it, we *sense* it.

But works of low art, or low works of art and culture, are *works that do not perform the above-described function* very well. The latter still belong to high art of a lower rank, because they were supposed to perform a function that they were unable to perform. By now, they are interesting as for as cultural history or the history of literature, or national or local literature, are concerned. In the latter case they bear some meaning for the historical consciousness of a group, an ethnic enclave, provided that they render meaning for them in a historical moment, or evoke in them the feeling of nostalgia and closeness that they do not evoke for a broader audience. But whether works are ranked higher or lower on the scale of high art, their function is the same. And it is the way in which they are made by the interpreters to perform their function that determines how they will be allocated on a rank in the hierarchy of works of culture. But it is not beauty (or the taste for the beautiful) that is ranked.[27]

Low culture was termed low in *the traditional distinction*[28] between high and low culture, which was originally associated with class-ranking. I would speak rather of mass culture or mass art. *The function of mass art is entertainment.* There are different kinds and varied levels of entertainment, as entertainment can also be refined, interesting, and sophisticated, as well as rude, primitive, and brutish. Sophisticated lovers of high art are sometimes also sophisticated consumers of mass culture. But they seek something entirely different in a detective novel or a sporting event than in Shakespeare.

I have spoken of sophisticated consumers, for mass culture (and art) is indeed *consumed*. Consumption here stands for quick absorption. One can remember for years the restaurant where one had a good steak, just as easily as one might recall a detective novel that one thoroughly enjoyed. But just as one does not feel the taste of the steak on one's palate in recalling the occasion of the meal, one rarely remembers the content (the story) of a detective story that one has read after work for the sake of relaxation.

Mass culture also knows ranking. Experts in mass culture distinguish between good and bad products. In this field, one can also have taste or not have taste. The producer has to make an effort to produce something that achieves the standard of being good. This does not necessarily mean sophistications. Mass culture produces for all ranks and for all consumers, for those with and without sophistication, for the man of humor and for the brutes. But there is something along the lines of "better done" and "badly done" in all genres and in all products.

Mass culture distinguishes itself from high culture in one very important aspect: the difference between creator, producer, and distributor seems to vanish. These days, high culture is also reproduced by the so-called "culture industry" and distributed in the market, while the distributors, as well as the mass producers, aim at the satisfaction of consumer needs. Yet this was neither the intention of the creator, nor is it incipient (or inherent) in the created work.[29] Irrespective of how many Beethoven records are produced and sold, Beethoven did not compose his sonatas for mass production, and he has remained the sole author of his compositions.

Mass culture mobilizes technological imagination and, in fact, also technology. The latest model here plays a far greater role than it does in high culture. The consumers of mass culture live in the absolute present tense, not just in fact, but also in imagination, although recently mass culture also began to employ and to instrumentalize nostalgia.[30]

I have made mention of works of art (and culture) which had not been accepted (or stabilized) through interpretation, and which address a very specific audience, with the well-known slogan "*de te fabula narratur.*" In describing this phenomenon I cannot find a better expression than "popular art." I mean thereby music such as tango or jazz which can be played and performed with the greatest virtuosity, as well as so-called "primitive" painting and folk art in general. In Europe in the 19th century and, for example, in Latin America or on a few Pacific islands upto the present day, folk art was written, composed, danced, and sung independent of high or mass culture. Popular culture was first country culture; later it became urban culture as well. Nowadays there are no more *Volks* left and, in all probability, country culture will lose its resources. Moreover, folk art becomes the easy prey of commercialization. Members of the Papua New Guinea highland tribes will produce rubbish for the market more readily than a postmodern composer.

But let us presuppose that the sources of popular culture will never dry out, for the urban milieu will prove to be as fertile a soil for new, and new kinds of, folk art as the small traditional village or the tribe once was. But the blooming of a kind of popular art is short-lived in nontraditional societies, for they – as part and parcel of daily life – are subjected to fashion, just as everyday life in general is. Certain works or types of popular cultures are normally absorbed by high art, others rather by mass culture.

It is questionable whether new works of high art can arise without having been inspired or fed by popular culture.[31] Since, as I have said, it has become even easier to commercialize popular art than high culture, the sources of high art may possibly dry up.[32]

There is a common feature of high art (culture) and mass art (culture) that distinguishes both of them from popular culture or folk art: they are both universalistic in the sense that they appeal to the denizens of all cultures (in the sense of the third concept of culture, to which I will soon turn), and that they are available everywhere in the world for those who seek meaning and for those who seek leisure and entertainment. In China the cultivated public reads Proust, and in France the cultivated public reads *The Story of the Stone* – both belong to high art. True, French readers will have a greater sensibility to feel certain nuances in *Remembrance of Things Past*, which they have ingested along with their own tradition; whereas the Chinese will understand certain layers of the *Story of the Stone* in a far deeper way than Frenchmen do – for they have also ingested their own tradition. Yet both the Frenchmen and Chinese will cling to both novels; both still seek out deep meaning in both, both will enjoy the sentences, the language, the game of words, the hidden non-metaphysical metaphysics of the fictitious universe.

And wherever you are, from Tahiti to Iceland, from New York to Bucharest, you can buy an Agatha Christie novel or watch on the television the series "Matlock" or "Dallas." You can discuss those books and TV series with the denizens of all cultures (in the sense of the third concept of culture), and you will understand what the other means; that is, you will understand even better than if you were to discuss a soccer match or a game of cricket, for not all countries patronize soccer and cricket. Yet all patronize American mass culture or are familiar with it, whether they like it or not.

Popular (folk) culture, however, remains the culture of difference, and popular art is the art of difference. This is not only because they are for the most part practiced in one place alone, and not in others, but because they are not absorbed in the same way as high art or mass art is, unless they are mediated by one of the latter. Folk art is normally collected by ethnographic museums, or as souvenirs by tourists. Once in a while, one goes to a folk music concert, but in this case popular music is no longer popular music. For, in becoming an exhibit, popular art itself wanders far away from its original source.

The Second Concept of Culture

The second concept of culture identifies culture with cultural discourse.

In the spirit of this concept, a "cultivated" or "cultured" person is not a person who writes poems or paints pictures, but a person who has taste in poetry or in painting, *who can talk about them intelligently, and in whose life reading, listening, and watching products of high culture occupies a pride of place.* But cultivated men and women do not talk exclusively about the works of high culture (only cultural "snobs" do that). In fact, they can talk about everything in a cultured way. They do not need to be literary critics; they do not need to contribute to the representative interpretations of works of art. Cultivated people can belong to any profession, to any walk of life.[33]

Cultivated discourse goes on in many places, both public and private. It is the culture of *conversation*. Conversation is the kind of discourse that is informal, that aims at nothing other than the exchange of ideas and interpretations, and is, in this sense, an end in itself. It is a kind of discourse from which no conclusions need to be drawn, neither in theoretical nor in practical terms. In a conversation, opinions either clash or support one another; no consensus is intended. A cultivated person is "created" or self-created in practicing this kind of conversation. For even if someone were to listen to good music every day, he would not be considered a cultivated person if he avoided the company of his fellows, if he failed to contribute to conversations or at least listen to them. Cultural discourse presupposes a "society," a group of like-minded and like-spirited people. They are not supposed to share an opinion (for if they in fact do, some of them will dissent provocatively, to provide the conditions for a discussion), yet all of them are passionately interested in *having a good conversation.*[34]

I repeat that the topic of the conversation is not necessarily high culture. In fact, everything can become the theme of a good discussion. But conversation as such is not necessarily also a cultural discourse. It becomes a cultural discussion if the topic of the discussion is transcontextual, if the participants do not aim at a decision, but they are ready to "catch the ball" of the conversation instead of monologizing. People sitting around the table in order to listen to each other's confessions, to subsequent monologs, do not conduct a cultural conversation. Cultural conversation is a dialogue; a psychoanalytic session or a spiritual "seance" are not cases of cultural conversation, nor is gossiping one. Quarrelling about a goal (in a soccer game) is not a cultural discourse, but to speak about the soccer game as such can be. A cultural discussion is not only transcontextual but also reflective and self-reflective. Our personalities are, of course, involved; but they are involved indirectly through our opinions.

Culture, in the sense of the second concept of culture, is, so to speak, *the main carrier of the dynamics of modernity*. This is why the concept (just as the phenomenon itself) first emerges in the era of the Enlightenment.[35] If, for example, the contestation of justice ("This is not just. Something else would be more just") were to have taken place only in political institutions, or the contestation of truth only in the schools or within the walls of universities, the Enlightenment could not have so successfully deconstructed the pre-modern edifice with all of its paraphernalia, or at least the process of deconstruction would have been far slower.[36] I mentioned earlier that in the pre-Revolutionary France of the 18th century, many dozens of constitutions were drafted. They were not only drafted, but also discussed in cultivated circles. All truly cultured people had to form an opinion about a prospective constitution – they had to come up with an idea of their own. But they also needed to form ideas about industry, dances, and cities, as well as about paintings, novels, religion, the clergy, Roman history, politics, and so on. In Russia, in the 19th century, a group of people in "cultivated society" could not go to sleep without first having discussed the questions concerning the existence of God and the meaning of life.

The constant waves of discussion, the exchanges of opinions, embedded the dynamics of modernity deeply into the everyday life of the circle of the learned elite. Critique animated the culture of discourse; it became its necessary element. When Kant revolutionizes philosophy with his three *Critiques*, in his system "critique" has already been the primary motion in the dynamics of modernity. Kant's Copernican turn itself was then discussed in the circles of cultivated men, and not only in Kant's own environment – whether or not the philosophical significance of the *Critiques* had been understood is another question. The culture of criticizing (of criticizing everything, in fact) is a necessary aspect of the cultural discourse. People quarrel with each other: they say both "yes" and "no," and they also tell you why they have said "yes" and "no" – but, I repeat, only in matters where neither "yes" nor "no" has direct practical

consequences, when no decision follows directly from approval or disapproval, rejection or apology. Indirectly, many things can and do follow
from cultural discussions. They undermine certainties, undermine strong
beliefs, they question, test, and query; yet they also enthusiastically
defend and embrace.[37] Although cultural discourse is reflective and as
such requires the mobilization of intellect, it is not a "brainy" exercise in
the wrong sense of the word. Enthusiasm and passion is, or at least can
be, invested in such discussions.[38]

The second concept of culture can easily be related to the first concept.
After all, the first concept of culture is also produced by the culture in the
second understanding of the word. Still, the two concepts cannot be
merged, for they are and remain distinct. Cultural discussion was said
to be the carrier of the dynamics of modernity – not just on the field of
culture, and even less merely in the field of "high culture," let alone "high
art." One can also speak – among other things – of political culture.[39]
Political culture consists first and foremost of the ability and the practice
to conduct cultured, transcontextual conversations about matters of
politics, irrespective of decision and irrespective, or at least seemingly
irrespective, of private interest.[40] Another reason why the second concept
cannot be merged with the first is the absence of bipolarity. There is
nothing similar to the distinction between high and low culture here. In
fact, to act in a cultured way (according to the second concept) is not
associated with ascension (climbing high) but with a change in one's
attitude. A group of people change their attitude to any topic at any
time when a cultural discourse is to be conducted. They suspend their
interest; they also suspend their private passions. Sometimes they even
need to bracket their preliminary knowledge and information to address
themselves wholly to the issue of the conversation, to "catch the ball" in
order to "throw the ball" of the conversation skilfully, and also meaningfully. It is presupposed that in a conversation of this sort everyone
relies on his or her mind alone. That is, everyone is going to think
through the issue from the viewpoint of his or her own convictions,
and still lend an ear – moreover, a sympathetic ear – to the convictions
of others.

From this, it follows that although cultural discourses cannot be
divided into categories of "high" and "low," there exists an *ethics* of
cultivated conversation. The first concept of culture does not include
ethics of any kind. One can create works of art, interpret them, read
them, or listen to them without any moral conditions. It is part of the
autonomy of art that it has liberated itself from morality, and the first
concept of culture restates this autonomy. Cultural discourse can rein-
force this. Moreover, it looks at the work of art as something "transcen-

dent" in relation to culture. Yet, cultural discourse has its own *moral code*. It is part of "being cultured" that a person follows this (unwritten or tacit) moral code. This is the moral code that allows culture (in the second interpretation) to avoid the paradoxes of culture that had already been detected in the first concept, and will be detected also in the third.

One could say that the second concept of culture is a "procedural" concept. Yet this is not an entirely fitting description, for there is no fixed set of procedures here. The procedural aspect is not formal, but rather ethical/moral. Men and women entering into a discussion of this kind need to suspend their private interests and prejudices (as far as they are aware of them), their grudges, and their sympathies. Suspending them does not mean eliminating them, but to abstract from them or – which is more viable – to *make them explicit*. The exchange of opinions is *not* meant to be value-free, but is meant to be conducted with *shields wide open*. Rationalization of interests and desires is best avoided if one openly declares one's preferences, and accepts that others openly profess their (different) preferences. It is part of the ethics of discussion that *one does not suspect the motivation of others*, but accepts the other's self-description at its face value.

To remain true to the ethics of discussion enhances the enjoyment of discussion, because we love to speak, argue, deny, give our opinion, judge, tell stories, interpret, and explain. But we enjoy all these the most if others pay respect to our ideas and our judgments, and if they do not suspect our motivations. It is the freedom, the equality, and the reciprocity of opinion exchange that is enjoyed, and it is enjoyed most *if no one cheats at the game*.

I have spoken many times of "exchange" as an "exchange of opinions." I said that the exchange is free, reciprocal (as all exchanges are), and in this sense also equal, since everyone has an equal opportunity to participate in the exchange. The norm of "equal opportunity" is in fact valid in cultural discussion. Everyone can participate, everyone gets the chance if he or she wants to speak. Yet in fact not everyone speaks, not everyone has the same skills of talking. The model, *the idea of equal opportunity, is represented in its pure form in the culture of conversation.* Opportunity is equal, yet still some will contribute to the discussion more, and more meaningfully, than others. The differentiation that results from equal opportunity is not painful here.[41] Since the situation of discourse presupposes the suspension of daily interests and passions (according to the ethics of conversation, which is constituted by the procedure), and the discussion group (private or public) is not located in a "workplace," an institution, but is a space just for discussion, hierarchization in factual access to speech does not cause much bad blood, for it has no consequences in one's life as a whole. After having finished the discussion, the person returns home, to the office, the university, or to another place.[42]

Just as the pure model of the modern social arrangement (equal opportunity) is in fact present in every group of people who enter into a free exchange of opinions, the free exchange of opinions is also the sole spiritual exchange in the modern world that can *remain untouched by commercialization.* Only one fringe aspect of the exchange of opinions is marketed – the exchange of opinions in newspapers and, lately, on the radio and on television. Yet these "exchange of opinions" are no longer the same kinds of exchanges of opinions as those taking place in typical cultural discourse. The exchanges of opinions are here normally directed toward something or by someone, adapted to the proper medium and, even in the case of a live show, cannot really remain spontaneous: someone is watching or listening, someone who does not participate. There are people out there to enjoy what the discussion is all about, who are, however, exempt from the ethical code of the discussion itself. The listeners and watchers are outsiders. The speakers are embarrassed. True, if one gets into the routine, the embarrassment does not show. Still, the discussion is not the same. Yet in a friend's apartment, or in a club where one gathers just for this occasion, there are no bystanders. Everyone is "in," a participant; everyone follows or is about to follow the moral code of the discourse. There is equal opportunity and, let me repeat, no commodification. The exchange of opinions is like the exchange of kisses, hugs, or nice words. It belongs to the category of nonmarketed goods. This is, perhaps, the greatest difference between the cultural phenomena encompassed in the first concept of culture and those encompassed in the second concept.[43]

Just as this concept of culture avoids bipolarism, commercialization, and commodification, it also avoids the fate of the first and third concepts. It does not prove to be paradoxical. Freedom is not paradoxical here. Giving and exchanging one's opinion freely in two senses (free from constraint and without getting paid) entails a weak ethos and, in addition, this weak ethos (for example, suspension of interest) does not call for a foundation. The question is, however, how the paradox of truth (which follows from the paradox of freedom) can be avoided.

Kant's *Critique of Judgement,* in the discussion on the judgment of taste, offers the best model for cultural conversation. The description of the pure judgment of taste, particularly the presupposition that it is without interest and without *"Reiz und Rührung,"* can also be read as a hidden imperative. A person who seriously wishes his judgment to be accepted by others must suspend everything related solely to his own position and experience from the grounding of his judgment. As is well known, Kant excluded the paradoxicality of the judgment of taste by advancing the idea that a judgment of taste cannot be discursively verified or falsified, yet we can still claim universal acceptance for our judgment, provided that we have first performed the "purification" of the judgment in the sense hinted at above. If we state that "this rose is beautiful," we claim that indeed it is; yet if someone else says about the same rose that it is ugly, we cannot disprove that it is ugly – nor can he or she disprove our judgment. We then have to accept that one cannot deny the justification of the judgment of the other even if one absolutely believes that one's own judgment is the right one. Judgments of taste can be contested, but not disputed.

Although in the *Critique of Judgement* Kant only speaks about the pure judgment of taste in the above sense, in at least one of his other works, in the *Anthropology*, where he is less bound by the system, he extends this model to the case of cultural conversation.[44] He speaks about cultural conversation as being about "the supreme sensual/ethical good."[45] Kant describes as the model of cultural discourse the conversation that takes place around a dinner table, where the enjoyment of food and wine on the one hand, and the pleasure taken in the conversation and in each other's company on the other, enhance each other. To continue in Kant's spirit: there is dignity in the conversation, for it has no prize; cultural conversation is thus the manifestation of social sociability.[46] In this sense, the world of cultural discourse is also "another world" – a fiction, a virtual reality. Yet this is a fiction shared among friends, and in this sense it is real. It is a reality in which virtuality and actuality coalesce. Here, utopia is actualized – yet only under the condition of the partial suspension of the pragmatic, the theoretical, and the practical pursuits in life. Partial suspension of the pragmatic is not total (after all, people eat, drink, and tell jokes). As for partial suspension of the theoretical: no one can prove truth, yet still believe in one's own judgment as true. With regard to partial suspension of the practical: there is no action proper; speech acts remain without consequences, yet there is a weak ethos that binds all participants. It is through the partial suspension of these claims that the paradox of truth will be avoided.

The second concept of culture looks very attractive. But this concept also has its down side. Since the conversation goes on as an end in itself, and everything can be the matter of reflective discourse, cultural conversation can turn into *bavardage*, small talk. Furthermore, discussion as an end in itself is a practice without responsibility, or with a very weak responsibility, for others. Finally, as the carrier of the dynamics of modernity, cultural discourse may go on negating everything; negation can be practiced like a major sport. The game may become destructive, cynical, or nihilistic.[47] In avoiding the paradoxes of freedom and truth, the second concept of culture is defenseless against accusations of banality and/or frivolity.

The Third Concept of Culture

All of the three concepts of culture are universals ("culture" as such is a universalized concept), but they are universals of different kind. "High" culture is a normative universal (it provides the yardstick) and "cultural discourse" is an optative universal (it provides equal opportunity); whereas the third concept of culture is an empirical universal (it encompasses everything that in fact exists).

The third concept of culture is termed, by György Markus, the "anthropological concept."[48] In the sense of the anthropological concept, all human societies are cultures insofar as they all provide their denizens with norms, rules, stories, images, religions, and so on. There is no culture in the singular, nor are there two cultures (for example, humanistic and scientific, or high and low), but there are cultures in the plural. Every way of life is a culture. Every people has a culture, and every tribe as well. Moreover, cultures are divided into "subcultures" – urban subcultures, religious subcultures, sexual subcultures, and so on. Just as there are no two identical leaves on a tree, there are no two families, or even two pairs of friends or lovers, who would not have their own subculture. Subcultures are normally perspective-bound; from one perspective, other subcultures can be detected than from another perspective.

True, each group of people conducts a way of life that is slightly different from the way of life of some other group, and entirely different from the way of life of most other people. But why do we call of them cultures? Why describe this empirical difference with an originally normative concept such as culture? To extend the term culture to all ways of life (and sub-ways of life) is certainly not an innocent move. It has a political message. Moreover, the political message is normative, although the term is employed as an empirical universal. For if all ways of life (and sub-ways of life) are cultures, all of them have to be studied and understood in their own way and in their own right. And once they are all understood in their own way and their own right, none of them will prove superior or inferior when compared with others. The *empirical* concept of culture(s) implies the *norm* first – namely, that each culture needs to be recognized[49] – and, secondly, that they need to be equally recognized. If every culture can be understood by its own standards (given that those standards make them "a" culture), cultures cannot be compared with one another. There is no hierarchy among them; no culture provides a norms or model or ideal for the others (for they cannot be compared). Those who still compare cultures and place one above another thereby prove nothing but that they have taken the wrong position. For they fail to look at the cultures from the inside alone, and superimpose upon them an alien standard instead (alien to the culture that will thereby be displaced to a lower level of a cultural hierarchy). This position is termed (and abused as) "ethnocentrism." If one ethnos provides the perspective from which the observer understands or appreciates another ethnos, the observer is said to have occupied the illicit position of ethnocentrism.[50]

I will now show how the anthropological concept of culture ends up in the same major paradox as the concept of high culture. The paradox of the concept of high culture resulted from its normativity as bipolarity. It had to exclude low culture, but could not. For it had to acknowledge taste as the final arbiter in matters of artistic beauty and quality, but could not identify the decisive taste either with the taste of everyone or with the taste of a few. To sum up, it became impossible to avoid cultural relativism, but it also became impossible to accept it.

The same paradox appears when one is thinking through the third concept of culture. Yet the path that leads to the recognition of paradoxicality is a different one. Since the anthropological concept does not know the bipolarity of high/low, but operates with the empirical – and nonnormative – universal, the paradox will appear through the thematization of the bipolars, universality/difference.[51] Needless to say, this paradox, just like all the others, is the manifestation of the fundamental paradox of modernity, of the paradoxicality of freedom as the foundation of the modern world which does not found.

Since the anthropological concept of culture encompasses all ways of life termed cultures, the modern concept of *equality becomes once again expanded*.

The first concept of culture was based on the recognition of the founding sentence of modernity: every person is born free and equally endowed (by the Creator) with reason and conscience. The second concept of culture was based on the model of political equality (which also offers equal opportunity): every person can cast his or her vote on the rose that pleases him or her, and make a case for this rose, whereas the others accept it or reject it – or prefer another rose.[52] The maximal extension of the concept of equality appears in the anthropological concept of culture. Here, equality is substantive equality. Every culture is equal to the other culture (on the ground that cultures, like men and women, are not comparable but different).

That there is a bad logic at work here is beyond question.[53] That every individual culture is unique, idiosyncratic, and cannot be compared with another as such, is certainly true. A culture as a whole can as little be compared with another culture as a whole as a person as a whole can be compared with another person as a whole. The whole is qualitative and not quantitative. It does not offer any standard for comparison; standards for comparison need to be quantitative and of the quantifiable. After all, equality is in itself a quantitative term. But from the circumstance that cultures cannot be compared with one another, it does not follow that they are of equal worth: firstly, because "equal," again needs a quantity for comparison; and, secondly, because "worth" is a category of value orientation. One needs to have standards of worth; one needs to know first whether a culture lives up to those standards, to find out whether this culture is "worthy" or how worthy it is.

One can recognize each and every culture as culture; that is, as a human culture that raises a claim for worth. This is a tremendous leap in the modern imagination, for it leaps over all the previous (pre-modern) kinds of imagination, which distinguished between human and nonhuman or subhuman cultures, religions, and people. The barbarians, the pagans, the primitives were frequently abused and treated as nonhumans – subhumans. The anthropological concept of culture turns against this unworthy tradition, and in this sense – in the eye of the moderns of today – the anthropological concept of culture as such is valuable; it is of worth. But the worthiness of the concept is one thing, and the acceptance of bad logic is another thing. I can recognize all cultures insofar as I recognize their claim for worth *without* accepting their claim for equal worth, and the "fact" that they are of equal worth.[54] The tension between two heterogeneous norms on the one hand, and between normativity and facticity on the other hand, is to be felt in every application of the anthropological concept of culture.

If someone states that all cultures are equally human cultures (to the same extent), and that this is why they are of equal worth, one has already committed oneself to cultural relativism. To speak about worth means to speak about the norms, rules, and values of a world, about their concepts of truth and the good, their ceremonies, their convictions, and so on. Thus, if I subscribe to the proposition that each culture is of equal worth, I cannot avoid subscribing to the proposition that none of them has a higher or lower kind of morality than the others, and that the truth claims of the convictions of all of the cultures are also of equal worth. As a result, what is good in one culture can be wrong in another, and no one can be an arbiter in this matter. What is true in one culture is in fact true – in this culture. What is true in another culture is in fact true in that other culture. And no one can be an arbiter in this matter either. No one is entitled to say about a culture that it accommodates far more true statements than the other. For example, if a culture accommodates plural concepts of truths, can it not be regarded as superior – if not in truth at least in freedom – compared with other cultures for which only one single truth (or concept of truth) exists? All such and similar questions are excluded from the relativistic argument guided by the third concept of culture. For, as I said, this discourse operates with the norm that no one can claim authority to decide upon such matters. Everyone is a member of one culture or an other; none of us is an outsider or indifferent. And since this is undoubtedly true, one needs to fall back on the statement that each culture has its truth (and good, and beauty), and this is the final word that one can utter in this matter. *Difference is understood as undifferentiated pluralism.*

For this interpretation, the anthropological concept of culture substantively limits the extension of the first and second concepts. Seen from the perspective of the third concept, the distinction between high and low cannot make any sense. In addition, the taste of the single person (judgment of taste) is no longer a point of reference, for the distinction by taste assigns judgment to the single individual. Yet, the anthropological concept of culture that is engendered does not accept the position of single individuals, but only of cultures, of cultural wholes. There are also serious limitations imposed by the relativistically interpreted, anthropological concept of culture on cultural discourse. Discussion concerning the worth of one culture or the other is dogmatically excluded, for this kind of discussion is already suspect, as a dangerous manifestation of ethnocentrism. Thus, the anthropological concept of culture, which extends the concept of culture to empirical universality as difference, also narrows it down, for it excludes approaches of normative universality and the normative distinction between differences.[55]

But this is not yet the paradox.

The anthropological concept is fully modern. It is far more modern than the first and second concepts of culture, which also emerged *in nuce* before the modern social arrangement settled in. The statement that all cultures are equal, that they cannot be compared, and that they are also of equal worth, is a thoroughly modern statement. No pre-modern society, not even in periods in which the dynamics of modernity were already in operation, would have accepted such a general statement – not even Hellenism, which subscribed to the equal worth of certain cultures (and religions) but, by far, not to the equality of all of them! To put it briefly (now mobilizing the third concept of culture against its own claim), all cultures prior to the modern one have been ethnocentric. Ethnocentrism is the natural attitude of the "natural edifice." Every pre-modern culture is ethnocentric, or has the conviction of being better, more cultivated, and more worthy than all the other cultures that they acknowledge (not to mention all the "cultures" that they despise as subhuman).

The term "ethnocentrism" was coined in the modern culture and only those cultures that accept that all cultures have a legitimate claim for recognition can be ethnocentric. It is first the modern/Western/European world that relativizes itself, its own culture, its own tradition, and its own truth, simply by coining the anthropological concept of culture, an empirical universal as a norm that Europeans should accept by relativizing themselves.

Why? A culture is ethnocentric as long as it has firm foundations, as long as the foundation itself is taken for granted (tradition, shared and unquestionable beliefs). But when freedom becomes the foundation – this foundation which does not found – a culture cannot justify itself as absolute through and with its foundation; it cannot justify itself by empirical means alone.

The empirical justification of the modern European culture was progression and the development of technology.

Yet (after WWII) when the belief in universal progression was threatened, when it turned out that modernity was going to devour the entire world with all of its cultures, the justification of the culture of the European world as the modern culture became problematic. The only justification that could have remained for Europe was to claim the position of the first occupant of modernity. Otherwise, its own culture, brilliant as it was, had no other claim but of being just one culture among many, with no specific privileges.[56] In a radical turn, Europe relativized its own culture. Extremist rationalist enlightenment (the globalization of the idea of modernity as universal progression) and extremist romanticism (the relativization of the European culture) appear in concert.

If – in the first approach – there are no yardsticks with which to compare cultures, the absence of yardsticks also eliminates the prohibition of comparison. In fact, there are no reasons why one should not prefer one culture to another.[57] And since this is so, the natural ethnocentric attitude reappears. Since cultures are incomparable, our culture can again be far better – at least for us – because it is ours, and no one has the right to interfere. Since the relativization of culture began in Europe, so far the only culture that has relativized itself is the European. In the end, however, Europeans can justify the privileged treatment of their own

culture with the gesture of the self-imposed cultural relativism of difference: "This is ours. This is our tradition. No one else should interfere."
This is a viable result if culture is understood in terms of the first and
second concepts of culture alone, and not in the sense of the third
concept. Yet, although cultural relativism sometimes refers to all types
of cultures, it normally concentrates on the third concept. The question is
not whether European opera or Chinese opera is superior, for high
culture has been universalized in fact, and cultural discourse cannot
be relativized, but only marginalized and treated with suspicion. Cultural
relativism prohibits the expression of preferences of certain ways of life
over and above other ways of life on any other ground than that this way
of life is "ours." Yet this claim sharply contradicts the tradition of enlightenment, a tradition that is not only European but also modern. Can one
say that a culture of violence, or of exclusion of pluralism, is as worthy as
a culture that restricts violence and admits pluralism? If denizens of a
culture practice violence and *freely* accept the exclusion of pluralism,
who has the right to call this culture inferior? Yet, human rights belong to
the tradition of modernity, but the modern state draws legitimacy from
protecting citizens against violence. However, modernity is in principle
based on symmetric reciprocity (which in this matter means that one can
accept the right of a culture to be different – which, for its part, is also an
acceptance of the right for one (culture or individual) to be different for
others, its own citizens or members included). In fact, the fundamental
values of modernity (the acknowledgement of universal human rights, of
political liberties, of symmetric reciprocity, of pluralism, of publicity, and
so on) have placed serious limitations on the recognition of the norm that
all cultures must be acknowledged as equally worthy in the sense of the
anthropological concept of culture. In the modern world, those cultures
in which the systems of norms and values do not stand the test of the
leading values of rationalistic enlightenment cannot be recognized as
having a worth equal to, or even comparable with, that of others. One
does not need to compare cultures with each other; one can simply
compare them with the major values of the Enlightenment in order to
distinguish between cultures (in the sense of the third concept). This
aporia appears to be strongest for the denizens of European culture, but
the paradox of romantic enlightenment versus rationalistic enlightenment makes its appearance in many other cultures of the world, particularly everywhere that a dominating culture accommodates various ethnic
and religious groups, and other subcultures.[58]

Universalism and difference are easily reconciled on paper. If a culture
rejects the recognition of human rights and the other legacies of the
normative heritage of the Enlightenment, and claims to have a worth

equal to that of all others, its claim can be legitimately rejected on the one hand. But, on the other hand, the rejection will fall short of being fully legitimate, for man is free to choose unfreedom. "Human rights," civil liberties, publicity, and so on compose the very cluster of modern political values that had been generated in the European/Western culture. Thus, if a fundamentalist culture can accommodate the three logics of modernity without acknowledging and granting human rights, civil liberties, and so on, to the extent that other cultures do, it still cannot be legitimately treated as unworthy. For this judgment would superimpose the cluster of norms on another culture that does not recognize their validity, and such a superimposition also contradicts the normative heritage of the Enlightenment and of romanticism.

In practice, however, every culture makes a decisive choice. This is just as much of a leap as are many of our other choices. There is no absolute foundation for the rejection of cultures that do not recognize the norms of the Enlightenment in full, but there is also no absolute foundation for recognizing every difference by its own standards. The decision that one normally makes – that is, the leap – is not theoretically founded but contextual.[59] In any given context, when the paradox appears and choice (in action and in judgment) is unavoidable, one chooses either the one statement of the paradox or the other as the foundation of one's decision. This is not a logical but an ethico-political choice in each case. And this means that the man or the woman who so chooses is taking responsibility for his or her choice.[60, 61]

9

Culture and Civilization II:

The Omnivorous Modernity

Among other things, I will now speak of culture in the understanding of all the three modern concepts. Culture also processes and distributes spiritual food and drink. This task was normally accomplished – and in part still is – in institutions such as schools of philosophy, workshops, and churches, and on ordinary festive occasions. Institutions process culture selectively; they distinguish between the healthy, spiritual food and the unhealthy, unsavory one.

Quite different criteria may be applied by the cultural wine-tasters, but some standards are always applied. Pre-modern cultures were far from being omnivorous; they managed on a very restricted diet. Some of the staple foods were of average quality, while others were considered better. Food and drink of the best quality was usually favored by the upper strata of the social world in which they had been processed – although not necessarily also created. People who "had tastes" came from those upper strata, but not everyone who belonged to those strata in fact had taste.[1]

In such circumstances, cultural food is roughly custom-made. It befits the rank and aspirations of the members of a cultural community. It defines their taste and, conversely, it is defined by their taste.

The early moderns have developed a highly critical attitude to traditional culture-processing. They resented the institutional distinction between healthy and unhealthy diet. For example, the Church should not prescribe which parts of the human body can be deployed, nor should the court decide which plays can be staged. Yet while the distinction between spiritually healthy and unhealthy food and drink was rejected, the distinction between more and less refined food and drink instead became reinforced. The first distinction was perceived as a limitation to freedom, whereas the latter distinction was understood as practicing freedom. Yet, the abolition of the first distinction (healthy/unhealthy diet) stripped all institutions – except the market – of this legitimated function of cultural food-processing. If the market remains the sole institution to process and to distribute culture, however, not only will the distinction between savory and unsavory diet be removed, but also the differentiation between refined and unrefined food and drink will lose its legitimacy. The Romantics of the 19th and 20th centuries are not ready to accept this either/or. They do not want any direct institutional interference with the freedom of artistic creation. Yet, this leaves them defenseless against the market. But they do not want to accept the "levelling" tendency of the market. They want a market that is not a market. They want an aristocratic democracy, a noble capitalism, combinations which never materialize.[2] The representative cultural drama or, rather, the myth of the unrecognized genius trampled underfoot by cruel market forces, by the uncultivated rude public opinion and the jealousy of the mediocre talents, was kept alive for more than a century. Many tears have been shed for young artists who starved to death while nowadays their paintings sell for millions of dollars, or for crazy composers whose loved ones would have preferred to offer their hands to undistinguished civil servants, while just a few decades later music-mad girls were dreaming only of them. But simultaneous with all the drama and mythology-making, the once staple diet had been entirely abandoned. Art became "free" of substantive interference – that is, "autonomous," free from religious, political, and other limitations and constraints – and in this sense the artist also became free. But a price had to be paid for this freedom.

These days, a mosaic of short stories has replaced the cultural drama. Genius-hunters have turned out to be just little fools. The painters no longer starve today in order to enter the Grand Gallery of Immortals tomorrow. These days, if one paints fairly well, one's paintings will be bought by art galleries, taken care of, and evaluated, and the same galleries will also take care of the painter's future – both artistically and commercially. The early modern project to open the gate before all kinds of spiritual foods but keep their quality well-guarded has not worked out as planned. Once the institutional processors ceased to distinguish between healthy and unhealthy (unsavory) cultural diet, no institution of processing and distributing could maintain the distinction between "low" and "high," "refined" and "unrefined."

Taste and interpretation are retrospective practices. The work, the text, already exists in thus-ness, and in this sense as a "finished product" to be subjected to a judgment of taste or interpretation. Yet, as already discussed, taste and interpretation based on a judgment of taste turned out to be fluid and ephemeral. And this fluidity, this ephemeral character of taste and interpretation, will be extended to the re-processing of the things created in the past as objects of "culture." As Baumann suggested, after the era of legislators and critics, interpreters will carry the day.[3]

If the spirit of technology were the sole imaginary institution of the modern age,[4] we could hardly understand how our culture became omnivorous. Technological imagination (the Heideggerian *Ge-stell*) is strictly future-oriented; in technology the last, the most recent, is always believed to be the best. The product of yesterday quickly becomes outdated and is soon destined for either the garbage bin or the museum. In the second case, however, it is no longer the technological imagination that is at work. The constant movement toward the new and the newest is one of the two major motives of contemporary culture. Yet, I repeat, there is another one as well, which moves in the opposite direction. In terms of the second tendency, as fuelled by historical imagination, the older something is, the more precious it becomes. This is true even for certain (but not all) products of modern technology. A late-model car is of great value, but the oldest model of car is of even greater value. Both novelty and *patina* are precious, and imagination plays a role in both cases. The newest is regarded as the best not just because of its greater utility but also because it carries the aura of a streamlined form of life, associated with "elegance," "luxury," and the like. And the oldest is regarded as the most valuable for very similar reasons; it carries the aura of a form of life that is already gone, a form of life that was elegant or simple, peaceful or dramatic, but by all means different from ours, a form of life which is no more. Projection and nostalgia are extremes, yet they belong together, for the present feeds both on the (close) future and on the (close and remote) past.

Historical imagination has opened up the past as a hunting ground for interpreters. By now, the past (or, rather, the pasts) stand wide open. There are no longer generally, normatively privileged pasts as they existed in the first half of the 19th century. The buildings of ancient Egypt or of ancient Mexico, the cave paintings of the Stone Age, Persian and medieval miniatures, pre-Columbian statues or nose-rings – it makes no difference: all spaces and all times are at the disposal of the interpreter. It seems as if, culturally, particularly as far as high culture is concerned, there is nothing to expect from the future. After the generations of Lukács and Heidegger, no one dreams about the renewal of cultural creativity, since it is now assumed – so far without much ado, and with even less regret – that the grand cultural resources of the modern age, particularly of Europe, have been exhausted, and that great works of art cannot be expected in the future. Even without subscribing to Hegel's remarks about the end of art, contemporary works of art are not expected to be creations of fantasy but, rather, undetermined or undeterminable objects or texts that allow private imagination to be unleashed.[5] To be sure, interpretation could not do anything with visions about the coming new period of art,[6] given that the future cannot be interpreted. Some eccentrics may still entertain hopes about the coming rejuvenation of artistic creativity, but one can barely discuss such an outlandish fantasy publicly.

Just as the omnivorous culture continues to feed on unlimited interpretation, historical imagination, which had originally opened up the past for interpretation, became vague or rather self-reflective. The oldness of the old, the "patina," still remains decisive, but the intimate relation between times and works is less emphatically sought. The more precise dating or attribution becomes technologically possible, the more it begins to lose its absolute significance. Whether a work of art is an "original" or an imitation is still very significant for the wallet, yet not so much for the taste.[7] It is not only the 2,000-year-old original work but also its 200-year-old imitation that is precious; both are old, both are supposed to be beautiful, both have "patina." The object, the thing, is by definition old if it has a patina, insofar as it elicits nostalgia. Whether a building is gothic, neo-Gothic, or neo-neo-Gothic still makes a difference, yet not in the same way and not to the same extent that it did just 50 years ago. What matters more and more is whether one can derive some meaning from it, and for whom and to what extent. The archeology of the interpreters becomes more and more timeless.

Interpretation of works of art (and of cultural objects) is a devotional practice. The object of devotion is the this-ness, the ipseity of the old text or the old thing – the interpretandum – and not its matter, content, or message alone. The devotion of the storyteller goes to the archetype. When a tale is recounted in several ways, as happens with myths and histories all the time, devotion is vested in the story that carries the greatest authority – just as the texts of the Apostles carry the highest authority, whereas the apocrypha gospels carry none. There is, however, an essential difference between the interpretations of sacred and secular texts. If the text is sacred, devotion goes not only for the body of the text, but also for the authority above and behind the text.[8] If the text is secular, devotion goes to the text alone – the text itself is the authority.

Still, all kinds of interpretations of all kinds of traditional texts are practices of devotion, regardless of whether the story, the text, the object itself is sacred or secular. Secular stories become quasi-sacred through and in the practice of continuous interpretation. This happened with the philosophical works of Plato and Aristotle, or with the fragments of Pythagoras in the ancient world. The more devotional the interpretation of the text becomes, the greater importance will be attributed to the real or fictitious author of the text. The converse is also true. If a text is attributed to someone of high reputation, the text has a great likelihood of becoming a chief object of devotional interpretative practices. The works of Pseudo-Hermes, Trismegistos, or Pseudo-Dionysius, the Areopagite, or of Ossian are familiar cases in point. The cultivation of the genius is the modern version of this ancient story. After all, the term "genius" stands for divine inspiration.

Interpretation ties "us" to the "other," to the real or fictitious author of the text or the thing. Normally the author is a person, although modernity invented and also cultivated "the people" or the "folk" as a collective author.[9] The "other," however, cannot be entirely other, but also has to be "us." What is entirely other cannot be "for us" the text of devotional practices. After all, "we" turn the text into "our" object of devotion through such practices; it is neither authoritative nor sacred, and as such is unfit for (devotional) interpretation.

Selection of the texts (things) worthy of devotional interpretation, and determination of the ways of proper or licit interpretation, belong to the tasks of processing spiritual food and drink; it is one of the major forms of institutionalized cultural activity. What needs to be determined are the following. Firstly, who is "us" and who is the other who belongs to us, or to whom we in the last instance belong? Further, which texts carry authority for us – without being sacred – as the sources of wisdom and as keepers of secrets worthy of, and yet beyond, deciphering?

The spirit of interpretation was not essentially modified until the last decades of the 20th century, and it remains to be seen whether the change was as radical as it now seems to be. Interpretation still remained devotional. Throughout early modernity, the work (the interpretandum) was regarded as authoritative and as the keeper of secrets – a kind of hieroglyph that offers itself for deciphering. Authorship (real or fictitious) remained crucial for authority. And to be sure, there is no reason to turn to an old work and to interrogate it other than the conviction that deep and surprising discoveries can still be made if one ponders over those sources and questions them a thousand times. A work of art or philosophy, and a text of religious worship, are always star witnesses. They can be brought back to the stand constantly, for one can expect that if only we would ask them new questions from a different angle, they could still come up with a fresh, original and surprising disclosure. Deconstruction as a kind of radical hermeneutics is a continuation of this practice by other means. Deconstruction often violates the text, reads the text against the text, yet – apart from the cases when works of contemporary authors are incidentally deconstructed – the most brilliant texts of deconstruction keep themselves conspicuously to the most frequently interpreted texts. This is particularly true about Derrida. Sometimes one has the impression that one is encountering an interpreter in despair. The star witness (be it Plato, the Talmud, or Immanuel Kant) stubbornly refuses to offer new answers, to disclose hitherto unrevealed secrets (revealed secrets are not secrets) if interrogated in the old fashion – that is, with eyes downcast, in a low and trembling voice, humbly. One has to bully the witnesses; one has to shake them so that they will finally offer new testimonies. An answer that one has received many times becomes boring, even if it was wise and deep at the beginning. The text that does not disclose new secrets (without disclosing them) is not a living text but a corpse. Deconstruction, as radical hermeneutics in general, is also a kind of devotional interpretation in the highest degree. It keeps the text alive through ridicule, irony, unmasking, negation – in a word, through provocation. There is still something new (in the old) under the sun.

Yet, although the spirit of interpretation has not been essentially changed from the era of Hellenism until yesterday, and it is an open question whether the present changes reach below the surface – *everything else did*. The broader the "us" (the quasi-community of interpreters), the less selectively chosen the objects (texts) of interpretation become. During the Renaissance, the distinction between sacred and worthy texts was already substantially blurred. Afterwards, the cluster of the worthy texts started to broaden and to grow. If "us" means "us Germans," then the saga of the *Nibelungen* and the fairy tales collected by the Grimm brothers will also be included among the worthy interpretanda. If "us" means "us moderns," then everything fathomable as "already modern" will be worthy objects of devotional interpretation. And if "us" means "humankind" (as happens in the anthropological concept of culture), then everything that was actually a human creation can eventually become such a worthy object, the carrier of authority and of secrets.

But who decides whether a text is the carrier of authority and the keeper of secrets? Who selects the texts that are worthy of devotional treatment? There is no longer an authority to select. In this respect, verily "anything goes." Take any statue, religious text, ceremony, verse, song, and the like, and question them in a devotional spirit – they are all expected to answer you and to disclose their secrets.

Modernity has become omnivorous because the institutions of text selection, text processing, and text preparation have lost ground and disappeared (*zu Grunde gegangen*, as Hegel would have said). Only the market, the great leveller, processes. The disappearance of the cultural elite was on the one hand the condition, and on the other hand the result of the *democracy of all texts*. At the beginning, the authority deficit of the traditional culture-processing institutions favored rather than hindered the emergence of elitist cultures. In fact, early European modernity was quite successful in its attempt at producing a cultural elite based on intellectual merit rather than birth. But by now this has become the matter of the past. In a dishevelled way, deconstruction still preserves the vestiges of the habits of the old cultural elitism. Even the slogan that there is no difference between high and low culture was at first "avante-gardist," for it still broke a taboo – perhaps the last one – and for two centuries it was the act of breaking taboos rather than anything else that both constituted and maintained the reputation of the cultural elite.

As long as there is a fairly well circumscribed "us," such as "us Jews" or "us humanists" (for example, Talmudic Jews and Renaissance humanists), there is still *a community of interpreters*. The community encompasses the living and the dead as well as the not-yet-born, given that the two latter groups are supposed to join the community. Although it has happened only recently that the expression "community of interpreters" has assumed a solid philosophical position, there is no longer such a community now, and there is none in sight. There are texts which are interpreted only by one single person; it is considered a feat if someone finds a very obscure piece of work that has not yet been noticed or interpreted by anyone. Other texts are worked over by members of groups consisting of the followers of famous contemporary or very recent interpreters. It rarely happens that two people randomly invited to the same dinner table by a late disciple of Immanuel Kant have read the same books, seen the same paintings, or have similar ideas about the same philosophical text. Cultural discussion becomes restricted, and almost impossible. Only experts in the same texts can communicate (in the same conferences all around the world). Instead of the community of interpreters, there are fragmented mini-communities – contingent, fluid, ephemeral groups, kept above water by academic, professional, or political lobbies. They interpret in the same way as Adam once worked: with the sweat of their brows – just to make a living.

Everything can be interpreted and worked up in a devotional practice, but by now it is the single person who seems to choose the proper interpretandum. The single person is contingent, is the interpretandum. This is how the great promises of the Enlightenment have come true. The merely "particular" no longer mediates; the individual relates directly to the "species." The "species" does not stand here for the empty category of "humankind," but simply encompasses everything that the human mind, spirit, or hand has created. The individual may choose anything, irrespective of the place and time of his or her birth. But, this does not mean that he or she in fact does so.

Although there is hardly a "present" in the traditional sense – for there is no steady position occupied by at least one generation – there are "presents" in the plural, for every eye of any naked "I" who looks upon all interpretanda from a spatiotemporal point (a point in constant motion) at which the "I" is standing (as in an airplane). This "I" can be naked insofar as it is stripped, and can present and represent the ever-present present precisely in this nakedness. Nowadays, a true king is unclothed, or rather no real king (of culture) wears the same clothes all the time. The cloth obliges, it ranks the person who wears it, it allocates him or her exclusively to the one tradition or the other. (True, jeans do not rank.) The real kings and queens of the omnivorous modern culture change their clothes frequently – namely, their reality is their nakedness; this is their "I", the viewpoint of their eye. They change period costumes; they slip from one period costume into another. These period costumes (the interpretanda) are not mediated with one another, because their choice can be contingent from the start. Yet the "I"'s choice of nakedness is not contingent, because *it stands for contingency itself*; it is not an attribute but an existential/ontological constant. The same person will interpret a Maya vase, a biblical verse, an ink stand from the early 1920s, from Ohio, or a movie of yesterday, and this will make no difference. It will make no difference *what* a person will pick as his or her next interpretandum, but it makes a difference *that* the person in question has freely picked his or her interpretandum. Existential/ontological contingency and omnivorous culture are the two sides of the same coin.

The paradigm of language is very poorly fitting for the task of properly describing this contemporary cultural universe.[10] In the cultural tower of Babel one constantly changes language. Language as such loses its power; the power rests on the sentence or on the speaker.[11] In the latter case, one needs to ask the question: Who is speaking? This is a well-known question in the tradition. The speaker is the carrier of authority; the carrier of authority reveals the authentic message. But in the case of a postmodern speaker, the message is not carried by the speaker – firstly, because no message is mediated by the speaker and, secondly, because we can hardly identify the one who speaks.

Let us discuss the first part of the above sentence. The speaker's authority rests on the fact that he or she alone is the one who speaks. The authority is empty, for it is simply identical to the naked "I" who speaks. The meaning of the interpretandum that comes to light through the interpretation is warranted by the single individual's whim. The single person who extracts meaning from the text can be identified as the *subject*. It is not the epistemological subject in a traditional understanding, for the ever-changing novel meaning does not necessarily convey new knowledge, and it certainly does not warrant, or even claim to warrant, the veracity of its exploits. The subject of world interpretation stamps the interpretandum with the image of its own face. Every interpreter pays with his or her own coins. He or she is the one who stamped those coins through his or her interpretation. The meaning drawn out from the interpretandum is his or her meaning or, rather, a meaning for him or her. Yet it is not "private." It is still for the others that this meaning is extracted, because the interpretation still remains devotional.

Still, who is the one who speaks? Is interpretation not a quotation of other interpreters, is the interpreter not wearing a mask? Is it true that he or she meets the text with naked eyes as a naked Eye? Do we see the interpreter? If he or she wears a mask, then certainly not. This is a question that has tortured moderns and postmoderns since the time of Kierkegaard and his character masks.

One can say that what becomes manifest in the series of interpretations by a person is the world according to this person, a world stamped with the face of the person, the subject. One can also say that the interpretative text is anonymous – that it is not only the interpretandum but also the interpretations that are the keepers of secrets – first and foremost, the keeper of the secret of his or her identity.[12] But even if we do not know who speaks, someone is still speaking. It is not the language that speaks.

If you want me to give a cheerful portrayal of the postmodern omnivorous cultural universe, I can present one.

As all the monads of Leibniz's metaphysical universe mirror the whole world, although each of them does it in his or her own unique way, from his or her perspective, so all significant people – as subjects in the sense understood above – present the whole modern world from the perspective of their self-chosen interpretandum, in their own unique way. All subjects (these unique worlds) together warrant the survival of the (post)modern omnivorous culture. I call those significant subjects the "kings and queens" of the omnivorous universe.

To avoid any misunderstanding, the naked kings and queens of the omnivorous universe, who take their pick from everything that surrounds them (from all things humanly produced), do not take over the functions of the traditional culture-processing institutions. They do not present the "proper" text (versus the improper one); they do not establish authority. They do not even create a new tradition, for they do not stand in a continuous and strong tradition, not even negatively. True, one always places oneself in a tradition whenever one picks an interpretandum from a tradition. But if one moves from the interpretation of a Chinese vase to the interpretation of Marx, or to the wooden statues of the Ivory Coast, one cannot but help merge traditions, even if one was socialized by only a few.[13] The interpretandum is then removed from the continuity of its own tradition, if it has any.[14] No "world tradition" exists.[15] The naked kings and queens of the universe of interpretation offer constantly ephemeral points of attraction.[16] Those ephemeral points of attraction (which feed on various traditions) are offered to other institutions (conferences, universities) for discussion, and are finally presented as "the thing that needs to be known." Ephemeral interpretations are mostly retranslated into objects of "knowledge"; for example, as prescribed reading for university examinations.

We encounter speakers who speak only in their own names, and draw back from pretending to speak in the name of an authority or in the name of (any) others. Here are the new interpreters, who abandon the divine mission of the prophet, and who also discontinue the divine vocation of Hermes. But without Hermes there is no hermeneutics. If personal meaning is squeezed out of all the open and no longer resistant pasts, by and through interpretation, interpretation ceases to be a proper hermeneutical exercise and prepares spiritual food and drink as "prescribed reading:" for the next conference and for the next semester – as knowledge without truth.[17]

Nietzsche once said that it is easy to dance in chains.[18] It is more difficult to dance after having been liberated from the chains. It is most difficult to dance if there is no choreography whatsoever. Without choreography just a series of free improvizations remain, for the dancer must improvise all the time. The dancers choose every move. They do not know whether their dance is pleasing or displeasing, whether it conveys a meaning to the onlookers. One cannot be sure of whether there is, or ever will be, an audience; one improvises, yet the theater can remain empty. Nothing is known in advance.[19]

Still, the naked kings and queens of the omnivorous culture – whether they make it to the top or remain unnoticed – are driven by the same spiritual hunger and thirst as the creatures of a monocultural universe. It is the hunger and thirst for meaning that they (we) seek to satisfy. While pillorying the fields of the "absolute spirit," one still tries to tell stories and one still asks the questions "Why?" and "To what end?" – all the questions that children ask and that adults fail to answer.

10

Culture and Civilization III:

Civilization

The concept of civilization is also twofold. It refers to both technological civilization and moral civilization.[1] Yet the twofold concept, although frequently discussed separately and sometimes even contrasted, refers to phenomena which presuppose one another, or are tightly related to one another.

Contrary to the two concepts of culture, the concept of civilization (in both of its aspects) refers to *everyday life*, the kind of everyday life that emerges and develops along with modernity. Civilization is also a bipolar concept, yet not in the same sense as that of "high" and "low" culture. High and low culture are supposed to exist in the same world, and yet occupy different places in it. Civilized or uncivilized behavior can also exist in the same universe, but it is presupposed that everyone could eventually behave in a "civilized" way in the self-same world. To behave in a civilized way is normative (for to behave in an uncivilized way means to fall short in minding the norms of proper behavior). But this is a norm that can be actualized eventually, that can be embedded in the daily life of all denizens of the "civilized world." The "civilized world" is normally contrasted with an "uncivilized world," or "the civilized social strata" with an "uncivilized social stratum." Civilization is a present- and future-oriented concept. Once upon a time, yesterday, or even today, there were cultures which have no semblance of civilization; there are still uncivil social strata – thus the story runs. But all this can be transitory. The modern world *as such* is a world of civilization. As a result, sooner or later all social strata and all cultures will learn civilized behavior. Everything uncivil, barbarian, or perhaps even savage will disappear from the modern world.

Thus, the concept of civilization, in contrast to the concept of culture, is progressivist, optimistic, future-oriented. And this conviction, I repeat, characterizes the idea of both the technological and the moral civilization.

Everyday life is guided and organized by a system of "objectivations," by which I mean the system of interconnected norms and rules that every man and woman needs to learn to understand and to use as a condition of adult life, of "independence" within a given narrow world.[2] The system of objectivation consists of three aspects: ordinary language, the use of man-made objects, and customs. These three aspects are obviously interrelated. For example, one uses man-made objects according to customs, and by using them one also explains their use or follows verbal commands, and so on. In pre-modern societies,[3] rank determines the concrete character and content of all the rules that are encompassed in the fundamental everyday system of objectivations. The nobleman and the lord use other objects, follow other customs, and speak another language (or speak the language in a different way) than does the servant or the serf. The higher one looks at the ladder of ranking, the more refined will the customs be that meet the eye. One can hardly speak of civilization here – for neither the idea of expansion, nor that of further refinement or progression, can be intended.

The birthplace and the time of conception of "civilization" are easy to detect. It happens when on the highest rank of the social hierarchy one begins to distinguish between uncivil and civil behavior, where civilization is regarded as a bonus, as a kind of "addendum" in refinement and in progression to the accepted employment of things, language and customs. Historically, civilization took off for its grand voyage in the courts of absolute monarchies, particularly in the French court, yet also in the small courts of the Italian and German princes.[4] The close relation between technological and moral civilization can be traced well here. The new attitude toward death and sexuality, as well as the way to use the spoon, the knife, the handkerchief, and the fork properly, were developing together, and they all became marks of civilized behavior. Cleanliness, one of the major assets of civilization, seems to be entirely technological (like the possession and the proper use of the bathroom). But cleanliness is traditionally also a moral metaphor. The terms "dirty" or "clean" refer to morals as much as to the body's appearance and odor. Sin has a bad odor. And the appearance of God, so Cusanus says,[5] is heralded by sweet fragrances.

The civilizing process in European modernity has developed in a rapid and dramatic way, perhaps because the European upper strata (before the emergence of the court civilization) were far less civilized in their everyday manners than the upper strata of traditional Asian civilization. Since European culture was a Christian culture, morality was regulated by the commandments and the authority of the Church. Civilization, however, is not based on commands, but on habits. Where there are many commands, there is less necessity for good habits to develop.[6] One subjects oneself to commands. If one fails to do so, one is guilty of sinning. Civilization has a different logic. One follows the optional norms of civilized behavior. If one fails to do so, one becomes ridiculous, not *comme-il-faut*, or shocking.[7] This is one of the reasons why European nobility remained rude and "barbarian" in comparison with Chinese mandarins, and had to go through a long civilizing process in the wake of modernity. The upper bourgeois and the nobility became "civilized" almost simultaneously. This already indicated (and also contributed to) the relativization of the estate barriers.

The norms and rules of civility (in the use of language, man-made objects, and interpersonal contact) are elastic and need to be followed in context. This is why it is not only "rudeness" that becomes ridiculous, but it is also a reason for laughter if the norms of civility are slavishly imitated or overdone, practiced out of context, or applied in an entirely empty, lifeless manner.[8] To put it simply, urbanity and civility are located in the rules but are embodied by the urban, the civil person, by men and women who behave in a civilized, urban way.

The words "urbanity" and "civility" themselves indicate the modern character of civilization. Urbanity is related to behavior in cities, civility to behavior in civil life. Politeness (*politess*) is a private value and can be thus contrasted with courtesy. The term courtesy (or courtship) refers to the norms of everyday life, centered around a princely court.

The more modernity develops, the less decisive and all-encompassing will be the primary everyday system of objectivation for the life of men and women. In the new social arrangement, where the function that one performs establishes one's rank in the hierarchy of stratification, where life within institutions based on the division of functions occupies a far more decisive place both in scope and in time span in men's (and later also) women's lives, "civilization," in the above double sense, assumes an ever greater importance. The rules of an institution also include some rules for behavior, the use of language, and of man-made objects, but those rules stabilize only the relation of men and women insofar as they perform their functions. One frequently says that "X" behaves as a "typical" bureaucrat, or a typical lawyer, or a typical businessmen, or a typical trade union boss, or a typical teacher. It is our experience that the performed functions also determine interpersonal relations to a great extent. The teacher is teaching, the bureaucrat is subsuming everything to rules, the lawyer is arguing, and so on. Still, interpersonal relations in institutions are never fully regulated by such rules. After all, men and women are not identical with their function; they do not relate to one another only *as* a function. When we bump into each other in an office, we say "Excuse me." When we want to get some help, we say "Please, would you be so kind enough to ... " We also play roles that do not simply manifest but also exaggerate our functions; we assume masks and play theater.[9] It is well known that the greater the role the use of objects plays in our performance, the less can we play theater, while the more interaction accompanies our function, the more opportunities arise to play theater. Sartre describes the waiter as an actor, but the lawyer in court is also an actor, and so normally is the teacher in his or her class.[10] The norms of civility can also include theater performance as their extreme manifestation.

Civility occupies the broader/narrower place that extends between playing theater and mere functional performance. Civility is required by many professions, but it still remains civility, because the requirement can be fulfilled in very different manners. For example, a bookseller needs to be polite (although he may sometimes be rude), yet to help the buyer, to advise about books, is not simply identical to "functional" performance but, rather, a matter of civility. In filling the space between playing theater and performing a function, civility allows (to a degree) for the unique human character to "shine through" the web of learned and practiced gestures.

One can behave in a civil or uncivil manner practically everywhere – in the pub, in the theater, on the street, and in the soccer stadium, as well as in all activities (dance, chatting, dining, playing with one another). The rules of civility and urbanity criss-cross all of the heterogeneous spaces where men and women meet or dwell. The rules of civility/urbanity also have a lion's share in establishing the character and width of interpersonal spaces (whether they are remote or close, intimate, or collegial), as well as their density (warm, passionate, hostile, cool). They also advise us how to move from remoteness to closeness, from intimacy to coolness and vice versa (for example, addressing each other by our first or second names). The norms of civility and urbanity make it possible that men and women in civil society can live among each other without always clashing in body, spirit, and soul. Conflicts are prevented in this way. For example, people are careful not to push others on the street, to line up at the bus stop or in the post office, and to behave in a crowd as if it were not a crowd. One also learns to read from gestures, to understand whether one is welcome or not welcome, to be aware of when one should leave, to find out what kind of gift is appropriate, and what would be too much or too little in a relationship (considering financial means, positions, closeness, age, gender, and so on). Moreover, one must do all of these smoothly, without hurting the average (not over-sensitive) man or woman.

These personal kinds of civil gestures act as a substitute for love to a certain extent, and protect against hatred to a certain degree. One can factor in the other person's vulnerability, even without knowing him or her, if one merely sticks to the rules of civility and politeness. And one can hide one's antipathy if one only keeps to the norms of urbanity.

In most of the cases enumerated above, moral civility is not related to technological civilization. But even here, the combination of the two aspects of modern civilization is not rare. If you have a car and another person cannot drive, you offer that other person a ride. You reciprocate letter with letter (handwritten letter with handwritten letter, typewritten letter with typewritten letter). You help the other person to carry heavy luggage, or open a bottle of champagne for him if he lacks this skill.

The matters of civility are small things, but these small things make modern life more liveable. Given that moral regulation is slackened, men rarely feel guilty, unless they are put to shame, and pangs of conscience become fairly rare.[11] Where the population density is always increasing,[12] where most of us live in apartment buildings in an urban milieu or in a metropolis, and become adjusted to walking and commuting constantly in crowds, life would be utterly unbearable were we not surrounded by the protective belt of civility. I think that constant civil unrest is more likely to occur in countries where the rules of civility have failed to develop.[13]

Civility and urbanity are also "good manners," not just in our relations with other people, but also as far as the use of man-made objects is concerned. The "civil" use is not a solely functional one. One can use a spoon according to its functions, but this is not enough. Rather, one has to learn to use the spoon according to good table manners. A civilized person has to know what to wear and for what occasion, all the more so because modern men and women now choose their own outfits, and more frequently than not dress themselves alone. Recently, even bourgeois women needed to learn how to wait for their guests at the dinner table.[14]

Yet, among all the man-made things which we need to learn to use both functionally and with urban elegance, _the human body_ stands out as the most important. The human body becomes a "standing reserve" just like all other objects of nature – in Heidegger's expression, inexhaustible[15] in its potential, malleable according to the wishes and whims of a "subject," that is reason or mind.

The civil use of the human body is not just about fitting the newborn's "raw material" into a "social" model, a practice as old as the human race, but about something else, and more. The "manners," the control of the body included, are not manifestations of an existence – for example, existence as a nobleman – but also *masks to hide existence*, to hide one's origins, and even to hide individuality. Manners no longer belong to men (and women), but are worn like dresses, perhaps the kind of dresses that, after a while, one is unable to strip from one's body. Romantics term these manners "conventions," although they are not conventional. Romantics also wage a war against conventions; that is, against manners becoming conventions after having ceased to be mere expressions of "being" such and such (for example, a nobleman).[16] Rousseau spearheaded the romantic movement. He was the first to abuse good manners as "masks," as borrowed costumes and the like.[17] But conventions also helped the assimilation of those in social strata who were formerly excluded from social acceptance.[18] If you control your body, then no one will be interested in your soul.

Foucault is the most recent brilliant critic of the disciplining of the body. Although he is not a romantic critic, his perspective is that of the Romantics. I find his descriptions not only illuminating but also insightful. Still, before joining him in his ruminations, I will briefly show the other side of the coin.

Among the two imaginary institutions of modernity (historical and technological), manners, conventions, and the different technologies of bodily control are the offspring of technological imagination. Only technological imagination treats the body as a "standing reserve." Romantic opposition (to abuse the merely empty conventions) is rooted in historical imagination and, as always, historical imagination defends a very modern idea, this time the idea of free individuality. A free individual cannot be subjected to control, because he or she is an independent subject. The slogan "subject" here plays a double role from the outset. Firstly, it is the subject that treats the body as an object (or standing reserve), but it is also the subject that one should liberate from being treated as an object. Both tendencies, opposite as they are, claim to be "humanist."

Foucault reverses the traditional Neoplatonian/Gnostic/Christian creed that the soul dwells in the prisonhouse of the body. Or, at least, he says that Enlightenment has reversed the relationship.[19] Now, since the Enlightenment, the opposite is the case, for by now it is the body that has become imprisoned in the soul. The soul, through rational control, through institutionalized disciplining of the body and constant surveillance, and moreover through scientifically legitimized oppressive practices, exercises an immense power upon the body, makes it malleable and obedient. The body is shaped by the whims of the soul. And those whims are oppressive.[20]

This, I repeat, is true. But something else is also true. The "innumerable petty mechanisms"[21] of the control of the body can be learned. They are indeed "technologies" of bodily control. This technology is not innate (no technology is). It is just like mnemotechnics. This offers the mind a relative independence. But Foucault is right: this mental independence also falls victim to the so-called applied social sciences: to anthropology, psychology, and sociology. But the same imagination (the "soul" or spirit) that imprisons the body can also liberate the body, for scientific technologies can affect the body in both ways.

The civilizing process can be followed, and was in fact followed, by a de-civilizing process.[22] In the same way that they appeared, manners disappear, conventions are dismissed, and the romantic imagination – seemingly – wins the day. But the body remains in the prisonhouse of the soul, be it fully controlled or (seemingly) not at all – because it is "reason," that is, scientific discourse, which decides how the body should be shaped and how not. And if "reason" decides on promiscuity, the body will follow as obediently as it once did in the Victorian era.

In the 19th and early 20th centuries, the disciplining of the body was tuned into the requirements of the social division of labor. Working-class children had to develop docile bodies for factory work, and not for horse riding. But all social strata (which were formed increasingly more in the institutions of education, rather than in the everyday life of their families) had to learn to control the body. Winston Churchill, for example, the son of a famous family, was savagely beaten up many times in a most elegant public school in order to learn discipline.[23] In fact, the educational system, the army and the navy, the factory, and the club, all institutions contributed to the disciplining of the body – and also of the mind.

The mind and the soul parted ways. The mind became a function of the body, or it became identified with the body. The ideas of education, health, well-being, ethics, success, performance, and "humanity" – that is, the "soul" – have set the rules for all kinds of learning. The principle of maximum output/minimal input, of "economization," of "rationalization" (in a Weberian sense), took care of the "result" as well as the selection, the quasi-Darwinian survival of the "fittest."[24, 25] The soul imprisons the body *and* the mind; but the soul can also allow them to be free.

Why, how, and to what extent were they allowed to be free? It is difficult to answer these questions, but it is less difficult to *date the beginning of the reversal of the civilizing process.* This happened in the famous year of 1968. In fact, all of the movements of 1968 were revolts against the civilizing process. Let me enumerate a few aspects of the movement: to destroy universities or to make a case for permissive education; sexual liberation; gay liberation; with an emphasis on youth, spontaneity, and "informality" in everything – in customs, in dressing, in social intercourse, and the like. The movement also attacked politeness and urbanity. The body was not defended by ceremonies from being touched – rather personal "touching," such as hugging, loving, caring, and discussing sex, became programmatic; so did the personalization of the environment, of the hair style, of clothing, of the kinds of entertainment, and of the consumption of drugs. By now, however, hugging, touching, and even "personal touch" have slowly disappeared, just as have the beards from men's faces.

Still, the old pre-1968 manners have not returned. Although not in everything and not everywhere, but at least in the USA (and also in some other parts of the world),[26] libertarianism had been replaced by a more rule-oriented, more rigid, more oppressive, yet also more democratic (far less class-bound) set of "civilizing mechanisms" than the pre-1968 one. "Neo-Victorianism" in sexual mores[27] makes fewer allowances for elasticity and personality than old Victorianism did, and mobilizes even the law for the implementation of sanctions, thereby colonizing intimate life.[28] The more intimate life is colonized, the more it becomes "illuminated" by the beam of public scrutiny, the more helpless the pure body/mind becomes, and the narrower its prison becomes.[29] The wave of sexual discourse, initiated already by the movement of "sexual liberation," has not ceded in times of neo-Victorianism; rather, it has become all-encompassing. The new wave of health control joins the trend of neo-Victorianism; one must gain bodily control by jogging, dieting, quitting smoking, and the like, and by believing and repeating all "scientific" nonsense that legitimizes the control of the body.[30] These days, smoking a cigarette is as much an indication of bad manners (even of sin!) as eating fish with a knife, or wearing breeches in the opera before 1968.[31] Finally, instead of the traditional "grand schools," now (with the exception of some Latin countries) specialized schools with highly technologized programs take care of the disciplining of the class-indifferent body/mind.

It seems as if a pendulum were swinging in the civilizing process, too. After the class barriers had been lifted, at least in principle although not in fact, the "conventions" lost their relevance. So did the old and rude technologies of creating docile bodies. Yet the pendulum that moved in the direction toward libertarianism – that is, in the direction of lifting the control of the body/mind beyond eliminating the strict class barriers – began to swing back. The spirit (ideology) invented new more freely accepted and more general controls, which do not leave any freedom for the person, however, for – unlike ceremonies – they do not protect the person from intrusion by the other. Instead, being afraid of ridicule, people become afraid of direct interventions into their daily lives, or into what has remained of daily life: the last vestiges of the intimate sphere.

Psychoanalysis belongs to these interventions as an everyday practice.[32] Through psychoanalysis, other kinds of therapies, and newly invented religions, such as scientology, the conceptual scheme of a person for self-understanding or for giving an account of oneself is entirely enframed.[33] The little self (the body/mind) of the person is bombarded from all directions. One can, however, expect that in the near future new movements might push the pendulum back toward a more libertarian position. Perhaps the questions of 1968 will be raised again, although surely with a different emphasis. By this I mean questions such as: What are we running toward? What is so urgent? What is success after all? or Why am I so concerned with the Eye of the other? If I am disapproved of, so what?[34] The pendulum will in all probability swing between the extremes of total conformism and total chaos, without reaching either end. If any of these extremes were to be reached and the swing of the pendulum were to cease, I think that modernity would not survive.

The imprisonment of the body/mind in the soul of ideologies is motivated and monitored by technological imagination. However, the counter-soul (romanticism, motivated by historical imagination) does not just hopelessly criticize the domination by rational control, but sometimes successfully reverses it too, as it happened in the world-wide movements of 1968. As long as the move of the pendulum is inspired by two conflicting imaginary institutions, there are no lethal dangers. Romantic/historical imagination can, however, enter into an unholy matrimony with technological imagination. This has happened in the in(famous) totalitarian regimes of Europe, first and foremost in Nazism and in Bolshevism.

A pendulum movement is also noticeable in historical judgments. Firstly, theories of totalitarianism almost entirely blame historical imagination – ideologies – for the horrors of Nazism or Bolshevism. Two decades ago, perhaps under the influence of Heidegger, they began to blame technological imagination almost entirely; this is by now the chief scheme of understanding.[35] In the most recent years, however, the "technological explanation" has again been dismissed, and the "historical imagination" explanation gathers influence once more.[36] But there is also a new tendency developing; namely, to avoid all explanations and to emphasize the total contingency of the emergence of totalitarian states and their survival.[37] Yet explanation with contingency works well if *only* the *emergence* of totalitarianism is discussed. Whenever the operation, the *functioning*, of a totalitarian system is under scrutiny, one cannot speak of "contingency." What is politico-historically contingent is not contingent in its operation. For if something functions, if it is reproduced, there must be some internal logic at work there.

I describe totalitarian systems as the offspring of the unholy marriage of two imaginary institutions (technological and historical) which, in this case, are not in opposition but, rather, act in concert. If one were to accept this description one could understand totalitarian systems as *irrational*, yet *not as contingent*. Irrationality stands for the unison of two entirely opposite imaginary institutions. Both imaginary institutions can guide rationally, but together they work irrationally. This is so because, at every moment, one or the other can gain the upper hand, and one cannot foresee which one and when. One can switch from one to another with ease: the "switch" itself does not suit either of them, but the switch is neither chosen, nor even noticed, by the person(s) who perform it. As a result, expectations can become null and void at every moment; all predictions are emptied out. The tomorrow becomes hidden, although it is constantly predicted and publicized as the "final victory."

Contingency means that there are many causes that criss-cross each other, and the result is not written on the body of any of the factors that contribute to the generation of a political system. Irrationality is not contingency. There are only two factors here, and these two factors are not causes. Moreover, irrationality is the denial of contingency. An irrational language does not make allowances to contingency; rather, it speaks the language of necessity or of destiny. The totalitarian language of collective destiny is as irrational as the language of historical necessity, not because "destiny" or "necessity" as such are irrational concepts, but because the "destiny" language uses the vocabulary of historical imagination while mobilizing it for the sake of technological imagination, whereas the "necessity" language uses the vocabulary of technological imagination and mobilizes it in the service of historical imagination.[38]

Totalitarian regimes are often termed empires of barbarism or of savagery. If "barbarism" means the absence of modernity, they were not barbarians. If barbarism means the absence of technological civilization, those countries can hardly be termed barbarian. One can rarely come across such docile bodies as in the Nuremberg party day ceremony filmed by Leni Riefenstahl, or in the May Day parades of Stalin's era. And nowhere were bodies more cruelly tortured and put under pressure than in totalitarian regimes. Nowhere was the mind/body more deeply imprisoned in the soul of ideologies and of evil maxims.

If barbarism means the absence of historical imagination, totalitarian regimes were not barbarians. What, then, is modern barbarism? I think that modern barbarism is in one sense the opposite of modern chaos. Modern chaos is the absence of all ethical powers, and it is characterized by the weakening of the impact of both historical and technological imaginations or, eventually, by their disappearance. Modern barbarism is, however, in my view, the unholy matrimony of the historical and technological imagination, where the carrier of the chief ethical power is the irrational (the fusion of the two imaginary institutions) itself. At both extremes, bodies and minds are threatened with something more final, more irreversible than the constant pendulum movement between the unattainable extremes of having been entirely imprisoned or having been entirely liberated from the prison of the soul. Namely, body and mind are threatened by losing the capacity and the opportunity to side with one imaginary institution against the other, or to cope with their contradictions and coexistence,[39] and thus to accept choice and contingency.

Until now, I have discussed technological imagination without touching upon the issue of *technological civilization*. Civility, urbanity, or the disciplining of the body (and the mind) are guided, or also guided, by technological imagination, but they do not belong, or only partially belong, to technological civilization. But most people do not associate the word "civilization" with the way in which one is walking on the street or dressing for an evening at the theater, or lining up at the bus stop, or jogging; but with washing machines, television sets, the airplane, and the Internet – that is, with technological civilization.

Technological civilization is normally associated with control, mediation, efficiency, rationality; being revolutionary on the one hand, while easing or alienating wealth, poverty, and freedom/slavery on the other hand. In the first cluster, I enumerated the objective characteristics of technological civilization (that is, the characteristics that are not bound to a perspective); in the second cluster, however, I enumerated the bipolar evaluation of the yields of industrial civilization from a traditionally progressivist/liberal and from the romantic perspective.

The first conception of technological civilization is founded in the dualistic description of the world as society/nature.[40] A new myth, a new *theomachia*, arises from this duality. Nature and society are believed

to be involved in an eternal struggle with one another; yet, finally, thanks
to technology, society will win the day. It is technology that makes society
able to control nature. And, so the story runs, society does not simply
control nature insofar as it subjects nature to itself, but also in the sense
that it can use the forces of nature themselves against nature – it can put
all of the resources of nature into the service of society/man.[41] This is
how nature becomes a "standing reserve."

The vocabulary of the new *theomachia* is indeed military. One conquers nature, one occupies new territories, one extends one's powers, and
so on; whereas nature fights back, it revolts, it wants to retrieve already
occupied territories.[42, 43] In the Darwinian theory of the struggle for life,
man is the latecomer, the most fit, and also the final winner of the
struggle.

Yet this is an optimistic vision that not everyone shares. The fear of
losing the battle always returns.[44] Technological civilization is civilization because it is society's weapon against the powers of nature. Through
the development of technology "man" – that is, "society" – acquires new
weapons, whereas nature cannot acquire any such weapons; rather, it has
to stick to the old ones, such as fire, water, and disease – the so-called
"evils." The new thought in contemporary ecology is not the idea that
society's control over nature is not a gain, or not solely a gain, for it is
also the cause of many losses (which I will soon briefly discuss), where
the losses outweigh the gains. Rather, the ecological argument is that the
weapon of technological civilization is (or becomes) a weapon of nature
against society. Ecological imagination simply replaces the old thesis that
society conquers nature by using the powers of nature with the thesis that
nature might be the winner of this battle by losing it entirely: technological civilization undercuts the condition of social-human life and commits suicide with the once seemingly so formidable weapons.

In the second understanding (mediation), technological civilization is a
civilization of *means*, not of ends. All assets of technological civilization
are means, and their value can be sought in their mean-character. Firstly,
they are indifferent in relation to certain goals or ends whose means they
are or can be. Here, modern thinking sounds similar to the first palinode
in Antigone: whether they are used for good or evil purposes depends not
on the means, but on those who use them for such purposes. Television is
not responsible for the increase of violence, nor is the production of gas
responsible for the gas chambers. Technological civilization is the civilization of means because it mediates between nature that is man-made
and nature that is not man-made, between different kinds of sciences
(knowledge), between "know-that" and "know-how," and, last but not
least, between men.

If mediated by the works of technological civilization, the intercourse among men becomes more apersonal and functional. The relationship of the passengers to the train driver is solely functional, whereas the passengers' relationship to the coachman was also personal, even if the passengers and the coachman were of an entirely different rank. One has a personal relationship to the dressmaker, but not to the creator of the machine-made dresses in the department store. Industrial civilization mediates itself more and more through industrial civilization. For example, advertising mediates the process of consumption at the second degree (it is already mediated by consuming processed food). Why is mediation "civilization"? For even the simplest cases of mediation are considered to be civilized. Just as it is more civilized to drink from a glass than directly from the tap or from the well (which is alright if someone is back "in nature"; for example, on an excursion), so (one believes) it is more civilized to inhale the odor of deodorant (the indirect, mediated smell) than the odor of the human body. Mediation has become associated with "civilization," and technological civilization is the "primus movens" of mediation.

Thirdly, technological civilization is characterized by "efficiency." But why is efficiency civilized?

The modern concept of civilization emerges along with work ethics. Work ethics puts a moral premium at work as a *technē* (not as a mere bodily exercise) on the one hand, yet also on the forms of civility surrounding the work activity on the other hand.[45] Civilized work presupposes civilized man and the civilized use of time, matter, and space.[46] To put it bluntly, it presupposes economizing. *Homo economicus* and *Homo faber* are the same man. To be efficient means to be civilized. Yet technological civilization is a means, not an end. It preserves the value of efficiency as a means value (and not an end value). This means that efficiency is, as an aspect of technological civilization, beyond ethics (beyond good and evil), and begins to live an independent life.

Efficiency, as the characteristic factor of technological civilization, became an essential aspect of civilization because of the moral evaluation of *Homo economicus* and *Homo faber*. Yet today, the efficiency value of technological civilization does not call for a *Homo faber*. In fact, the great efficiency of technological civilization makes the image and the reality of *Homo faber* superfluous, or at least marginal (as an artist, for example, who is *not* efficient).

Technological civilization is *rational*. But what does this mean? And why is rationality associated, without much ado, with "civilization"? And why do modern men and women share the belief that the more rational we are, the more civilized we become?

The conviction that the rational man is more virtuous than the one who follows his instincts is as old as philosophy.[47] True, the "civilized" man is not the "virtuous" man. The civilized man, to speak with Kant, pays with counterfeit money; but the counterfeit money, although not of real value, is at least an imitation of the value, and thus better than none.[48] The civilized man pretends or seems to conduct his life according to the dictates of practical reason (even if he does not). A rational/ civilized person is predictable and reliable. Technology has no instincts, it is functional; the way a thing of technology operates is also predictable and reliable. One cannot rely upon natural powers. There may be warm, or sometimes freezing, weather on the same day of each year. The heating is reliable, and you are in control of the heat; the more perfect technology becomes, the more reliable the heating becomes.[49] It is rational; its work is not dependent on the whims of nature – human instinct or natural forces. Briefly, it is civilized.

I think that *reliability* and *predictability*, those fairly traditional conceptions of rationality, legitimize technological civilization *qua* "civilization," rather than just means–end rationality. Renowned critics of industrial civilization have contrasted the "mechanical" character of modernity with the "organic" character of the pre-modern world.[50] But this contrast can also be evaluated in favor of the rational character of technology. After all, the organic is associated with the instinctive and unpredictable, whereas the mechanical is associated with predictability and reliability, precisely because it is mechanical – functional, but empty.

It is difficult to detach the understanding of technological civilization from technological imagination in general and its expansion to the whole modern world, first to the institutions of the world in particular. But if one tries to avoid this expansion (which, as a matter of fact, cannot be entirely circumvented), the idea of technological civilization as a rational civilization will become more obvious. After all, technological civilization, in a narrow and direct sense, is only means (mediation) and has no direct relation to the goals or ends: it is not chosen so that the ends can be achieved, but forged or created as solutions to technological problems. Problem-solving and the achievement of ends require two fairly different kinds of rationality. In the case of problem-solving, the ends are, rather, glued to the means, sometimes not even rationally, by trial and error or imagination, unless the ends are also technological (for example, this kind of software is needed for that purpose).

Rationality is not the absence of imagination. The things encompassed in the world of a technological civilization are frequently created not only with inventive (as opposed to repetitive) thinking, but also by creative imagination. Their rationality becomes devoid of imagination only in the moment at which they are "there"; that is, in mass production. Produced *en masse*, the product must be reliable and/or predictable (rational in the sense of a virtuous man). At the moment at which a product of technological civilization leaves mass production, the "first" users still need to stretch their imaginations, yet the need for stretching imagination ends quickly and the thing is taken for granted.

Technological civilization is revolutionizing. Revolution and progression (as cumulation) are, however, far from composing two straight lines that lead in the same direction.

Technological civilization expands further and further – it encompasses more and more domains – and in this sense its "progression" is taken for granted. We now use things that were not in use yesterday. It is also taken for granted that technological civilization has an intimate relation to science, and that since science grows and expands, develops, and undergoes revolutions, so does technological civilization. Yet technological civilization is far more intimately intertwined with the daily life of men and women than science ever was or might have been. Science provides the dominating world explanation in modernity,[51] and thus everything can be legitimated by science in the last instance, technological civilization included. But technological "civilization," with its capacity for control, mediation, efficiency, and rationality, (in the sense of predictability and reliability), is actually *there*. The products of the technological civilization are the matter-at-hand (*Zuhandesein*, in Heidegger's expression). One does not need to study anything to be aware of their mere *presence*.[52]

Revolutions in technological civilizations[53] radically change the way of life of men and women. For example, the development that began with the separation of workplace and household, and finally ended with the mechanization of the household on the one hand, and the socialization of household activities on the other hand,[54] has essentially contributed to the total change in family structure,[55] to the metamorphosis of the relation between sexes, and even to the expansion of legislation.[56]

Currently, the revolutionizing of communication and of information is the "mobile," the progressing, territory of technological civilization. The latest revolution (civilizing paradigm change) has opened a new route for progress. This time, progress contains less replacement than it did during the revolutionizing of the household.[57]

Thus far, the description of the complex character of technological civilization[58] has seemed to be value free. But this is just the tip of the iceberg. Every serious discussion of technological civilization collides sooner or later with issues arising from reflection on the nondialectical contradictions of this civilization. Let me also refer to these as paradoxes (or insoluble antinomies) – technological civilization is easing the burdens of men/technological civilization alienates man; technological civilization creates wealth/technological civilization impoverishes the Earth; technological civilization liberates us/technological civilization enslaves us. And behind all these questions the Main Spectre looms large: this is the Spectre of Identity. Who is "us"? "Us" Europeans? "Us" humankind of our generation? "Us" humankind of all generations? "Us" as all living creatures on Earth? "Us" as the Earth itself?[59]

The antinomy of *easing/alienating* refers to the *burden* of man, particularly to the burden of work.

The advocates of technological civilization point to a blessing that can hardly be denied: technological civilization takes most of the burden of work from man's shoulders. The curse of Adam has been lifted by Adam. Whereas self-maintenance and self-reproduction alone once used up bodily strength, whereas pain, fatigue, and exhaustion of the body crippled men in early youth, by now machines have taken over the difficult and crippling tasks, man is in control, and he remains young and healthy for a long time, and dies in old age. The curse of women has also been partially lifted. Now you can bear a child with less pain, childbirth is no longer dangerous, and one can make love without bearing children, and enjoy one's body in all the ways one pleases. There are fewer chronic and incurable diseases; suffering from bodily pain can be alleviated. One does not even understand the meaning of the sentence that expressed the common experience of men and women for a very long time, that our Earth is the vale of tears.

The critics and enemies of technological civilization will point at the loss which can hardly be denied. The great weight of suffering and pain has been lifted from the body just in order to be imposed as a heavy burden on the soul. Men have become alienated from nature. They do not accommodate the rhythm of nature (which is also the rhythm of their bodies), but the rhythm of artificial things, their own creatures. They lose control over their creatures. They lose the capacity of a natural "movement." They consume "unnatural" things. Food can turn into poison. And what is more important: as far as man's relation to Nature is concerned, the famous predictability of the things of technological civilization breaks down. The movement of each and every artificial thing may be predictable, yet the universe of technological civilization as a whole has become entirely unpredictable. And everything that is unpredictable is dangerous. Life has become longer, yet the same factors that have contributed to the prolongation of life will shorten human life tomorrow, or even condemn the human race to extinction. The alleviation of the burdens of work and pain (of the curse of Adam and Eve) can lead (or, more emphatically, will in all probability lead) to the exhaustion of all natural resources, and finally to the complete denaturalization of man, to the absolute reversal of all the benefits of technological civilization. Losses will outnumber blessings. (They already do.)[60]

The advocates of technological civilization then turn to another, yet related, argument. Just as the labor process is no longer burdened with pain, suffering, fatigue and exhaustion, sickness, and brevity of life, as it has been every where before our era, so it increasingly produces a greater *wealth* of material and spiritual things, putting all into the service of man. But the accuser will answer that the quantity of things for use is in itself not yet "wealth," because human riches do not consist of the quantity of things at hand but, rather, of the refinement, the manifoldness, the depth of experiences. The use of the things at hand is taken for granted; their essence is not reflected, and their essential merit and importance never queried. Man becomes the appendage of things, and the more things we have, the more "appendage-like" our life experience and behavior will become. This appendage-like, reactive, superficial life can be termed "alienated" in the sense that the essence of the human individual becomes external to his or her existence, just as in the case of madness. Alienation is madness, although undetected, for if everyone if is mad, madness goes on unnoticed. Technological civilization empties out life through alienation; the exister loses his or her second and third dimension.[61]

In the minds of the advocates of industrial civilization, this civilization is liberating; in the minds of its adversaries, it is enslaving. Their respective arguments follow from those already mentioned.

Industrial civilization liberates man from the cave of nature, from pain and toil, from the fear of early death. And what is most important is that it frees up time for us, it sets us free from being home-bound and Earth-bound, to sum up the argument put forth by the advocates of industrial civilization. The opposite of all this is true, thus speak the adversaries. Instead of having liberated time, technological civilization puts us under constant time pressure, where in to be no longer home-bound and Earth-bound is not a gain, but a terrible loss. Instead of being at home, we become alien in the world; instead of being free everywhere, we are slaves insofar as we remain alien (like the old Hebrews in Egypt). The loss of certainty and the security of Mother Earth is no freedom. No things, not even the more extravagant things, can warrant freedom.

These were briefly the antinomies (or paradoxes) of technological civilization. Both "sides" are one-sided. Rationalistic apologies are flat; romantic outbursts are ridiculous. As with almost everything in modernity, technological civilization is both a gain and a loss – and there is no way to compare them. Still, it is legitimately termed "civilization."

Moreover, this is a kind of civilization which is, or at least can be, commonly shared by all "cultures" (in the sense of the third concept of culture). Technological civilization is shared by cultures in which both the advocates and detractors of technological civilization are embedded in the dynamics of modernity.

It is normally accepted without much ado that the modern world is rationalistic or rational. Whether the three concepts of "culture" and the concepts of "civilization" fit the bill of rationality still remains an open question.

Let me sum up a few results of the previous discussion. Civilization can generally be called rational insofar as predictability and reliability are important aspects (and even determinations – definitions in the sense of the German word *Bestimmung*) of rationality. One can admit that civilized or "urban" behavior is more rational than its absence, and that the things of technological civilization work in a rational manner in the short run. Yet, I have added that the complete fusion of technological as historical imagination results in utter irrationalism (as happened in totalitarian states); moreover, that what is rational (predictable and reliable) in the short run can turn out to be unreliable and unpredictable in the long run. (So far, we do not know for certain what the lasting consequences of technological civilization will be.) This is not a statement in support of the ecologist's doomsday scenario, but is only a statement of *je ne sais quoi* – namely, that this scenario cannot be dismissed as an entirely absurd one.

Under the heading of the first concept of culture, the distinction between "rational" and "nonrational" does not makes sense, unless as orthodox Hegelians we think of works of art as the manifestations of Reason in history. One can admit that our contemporary culture is more reflective and less creative than in the era of early modernity, but reflectivity in itself is no more rational than creativity, unless one accepts Nietsche's all-encompassing judgment about Socratic/Alexandrinian anti-culture as the prototype of rationality. But we can choose not to underwrite either Hegel or Nietzsche, and accept a concept of rationality that "makes" creative periods more rational than reflective periods. One could insist that becoming omnivorous and squeezing meaning out from all possible and impossible texts is an exercise of "reason," given that it is meaning or sense that we need to squeeze out from those texts. The desire to "render meaning to our life," the need for meaning and sense, is rational in the sense of "*vernünftig*," but it is the needs and the desires (the emotions, feelings) themselves which are "*vernünftig*." But from this it does not follow that meditation on the imago of the Redeemer in a medieval painting could be understood, conversely, as "*unvernünftig.*" In the spirit of the third concept of culture, either all cultures are rational or none of them are. If keeping oneself to norms and subjecting oneself to rules is "rational," all cultures are rational, for without this kind of rational behavior they cannot survive. In fact, the specificity of the modern world's rationality fits the bill of the second concept of culture in particular, and the dynamics of modernity in general. To concede that Truth (and the Good and the Beautiful) is not absolute and cannot be taken for granted – and, furthermore, that one can make contradictory cases for something without being branded as a heretic or madman – this attitude, conviction, and practice is truly modern, and can be described as rational in a modern sense. Since the modern world is based on freedom which does not found, moderns, as already discussed, can establish an *archē* and build a system on this *archē*, using it as a pillar to support good arguments. By "good argument" I do not mean argument in the narrow meaning of the word. Given that a story is also an argument, pointing at the "*Sache selbst*" can also sense an argument, reciting a poem as well – in fact, almost everything has the force of an argument, if it makes plausible that what we want to present as true (as our truth) is in fact more true than the other truths presented by someone else. It is not very important what kind of form such a "discourse" takes. It can be conducted according to strict rules, go on as an "anarchic" conversation, or take place both inside and yet outside institutions. What is important is the openness of the debate and the conviction that every truth is fragile (not relative!) except the moral truth.

In this sense, I subscribe to Habermas's distinction between instrumental, pragmatic, and communicative rationality – but with three important provisos. Firstly, argumentation – as with discussion in general – is rational insofar as the partners to the discussion remain aware of their fallibility, and of the fragility of their arguments and their respective truths. Secondly, one remains aware of the nonfounded conditions of one's foundation; namely, that the whole process of argumentation rests on something that cannot be proven, or – which amounts to the same thing – that many "final principles" can equally be proven. Finally, being "*vernünftig*" is a way of life, the logic of the heart included. The modern culture is rational under the condition that the participant to the cultural discussion keeps in mind that freedom is not just the condition of rationality, but also the limit to reason.

But Reason is not identical to reason. Among all the other differences, there is *warm reason* and *cold reason*. Cold reason is reason without Eros; warm reason is reason with Eros. Merely procedural argumentation mobilizes cold reason. Conversations about taste (Kant's luncheon parties, for example) mobilize warm reason. Cold reason is arguing *about* (something), warm reason is always *talking to* (some other). Let me concentrate briefly only on the third concept of culture. I said that all cultures can be termed "rational." By this I meant – just as do all theorists who operate with the third concept of culture – that the rules of a society are applied to those members of society to which they in fact apply, and that they are applied[62] consistently and continuously. But modern culture is also rational in addition, insofar as it becomes general practice to test and to query accepted (traditional) norms and rules, statements of facts, certainties, and concepts of the Good and of the True. I have termed the first kind of rationality "rationality of reason," and the second kind "rationality of intellect."[63]

It is an illusion to think that since rationality of intellect (assuming the form of the dynamics of modernity or, to use Nietzsche's language, of the vehicle of "nihilism") is a modern kind of rationality, it is the sole kind of rationality remaining on the stage. In the main, men and women still take many things for granted. They accept certain rules as if they had been predestined, but they do not know by whom. There is also a tendency toward conservatism in the modern world, as a protection against the constant trend toward the revolutionizing of minds, forms of life, customs, and so on. True, the dynamics of modernity will also become a habit, but there are many other habits that men and women are reluctant to give up. In simple issues, such as in changing drinking or eating habits, people can prove to be extremely conservative. This conservatism, although frequently abused by the priests of constant innovation, plays a very important role in modern life. There is a limit to malleability, to the elasticity of the human form of life and character, and there is a limit to the speed of the constant revolutionizing of daily life as well.

As a matter of fact, the two kinds of rationality (rationality of reason and rationality of intellect) must adjust to one another to a certain degree. The defense of the tradition is now rarely based on pointing at an authority. The one who defends the tradition frequently gives arguments for the superiority of the tradition, or tells stories about the tradition in order to legitimize it. In addition, rationality of intellect, mobilized by the drive to revolutionize the way of life in new waves, can also mobilize tradition, and even reinstitutionalize tradition through revolutions. For example, the social democratic welfare state has won a difficult victory against free-market liberalism after WWII in many European (and not just European) states. In this sense, social democracy has changed everyday life. But the change in daily life has pointed in fact toward the defense of certain traditions. It has been conservative in comparison to the all-around revolutionizing madness of free-market capitalism. Yet, although both rationality of reason and rationality of intellect assume certain features of the other, they still remain distinct. And this distinctiveness is essential. For, whereas rationality of reason has empirical certainties, rationality of intellect bases its de-legimating claims on counterfactual certainties. Neither empirical nor counterfactual certainties are certainties in the old sense, for if they were, argumentation and discussion would be irrelevant. But it still makes a difference if a certainty is "positive," already there (even if queried and tested), and if a certainty is just recommended, if it is entirely new. Rationality of intellect is also destructive. It wants to destroy the "real" and the old. Rationality of reason is also destructive – it wants to annihilate the propositions of rationality of intellect at the stage of gestation. Modernity needs the family quarrel of the two kinds of rationalities badly, just as *it needs both kinds of rationalities*. This is just another way of saying that modernity needs to maintain itself between the two extremes of rigidification and chaos.

11

Worldtime and Lifetime[1,2]

In his now famous lectures on time, delivered in 1924, Heidegger dramatically and drastically contrasts "objective" time, the empty, physical time, on the one hand, and the time of *Dasein*, time as life, on the other hand.[3] The distinction is not entirely new, but the way it is done by Heidegger is. Heidegger offers here, and in *Being and Time*, a fundamental/ontological analysis of time. He thereby meant to formulate a concept of time which is, in fact, *The Time* of the *conditio humana* (*Dasein*). Only from this perspective could he reject other conceptions of time; for example, that of Hegel.[4]

Time is a historical concept, and thus changes its determinations historically. There is no meaningful concept of time in metaphysics. There is no conception of time in Platonism.[5] Aristotle's time concept is twofold. It is the concept of lines on the one hand, and the concept or "now" in relation to action, one of the categories which have been later quoted as the category "time," on the other hand.[6] There is no "time" in 17th-century metaphysics, whereas Kant understands time, as well as space, as the *a priori* forms of "*Auschauung*," which are in the last instance imaginary entities (*ens imaginarium*). It is the "imaginary institutions" of modernity, primarily historical imagination, which place time at the centerpoint of philosophical reflection. But this development is coeval with the demise of metaphysics.

Time is a problem in metaphysics only indirectly. It is related to demise, disappearance, unsteadiness, motion, and change. Motion and change, in all its forms – from locomotion to *dynamis* – are central categories in ancient metaphysics and, to an extent, also in the 17th century – for example, in Leibniz. But pre-modern imagination was hierarchical through and through, and in this hierarchy the immutable, immobile, and eternal had to occupy the highest place. To be in motion is to be temporal. Time is then something that "devours," that destroys, that makes things disappear. Victorious time shows itself in the ruins.

The Greek/Roman concept of time is not really a concept of time, but a concept of motion, or of the forms of motion. The circular motion, the constant repetition of the same, is the most elegant concept of motion/time, and it is most easily accommodated to metaphysical thinking. Both Hellenistic Epicureanism and Stoicism were thinking time in terms of circular motion. The "eternal repetition of the same" was sometimes understood as if, in fact, all events would repeat themselves whenever the circular motion started anew.[7] Time, then, is the accomplishment of this motion.

The Jewish/Christian tradition introduces a different concept of time. It comes from the "East." When discussing earlier the stages of historical consciousness, I referred to the Christian stage as historical "consciousness of unreflected universality, the universal myth."[8] This description refers to the appearance of three-dimensionality in historical imagination and historical temporality: Creation as past, salvation as the present (after Christ), and the last judgment as the future. It is entirely unimportant how the time span was in fact divided (for example, as to whether they were thinking the present as "very short" in comparison with the past – since Creation – as happened in early Christianity or, rather, very long, long beyond imagination, as later).

But this was not the sole anti-Greek tradition that finally entered European thinking and somehow prepared modern historical imagination. After a long battle with Gnosis and Manicheism, Christianity finally took over the Jewish concept of history, which was a _linear concept_, in which linear development was believed to have always been _interrupted_ by dramatic, "revolutionary" events, which changed the development itself. Jewish history is history in Time. The biblical time is (also) historical time. There is no absolute schism between Divine Time and Historical Time. God is eternal, contrary to Greek gods, who were just immortal, and as eternal, stands outside time. But God works though time, since He works through the lives of His people; it is His people who have to accomplish the divine work. Time as historical time, rather than the quality of the category of Being, or a quality of motion, is the concept of time that the Middle Ages inherited from Judaism. Furthermore, the time in Judaism is not "private," not experienced time; the single person is "in time" insofar as he or she occupies a place in the continuity of generations. It is the age of the single men and women in the linear and continuous change of generation that is "counted." God promised _long life_ on this Earth for those who show respect to their parents; that is, who show respect to time as to the continuity of generations. There is also "eternal repetition" in Judaism. But it is not the events that repeat themselves, but the stories told. The Bible always needs to be read from the beginning. Every year (a repetition) also brings the repetition of the same stories. Story-telling encapsulates history. But the story that is told in circles had been developed in a linear way and it is only relatively closed in and through the present remembrance.[9]

To be sure, Hellenistic Greek and Roman historians have also practiced linear history writing. They also identified turning-points in histories "*ab urbe condita.*" These were also histories of people, written for the same people. Among them also, the history of *The Jewish War* by Josephus Flavius needs to be mentioned. Yet, the future dimension was absent from these histories. The stories never became collective experiences through ritual story-telling; they were not embedded in a divine plan.

The Jewish/historical time relates to transcendence, and yet has no metaphysical dimension. The Christian elaboration of this concept of time reintroduces, however, some metaphysical issues and, in addition – and this is not unrelated – also adds an *existential aspect* in the understanding of time. The fear of death plays no decisive role in the biblical stories, nor does the concern of man with the shortness of life, with the after-life, with the resurrection of the soul and/or the body. The fear of death, the shortness of life, the ideas that were central in the Hellenistic philosophical schools, overdetermine the historical concept of time. Time is both historical and personal time, the time of a people, the time of each man and woman. The care of the self is the care of one's time, care for the use of the short time that one spends on Earth.

While facing the after-life, eternal salvation and damnation, the short journey becomes absolutely decisive. As far as the fate of the world (worldtime) is concerned, it is only Satan who fights against the limitedness of time: the end result of the worldtime is salvation – time works for God, not for Satan. Satan must act fast, for his time is limited.[10] In the "lifetime," however, salvation is not granted; it is not the "outcome." One can also be damned. There is little time to put sins right, to act such as to avoid damnation.[11] To sum up: there is already a tension between the concepts of worldtime and lifetime in Christian imagination, although the two concepts of time are mythologically bridged. But from this difference a gap opens up in modern times.

Without engaging myself in the long story of the modern concept of time, I will do it only in a "shorthand" way.

The concept of time in classical mechanics is the objective concept of time pure and simple. It is an absolute concept. The infinite universe is like a container, in which time always "exists." Time is the sum total of all of the motions and changes that are happening within the container, which means that everything exists "in time"; that is, within the unknown container.[12] We are infinitely small, and life is infinitely short, in the (impossible) comparison with the container (time/space) itself.

Historical time, on the other hand, begins to be divided into *prehistoric and historical time*. Prehistoric time is not external to the world, to the universe – not even to the Earth. Rather, it is external to the things which are "ours." To divide up time into *prehistoric and historical* time from Bacon to Hobbes, Vico to Rousseau, was the prelude to the grand narrative; it was the first manifestation of modern historical imagination. It already performed the task of legitimation and de-legitimation, an essentially ideological function, although it was devoid of mythological roots – both metaphysical or transcendent ones. The concept of time of technological imagination (progress, truth as the offspring of time) appeared simultaneously.[13]

The dividing line between objective time and lifetime is not exactly the same as the dividing line between the time concepts of technological and of historical imagination. Technological imagination frequently co-constitutes the concepts of historical time (for example, through the idea of universal progression) without controlling them in full. The concept of "objective time," on the other hand, seems to be fully technological. It is, after all, the "measured time." In the quantified time, measuring and quantifying are typical "technological" categories. "Objective time" is not existential: it has no relation to men, nor to the single exister, nor to people; it is a speculative concept of time with no practical relevance.[14] This concept has no function, and it seemingly has no use, except in space physics. Still, it does have a use, albeit a negative one; it constantly confirms the death of God; it offers a concept of time that excludes God, that makes Him (to speak with Laplace) superfluous in the universe. *It pushes God back into history and into the world of the single exister.*

Let me return to Heidegger's lecture on time in 1924, and to his elaboration of time in his *Being and Time* in 1927.[15]

In this scenario, lifetime is *Dasein* itself, and worldtime is mechanical, objective time. Time, as lifetime, becomes sense (meaning). There is no more meaning *in* life, just as there is no more happening *in* time. *Dasein's* historicity is the opening of sense/senselessness. "The analysis of Dasein's historicity tries to show: this being is not temporal because it 'stands in time,' but, conversely, it can only exist historically because its being is fundamentally temporal," (trans. A. H.) writes Heidegger.[16] *Dasein*, of course, is *also in* time, for it needs the watch and the calendar in order to exist. But it can be only in time, for it *is* time. Heidegger approaches the question of time from the perspective of everyday life, and this is why objective time is pointed out as the watch and the calendar, and not as the speed of light.

It is obvious that the aforementioned differentiation between lifetime and worldtime is very contemporary. For our peasant ancestors, the four seasons of nature were intertwined and interchangeable.[17] There was no watch; one oriented oneself by the sun. The yellow grain indicated that these was a time for harvest, just as menstruation indicated that there was a time for a girl to marry. The fact that life is limited, and that we are going to die, is no novelty. That humans stand under time pressure is commonplace. What, then, is new in Heidegger's distinction between lifetime and worldtime (objective time) after WWI?

The discovery of "lifetime" as distinct from objective, measurable time, as the time of *personal experience*, preceded WWI. I could trace it back to Kierkegaard,[18] yet its first *debut* in literature was beyond any doubt in Flaubert's *Education Sentimantale*.[19] Bergson's discussion of subjective time *qua* stream of experience, Husserl's conception of the lifeworld, and the combination of the two conceptions by Alfred Schutz[20] show the popularity of the idea. The classic portrayal of the pre-WWI experience of time was and remains Proust's *Remembrance of Things Past*. The new time experience had been thus "eternalized."

There is but a nuance of difference between the pre-WWI and post-WWI conceptions of lifetime, but this difference is decisive.[21] Both the Flaubertian, Bergsonian, and Proustian "lifetime" as *Erlebnis*-time, and the Heideggerian lifetime as historicity are contrasted with "objective time," clock time, calendar time, and mechanistic time. In both cases, "Lifetime" is, or at least can be, authentic, whereas objective time is either inauthentic or indifferent to authenticity.[22] However, subjective time as experienced time denounces history, and life *as* history (not just life *in* history) as inauthentic. The pre-WWI lifetime conception is "decadent," to employ a Nietzschean word, whereas the Heideggerian time conception is "avant-gardist." The latter turns the experience of subjectivity into a destined fate (*Geschick*), into something sent, or self-sent, into teleological time, historical in a deeper sense, more precisely historical in the meaning of "sense." Time as *Dasein* does not turn its back on history, as on something external and mechanical, but becomes history itself. For Proust, meaning is meaning-rendering, whereas meaning rendering is subjective, and strictly individual; furthermore, it happens in retrospect, in grasping and thus *eternalizing* lost time. "Time" and "time" differ from one another according to their density. Density is experience and remembrance (just another experience). But remembrance is not like *Geschick*; just the opposite, it is always in shambles, it consists of mosaics which do not fit. It can be always overwritten – there is no *telos* there. The ephemeral, the contingent, is and becomes the text of recollection, and it does not lose its ephemeral character, its mosaic-like feature, in the infinite stream of remembrance. The streams do not lead in a direction; there are many streams. Yet they do not annul one another, because it is not the direction but the remembrance of memory and the experience stamped on it that is important. If you ask the "lifetime" of Flaubert, Bergson, and Proust the question, "Where are we going?" there will be no answer, not even "Nowhere."[23] Heidegger's lifetime is activist. It decides about its authenticity and/or nonauthenticity. In *resolve Dasein* returns to itself, chooses its tradition, and creates an authentic history along with its generation.[24]

I have dwelled for quite a while on the difference between the Heideggerian understanding of "lifetime" in the 1920s, and that of Flaubert, Bergson, and Proust.[25] There is a historical sequence in the appearance of those two conceptions on the stage.[26] But by now "the order of appearance" has lost its significance. One can understand lifetime both in the pre-WWI and post-WWI versions, and one can also contrast it with worldtime in several ways. Characters choose their "lifetime" interpretation according to their character and experiences.

Time exists only for man. This is an old wisdom – not only in a world in which God is dead, but in all possible human worlds. God is timeless (eternal) and the whole of human history exists simultaneously in His eternal mind. The sequence of the simultaneous is human experience. Or, to employ a more archaic metaphor: time is spun as the sequence of events – but both the thread and the pattern of the end product is there before destiny starts the work of spinning the tapestry; yet the result is hidden from the human eye.

It is certainly "vulgar"[27] to speak about time as the sequence of events. But this flat statement (time is the sequence of events) can serve as a starting-point. There is no time without something being "earlier" and "later." It is not just that the calendar cannot operate without "earlier" and "later" – nothing does. We are children earlier in life; later, we are adults. The sexual act precedes the birth of children; dying is earlier than being dead. I would add that "earlier" and "later" (I will come to speak about this later!) has no analogy in the concept of space. (The designations of "right" and "left" are not analogous to "earlier" and "later." And, of course, being close and remote in space is analogous to being close and remote in time.) Moreover, "continuity" and "discontinuity" are also both spatial and temporal concepts. Yet, I repeat that "earlier" and "later" are only temporal.

This "vulgar" concept stands out as the *differentia specifica* of temporality, a *differentia specifica* which is there both in the concept of lifetime and of worldtime. There is "earlier" and "later" for us just as it was for all human beings, and always will be.[28]

Earlier and later are *primordial historical categories*. They are the only primordial historical categories of temporality. And they are relative and relate to *concrete* things and events. The "earlier" and the "later" are categories that are unfit for metaphysical use. The question of what came first, the chicken or the egg, is totally irrelevant in terms of the categories earlier and later, for in terms of these categories (which are always in relation, and never absolute or categorical) one can only ask which was earlier: *this* egg or *this* chicken. And then one is certainly expected to give a straightforward answer.

There are synchronoptic world histories; and there are maps showing what has happened in China, India, Mexico, England, and Russia at the same time. But it would be nonsensical to say that the Maya kingdom collapsed earlier than Czar Peter's ascension to the throne of Russia. Historical events happen "earlier" or "later" if they belong to the *same* story. Earlier and later are temporal categories of narratives, or at least of *possible narratives*. If one can at least tell a common story of two events, if two (or more) events could at least be connected by a chain, one can reasonably speak in terms of "earlier" and "later."

By now, all of the cultures on Earth have become synchronized in the sense that they have become coeval. It makes sense to say that the collapse of the Soviet Union happened earlier than the democratic elections in South Africa.[29] The best indicator of the world becoming "one world" is that there are significant events in every place of the world which can be connected with other significant events on the time scale of "earlier/later" and that this would make sense. One could tell a common story of the world after WWII. But this story would still be a sketchy one, although meaningful and significant, since each and every place in the world offers their events and happenings to other stories. And so does every exister's life. That I am born earlier or later than someone else is of interest in my contact (connection) to this other person. For my birth and his, mine earlier and his later, can be connected in one single story only if *we* two are connected. This connection can be personal, but it can also be an "ideal" encounter. I could not read a book in my childhood which was written later, and I could not personally experience happenings earlier than the first records of my memory.

The narrative that connects the distinction "earlier/later" can be causal as well as argumentative. In fact, it was Hume who first said that the causal relation is a narrative of earlier/later. What happens earlier is the cause of what happens later: or, in a teleological narrative, what happens later is the cause (final cause) of what happens earlier. Whatever happens later than X cannot be understood as the efficient cause of X. In argumentation, the conclusion comes later than the propositions. If the conclusion comes earlier than the proposition, one is moving in a "vicious" circle.

I said that the distinction "earlier/later" makes sense in concrete contexts, that there is no "later" or "earlier" in general; only in something, of something. I could have added that "earlier/later" is also relative to the speaker. The speaker says: earlier, later. I told you earlier; I will tell you later. The speaker's position can be described as the position of the present. "Earlier" and "later" are relative to the present. They can be described as no-longer-present or not-yet-present. But this is not so. For the speaker can speak in the past tense as well as in the future tense. I can tell my friend to come and visit me tomorrow. He says, "I will come in the afternoon," and I answer, "Please, come earlier." In this case I am speaking in the future tense (I expect my friend tomorrow), but I do not relate the "earlier" to the present, but directly to the "later." There is no "present," then, between this earlier and the later.

The human exister is a crossing point of many heterogeneous kinds of earlier(s) and later(s). At the moment of my birth there is (for me) no earlier. In fact, before the first memory trace there is no "earlier." The first memory trace is the "earliest." It is not related to the "present" unless the person him- or herself *is* the present (not as *Dasein*, but as a single exister). For the dying man, there is no such thing as "later." (An afterlife is not the later of the concrete body/soul that we are.) *Life itself* can then be described as the intersection of earliers and laters. You make a promise earlier; you keep it or do not keep it later. Every process of learning is a series of earlier(s) and later(s); so is every experience. This cavalcade of heterogeneous series (stories) of earliers and laters is responsible for the twofold subjective time experience. The more one learns and the more one experiences, the more "the earliers" will accumulate, the more one gets the impression of "how much" time has elapsed, and "how fast is time running away." The years which are said to go by are just the numerical embodiments of the earlier/later relationship. That we are getting one year older gives us the impression that one year has been added to the "earlier," yet also taken away from the "later." As long as someone is young, it is a great joy that one year is added to the "earlier" (for learning and experiencing is the chain of later/earlier). If one is confident that one has accumulated enough, and that the earlier(s) and later(s) have assumed a good balance, one begins to worry when increasingly more years are added to the "earlier" because "time goes by." But panic grasps the mind if "time goes by" without the accumulation of the earlier(s), where the "earlier" remains thin: this is called "wasted time."

Things can happen "too early" or come "too late" in life. Coming too early means that there was not yet time for it; coming too late means that there is no longer enough time for it. In both cases the problem lies with the difficulty or impossibility of inserting something (a possible experience) into a sensible life story.

The "earlier" and the "later" are often substituted by the terms "before" and "after." Before and after are also spatial expressions, whereas earlier and later are only temporal. I think, however, that earlier and later are the primordial categories or experiences of time (temporality), because of their elasticity and indeterminacy. Mostly, one can substitute before and after for earlier and later, but one needs to add *a determination* to them. For example, that I come earlier than Christmas is not identical with that I come before Christmas, because it can mean that I come just before Christmas or many days (many weeks) before Christmas. I cannot replace the sentence "I come later" with the sentence "I come after" because in saying that I come after I need to say what it is after, and whether it is shortly after or long after.

I think that objective and measured[30] time, the through and through quantified and homogeneous time, is processed from the experience of earlier and later by extracting its essential elasticity, its concreteness and indeterminacy. Before/after, the spatialization of the temporal categories earlier/later, lend themselves to homogenization and quantification of the time experience better than do the primordial categories of earlier/later.

On the ground of my former rumination, it stands to reason why I have my doubts about the Heideggerian distinction between the authentic and the nonauthentic temporality of *Dasein*. Running toward death or being-toward death is also, in my thinking, one of the aspects of authenticity. But running toward death is running toward the intersection at which everything becomes earlier, with nothing later remaining. Authenticity is not just this running ahead, but is also resting on the "earliers" which were accumulated at the moment toward which one is running ahead. Authenticity, in my conception, is also "to run ahead," not as being-toward-death but as being-toward-the-earlier, being toward the density of the earlier(s) with no later.

Even if "earlier" and "later" are not necessarily related to the present, they can be. In the manifold heterogeneous uses and experiences of earlier/later, an outstanding one is the experience of past/future. What comes later is the future; what happened earlier is the past. If earlier/later are indicating past/future in relation to the present, the earlier becomes no-longer and the later not-yet. In fact, the present is nothing but the intersection of the not-yet and the no-longer. The present is as elastic as the not-yet and the no-longer, because it depends on the concrete content and quality of the thing earlier (no longer) and later (not yet) that a present in fact is. How long can I dwell in the present? Is the present extended? It is not always extended, but it can be. We can speak of the present age. Then the not-yet is the future age, and the no-longer is the past age. The present age can last for a long time. It can last longer than the exister. I can also speak of the present in the sense of "just now." If I do this, the present disappears into the unimaginable and unexperiencible infinitely small.[31]

The "earlier" is recollected in remembrance and memory. It is (in a double sense) impossible for the exister to live in the past alone. He or she cannot recollect without the present and future. If he or she has no future he or she dies, and ceases to remember. And he or she cannot live in the past alone, because the traces of his or her "bygone" experiences are enlivened more frequently than not, brought to the surface, and also modified and interpreted by the representative (and sometimes even less representative) others. History is always shared. One remembers an experience regarding one's relation to others, and one remembers along with others. Thus the earlier as bygone – as past – is shared, but rarely fully shared: shared with some, but not with others, shared with some who are no longer. Some others rob you of your past, for they look at your bygone experiences with an entirely alien glance. They change your past; they destroy the buildings of your remembrances, so that only ruins are left – as they can also find for you a lost rose among those ruins. Thus your past, the hunting ground of your remembrance, is always endangered. You have to protect it against attacks, but if you protect it too much you endanger it too. *Lived history is the greatest blessing (and luckiest thing) in life.*[32] Lived history happens if two (perhaps a few, but not many) men or women live together so that they share experiences, mutually work on their past, and become transparent for one another so that their bygone experience is not endangered. They do not feel the lack of time; they do not say that time goes too fast or crawls too slowly. They do not complain that something came to early or something came too late, for they do not notice time, since they are living history.

There is no absolute present tense in the exister's experience of time, with the exception of the few minutes of happiness in which time and eternity cross, and "time stands still."[33]

But I have said[34] that contemporary, postmodern men and women have resolved to live in the absolute present tense. I now have to briefly explain how this is meant.

The modernist man who was clinging to the grand narrative pretended to know what will happen to the human race in the distant future. He lived (in thought) in this distant future. He drew "knowledge" about the distant future from the story of mankind. Thus, he looked into the past as to a storehouse of frozen memories, of the finally stamped and understood series of events which, out of necessity, lead to the future. The present did not count. It was an intermediary stage. The only present that existed was merely personal (one has to make a living). But the present-as-such has not fired the imagination. And historical imagination needed a spark to burst into flame.

I spoke about the synchronization of the present world. Since the whole world has become modern and coeval, the whole world shares the "present age." It is the heaviest "present age" ever carried on the backs of historical people. The task is to reduce the gap between the ideal of modernity and the actual empirical state of modernity. This means that one takes responsibility for the present.

Modernity has set in; the "present age" is here and now. The future of the present (to close the gap between the idea of modernity and its facticity) is not distant. It is not a remote point on the horizon; it is not something that happens – if it happens – much, much later. Closing the gap is approximation. One always approximates. The work of Sisyphus is to approximate. One approximates in view of the future. It is a long journey, and the end of the journey is not in sight, yet one knows *what* the end of the journey is to be. No imagination has to be set on fire. The goal is the future-of-the-present, for it is the accomplishment, the "end" of the present. This is a simple state of affairs. And this is what I meant when I said that we (post)moderns are living in the absolute present tense, Historically, there is absolute present tense (which includes the past of the present and the future of the present). Yet the fundamental existential temporality of men and women has not changed.

This conclusion – if it is a conclusion – may be surprising. For I took as my starting-point the fundamental distinction between worldtime and lifetime, between objective time and subjective time, between measured time and temporality as historicity. I emphasized that these distinctions are modern, that they appear directly before and after WWI, and I even offered a sketchy picture of them. I do not deny that many experiences have been transformed and have taken on a new shape. But I speak of the fundamental time experience of the exister. And, so I believe, it still remains the primordial experience of earlier and later, and the constant toil or pleasure to put the earlier(s) and the later(s) into pretty chains, to connect them with loose threads, tie them by narratives with causality or teleology, the more the better – to tie them together, to be their recollection

of times bygone, traces of myths, stories of the Earth, of the con/stella-
tions, be they genetic codes, friendships and enmities, wars, mystical
experiences or fictions, stories of stories, and fairly tales. They are all
put together, combined, or set apart in imagination, just as they combine
themselves, set themselves apart, and recombine themselves earlier/later –
in short, they change. The change of the existers is time; the change of the
world shared by the existers is historical time. The change as such is
worldtime – but this is no time. The time of existers is finite; historical
time is finite. The change in worldtime can be finite and infinite. But
where is eternity?

12

Space, Place, and Home

The early modern world was born together with the revolution in the perception and concept of space, with the Copernican turn. The dramatic changes in man's time experience and concept of time followed only two centuries later.

The metaphysical systems of the 17th century had not yet faced the challenges of historicity. The fundamental and unanswerable question of Hegel and Kierkegaard, "How did eternal truth appear in time?" which later signalled the end of metaphysics, was not raised until the French Revolution or – in part – by Rousseau and Condorcet. But the "problem of space" was there right from the beginning of modern times.

By the problem of space I mean, firstly, the distinction between the concepts of *place* and *space*. The Aristotelian category is the category of place, and not of space. Neither the Greek/Roman Cosmos nor the Christian divine universe is a "space" or is "in" a space. God creates all things; He creates the heaven (sky) up there, the Earth down here, the sea, the fish, and the underworld down there. The concept of space appears with the thought of the infinite universe. From then on, the heavenly bodies are placed into a "space," and in Newton's universe space becomes the "container" other than time.

Physical space and metaphysical place coincided in ancient cosmology as well as in the Christian divine universe. This natural and easily sensitizable space/place conception had to be reworked and rethought after Descartes in 17th-century metaphysics. The reorganization of the metaphysical topology was to accommodate the modern concept of space, and as a result the hierarchical spatial arrangement of the universe had to be sacrificed. Thus modern metaphysics became less sensitizable and more abstract than its predecessors. Even Platonists and enemies of the mechanistic–Newtonian conception of the universe, such as Leibniz, abandon the graphic image of the metaphysical cosmos from "up" to "down," of the series of emanations of hypostases, and replace them with perspectivism, whereas totality, the Uncreated Monas, is not located in space but conceived of as the whole (as all perspectives together). Metaphysics thereby contributed to its own demise in reorganizing itself and accommodating itself to the mechanistic universe. Of course, "high" and "low," and "up" and "down," as elementary categories of orientation, preserve their metaphysical connotation of sacred/profane, light/dark, and noble/base – the very distinctions that predated metaphysics.

The opening up of infinite space made the human world shrink.[1] Simultaneously, man's allotted place (the Earth) began to be expanded. Exploration of the unknown territories of the Earth meant a drastic expansion of the human habitat for the Europeans of early modernity.[2] The thought of the eternal recurrence of the same, which had been expelled from the image of temporality roughly at the same time, became the truth about the perception of place. Our place, the Earth, was now thought as being rounded. It no longer had an end; it turned out that while travelling in one direction one would always return from where one had originally started, to begin once again.

Kant made the distinction between "knowing the world" and "having a world."[3] The opening up of infinite space, on the one hand, and the discovery of the unknown territories on the Earth, on the other hand, was at first a revolution in knowing the world. Learned men and women began to see the world and their place in the world in a different light. This meant at first that a huge gap was created between knowing the world and having a world. Kant, who wrote innovative books on the universe, on world history, and gave lectures about London Bridge, said that the world that *he had* was Konigsberg.

The *gap between knowing the world and having a world* constantly became wider, both in spatial and temporal experience. In fact, time is perceived and thought of as if it were space. One refers to remote worlds as those of faraway and scarcely known places on our globe, just as also to even lesser known worlds of times long gone. In both cases, the other world is at a distance. In both cases, the world-in-distance enflames imagination, just as it also elicits nostalgia, curiosity, the wish to be there, the wish to expand the world that we have. One can translate – in imagination – places, past times, or faraway continents into virtual places. Virtual places are present; they are *here*, not there. They are here *as fiction* without being fictitious, as the effective world of imagination. Fiction is not fictitious if it contains the image of things that are supposed to be actual/real. And the world of imagination is effective if it becomes intrinsic to existence, to life, to the "now" and its before and after.

Printing, the emergence of the Gutenberg galaxies,[4] has expanded virtual reality far beyond the world of myths and fairy tales; it has become a virtual reality that is known as having been as actual as ours, somewhere else and in another time – that those worlds were worlds once upon a time, or are worlds in a remote place that other men "have," just as we have ours. We have ours, but we know theirs; in this way we also have theirs – yet as *a virtual world*, which, as a virtual world, belongs to the actual world that we have. London Bridge has not belonged to the world Kant that "had," but the *image* of London Bridge did. It did because Kant translated his "information" into oral communication; he was conversing in Konigsberg in the early morning with a few young boys about London Bridge – thus London Bridge became a shared reality in Konigsberg. That is, the gap between the world that we have and the world that we know was connected by a *corridor*, filled with books, stories, and descriptions. The hunger for letters, stories, and descriptions is also the hunger to fill the gap between the world that we know and the world that we have. But in fact the gap is not filled. While swallowing the letters, one knows more and more about the remote world, but this knowledge expands mostly at the level of knowing, and not of having the world. Even the virtual world that one "has" is limited (because we are limited). In addition, the more one wants to expand one's world within a virtual space, the less intensive having the world becomes.

Extensity and intensity are at cross-purposes. The expansion of the virtual space (place and time) does not also result in the greater density of the experience of "having" a world. Somehow, however, intensity and extensity need to be reconciled, and some balance needs to be worked out. As Kant said, Konigsberg is a good world to "have," because it is somehow the microcosm of all the important things that are going on around the world that we know. One can have a very dense world which, on the contrary, is far from being the "microcosm" of the world that one knows.

There were certain places in Europe that played, in fact, the role of the *representative microcosm*. There were times when Rome played this role (particularly for the Germans), and also London, but first and foremost Paris. Men and women were longing to go there, because in those places "having a world" got closest to "knowing the world." The gap was not as great – at least so it was perceived. While walking on the streets of the "eternal city," in the city where the Bastille once stood – or in the city of the Parliament and of the Bank of England, the center of the new Empire – one was in a privileged position. One not only read the books, but one was also living in those books.[5]

An important difference between the relation with the "remote" past and the "remote" place soon made itself known. The distance in time was constantly increasing, whereas the distance in place was constantly shrinking. Historical imagination opens up new pasts that we know slightly but do not have, or cannot have without changing place; whereas technological civilization changes remote places into close places.

Distance is always measured in time. "How far is the next village?" you ask a highlander of Papua New Guinea, and he will answer "Two days distance." How far is this village now? An hour by car. The next village was remote; now it is close. How far is Paris? Two weeks distant. Nowadays, an hour by plane. Paris was a remote place; it is now close. The unbridgeable gap (in time) seems to be bridgeable (in space). The entire globe is accessible. It is small. One can get everywhere, and so one will. The craze of tourism is not just a pastime or a way to fill the empty hours of boredom. It is also a mad attempt to fill the gap between the world that we know (about) and the world that we have. If you visit this place, you are there. This is not a virtual journey, but an actual one. You are really standing there. You see with your own eyes. You capture it – you let your picture be taken with the Coliseum in the background.[6] One must be there *in body*, not merely in mind. One has to experience *in body* the shrinking of the Earth to get the illusion of having an actual and not a virtual world.

Contemporary tourism is not motivated by the desire to find the "microcosm" of the modern world. In order "to have a world" as a microcosm, one must stay in one place for a while, do things other people also do, live a daily life. A journey such as the Italian journey of Goethe lasts for seven years. In seven years one may manage to "have" a world, one may live in this self-selected microcosm to a certain extent. But contemporary modern tourism is different.

Modern/postmodern tourism is not the reason why the mythological places are losing their privileged positions as representative of "microcosms" of the modern world but, rather, the result of a slow erosion of the privilege. Paris is still Paris, and it still works on its own myth, but "to be in Paris" no longer has the same significance as it had 100 years ago. The modern world, as it is now understood, can be found everywhere, or at least in many places. Everywhere there are the same hotels, the same menus, and the same cinemas. Also there is a kind of English spoken everywhere, yet all places also offer their "specialities," their mostly artificially kept local traditions such as dances, bull fights, camel rides, and so on. In addition, one has the opportunity to see all places without in fact being there, without stretching one's imagination. I see Paris almost every day on the TV screen.

Once upon a time, Paris was a privileged place, for it was there that one could inhale and exhale the "contemporary" world as a whole, together with its most significant past (tradition). Venice, Florence, and Rome were also privileged places, for they presented – in a spatial nutshell – the great treasures of the European tradition. But in an omnivorous culture one can find interpretanda everywhere; a kind of tradition, or at least a kind of object of interest. Promiscuity was also substituted here for monogamy: one tries one city for a few days, then another one, and then a third – one does not remain faithful to any one of them.

Modern mass tourists move in the "actual world" (whether Paris or the River Amazon) as if it were a virtual world. Although they are there in body, for they endure the small hotel rooms that lack comfort, or the heat and the mosquitoes (this belongs to the experience of being there in body), they do not quite "have a world." They would not be able to maintain themselves in these worlds. They do not speak the language; they do not understand the gestures without further explanation; they cannot sing the nursery rhymes. They return from there to their "normalcy" just as one returns from a virtual world to the world of action. For one "has a world" only if one can change it, not only for oneself, but also for the denizens of the world. Kant could act such as to influence his fellow citizens in Konigsberg, yet he could influence the passengers crossing London Bridge as little as he could influence the universe. The readers of Balzac can dwell in this world, but they will not influence the acts of the characters in the novel. Goethe, who spent seven years in Italy, could influence his Italy in a few days, as well as that of a few fellow Italians. But a tourist running through the Louvre is just a number in the statistics of the French tourist industry. Something extraordinary needs to happen for a tourist to "have a world" in a place of his or her visit.[7]

I have described mass tourism as a mass movement to bridge the gap between knowing a world and having a world, to diminish the distance, to bring all things "close"; that is, familiar (I have seen it, I have been there, I visited it, I know). And I came to the conclusion that in fact those "close" worlds slip from their fingers: we can stay there, but we do not inhabit them. However, two transformations do take place. Firstly, the dense microcosms of significant places lose their privileged positions (places), yet instead there appears a common world of the "united tourists," a shared world, a world that many million people "have," in which they can position themselves, which they understand. The shared world of the "united tourists"[8] is a separate world. I speak about the world of the united tourists, but not only "tourists" are tourists. So are international businessmen, jetting lecturers, and regular conference participants, people who constantly move around the globe, jumping from hotel to hotel, from business dinner to business dinner. But to be a member of the club of the united tourists is not linked to high professionalism or a substantial income. Moving from the countryside to the city, from the city to the suburbs, or from the suburbs to another city, *transforms a person into a tourist in his or her home country.* And if emigration/ immigration were to be solely determined by personal preference or choice, the whole globe would by now be in constant motion, with people seeking work here and there, trying to succeed in different places. Americans can eat with chop sticks, and Chinese with the knife and fork, one wears Indian dresses and Eskimo hats, drinks herbal teas made from oriental spices, and practices the religions of a remote place. This "united mass tourism" is also frequently termed multiculturalism.

The change in space experience and the change in time experience in modern life are generally not just intertwined, but barely discernible. Good examples of this are the revolutions in telecommunications and transportation. But as there is a novel time experience that can be linked only indirectly to space experience (the distinction between subjective and objective temporality), so there is an essential space experience that is only indirectly linked to time experience, but plays an absolutely decisive role in the conduct of the lives of modern men: *urbanization.* How radically the modern metropolis differs from the traditional urbs (city) is a topic that has been so wisely discussed that I cannot add anything of substance to it. But it needs to be mentioned that urbanization has contributed to the relativization of home experience. Given that in a metropolis everyone is a stranger, if one leaves one's closest environment, workplace, family, and entourage of friends, one can also behave as a "universal tourist" in the city of one's birth. Urban sociology is frequently practiced by "natives."

The question remains as to whether there is a privileged place for modern men and women, a place that could still be described as the center of their world.

Just as the self has become de-centered, so the world-one-has (and not the world one just knows) has become de-centered. Traditionally, we have called the center of a world that we have our "home." But where are we at home? Do modern men and women "have" a home?

I referred to the de-centered self not in order to find a good metaphor, for an entirely de-centered self has no identity (whereas an only and rigidly one-centered self(s) identity is also inflexible and rigid). Similarly, an entirely one-centered world (which one has) differs absolutely from the world that one knows. An entirely one-centered world displays a rigid continuity and a rigid identity (collective world identity). If the world is many centered, so that no center has a privileged position (in the world that we have), there is "multiculturalism," for all centers are de-centering identities but, in all likelihood, men and women are nowhere really "at home." If one is never at home, one only has left the united world of tourism, in which one can act, understand, or move with some confidence. But since the united world of tourism is through and through a modern virtual and actual reality, it has *no tradition*. A man or woman who lives in no other world center but that of the united world of tourism will live without tradition. A person without tradition is a person who lacks historical imagination and must live exclusively on the meager ideological diet of technological imagination. This means that without setting foot on one (or two, or three) privileged points or centers on Earth, one will lose the double-bind.

The center is called the home. The home is "close." The farther away something is from "home," the more remote it becomes. I repeat that I speak of close and remote in the sense of "having a world." My "close" friend can be far away and I can still share[9] a world with him; whereas my next-door neighbor in an apartment house in a metropolis can be a total stranger.

The simplest way to distinguish the "close" from the "remote" is by the *length* of communication of the same information. Assume that a person wants to tell something to another person, something which is – for her – of great significance. The closer the relationship is, the briefer the length (the path) of communication is, for "close persons" understand one another without words, by allusions, in an abbreviated manner – they speak shorthand. Yet, the length of the path of communication itself does not decide as to whether the common ground of the interlocutors is a "home," or whether they share the united world of tourism. The second criterion that distinguishes the close from the distant in communication is whether the communicated message belongs to the function that a person performs in the division of positions and ranks of the social arrangement. If two people can communicate in shorthand, but neither of them at least enters a communication about the function that he or she performs, the length of the communication will indeed be a good seismograph that signals closeness or remoteness.

Obviously, closeness/remoteness is not one-dimensional. Two persons can be brought up in the same culture, in the same real or metaphorical "home," and thus can communicate with one another without further explanation, understand each other through gestures, and take many things for granted – but in addition they can be childhood friends, or sisters or brothers, just as they can also be strangers who happened to meet yesterday by accident in a café. The communication between the interlocutors will be shorter in each and every case of "closeness" than in the case of an accidental encounter, because the less the distance is, the more things are taken for granted.[10] Yet, different things can be taken for granted, and the communication can take place on different levels. The abbreviation of communication indicates whether mutual understanding is also spontaneous or instinctual. The less I know about my interlocutor and she of me, the more rational my communication/conversation will be, in the sense that I will make mental efforts to read the signs of the other person, and read them properly, and I will also make great mental efforts, conscious efforts, to emit signs that can be understood by my interlocutor according to my intentions. The less familiar the encounter is, the less I can be sure of being understood according to my intentions and the more cautious I need to be.[11]

There is a center (or there are a few centers) – we have a home, a tradition, an elastic group (ethnic, national, or religious) identity – if there exists a periphery or many peripheries, if there are traditions other than ours, if there are identities other than ours, if there are places where we are not at home, where we are strangers or aliens. In the absence of alien places, we know that there is no home.

In the traditional world, the home and alien places were strictly and traditionally separated. There was no need to leave home and then return in order to realize that one either had or did not have a home. But in the modern world the question of home "being at home" *becomes a question.* And since it is a question, it can be answered in different ways.

It is a question because one leaves home (and one either returns or does not). To return also means to recognize. One recognizes that which is familiar is in the "strange."

What were once immortal stories of mythological significance now become daily occurrences.

In the old myths, *recognition* occupies the place of a primordial emotional and intellectual experience. In Plato's representative dialogues it is the philosopher who acquires the ability to recognize the idea (of the Good) that he saw before birth; Orestes and Electra, and Orestes and Iphigeneia, recognize each other. According to Aristotle's *Poetics* it is the "recognition scene" that makes tragedy great and forceful.[12]

Why is recognition a "spatial" experience? Something very close to us is lost (or goes away, or we are the ones who leave home) and then, suddenly and unexpectedly, we meet. We meet in the body (even the ghost of Hamlet's father has to appear in the body). We are close, we see each other face to face; everything gets close except the mind. And then, as suddenly as a flash of lightening, we recognize one another, embrace, and kiss – it is the unity of the body, the side-by-side, the absolute vicinity, that stamps recognition.[13]

We recognize. The great triumph of recognition is not just the great triumph of love (that the beloved is *close to our heart*), but also the triumph of home. Let us go home to our Father's house, says Plotinus.[14] The Gnostic hero leaves the exile of the Earth and goes home to the source of Light; redemption is also homecoming. Homecoming is the most ancient, the most primordial source of joy. It is also salvation.

In modern times, homecoming becomes a matter of routine. We return from our workplace or from a holiday or, conversely, we return for a holiday. We return from another country to visit our parents. We speak another language and then return to our mother tongue. But what has remained of the great joy? What about the felicity of the moment of recognition? Do we still have a home? Or do we live (as does the Gnostic wanderer) in our eternal exile? Can one live in exile if one has no home? And what do we recognize in returning home (if there is a home)? Are we homesick? What kind of sickness is this?

Homesickness means that one is longing to return home. But it could also mean that one is getting sick of being at home. The moderns are homesick in both understandings of the word. This emotional relation to the centerpoint of life (in place), both its attraction and its repulsion, is one of the recurring experiences of the paradoxes of modern life, such as the fear of freedom and the fear of unfreedom, the desire for independence and the desire to belong, of individualism and communitarianism. Again, there is no single tendency that leads in one direction or the other but, rather, a pendulum movement; certainly not in each and every person's life – because much depends here on psychological or moral character – but in cultures (of universality or difference, of individuality or collectivism, and so on), where the rhythmical recurrences of the two extremes, one after the other, are frequent.

The center in place (home) stands for all of the other centers, and not only metaphorically. Homesickness (in a double meaning) also stands for the experiences (desires) that motivate men and women in many other instances: in turning their backs on one extreme in order to embrace another, and vice versa, in a fairly rhythmic motion. (Again, I do not mean that every single person follows this rhythm.) To be sure, modern men's relation to transcendence is also one of the manifestations of homesickness: one can rejoice because God is dead, one can experience the death of God as the liberation from an other-worldly authority, as freedom. Yet, one can also be filled with anxiety while longing to go back to the bosom of the protection of the Certainty, the Absolute. One can vacillate between those extremes, as one can experience both feelings simultaneously, and one frequently does.[15]

Homesickness is a melancholy feeling. One suffers because one is living far away from something that one calls "home." If one were only there in the familiar place and not here in an alien and strange world, one would be filled with joy and happiness.[16] And if one feels sick of being at home, this is also a melancholy feeling. One suffers because the distant, the faraway, the unknown and the unexplored places promise joy and happiness. In both cases, one feels a *lack*, an internal empty place; something is missing – the most important thing is missing, and life becomes empty. Why is life "empty"? Why do we all employ the metaphor of the "empty" space? Emptiness reads that "nothing is there." Obviously, something is there. The feeling of melancholia or depression is also something; it is "there." Does "empty" mean the absence of continuity? Continuity of what? Of the personality? Or, perhaps the "soul" is empty because the center is missing.

If something is happening "there" or experienced "there," the *what* of the experience is not a presence but an *absence* – the absence of the center, or the absence of the source of joy. If the source of joy is absent, one cannot say "yes" to life, even without having any concrete cause or reason for despair.

One would believe that a person might suffer from depression, from the "emptiness inside," if he or she is incapable of experiencing joy or happiness. But in fact, depression, or melancholia, is more likely to grasp a man's or woman's soul if they are – or at least believe that they are – capable of joy and happiness. It is only that the root or the source of happiness is "out there" it is far away, beyond one's grasp. It is the *distance* from happiness, even from the promise of happiness, that makes the "homesick" melancholic.[17]

"I would be happy at home," one says; "I could be happy if I could only leave home," says the other. There are also frequently two persons in one. "If I could only return to my native city," says one; "If I could only leave my native city," says the other. "If I could have a family, if I were only surrounded by my children," says one, "If I could only get rid of the prisonhouse of my family," says the other – and these two may be two in one. "If only life had not have changed since my youth," says one, "If only life had changed more since my youth," says the other – and they are often two in one.[18]

The modern world is the world of *diaspora*. Since we are born contingent – and are also aware of our contingency – we are strangers, aliens, wherever we are born. Since we are aware of our finitude and have lost our faith in the after-life and, furthermore, because we experience transience[19] every day, we feel like visitors in this place. We are suffering from the thought that our journey on Earth is always cut short.

"Short" is a spatiotemporal expression. Short for what? Nothing is short in itself, but short for something. Most people say that life is short because they would like to continue living. But, in a deeper sense, life is short because one cannot overcome the feeling of being alien. One cannot become "familiar" with the world and with other significant men and women in one's life, and one desires other places to "explore."

The universal mass tourist is not a stranger, nor is he homesick. He understands as much as he needs to understand. He worries, but he is not melancholic. He is happy in the sense that he normally has a good time. He worries because life is short, and he will not have a good time 100 years from now.

For the homesick, life is short because of the distance; life is too short to transform the world that one knows into a world that one has. As long as I feel myself to be an alien, a stranger, as long as I fail to understand men who are closest to me, there is no home in which I could rest, even if I were to be formally "at home," in my birthplace, in my city, in my street.

Life is short, in relation to the capacity of modern men and women to have a world.[20] One never has a world in full. Homesickness is a melancholy feeling elicited by the awareness that life is too "short" to become familiar with it, to understand even one single person.

Life is "short" – but it is not always "too short" in this existential understanding of "being short." One can experience the shortness of life only quantitatively. Life is short in this primary sense if one does not live for 100 years. People try hard to live for 100 years or more, but this is an inauthentic perception of the relative "shortness" of life.

The authentic perception of the shortness of life (life is too short to have a world) arises only in men and women who desire to have a world; it does not arise in the minds of the universal mass tourists. If one is aware of being alien and still longs (desires) to be more familiar in the world – whether in one's own or in "other" worlds – the shortness of life is not quantitative but qualitative. And this quality is termed the *transience* of human life. It is this *quality* that a modern person has to learn to live with.[21] We do not return to the warmth of the stable, just as we do not return to our mother's wombs. We will never be protected, nor will we be dumb or ignorant if we do not want to be. We can return "home," but this will not be the home or the warmth of the stable. Many things will remain familiar and many things will change. No one will we know absolutely, least of all ourselves. We will not have a world in the way in which we once did. We will keep our distance, and also suffer from the distance. The bodies, after having touched one another, will part. We are born, and we are born moderns. The umbilical cord has been cut in a double way by modern men and women.[22]

Remoteness and closeness in exterior distance, and remoteness and closeness in interior distance, are in constant interplay. In this sense, space/place experience does not differ from time experience. The historicity of the exister is as much spatial as temporal. From birth to death, we are here, and not there. We are here in body. We have set foot on Earth for a while as some/body. Having set foot on Earth as some/body is an internal experience. We do not need to see ourselves in the mirror to know that we are extended beings; we are living among extended beings like ourselves. This is the human condition. So is the conflict between interior and exterior.

The metaphysical and, generally, the religious descriptions of the relation between interior and exterior have problems with the body.[23] The interior is the "soul"; the soul has no extension. The interior is the spirit (nous). It is, by definition, spiritual. It is again a substance (or a faculty), and has no extension. In Spinoza the substance has two attributes – thinking and extension. Thinking is by definition nonextended. The problem with the body is that it is extended. Yet, although it is extended, the human body cannot be understood in the same manner as all other bodies (the bodies of nonhuman animals included). The interiority of the bodily experience – that is, the internal spiritual experience of our own extension – needs to be addressed as a problem. In addition, emotions and feelings are also bodily sensations, yet they are interior and some of them are spiritual. Extension is then something effective "inside" as well as "outside" – there is a connection. Finding the connection implies the so-called mind–body problem, as well as the problem of space/place or of extension.

An already quoted passage by Foucault comes to mind again here:[24] in modern times, the body is imprisoned in the soul. Whatever else this observation refers to, it says something important about the change in the perception of the interior/exterior relation. As long as the soul was imprisoned in the body, as long as this was the dominating understanding of interior/exterior, the soul was always the "interior" and the body the "exterior." But what if one can imagine that the body is imprisoned by the soul? This would mean – if we were to follow the metaphor literally – that the body becomes the interior and the soul the exterior. In fact, however, it means something else: it means the relativization between external and internal, exterior and interior, the disappearance of the traditional puzzle of the body. The soul and the body become indistinguishable. It is in this sense, too, that modern culture is "materialistic" and not "spiritualistic."[25] The other sense is that men and women prefer material goods to spiritual goods. But this difference is also relativized. It is less and less possible to point to spiritual goods that are not "material"[26] – with the sole exception of the eternal felicity of the soul. But even religious men and women now rarely entertain this idea of spirituality.

The name Sigmund Freud symbolizes the modern revolution of the relativization of the corporeal and the spiritual. He was the most significant among those prison guards who released the old prisoner (the soul) from the prison cell (the body), now to send the body into the prison cell of the soul, or at least to unmask the body as a phantom soul, and as its own prison guard. This was the most effective reversal of metaphysics of them all.[27]

Freud presents a spatial map of the soul. All of his major metaphors are spatial.[28] For example, he speaks about the conscious mind as the "tip of the iceberg," he describes "the ruins" of already sunken experiences that one can detect in the psyche, and so on. The spatial arrangement is also temporal. For example, the id is not only spatially deeper but also temporally older than other parts or levels of the psyche. And above all, the external/internal relation is relativized; for example, the same particular psychic experiences are rendered in all types of childhood development.

Just as the body, the corporeal existence, the extended thing "between" the merely material things and the spiritual soul, remained the great and insoluble mystery of metaphysics, so did the "soul" or psyche become the mystery of modern times. One must find the extension for the soul and understand the soul as a *spatial* phenomenon, a phenomenon that can be pinned down and fully understood – for only that which is extended can be fully understood. The merely "internal" is to be deciphered as an *epiphenomenon*. This is the direction that the solution of the so-called mind–body problem also takes.

The Freudian spatiotemporal understanding of the psyche also relativizes the relation between close and remote in a stronger sense than does historical imagination.

The remote exists (in historical imagination) insofar as it is *here*. Without seeing the traces of something, one cannot feel the absence (the lack) of this thing, one cannot dream oneself into a bygone world, "far" in the past. Yet one needs to "see" the traces just to feel the absence, to know about the remote without knowing it, to "present" the remote.

But in the Freudian scenario the traces do not need to be seen or known; they are not conscious. They are only negatively "presencing" in the understandable personality disturbances before they are detected through the disturbances as their efficient (and sufficient) cause by the analyst. For example, the mythologically/historically remote killing of the father is omnipresent, for its traces are detectable in the repetition of the same story in the early years of every (male) child.

An unconscious trace as a temporal occurrence must also have a "place."

The consciously received trace – for example, the burial place of ancestors as a trace of their "world" – is "placed" in the mind "from the outside" even if the desire for such a trace, the desire to expand the world that one now has, comes from the "inside." Yet the place of the unconscious trace is "here"; it is "within" somewhere, it does not come from the outside. To put it better, only the *conditions* that may mobilize the trace and illuminate the internal memory come from outside. This motive is a quasi-repetition of the *concept of hereditary sin, yet in reverse*. The killing of the father is inscribed into our soul/body. The remote is close, yet it is not inscribed as a sin but as suffering.[29] *The two concepts of evil change place*. Evil as moral evil is transformed into evil as suffering, while the evil that originates in the evil soul is again transformed into the evil suffered by a soul/body. The fathers have eaten sour grapes and the teeth of the sons are set on edge indeed.

The Freudian logic is even more interesting than the former description. Since the remote is close and the evil gets close in the form of suffering, to liberate a man from this suffering requires a change in the topos of the "complex" – the unconscious need to become conscious, the Id to be turned into Ego. Freud expresses this in spatial terms, and rightly so: *"where* id has been, ego should be."[30] Liberation is the spatial extension of the Ego, the occupation of the Id-territory by the Ego, the liberation from the past by the present. If the historical is not only temporal, but spatiotemporal, and if the space in which the mythological/historical is constantly dwelling is "in" the "inside," and if the locus of the past-as-close is the locus of suffering, the inside needs to be cleared of the ruins of the past. It needs to close the shop of remoteness as the closure and make itself scrutable. It needs to make itself matter-of-fact and future-oriented. The healing is the abandonment of the double-bind (in the psyche). It is to translate the psyche into something rational and technological.

As with every kind of liberation, this also has its price. If the liberation were to be crowned by success, one would produce the universal tourist. True, the psyche of the universal tourist does not suffer; it is not melancholic. Moreover, the universal tourist is not even a dangerous species.

Universal tourists do not kill by being motivated by unconscious, obscure, and primordial impulses. They will kill, if they will, only in cold blood.

I have scrutinized Freud's thoughts only marginally and one-sidedly, from the perspective of his topology, the remodelling of the internal space alone. But this aspect, namely Freud's relativization of the categories of internal/external,[31] soul/body, remote/close, and historical/spatial, has changed the modern perception of space experience.

The assessment of the healing practices that follow from the Freudian philosophy is beyond my concerns and competence. To be sure, not everyone can be "healed" not everyone will become a "universal tourist." And there is no reason, if only on this count, to be overly optimistic or overly pessimistic about the future of the specimen of *Homo sapiens*.[32]

In the Freudian vision evil is in us; the "alien" is in us. But the alien is not the devil or evil; it is suffering. It is the suffering the cause of which is unclear, the suffering that we cannot understand, the suffering that is not "rational." When is suffering rational? What is "outside" that gives reason to suffer "inside"?

In the metaphysical and religious tradition, human suffering is caused by the evil outside *and* inside. But if there is no evil inside other than suffering itself, suffering is either caused by uncured sickness or by some powers outside. This is, or becomes, the common conviction of the 20th century. This is no longer Freud. Freud was the protagonist of a revolution (the revolution of the reversal of the body/soul relationship), but this revolution – which transformed, through the corporealization of the psyche, the "evil inside" into the "sickness inside," while preserving the evil outside – happened to be one of the manifestations of the spiritual transformation summed up by Nietzsche as the "death of God." After the "death of God" the balance between outside and inside will be disturbed. The disturbed balance could be restored either by the re-spiritualization of the internal space (there is evil inside) or by the rationalization of the body, the things (there is just sickness, no evil), outside. One can say "Repent" (inside!). And one can also say "Rationalize everything" (outside!). Historical imagination bars the second option; technological imagination bars the first. The imbalance remains.[33]

13

Law, Ethos, and Ethics:

The Question of Values

Max Weber's proposition that the modern state has been legitimated by law is frequently quoted. So is the thesis of Habermas,[1] that in modernity only justice is left of morality. Habermas's dictum can be also interpreted in the following way: in modernity, among all the virtues, only the virtue of justice preserved its relevance. MacIntyre's position[2] is even more radical. Moderns, he says, do not even understand the meaning of ethical expressions and moral words. Moral terms made sense only in a world in which men and women received the *telos* of their life in the cradle. Without an intrinsic teleology of human life, moral expressions are like splinters, put together at random or not at all. MacIntyre expands on this idea in denouncing liberal discourse as mere procedure, as a power that imposes its domination on all its possible alternatives.[3,4]

In what follows, I reflect on these three propositions without entering into the discussion of the concrete propositions of their most representative advocates.[5]

The proposition that the modern state or the modern kind of domination is legitimated by law suffers from overgeneralization. For example, the totalitarian states are not legitimated by law, but by charisma and ideologies.[6] In addition, legitimation by law does not specify *what kind of law*. That nothing is more important than to have steady laws is a very ancient idea – one can find it in Aristotle and almost all of the Roman authors. The old Jewish states (the old Israel and Juda) were legitimated – among others – by the Mosaic Laws, and in the case of a fundamentalist Muslim state such as Iran, one could say that it is legitimated by the law of Islam, the Sharia. But Max Weber's idea of "legitimation by law" refers to something else, something really modern, something that goes back to the contract theories. The idea is not that domination is legitimated by law full stop, but that the law legitimates domination *provided that* it is itself based on the agreement of the citizens of the state. Whether this agreement is an initial agreement which cannot be taken back, or a kind of tacit consent, or whether the initial agreement can lose legitimacy, or whether it needs to be renewed, are different questions. Who must be the highest authority, the sovereign, is again a separate and disputable issue. But the laws that legitimate the modern state are supposed to be nonideological, secular,[7] "positive," and rational.[8]

Domination is fully legitimated by law in a modern sense under the condition that the state is secular, that it declares its indifference in matters of religion and ideologies.[9] The law is not the arbiter of truth or of goodness, but of justice. Domination is legitimated (by law) if a considerable majority of citizens subscribes to the idea that the state should remain indifferent in matters of faith and truth. This idea can also be formulated in a positive way. The citizenry of a modern state is not homogeneous. They differ in religion (where there is only one religion, there can be disbelievers and atheists), in their conception of good life and happiness, in their convictions, in their commitments to goals, and so on. A modern state is legitimated if people of different faiths and different commitments, different concepts about truth and happiness, are equally protected by the law or equally persecuted and punished if they break it.

Equality before the law, the famous battle cry in the era of early modernity, claimed the abolishment of the estate/class-specific legal systems, and the establishment of a general system of law that was equally valid for everyone. But in fact, equality before the law is not just about the generality of the law, but also about "abstraction." Abstraction means that acts that are ethically repugnant for one way of life – or, moreover, intolerable – yet not for others, should be removed from the authority of the law.[10]

The abstraction of the law means to divide law and morals. Law is general; morals are community-specific. Of course, there is no legal system that is entirely independent of the moral/ethical consensus. If it were, domination could not be legitimated by law at all. Law (the legal system) needs to follow an abstract ethical consensus or near consensus.

That the modern state (form of domination) is legitimated by law does not mean that all laws are legitimated. If this were so, the world could not be modern. One pursues the practice of dynamic justice if one asks questions about the justice (legitimacy) of one or another statute of law. Legitimation by law is most eminently directed toward the citizen's opportunity and capability to annul a law, to replace one law with another if the sense of justice of a considerable majority signals that the law is or has become unjust. In this manner, laws and the legal system itself acquire the aspect of temporality. A law could have been just yesterday, but is no longer just today. The law is not sacred. (This is one of the meanings of the secularity of the legal system.) There can be a basic law – a constitution – which remains more permanent and serves as a continuous reference point for the changes in the legal system. There can also be "conservative" institutions (such as constitutional courts) which guard the fundamental law against change or against serious interference or gross neglect by the authorities of legislation. Legitimation by law includes the division of powers, the relative – or total – independence of the judiciary. This independence can mean independence from the legislative or executive power, but it can also mean something very spiritual: independence from fear and anger, interest, and advocacy of ideas and truths. That is, again, indifference for everything else but justice.

A system of domination is legitimated by law if the citizens are roughly law-abiding. They are roughly law-abiding if they do not practice illegalities with continuity, and if, provided that they believe a law to be unjust, they seek legal ways to change the law. The more legal ways a state allows for people to change laws, the greater is the legitimacy of the state. Yet, the more illegalities men and women practice with some continuity, the less legitimacy will the state have. In fact, the two tendencies can exist or even develop together. If illegalities are increasing, then even the overabundance of channels to change the laws can contribute to a deficit of legitimacy, insofar as chaos, insecurity, violence, and uncertainty may result.

Given that the legitimacy of the modern state is not based on inherited authority, it is not blessed by God, nor is it traditional in any sense. The legitimation of authority is functional and rational. The state is supposed to ensure the security of the citizen inside the state, and against the external enemies of the state. This is its main *function*. Modern society or the modern social arrangement is, as we know, functionally organized. The political activity of the citizen is *transfunctional* in the sense that it does not belong to the position that one occupies in the institutional hierarchy, but the politicians who are elected to a position in the political/ institutional hierarchy are duty bound to perform their functions as functions and to perform them well. They perform their functions well if they provide the conditions for both the citizen's freedom and his or her security.[11]

There is one ethical minimum for all citizens of a state: to be law-abiding. The law is not concerned with anything more or less, which simply means that in the eye of the law a person is ethically in complete order if he or she never breaks the law. This follows from the abstraction of the law, from the elasticity of the modern legal systems to ensure pluralism of lifestyles and concepts of the good. The law is not interested in whether someone is a good person, not even whether he or she is a good citizen. The law is not interested in one's actions inside the framework of the law, and even less in one's motivations.

Politicians do not differ from all other citizens in this respect. Yet, since they normally also participate in the activity of the legislative, executive, or judiciary powers, and thus their functional and transfunctional activities in fact coalesce, while their functional activity is to preserve the conditions of free equality and security in the state, breaking the law has a morally greater negative weight in the case of a politician. It is a matter of "honor" (not of virtue) not to break the law.[12] That in fact this is not the case, that professional politicians in several modern countries have not developed a sense of honor that would motivate them against breaking the law, even if they had a great opportunity to do it and in addition remain unpunished, is an empirical matter. But if politicians infringe upon the law regularly (for example, if they are corrupt) legitimation can break down unless the citizens themselves have no higher moral expectations.

The two branches of modern enlightenment, rationalistic enlightenment and romantic enlightenment (their smaller branches included), are fighting a never-ending battle over modern law, legitimation by law, and above all about the ethical relevance and irrelevance of law.

I will touch upon only a few major points of this rich and inexhaustible discussion. It can be expected that those two extreme opinions here also produce some pretty antinomies, that we can surely understand them as additional manifestations of the paradoxicality of the modern world – more precisely, as the manifestation of the paradox of freedom.

The antinomy of the application of (modern) law is simple as well as being simply irresolvable.

Rationalistic enlightenment argues as follows: the formalism of the law warrants equality before the law. Equality before the law is the warranty of equal freedom. Romantic enlightenment argues as follows: law equalizes the unequals (precisely as the market does). Every person is unique; there are no two equal acts. To apply the same paragraphs if two people do "abstractly" the samething, to let them go through the same procedure, is outrageous, for no two men ever did the samething.[13] The most sacred treasure, the dignity of the single person, is then infringed. And this also infringes human or personal freedom. Moreover, the judge is placed in the morally impossible situation of doing justice to a single individual from the standpoint of a law (or laws) which are simply "there" and will be reconfirmed in their universality (generality) through the singular judgment as if judgment were resulting from a syllogism.[14]

Rationalistic enlightenment argues as follows: the very existence of formal and positive law sets men and women free. They can do whatever they want unless they infringe the law. They are free to follow all their wishes, let lose their drives. No one will interfere with their conduct of life unless they violate the law. And one rarely needs to violate the law in one's pursuit of happiness.

Romantic enlightenment argues as follows: the claim that everyone can do whatever he or she wants unless he or she violates what the law indicates that the legal system as *a formal system* is entirely alienated from human life. Under such conditions, the only reason why men and women will not wrong their fellow creatures will be the fear of punishment, and if they can wrong them unpunished, they will do it. All ethical motivations will become negative. Ethics itself (ethos, morals, and morality) are going to die out as a result. They will no longer be needed. If regulation by alienated law is to remain the sole common guide of human behaviour, modern men will be entirely outer-regulated. Since fear of punishment is not an authentic internal motivation, conscience is going to disappear. Finally, regulation by shame will also become sporadic and superficial.[15]

The question is not whether the description of enlightenment rationalism or that of its romantic opponents is more precise or more accurate. I will show later that, as far as I can see, neither of them is accurate. The conceptions are antinomic because both of them rely upon freedom as the foundation of modernity. Both draw relevant conclusions from this, concerning tendencies that might coexist at the empirical level, but which contradict *one another at a theoretical and evaluative level.*

Beyond restating – mostly unwittingly – the paradoxical character of modern freedom once again, the controversy between rationalistic enlightenment and romanticism is of interest because it raises a few specific issues concerning the fate of ethics, morals, ethos, and morality in the modern (postmodern) age.

Modernity is frequently accused of "immorality." Apart from vulgar forms of abuse, a few sophisticated issues are also raised. Let me start with the observation that a person can survive, – and moreover, can also become a respected member of society and a citizen – without ever having been confronted with one single moral norm, without ever having been motivated morally. A person can live alone, in an apartment house in a great metropolis, where he or she works hard, climbs upward on the ladder of advancement, goes to vote every time there is an election, and has satisfying – although superficial – sexual relations with one or more persons, doing all of these without having one single nonfunctional, nonformal contact, one single contact where he or she can display emotions, a sense of caring for someone, a single virtue. The only ethical condition that such a reason satisfies is a negative one – such a person does not violate the law. A person like this is neither bad nor good; he or she is not a decent person, nor is he or she a good citizen. The fact that someone like this does not violate the law is not of moral relevance because the motivation is not moral, but in all probability a matter of convenience and of rational interest. In fact, the sole motivations of men and women like those described above are interest and convenience.

Thus, a merely law-abiding moral person performs way below the level of the attitude that Kant once termed "legality." "Legality" means that a person does all the things that others might do out of duty, yet he or she does it without moral motivation, just dutifully. He or she does it not just because it is in his or her interest but perhaps also because he or she likes to do the right moral thing. One can act ethically far beyond the level of remaining law-abiding if one assumes the attitude of mere "legality." For example, one tells the truth while there is no law against lying, and a merely law-abiding person can freely lie if it is in his or her interest, or as a matter of convenience. The modern world is a world – or at least has the tendency to become a world – in which morals, ethics, and morality become *redundant*.

This is indeed a possibility, one of the tendencies of the modern world. Yet, there are other parallel tendencies that exercise their influence in the opposite direction.

Here immediately we have the issue of justice. Normally, people do not simply go to the polls. They also participate in the practice of legitimating and de-legitimating norms and rules in the discourse on justice. They frequently utter the sentence, "This is unjust – something else is what is just, or is at least more just." Since the dynamics of modernity are omnipresent, so is dynamic justice. And if one person insists that a law is just or unjust, his judgment or opinion needs to be based on something that might also imply an ethical quality. Moreover, one can be stubborn and adamant in claiming justice for something, and this stubbornness itself may be associated with a traditional virtue, the virtue of justice. One is then inclined to side with Habermas that, among all virtues, the virtue of justice has remained relevant and is still practiced.

But which justice, of what kind? – so MacIntyre asks. I do not believe, however, that this question is relevant at this point, since it is enough to admit that every claim for justice is motivated, or at least can be motivated, by something other than self-interest or convenience. To disclose that a valid norm or rule is unjust manifests a motivation other than convenience. And since one frequently queries the justice of norms and laws which do not touch upon one's interests, the motivation of the de-legitimating claim cannot be interest. I do not even mention the possibility of querying the justice of rules or laws which otherwise sense the interest of the person involved in the contestation. I say only as much as a person can say, "This is unjust. Something else would be more just," emphatically, without having a personal stake in changing those rules or laws.

Let me return to the issue that there is "something" on the ground of which one insists that another rule or law would be better and more just than the standing ones. If someone says "This law is unjust," and the other asks "Why is that so?" the contestor cannot answer "Because it is unjust." And not just for logical reasons – not only because this would be a redundant answer, but because the foundation of the de-legitimation is normally prior to the act of de-legitimation itself. Whenever someone says "This is not just," and wants to make an argument to support his or her claim, he or she has to refer to an *archē*. What is – what can be – the *archē* in the case of justice? This question can be answered easily in a historico-empirical way. Whenever dynamic justice has been mobilized, those who have disclaimed the justice of a norm or law have always taken recourse either to *freedom* or to *life* – more precisely, to the value of freedom and/or the value of life (chance).[16]

It is no wonder, then, that in modernity where both values (freedom and life) became universal, dynamic justice and its practice became a commonplace. The continuous contestation of justice indicates that reference is constantly made to two universal values in one of their several interpretations.

Thus, the accusation against modernity that it can be maintained without one single virtue or value withstands neither the theoretical nor the empirical test. There is at least a third motivation "behind" human actions in addition to convenience and self-interest, and this is justice – a sense of justice, to claim justice – even if justice in a concrete case is indifferent to the person's convenience and self-interest.[17]

But what about those values to which one has to have recourse if one wants to argue for or against the validity of a norm, rule, or law?

Let me begin with the rules and norms themselves. Since we have presupposed until this very point that the accusations of contemporary pedestrian romantics are true, and that the modern world and modern persons can survive and behave well, if they are just law-abiding, we must also presuppose that the norms which are de-legitimized are legal. Take, for example, a divorce law. Men and women can say that a divorce law is unjust, for certain reasons, and then some will refer to freedom, and others to life chances, but everyone will refer to a *value*. The disclaimer asserts that the law itself (in this case, the divorce law) was once legislated on the ground of an interpretation of freedom and/or life chances which were already wrong at that time or, alternatively, became outdated. The disclaimer implies that all norms are related to values, that laws secure the validation of certain values held by the majority population, and that this was – perhaps – also the case with the original divorce law, and yet is no longer the case. Whenever one de-legitimizes a rule or a law, one also questions the value-interpretation behind the law. This means that no law can become absolutely "positive" in a world in which the contestation of justice is widespread. True, the law is positive in the sense that as long as it is there, it should not be infringed upon. But it is not necessarily also positive in a narrower sense. The fact that it still exists is not yet the proof of its legitimacy, or full legitimacy, for it can be strongly contended.[18]

But what is a value? And what has value to do with ethics, morality, with morals and moral motivation?

Value is a modern expression. The term "value" became widespread in moral discourse from Brentano through neo-Kantianism, Nietzsche, and Max Weber, until Scheler.[19] Nietzsche spoke about the re-valuation of all values,[20] whereas Scheler devised a substantive value ethics in opposition to the merely formal ethics of Kant.[21] Although every philosopher adds a special tint and hint to a category, there are not simply common elements in the employment of the concept of value, but these elements are, in my view, indispensable for the understanding (and the construction) of the modern world.[22]

The concept of value has in part replaced the traditional concept of "good" or "goods" still used in classical German philosophy, along with the distinction of "substantive good(s)" and moral good(s), which originated in the Latin *bonum* (bonus). The opposite term, however, (*malum*) went out of use. The tradition of the concept of good(s) goes back to Aristotle. It occupies a "natural" place in the philosophies of the "natural edifice." Since the natural edifice is hierarchically structured, the different kinds of "goods" are also hierarchically ordered. Whatever men are striving for are goods. But there are lower and higher goods. The supreme good toward which everyone is striving is, as we all know, happiness. After the deconstruction of the "natural edifice" (and this is already a closed chapter in Kant), it is difficult to keep the hierarchy of the substantive goods in place.[23] The so-called substantive goods are no longer linked by a teleological chain, and the pride of place of the supreme good remains unoccupied, or can be occupied by different goods.[24]

Value is a splinter-concept of the good. It is a concept of good without its traditional teleological hierarchy. One encounters different forms of life in the self-same world, and all of them occupy the same level. They are not hierarchically organized. At least this is the model of the modern world, and where the empirical reality does not match the model, and the contestation of justice is going on. For it is not just if certain ways of life and their value hierarchies are – in principle – placed higher than others, provided that all of them are law-abiding.[25,26]

One can keep both the concept of good and that of value. Nietzsche in fact did, and did it in a polemic way.[27] But Nietzsche's project was the reversal of the value-hierarchy and not the abolishment of this hierarchy.

Let me return to the point that modernity also accommodates different value-hierarchies insofar as it accommodates different forms of life. In addition, the single individual can choose for himself or herself a simply personal value-hierarchy. That the construction of a personal value hierarchy is often blocked, and personal value hierarchies are, *in nuce*, levelled by secondary social forces (market, education, media, and so on) is true, but cannot be discussed here.[28]

Thus the concept of value is a splinter-concept of the concept of good, arising from the pluralization of ways of life, the personification of hierarchies of goods, the constant change of these hierarchies, the marketing and secondary coding of evaluations, and the multiple identities.

One makes a distinction between something "having a value" and "being a value." The goals that we are striving for "have" a value, but they are not values. In fact, we rarely covet values; we normally covet ends which are value-related. In this sense "value-related" is closer to what the ancients termed "substantive goods." Thus we covet a new apartment, we desire that X should return our love, we want to become lawyers, and so on. All of these goals are value-related, whereas we rarely covet values such as education, health, and love as such. Max Weber described the traditional action as "value rational," yet I think that only modern actors act in a "value rational" manner, for only in the modern world can one covet goals which are value-related, yet not inserted in a firmly set chain of the hierarchy of goods. For the ancients, coveting wealth was identical to coveting this or that kind of wealth (due to the social hierarchy): today, one covets wealth in absolutely everything that can be turned into cash. Thus "wealth" is a value, and is as a value related to different acts of coveting wealth; it makes them understandable and "rational." Still, one does not covet "wealth" as such, but at one time a yacht, at another time a managerial position or a house in the country, and so on. One chooses the item that one covets most among value-related things according to the dictates of fashion, by a concern for gain, and also by personal taste or even whim. The value-related things that one covets can be hierarchically ordered (the person can have temporal or other preferences) or not (instinctual preferences). Value-rational action does not preclude the possibility that preferences will be determined by "sense" or "instinct" and not by calculation. *The story of someone's subsequent and simultaneous choices of value-related things is one of the most characteristic stories that one can tell about the life of a person.* It is one of the strongest identity-constituting stories.

Wealth and Health are the most traditional goods or values. So is Love (or Friendship). So are Liberty, Justice, Life, Beauty, Goodness, Truth, Wisdom, Family, and Salvation. In the modern world a few other values were added to the list, such as Equality, one's own Nation, Democracy, Humankind, Work, Culture, and so on. It is already obvious from this sketchy list why values are not just goals that one is coveting but, first of all, value ideas to which the goals that one is are coveting are related in the sense that they *regulate* or guide the choice of goals, although not always also the choice of means. The Kantian concept of *regulative practical ideas* can be of help in understanding how modern values work.

The traditional values (formerly "goods") are also ends (goals). One covets health, wealth (in its determined fashion, such as land), friendship (of a certain quality and kind), and liberty (in a political sense). And raising a family (particularly sons) is also "natural" goal. One can also live in the constant expectation of salvation even if salvation is not a goal that one could covet, but the gift of Grace.[29] One does not covet humankind or Democracy (if there is already one), nor Culture as such. But one's choice of value-related goals is or can be regulated by the universal values of Humankind, Culture, or Democracy.

There are values that are of moral relevance, there are others that stand in a moral relationship (positive or negative), and finally there are values that are also virtues. On this latest count, Habermas's dictum that of all the virtues only justice has remained makes sense. For among those goods which were also (traditionally) virtues, *only justice remained both a value and a virtue.* Love is a value, but it preserves its ethico-moral connotations only in some forms of life, in some philosophies. Kant, for example, does not acknowledge love as a moral motivation. Obviously love also can motivate against obedience to the moral law. And this is said not only about erotic love, but also about *caritas* (a main virtue in the Christian tradition).[30] Friendship, a chief virtue in Aristotle's ethics, has lost its strong ethical content for some but not for others.[31] Work has assumed a high ethico-moral standing in early modernity and become a virtue,[32] although in our times it has begun to lose its virtue character. Work still remains a value, at least in the dominant modern forms of life.[33]

But from the circumstance that Justice is the sole, chief value that also has remained a virtue, it does not follow that Justice is the only virtue of or in modernity.

Let me return to the distinction between substantive goods and moral goods. Substantive goods stand in a value relation, for in coveting those goods we are guided (or regulated) by the value to which the act stands in a relationship. I take preventive medicine seriously, go to the doctor even if I do not feel sick (related to the value Health). I participate in political decision-making (the value of Liberty and Democracy). I stick to my convictions even if the majority is against me (the value of Truth). I confide my secret to one person who seeks my friendship (the value of Friendship). I employ the same strict standard to everyone who seeks employment (the value of Justice/Equality). I do something exclusively for another person's sake, absolutely forgetting myself (the value of Love) – And so on.

In most of the simple acts enumerated above sometimes, or perhaps frequently, certain virtues other than justice need to be mobilized. And – which amounts to the samething – certain vices other than injustice need to be eliminated or suppressed.

To make a just judgment, for example, in the case of an appointment, one frequently needs to suppress one's prejudices and self-interests and to mobilize good judgment (*phronesis*), which has also remained an intellectual virtue in modern times. Sometimes (if one stands under an ideological pressure, for example, that of being politically correct) one needs to be courageous to be just. Confidence also requires a display of courage and a readiness to listen to the other person if he or she wants to confide in you; it demands that you give away a part of your time for the sake of friendship. When participating in decision-making one has to learn to suppress anger, to display the virtue of patience, to suppress one's personal interests and biases, and also to cope with boredom, the feeling of having wasted one's time. Every value-related act *may* require the mobilization of virtues other than justice, first and foremost the virtue of *courage*.[34] And many of them also require the virtue of *self-sacrifice* in three major forms: sacrifice of money, of time, and of work.[35]

The virtue of courage in its form of civic/civil virtue is in fact, aside from justice, the most outstanding virtue in modern times. Military courage has remained a virtue (in war) but, in addition, the virtue of civic courage is constantly required, for it needs to be exercised at *all levels* of modern society and in *all times*. The display of courage does not necessarily require self-sacrifice, but the "acceptance" of self-sacrifice as the possible result of the act of courage is a risk taken by every person who displays civic courage.[36] But civic courage (contrary to military courage) is a kind of courage where one accepts the risk of self-sacrifice, but does not accept the risk of sacrificing others, at least not directly.[37]

The most distinguished position of civic courage among all of the other virtues (except justice) in modernity follows from the structure of the modern social arrangement and from the pre-eminence of the dynamics of modernity.

Since the de-legitimating gesture to say "no" to the extant, and the legitimating gesture to say "yes" to the not-yet-extant, have become everyday occurrences in modern times, since (and where) it has become accepted that modernity is not destroyed by negation but thrives on it, every citizen can in principle be engaged in the process of legitimation/de-legitimation. If this possibility becomes an actuality, there are no more revolutions. The new is no longer born in blood; the sacrifice of life is no longer required. But at any time when a new kind of contestation is put on the agenda, or an old kind of contestation is put on the agenda in an entirely new milieu, those who initiate the process of modernity's dynamics need to display courage. As a result, the dynamics of modernity cannot present themselves in an unperturbed form unless there are persons who display courage whenever a new contestation is initiated; if, that is, the "hardened hearts"[38] of the old powers of tradition fight with all their might against the new or the uncommon idea.[39]

The tendency toward the generalization of modernity's dynamics results in the incomparably greater demand for men and women of courage, and also in the lesser extremity of the sacrifices.[40]

Just as the dynamics of modernity have promoted civic courage to the status of the most distinguished virtue, so did the modern social arrangement. It was said in chapter 2 that in the modern arrangement everyday life loses its major significant role in preparing men and women for their social functions, because it is the function that men and women occupy in the division of goods, social places, and services that determine the positions to which men and women are allotted in the social hierarchy. In Foucault's terms, the main power relations and the most sophisticated forms of domination are constituted in the sphere of social institutions other than the family. This development results in the shrinking of the authority and of the social importance of the family, along with an increase in its emotional importance.

Civic courage is displayed not just in politics, but in all of the institutions where the social hierarchy of ranks, income, and prestige are now constituted. These are the relations of subordination and superordination. It is here that injustices frequently occur, where people are abused, where biases reign supreme. These are the relations of subordination/superordination, the territories of infights and of fierce competition in which men and women lose or win their battles, in which they are humiliated. It is in all such institutions, from the schools to the courts, from the factories to the governmental offices, in every workplace, everywhere where you buy and sell, borrow or lend, where you lodge an application with an organized political group or an association – in fact, in every place and in all activities where modern men and women spent most of their lifetimes – that civic courage needs to be displayed. And this is so not just in confrontation with bosses, but mostly in confrontation with one's own colleagues.

Furthermore, precisely because all men and women are born free, and they are all equally endowed with reason and conscience, precisely because modern social relations are in principle (if not in fact) primarily the relations of symmetric and not of asymmetric reciprocity, that courage ceases to be a status/virtue. It is no more exclusively the virtue of the noble, that of the male members of the higher ranks. Everyone can display courage, men and women alike, and in every social position. Moreover, to display courage is virtue and merit in everyone. Courage as a democratic and a general virtue is the civic virtue of courage. This is why it is a modern virtue.

But what is courage? And what is self-sacrifice? Is the stuntman who puts his life at stake every day courageous? Is he displaying the virtue of self-sacrifice? Listening to our moral sense we would answer in the negative, and this was also Aristotle's answer. But since he was thinking in the framework of a hierarchically ordered system of goods, he explained his answer with his theory of middle/measure. Bravado is not courage, because the man of bravado is less afraid than he should be. In a nonteleologically ordered world of splinter values, the answer sounds more simple. Valiant behavior, the readiness for sacrifice for something or for someone (and mostly also against something or against someone), is called courage if it is related to a value. Courage is as a virtue an *end in itself*, because one is courageous not in order to achieve a goal. Yet courage is also *not an end in itself*, because it is regulated by the value to which it as a virtue relates. A stuntman is a stuntman just because he likes a stunt. His bravado resembles courage, but it is not courage – for it has no relation to a value. To "show" my courage, to take pride in it, or even to prove my own soul[41] are not values in the sense in which we use the word, for they are not "splinters" of the once teleologically organized system of goods. Your family is a value because your family is one, your country is a value for a country is one, your truth is a value for a truth is one, justice is a value and a virtue, equality is a value, human dignity is a value (a moral value), and the freedom of the personality is a value (as the representative interpretation of freedom). If it stands in a relation with any of those values, the valiant act equals civic (civil) courage. To tell the truth, to speak your mind, not to succumb to pressure or brainwashing, to blackmail, and so on – these are all value-related acts. They are related to the values of equality, freedom, and human dignity: in defending these values you are courageous and your sacrifice is an end in itself, yet it is also regulated by those high values.[42]

In modernity the concept of value cannot be meaningfully replaced by the concept of norms and rules.[43] There is no human world without norms and rules. The different categories of value orientation (good–bad, good–evil, true–false, pleasant–unpleasant, useful–harmful, beautiful–ugly, and the like) can also be described in metaphysical terms as the "accidents" of a "substance." The positive side of the categories of value orientation are the "accidents" of our customs and of our norms. To obey them means to do the right thing, to think well and to act well. To disobey them – or to obey the norms of the stranger or the enemy – means to act wrongly and to think wrongly. The rules must simply be applied, whereas the norms also include the "directions for use."

In modern times, only acts of technological character remain entirely rule-directed. Administration, the army, and production are, or at least show, a tendency to become rationalized[44] and, as a result, mainly rule-directed. Yet all of the nonrationalized aspects of life – from politics to sexuality – have become simultaneously less and less rule-regulated. There are still norms that one needs "to live up to," but they are less specific, less concrete. They are mostly abstract. That science became the dominant world explanation of modernity, and that religion lost ground as the agency responsible for organizing daily life, grossly contributed to the abstraction of norms. By now, single persons *qua* single persons need to choose among many possible paths of action, all of which may be in some way "good" or "useful"; no directions for use alleviate them from the burden of responsibility for their own lives.[45]

One could say that values are shorthand versions of abstract norms. (For example, the value "family" stand for "do everything for your family's sake," where the issue of *what* this "everything" consists of remains undetermined.) But such value-related, abstract quasi-commands are maxims rather than norms in a traditional understanding. They guide a person's life in many kinds of actions, as well as non-value-related ones. Norms proper are either imperative or optative. A maxim as the guiding principle of a person's life is not optative or imperative but, rather, regulative. A maxim can be related to a hypothetical imperative and, as Kant said, it can also be checked by the categorical imperative so as to qualify or not qualify for it. But in the latter case it needs to be a moral maxim proper.[46]

Yet values in their employment as maxims of a form of life are normally not of a moral character. For a maxim to be of a moral character, the value itself also needs be moral. Whether this kind of scenario is relevant in modern times is a question that I will soon discuss briefly.

But let me first return to the initial question of my ruminations on the status of ethics in the modern world. Is the demise of all ethical regulations, norms, rules, values, and virtues possible? Can all of them be replaced by law alone? Is it possible to think a world in which the only wrongdoing is to violate the law?

One can perhaps *think* that Law remains the sole value, and that the sole moral maxim will be to remain law-abiding. But to think something (if it does not contain logical contradiction) is not difficult. It is not astonishing that *imagining* things is more difficult then thinking those things. In matters that concern knowledge about the universe, thinking and imagination parted company a long time ago. We have learned to think things that we cannot imagine, and we have already learned that many things that we can imagine (for example, mythological things) we cannot properly think. But in the human world the divorce between thinking and imagination has not occurred. More precisely, it has occurred in theory alone. And this is suspect.

To cut a long story short: in principle, I can think a world in which Law remains the sole value, but I cannot imagine a world like this. Our world is certainly not like this.

I have already spoken about contemporary value pluralism, about the chief virtue of civic courage, about other virtues, all related to values, about maxims (among which I also mentioned moral maxims), and also about abstract and universal norms that cannot be replaced by an article of Law. Needless to say, the norm that one should not lie is even now not restricted to the prohibition of perjury. Earlier[47] I also mentioned the norms of civility/urbanity, which although not directly ethical, contain an ethical component. But all of these are still meager instances. One does not enter the ethical relation incidentally or by accident; one is still constantly reinforcing ethical relations in action and in judgment.

I would distinguish between dense ethos and weak ethos. In a pluralistic human universe such as the modern one, there are communities with a dense ethos and others with a weak ethos. Religious communities are normally characterized by a dense ethos, and so are republics in times when they are constantly threatened by mortal enemies. Organizations of people who are "held" together exclusively by the institutions where they normally perform their functions have a weak ethos. The same person can live in a community with a dense ethos (for example, in a kibbutz) and work in a workplace with a weak ethos (for example, in a department store). Yet, also, where there is a weak ethos (in a department store) there exists a web of norms and rules. True, if one leaves the workplace, one also leaves those norms/rules behind; although not necessarily – for example, many schoolteachers are schoolteachers everywhere they go.

To live in the web of a dense ethos is nowadays more exceptional than before. But it exists. Yet, all of us moderns are living in the loose web of a weak ethos – but an ethos all the same. Furthermore, the ties between the different ways of life are also webs of a weak ethos, except in cases of a continuous mortal threat. Situations of mortal threat were termed "borderline situations" by Jaspers. Borderline situations can also be sudden, just as it can also happen that the single individual has to face them alone. In such a case, it is not the collective ethos but personal morality that has to stand the ultimate test.[48]

Children are brought up either in a dense ethos or in a weak ethos. Nowadays, it is mostly in a weak ethos. "Permissive education" on the one hand, and the de-civilizing process on the other hand, have grossly contributed to the weakening of the ethos in the most representative of dominating ways of modern life. This is why it has become common parlance to accuse the modern world of "immorality."

Critics normally *identify "ethics" and even "morality" with the density of an ethos*. They believe that the more restrictions, the more imperatives these are, the better will be the mores; that is, morality. But "mores" is not like ethics, and it is even less identical to morality. The firmness of a modern ethical culture does not depend on the density of the ethos, on the number of restrictions, or on imperatives. Nor does it depend on the number of people of the highest morality (which we do not know anyhow). Modern ethical culture is firm (a) if the moral norms, albeit few in number, are respected, (b) if disrespect for those norms meets public disapproval without legal sanctions, and even without social sanctions with the exception of the disapproval itself, (c) if it lies within the discretion of single individuals to live up to those norms in their own ways, and (d) if there are no norms and rules the observance of which implies the use of men and women exclusively as means. The main ethical issue is not how much one ought to promise, but whether one keeps the few promises that one has made to one's fellow creatures.

Modern men and women live together. One still lives with one's fellow creatures, not just in the family but everywhere. For even in institutions where men and women perform only their functions, one does encounter a web of transfunctional human relations.

It is true to say that the status of the "nonperson" has also become democratized. Just as, for a lady in past ages, a servant was a "nonperson," so can all persons with whom one has only a functional relationship retain the status of "nonpersons." One does not notice their faces; one does not know their names. And we all know that a person becomes a person for us if he or she has a face and a name, if he or she can be recognized among very different circumstances, and not just in his or her "proper places;" for example, as a customer, as a post office clerk, as one violinist from the orchestra, and so on. It is impossible nowadays, particularly in a metropolis, not to view many persons (perhaps the greatest number that one formally encounters in a day) as nonpersons.

The norms of civility differ from the ethical norms insofar as they also are related to nonpersons of the democratic kind. One is not rude to the postman; one does not push the customer over; one does not laugh in the face of the violinist even if he plays out of tune. The ethical norms, however, guide intercourse among persons; that is, persons in a transfunctional relationship in which they have at least *a face and a name*, even if we know nothing about their internal lives and are not interested in their inner motivations.

It is not difficult to enumerate a few still valid and constantly validated moral norms and values which do not figure in any codes of law, and the infringement of which does not carry legal sanctions. These norms are not "applied" because they are orientative. They orient us in human intercourse between "what is right" and "what is wrong" in the interaction between humans. Normally, they do not require much from the person – certainly not self-sacrifice, not even the neglect of his or her own basic life interests. Still, they are all important. For how well or how miserable men and women feel themselves to be in our world depends to a fair degree on the honoring or dishonoring of such elementary ethical norms.

The most general orientative moral principle can be formulated as follows: "care for other human beings," and – in the form of an interdiction – "do not harm another human being on purpose." These principles are orientative, for they do not tell us what is to be done and what is to be avoided. Moreover, they are orientative because it is always in the power of the individual person's discretion as to whether exemption from the orientative principle is warranted. For example, one can harm a person on purpose in case of justified punishment, be it moral or legal, and so on. But all these examples, exclusions/inclusions, are mainly of logical importance or are matters for argumentation, for one must presuppose a certain "moral sense" that does not give absolution easily if one makes an exception from this principle.[49]

This main principle or maxim includes several others. The following are examples. (1) Do not humiliate a person, or do not put a person to shame (without strong moral reasons). (2) Respect another person's sensitivity and autonomy. (3) Do not patronize others. (4) Do not make others dependent on you intentionally. (5) Help the other person to "save face." (6) Do not show your contempt for another person unless morally justified. (7) Learn to express your love, respect, and appreciation for the other person. (8) Do not try to break another person's will. (9) Do not pretend feelings for gain. (10) Admit that everyone deserves recognition. (11) Alleviate the suffering of others according to your abilities, and so on.

The norms of reciprocity also surpass the level of mere civility. One reciprocates what one gets, but by no means should one always reciprocate a thing or gesture with the same thing or gesture that one received but, rather, with something nonquantitatively but qualitatively "equivalent." One reciprocates greetings with greetings, an invitation with another invitation, friendship (if one can) with friendship, a kind of gift with another kind of gift. Yet one can also reciprocate charity with a blessing, a present with saying "thank you," and so on. The norm of reciprocation is perhaps the oldest moral norm in human intercourse, yet it is still valid. Not to reciprocate is still a vice – the vice of ingratitude. Reciprocating still means to fulfill the norm, since if one reciprocates in one way or another, one is "all right." But to add a plus to the gesture of reciprocation is a virtue, and is called gratitude. Gratitude always implies the element of a free gift. In my mind, *gratitude is the most beautiful virtue*. It is beautiful because it always entails the element of a *free favor*.[50]

Without men and women who are roughly following the orientative moral principles briefly described above, one could hardly speak of ethics in contemporary human intercourse. But they are not infrequently, although perhaps roughly, followed, for the validity of the orientative moral principle is not denied. Ask anyone whether one should care for someone or not, or whether one should harm others on purpose or not – one cannot doubt what the answer of the overwhelming majority will be. These are the norms that most people learn as children, and usually never ever forget, whether they fulfill them or not. You were told as a child not to torture your sister, not to be cruel to your brother, to respect your mother's sensitivity, and so on. You learned this before you could have had the faintest idea that laws exist. And this is the *moral knowledge* that one normally also passes on to one's own children.

Let me return for the third time to the question of *ethical powers* (*sittliche Mächte*) in the Hegelian sense.

The balance of the modern world can be preserved. That is, the modern world can survive if the three *integrations* of the modern world, family (community), civil society (society), and the state (political body), preserve their ethical power. The question is not whether those integrations have the status of values, because "ethical powers" are specific kinds of values. Firstly, they are values to which the virtue of courage and the virtue of self-sacrifice are related. Moreover, they are powers because men and women are expected to be ready to make the highest sacrifice, the sacrifice of their own lives, on the altar of ethical powers. But there is another reason, too, why those three values are (or need to be) values of a specific kind. They need to be shared, or at least *shared by a considerable majority* of a nation or of a state. One can opt to choose or not choose many other values. Culture is value for some, while not for others. Love can be the value of a few, and not of others. The same applies to Religion, Beauty, and many other values. Besides, the value hierarchy itself is supposed to be constituted by the individual. But the three ethical powers that require the greatest sacrifice need not only be shared, but are supposed to occupy a top position, a position among the *supreme values* in the value hierarchy of every citizen. And even if this is not so in fact, it needs to be so at the level of the regulative idea. One needs to presuppose that the three ethical powers in fact occupy a place among the supreme values of each citizen. If one cannot presuppose this, if the choice of the three ethical powers is meant to be personal, then someone will choose them, someone else will not. In one value hierarchy they will figure among the values at the top, whereas in the value hierarchy of others they will occupy a lowly place, if they feature at all. If this is the case, then a nation, a world, or a state lacks *ethical cementing*.

Ethical cementing is not the same thing as a dense ethos. The family can be an ethical power without the strict norm of monogamy or virgin marriage. The state can be an ethical power without a supreme personal sovereign, without nationalistic/ideological education or a strong image of an enemy and the organizations of civil society (for example, the jury system) can be a high and shared ethical power without capital punishment. I would go even further and say this precisely because a great variety of forms of life (with a weaker or stronger ethos, respectively) can be accommodated in a modern state by a modern nation. And precisely because every individual has the right and opportunity to establish his or her value hierarchy in a personal way of life, it is it absolutely necessary that a few values assume the position of an "ethical power," and that those values should be shared by everyone – even if not in fact then certainly at the level of ideas. For if this is not the case, I cannot fail to repeat that there is nothing left to cement an overarching modern integration – first and foremost, the state. The state, and as a result society, can easily erode and fall into anarchy. And once it has fallen into anarchy, modernity loses the most integral and original aspect of its legitimation: *to provide law and order along with freedom.* The question as to whether there can be shared ethical powers in modern states and nations is crucial, because it is decided at this juncture whether it is possible to provide law and order with political freedom.[51]

––––––––––

Whereas for Hegel the link "in the middle" between family and state, namely civil society, has warranted the possibility of survival, most critics blame "the middle" – that is, capitalism, commodity exchange, and the institution of the market – for the demise of the ethical powers of the state and of the family. They also blame these for the dissolution of norms, for the breaking down of ethical ties, for anomie.[52, 53] As a result, so it is said, modern men and women became motivated by self-interest alone; they became materialists, sensualists, hedonists. Generally, cultural critics distinguish stages in the deterioration of the modern ethical life. First came the motivation by interest with its Protestant ethics and asceticism,[54] but by now sensualism and hedonism have the upper hand.[55]

Different things are meant by sensualism and hedonism – some of them vulgar, some of them quite subtle. For example, men and women are interested only in their material well-being and "nothing else;" they are concerned only with their bodies and not with their souls. They are aiming at immediate satisfaction; they cannot withhold satisfaction. They seek pleasures without selection, they became indifferent to "spiritual" things, they are infantile, they are narcissistic, and so on.

Now, even if all of the accusations were true as described, most of them could not be taken as a proof of ethical decay, with a few exceptions. If it is true that men and women are interested only with their material well-being, then politics, the care for *res publica*, can be exhausted by the care for the general (common) conditions of well-being. In this case the pursuit of public interest is about to secure the best conditions for the pursuit of private interest.

It is difficult to deny that there is some truth in this accusation. Among the major issues of politics, economical issues and those of social policy occupy a pride of place. With politics, it is often mainly about balancing the budget, about taxes, social security, and the like. Among all categories of justice, distributive justice begins to play a dominating role. Yet there are also ethical aspects in the contestation of distributive justice. True, they cover only a very small territory of public ethics and require very little ethical concern by the citizens.

Furthermore, if it is true that modern men and women cannot withhold satisfaction and cannot select among pleasures, this would mean that the personality as such is falling apart. A person who cannot withhold need, desire, or satisfaction and does not select among pleasures lacks, in particular, the capacity to make promises. And whoever lacks the capacity to make promises is incapable of taking responsibility. Given that there is no ethics without taking responsibility, one could be justified in speaking of the decay of morals – provided, again, that the accusation is true. I do not know whether it is true.

But even if no other regulation remained in modern times than regulation by law, and even if everything that is not punishable by law was not only legally but also morally permitted, if no act, no attitude was morally approved of (because one does not approve of a law-abiding person, although one disapproves of the person who breaks the law) – that is, all the norms and rules were homogenized in one single set (the legal) – if nothing else motivated men and women to obey the law other than the fear of legal sanctions, there would still remain an ethics of sorts. But, let me reiterate: an ethical world like this can be thought of, but one can hardly imagine it.

14

Happiness, Perfection, Authenticity:
An Ethics of Personality[1]

The deconstruction of the "natural artifice," the pre-modern social arrangement(s), also resulted in drastic changes in the concept (and perception) of happiness and the idea of human perfection.

In the pre-modern social arrangements of "high civilizations," happiness and perfection were conceptually related; both of them occupied the supreme place on the teleologically/hierarchically ordered paths of life.[2] For simplicity's sake, I illustrate this model using the example of Aristotle's ethics.

The free man stands on the highest level of the hierarchically ordered space of human creatures; he is the political animal, he is the possessor of *logos*. His path is teleologically devised. He can be perfect if he becomes a completely good person by practicing all the virtues of good persons and becoming the best character (*heksis*), called the *megalopsychos*. The megalopsychos is perfect. He is ethically perfect. The ethically perfect is the embodiment of goodness and beauty. If someone is ethically perfect, he does not lack any perfections. A modern man or woman could object that a perfect gentleman or gentlewoman also lacks many perfections. For example, he or she is incapable of making beautiful statues like a sculptor, or writing beautiful poems like a poet. But for the ancient mind, and thus for Aristotle, no one is or can be more perfect than a perfect gentleman.[3] A perfect ethical gentleman also has a choice between living a political life or a theoretical life. In Aristotle's scenario, a gentleman living a theoretical life arrives at a higher level of perfection than a person who conducts a political way of life; although both of them are perfect. They are "autocephal"; that is, enough for themselves. They are in no need of anyone or anything else.

Being enough for ourselves is to be perfect. After all, no one can add to or take away from a perfect statue. The statue is perfect exactly the way it is: it has achieved the *telos* of the statue exactly the way it is.[4]

And, Aristotle goes on, who is a happy person? After having rejected other opinions (for example, the hedonistic concept of happiness), Aristotle says that the morally good and virtuous man is the happy man (provided that he also possesses certain goods of fortune, such as medium wealth, health, and the like).[5] True, in Aristotle's philosophy ethical perfection itself requires similar conditions up to a degree. A very poor person lacks the conditions for becoming ethically perfect (for example, he cannot exercise the virtue of liberality), as does the cripple. The happiest is of course the free man/citizen, because he is the most perfect, he can arrive at the *"telos* of man."

A very similar scenario characterizes the Hindi, the Buddhist, the Jewish, and the medieval Christian/feudal conceptions of perfection and happiness. The connection also works well in a negative way. For example, in the Judeo-Christian scenario, only God is perfect. Men are by definition imperfect. (In the Christian theology they are born in sin.) To simplify a little: men are imperfect because they have a body, and the body infects the soul with its own imperfections. But there is a way toward perfection that one can follow, and this is the way of morality, just as it is also the path of faith. This worldly happiness is relative, but the good ones who have faith can gain eternal life in Paradise, eternal happiness and blessedness.

One can still encounter the bits and pieces of this once so homogeneous conception in Kant, where its splinters are all thrown into the cluster of the postulates of pure practical reason. Full obedience to the Moral Law is perfection according to Kant; we do not know, but we do doubt whether anyone was ever so perfect. At any rate, the man who mostly obeys the Moral Law deserves happiness, although he is not happy.[6] One has to postulate eternal life, the immortality of the soul, to make a case for the coincidence between goodness and happiness – and also for another reason. Even after the so-called "revolution of the mind"[7] which makes man identify with the imperative of the Moral Law, in practice it takes infinite time for the sensual and interest-oriented nature of man to reform itself and to obey the Moral Law without resistance. Also, this development – the approximately infinite progress in moral perfection of the single person – requires the postulate of immortality of the soul.

Kant's attempt at somehow "saving" the traditional connection has proved the opposite; namely, that the once integral moments of a homogeneous vision have fallen apart. They have fallen apart in two decisive ways. Firstly, perfection itself is pluralized and ethical/moral perfection no longer includes perfection as such; secondly, happiness and ethics (morality) have parted company, and different and new concepts of happiness are emerging and coexisting, which take more cognizance of the experiences of men and women in modern times.

Who is perfect? Who is perfect in what?

A new perception of the ancient Greeks and Romans in the times of the Renaissance brings back the idea of human perfection. The analogy with works of art again presents itself. As a statue or a painting can be perfect (nothing added to it, nothing taken away), so can be a human person. Yet, contrary to the ancient model, the concept of perfection itself becomes pluralized. Perfect in what? Vasari's book about the life of the famous artist signals quite radically how things have changed. He makes a case that the most perfect artists are not very perfect beings in the ethical sense; they are ambitious, envious, vain, and resentful. "Perfect" begins to indicate "fully accomplished"; it does not mean "to be good", but "to be good at something," whatever this something may be. The word completely loses its ethical tint. One can be a perfect impostor as well as a perfect gentleman. And the term "perfect" suffers not just of pluralization, but also of a complete devaluation. "Nobody is perfect" is not just an apologetic commonplace, but becomes the deep conviction of modern man. In a dissatisfied society, one is dissatisfied with oneself as much as with others. Where there is no fixed end to reach, there is no end at all. Even if there were such a thing as perfection, it could never be achieved. Even the best, the most accomplished, suffer the humiliation and the pains of Sisyphus. "Nobody is perfect," but the less clever ones are still chasing perfection. They do not reach it, however. The more you chase it, the less can you reach it. There is no fulfillment, no satisfaction, no bliss. Perfection and happiness have thus parted company. Men and women who can show little accomplishment in life may still believe that those who have accomplished something in the public eye "are happy." This is a false conception, not because those who have accomplished something cannot be happy or are less happy than others, but just because happiness and perfection have entirely parted company. They are neither positively nor negatively linked to one another.

Nor is happiness linked to morals any longer. One cannot say that the decent, good people "are happy," just as one cannot say that "the decent, good people are unfortunately unhappy these days," for there is again no direct tie or connection between decency (goodness) and happiness, since happiness has ceased to be an objective concept.

In the traditional world, happiness used to be an objective concept. According to the archaic conception, the wealthy and the mighty are the happy ones. The gods are the most happy, because they are the most mighty. But the wise Solon questioned the truth of the traditional concept. Because men are mortals; they never know whether they are keeping their might and wealth or losing it during their lifetime. Thus no man was ever happy before death. How can a man be called happy while still alive? The classical answer is that if he is virtuous (perfect in virtues), he is also happy. Everyone in a city knows who the most virtuous men are – thus everyone knows who the happiest of them are.

This whole concept broke down along with the ancient social edifice, although this breakdown was conditioned by other occurrences also; firstly, by the emergence of *subjectivity*.[8] The concept of happiness is no longer objective; it becomes subjective. People *feel* happy or unhappy. In modern times, if I tell someone "You are happy," and they answer "No, I am unhappy," one cannot object that the person has assessed his or her being happy/unhappy wrongly. For one *is* happy now only if one *feels* so. As long as the concept of happiness is objective, it is not just possible to live a happy life, but everyone is entitled to describe his own life or the life of someone else as happy/unhappy. But in modern times, where happiness has become subjective (a feeling), no objective criterion determines whether or not someone lives a happy life. Subjective criteria, chiefly the constitution of the person, his or her inclinations and emotional propensities, make that person's life happy or unhappy. Wittgenstein said that the world of a happy person differs from the world of the unhappy person, because the world of the former is a happy world.[9] Prior to modernity, this sentence could not have been uttered by a person with sane mind. Happiness is personality-dependent. So is ethics. But it is by no means necessary that the same personality should be inclined to happiness and to become a decent person. Many decent people have no happy constitution, and many people with a happy constitution are not quite decent. The world of the unhappy can be ethical, and the world of the happy unethical. In a way, Wittgenstein points to this possible connection without spelling it out. For the happy person feels himself or herself to be in agreement with the world. But whether it is ethical to feel ourselves to be in agreement with the world is highly questionable, or at least it can be problematic.

To say "yes" to life is by no means identical to "being happy." For saying "yes" to life is also to say yes to pain and suffering, primarily to our own pain and suffering. The world of a person who says "yes" to life is not necessarily also a happy world. Nor is it an unhappy world. And certainly, saying "yes" to life stands in no direct connection with being a decent person.[10] A decent person can say "yes" to life; yet, those who believe that our world is the vale of tears can also be decent.

But one does not need to have a happy constitution to feel happy from time to time. Men and women who do not have a happy constitution can feel happy for a moment, for a second, for a short time, where "time" stands at the meeting point of time and eternity. The representative story of the modern dissatisfied man who never reaches perfection and the totality of pleasures in his lifetime, who can never accomplish all that he desires (whether he has one life, two, or five), the story of Faust (by Goethe), culminates in the experience of the happy moment.[11]

There are different kinds of happy moments in the modern man's life. The first kind is an exceptional occurrence of need satisfaction and delight, mostly when it happens for the first time. If the same experience happens for a second or third time, it is still need satisfaction and delight, but the incommensurable striking feeling of "happiness" cannot be repeated. Some examples are if one makes love with a beloved for the first time, if one's book is published for the first time, and if one sees the city of one's dreams (for example, Venice) for the first time. The other kind of feeling of happiness can be called "felicity." The feeling of felicity is not diminished if the same or a similar thing happens to us, or if we repeat the experience. The great moment of happiness when listening to music can be even augmented instead of diminished if we listen to the same sonata five times. The same can be said about moments of religious/mystical experiences. The two kinds of happiness can also be fused in the subjective experience.

The more subjective happiness becomes, the more its value depends on the inner life of men and women. In case of emotional impoverishment, the "internal rooms" shrink. Happiness still remains subjective – for the objective, generally valid ethical models of happiness are lost. Yet the market, the media, and public opinion provide panels and stereotypes for happiness. People will then feel happy if they are supposed to be happy. One could say that the archaic model reappears: the mightiest, the wealthiest, and the most renowned ones are called the happiest of men. The stereotypes, however, are not only *descriptions* of "being happy," but also the *prescriptions* for "feeling happy." One should feel happy if one approximates to the stereotype of a "happy" life or even the stereotype of happy moments. One tries hard to feel happy when someone is supposed to feel so (according to the mass-produced and marketed stereotypes). The tension between the prescription to feel happy and the absence of the expected feeling of happiness, or even of joy, is a discrepancy that the person who suffers from this discrepancy hardly understands. Rather, one feels oneself to be inferior; something must be wrong with us "inside." This discrepancy between the panel prescription to feel happy, and the absence of an actual feeling of happiness, or even of delight and joy, can lead to depression and to the crisis of a weak and shallow personal identity.[12]

Conditio moderna is also *conditio humana*. The constituents of the human condition (*Dasein*) cannot disappear in the modern condition, but they can be grossly modified. This also happens with the teleological and causal constitution of personality, where teleological constitution stands for freedom and causal constitution stands for unfreedom. Religions and philosophies agree on this count.

Let me first look at the traditional picture. A person is teleologically constituted insofar as he is "pulled" by the model of perfection from "above"; the more he reaches the model, the idea that "pulls" him, the more perfect and free he becomes. Freedom means independence (in Plato and Aristotle), or (as in Stoicism, Epicureanism, and also Buddhism) a kind of indifference. A person is causally constituted insofar as he is "pushed" instead of being pulled. He can be pushed by his desires, by external circumstances, by false opinions and judgments, by the whims of fate. In Spinoza's vocabulary, the person who is pushed is pushed by his passions. The word "passion" indicates passivity; the unfree person is "the slave" of his passions. The teleologically constituted personality translates his passions into actions (in Spinoza's case, this is due to adequate knowledge).[13]

Spinoza's construction had already resulted from the breakdown of the teleological model of human perfection. But as a metaphysician he had to derive the possibility of a freely (teleologically) constituted self from adequate knowledge of the substance (god as nature). After the deconstruction of metaphysics, this became impossible. The old model no longer described the experiences of men and women who became aware of their contingency.

The new model, which does justice to the experience of contingency, is the model of philosophies of existence.[14] The philosophies of existence do justice to the modern condition insofar as they preserve the distinction between "being pulled" on the one hand and "being pushed" on the other hand, without offering an essentialist picture[15] of man or a general landscape with distinguished teleological paths.

Here I briefly describe one model without suggesting that there cannot be others. This is my model, fashioned on Kierkegaard's conception of an existential choice.

The model of the teleologically constituted self is the person who chooses himself/herself and lives up to his/her choice, in becoming what he/she already is (has become) through his/her choice. It is not an image of perfection, not the ideal – not Reason, knowledge, Goodness, or truth. It is none of these things, but the choice of one's self that will pull the person who has chosen himself/herself. Teleology becomes personal (to become what you are, says Nietzsche),[16] it is not perfection, yet in a way it is, for a single person fulfills his/her destiny in becoming what he/she has chosen himself/herself to be or become. The perfect self (being oneself) is the Centerpoint, the centerpoint of the personality. To be pulled by one's own *destiny* means to be destined.[17] But this is not destined from the outside but, rather, destined from the inside, by one's own choice.[18]

But how can one translate the "push" into "pull?" How can one overcome "determining factors" if one no longer accepts the old recipes, such as suppressing drives, being entirely rational, becoming indifferent, and so on? The choice of the self means the choice of everything that one is: when I choose myself I choose all my determinations – I choose my drives, my infirmities, my mental abilities, my neuroses, just as I also choose myself *as* my self, with all of the predeterminations that define it: my age, my birthplace, my family, my religion, and so on. I choose all my determinations, and I say, "Here I am, as I am, what I am; I am this and this, and have become what I am." For example, "I am a poet, I am a philosopher, I am a politician – or I am a good, decent person."

The existential choice of the self (the personality) is a *leap*. It is not determined, although it does not take place without conditions. One can and cannot be aware of the leap. Authenticity means to remain true to the leap, to one's choice of oneself. *Authenticity is to remain true to oneself.* Authenticity has become the single most sublime virtue[19] of modernity, for authentic people are the people who remain true to their existential choice, who are pulled and not pushed, who are personalities. This also means that they get as close to perfection as a modern person can. The existential choice of the self establishes the centerpoint of the self (the centerpoint occupies the place of norms or ideas, and so on), and in becoming what he/she is, he/she approximates the center. This does not mean that he/she hits the center. Perhaps no one hits the center, and if anyone ever does, we do not know. (Maybe he or she does not know it either.)[20]

Kierkegaard says that if one does not choose oneself, others will choose on one's behalf. Those who do not choose themselves are pushed; they are determined. They are *das Man*, or the other-directed men – and almost all philosophies find a telling description for what they are. Yet as perhaps no single person is only pulled and never pushed, it is also very unlikely that there are people who are always and exclusively pushed and never pulled. But we can speak of people who have existentially chosen themselves if they are mostly pulled, if their personality shows that they are pulled, if they become what they are, if they are authentic (even if sometimes they can miss the center, be pushed, if *das Man* acts and lives in all of them, if all are at times also other-directed, and so on).

The modern personality structure that I have described so far is the model of a *free personality*. He or she is as free as a human person can be, as independent and authentic as a modern person can be. But this does not mean that he or she is also decent or good. For the modern personality structure of the "pull" is not identical with the personality structure of good persons. This could have been expected. For, as I said in advance, perfection itself has been pluralized in modernity. There is no all-around image of perfection; one can be perfect, or nearly perfect, in something, yet not in many things or everything. The relevance of this remark will now be clarified.

One can choose oneself under the category of the particular. For example, I choose myself to be a philosopher, and I become what I already am, a philosopher (or a poet, or a politician, or a perfect lover). It is important that in all cases one does not choose something outside of the self but, rather, that one chooses oneself. I do not choose philosophy, but myself as a philosopher. Of course, having once chosen myself as a philosopher I will be passionately interested in philosophy. That is, I choose myself as being good (perfect) at something. I am authentic if all my subsequent choices are related to the "pull." This is certainly not an ethical choice, although it has ethical implications. First, it mobilizes the most sublime virtue (authenticity), yet it may also require the practice other virtues. A painter can betray his choice if he begins to paint rubbish for money, or because of pressure from a totalitarian dictatorship. If he does so, if he lies with his brush; he loses himself and thus becomes an "existential failure."

The modern decent (good) persons are the persons who have chosen themselves as decent persons. They choose themselves entirely and they say, "As I am, I am a decent person and I will become what I am." He/she is pulled and not pushed; he/she is authentic. To choose oneself as a decent person is to choose oneself under the category of *universality*. Not because one chooses universal values, but because the choice of oneself as decent person is not the choice "to be good at something," but the universal choice "to be good." But if one chooses oneself as a decent person and becomes what he/she has chosen himself/herself to become, he will not become "perfect" as such. True, there can be men and women (there are) who choose themselves as being good at something *and* also as decent persons. If they are lucky, the two choices will not collide; if they are unlucky, they might.

What does it mean that a person has chosen him- or herself as a decent person? What does it mean to be good (decent)? People normally know the answer to the second question, although they will have difficulties formulating it. The first question is more philosophical.

Socrates entered into a controversy with Callicles and Thrasymachos, whether it is better to suffer than to commit injustice, whether it is better to suffer wrong than to wrong others. Socrates proves that it is better, yet Callicles and Thrasymachos prove the opposite. It can be equally and rationally proven that it is better to suffer than to commit injustice, and that it is better to commit than to suffer injustice. The arguments for and against the dictum of Socrates are equally strong. Socrates "solves" this paradox, by antinomy, by choosing death instead of committing wrong. Decency itself proves decency, nothing else does. Yet indecency is also proven, and by the majority of men. So what? Why does someone choose to be good? The question is unanswerable. The sources of goodness are transcendent. Kant came to the same conclusion, for he could not resolve the antinomies of our practical reason but by a metaphysical device of distinguishing absolutely between *Homo nuomenon* and *Homo phenomenon*. Post-metaphysical thinking cannot accept this solution. What, then, is the philosophical solution?

In a world founded on freedom which does not found, philosophes choose the foundations. The foundations of moral philosophy are not chosen by philosophers, however. The foundation of every philosophy of morals is the decent (good) persons themselves, irrespective of the understanding and the theorizing of their goodness. The foundation resounds: decent (good) persons exist. The question is: How are they possible? Traditional metaphysics could answer this question; postmodern philosophy cannot answer it directly but only indirectly. The indirect answer sounds as follows: good (decent) people are the people for whom the dictum of Socrates (which cannot be proven, or the opposite of which can also be proven) is true. Good persons are possible because there are men and women for whom the dictum of Socrates is true.

Since (modern) good persons are the persons who choose themselves as good (decent) persons, neither the ethos nor the value system of the (modern) world increases or decreases their numbers. Here I am in agreement with Kant's intuition: the good ethical order can promote legality, yet not morality. Yet, without morality there is no legality.

Contemporary moral philosophies (particularly analytical philosophies) center around the issue of moral/ethical argumentation.[21] The dividing line between dialectics and rhetorics is thin. Whenever one argues, one wants to persuade others to accept the result and to judge and act according to the result. Ethical/legal argumentation is, of course, not just a philosophical practice. In our "reflective age,"[22] where the dynamics of modernity is always kept in motion, the only nonviolent method of contestation is contestation by argumentation.[23] Arguments are weapons in political fights.[24] In a democracy arguments decide – at least on the surface[25] – what kind of measures will be taken. The members of the parliament, of the council of ministers, the economic and political advisers, all of them fight with arguments. One argues for (or against) a social policy, one argues for choosing this plan for city development rather than another, one argues over sending troops to this or that country, one argues for and against almost everything.[26]

Argumentation can help to persuade the undecided; it can bring hidden aspects of the matter in discussion to the surface; it can give a good weapon to the mouth or pen (not the hand) of those who have a vested interest in something but are in need of rationalization. There is only *one thing good arguments cannot perform: one cannot prove by arguments alone that the decision supported by the argument is the only true or the only right one*. But arguments aim exactly at the *impossible*: to prove that only the decision for which they are to argue is, in principle, right – or at least that argumentative discourse can decide what is right. The participants in an argumentative discourse pretend, sometimes unknowingly, that argumentative reasoning, *Reason itself*, decides the *ultimate questions of right/wrong, true/false*, in all matters of public life.

But *conditio moderna* has not changed *conditio humana*, although it has reversed the structure of social arrangement on all counts.

Let me return to the starting-point of this book. Aristotle's observation that one can conduct a rational discussion with a rational result only under the condition that there is an *archē*, a primal principle, which we take as being self-evidently true, is an observation concerning *conditio humana*. Reason is a powerful weapon, but it is powerful within its own limits. No ultimate truth can be established by reason. Whenever one argues for or against an *end*, an evaluated goal, a project, a program and the like, one needs to be aware that the argument can go on *ad infinitum* (and none of the parties will ever win, unless they use forces other than the force of the argument) if there are no values or evaluated ends that are accepted *before* the argument. If one already knows what the end should be, what the good is, what the truth of the matter is, one can well argue for this end. So can others who evaluate another end for their end.

In the modern condition, the relation between *pistis* and *logos* has been rearranged. *Logos* stands in the foreground, and *pistis* in the background. This reversal follows from the dynamics of modernity; it is required by it.

The abandonment of the argumentative practice, of the practice of discourse, would mean the abandonment of the dynamics of modernity also, of modernity itself. If I say that one normally argues for something that one has already accepted as true, good, or correct, I do not mean that arguing for the sake of those things is useless, redundant, or ridiculous.[27] Just the contrary; this is exactly what is required by the spirit of modernity. But if one concludes from all this that in the modern world Reason reigns supreme, or that we in fact prove with reason either truth, goodness, or rightness, particularly in matters of historicity, one will overstretch oneself, for one will mentally exempt the modern condition from the human condition.

Without pistis there is no logos: this remains the human condition now as well. Here I do not speak of *pistis* (faith) as contrasted with *knowledge*, as usual. I do not identify it with *will* either, but speak of it contrasted with or pairing with argumentation, such as *arguing or accepting according to the leap of faith*. For, in contrast to all other kinds of reason, argumentative reason is the *modern* kind of reason par excellence,[28] and this is why it is better to remain aware of it, that this particular employment of reason is the most *inseparable* from faith among all the other kinds of reason and their employment.

The reversal of the relation between Faith and *Logos* could be best formulated as follows: if *Logos* stands in the background, the starting-point, the nonrational foundation of argumentation, sounds roughly like the following: *I believe because it is not absurd.* (*Credo quia non absurdum est.*) Everything which is not absurd can be proven by arguments rationally.[29] One first has to accept it as self-evident.

But when is a social, political end (project) absurd? And how do I know that it is absurd? After all, absurd things can also be proven rationally. For example, the Marxian project of the de-alienation of society and the withering away of the state and all human institutions could also be proven rationally. Sometimes, some project, ends, or goals unmask themselves as absurd without having been obviously absurd when they were first "proven" by arguments. On the contrary, many projects were first regarded as absurd and turned out not to be absurd later. When is an evaluated goal, end, or project for or against which one argues absurd? How can they be recognized as absurd? Since everything can be argued for rationally (unless it entails a logical contradiction) and all ends and goals are by definition contingent because they are "history" in *futurum perfectum*, and historical events and institutions are contingent, one can argue for and against all ends or goals rationally.

But when I suggested that *"credio quia non absurdum est"* is the modern principle which guides *initial faith* – the faith that precedes argumentation – and also suggested that here and now the relation between *logos* and *pistis* had been reversed, I had in mind *not facticity, but validity.*

In the pre-modern social arrangement, most things that really matter are taken as self-evident: the cosmos, the mores, the institutions, the way of life. This means that these things are accepted as good and right by *faith.* Men were not really responsible for their faith because they received knowledge by faith. The moment one began to use one's personal reason, one assumed an enormous responsibility. Personal reasoning, proving and disproving, reasoning as such, and most of all reasoning about certain ends,[30] endangered their world, its sheer survival. The knowledge of good and evil and the capacity to discriminate was mostly subjected to authority. To argue against such an authority was mostly suspected to be the work of the Satan. To summarize: one had little responsibility for faith, but enormous responsibility for reasoning.

In modernity, the opposite is the case. Reasoning for or against concrete aims and goals is a matter of course. We all do it every day. We can argue better or worse; but even if we come up with bad arguments, our responsibility is small.[31] We will be soon corrected. However, *we moderns carry enormous responsibility for our faith.* This is why the *"credo quia non absurdum est"* is a normative and not an empirical statement. It means that one carries great responsibility for the ends that one has accepted by faith prior to the process of argumentation. The ends should not be absurd. "Nonabsurd" first means to be nonabsurd pragmatically (an end which is not impossible to reach); but it also means *nonabsurd in the moral sense.* Which aims are morally absurd or, to speak Kant's language, "morally impossible"? The answer is: all the aims the realization of which, or the approximation of which requires, by definition, the use of other persons as mere means. *Those aims are morally possible which do not in principle require the use of other persons as mere means.* They are morally not absurd.

The responsibility of men in postmodernity is essentially the responsibility for the investment of one's Faith and not of the exercises of Reason. One can put one's faith in the most incorrect (most absurd) end, and still argue for it splendidly. The Devil reasons well. But reasoning is no longer the work of the Devil, but is now the commonly assumed exercise of modern men and women.

Reason does not decide the ultimate questions of right/wrong, nor does faith. One needs to take enormous responsibility for one's faith in matters of good/evil or right/wrong precisely because certainty is *not there,* because one leaps into one's own certainty (truth) for which one takes full responsibility.

There are two kinds of responsibility: retrospective and prospective. One has retrospective responsibility if one assumes responsibility for one's past deeds. However, one has prospective responsibility if one is in charge: I carry responsibility for this thing in the future (my country, my fellow passengers, my children). Responsibility is associated in both cases with the word and the act *to respond*. I am responsible – I answer for it.

Both kinds of responsibility can be personal and/or collective. One of Balzac's heroes, Rastignac, said once that no one is responsible for collective crimes. He referred here to the crimes of capitalism. There are three interesting new features in his statement.

Firstly, he assumed that *we*, the speakers and not just the enemy, can commit collective crimes. This assumption signalled a novel feature of modern (at that time, European) culture, namely self-reflexivity. We can describe our deeds as crimes – not sins committed against God, but crimes committed against others as well as ourselves, our fellow creatures.

Secondly, Rastignac insisted that there are crimes for which no one is responsible. Perhaps this is because there is no one to ask the question we need to answer, but mainly because the criminal actions have no alternatives. We cannot say that this is wrong and that something else would be good instead, because we do not believe that something better could be the case. We deal with an historical phenomenon as with *historical necessity*. Crimes necessitated are still crimes, but because there is no free will to avoid them, no one is responsible for them.

Thirdly, where everyone participates in a crime, no one as a person has committed a crime. A collective crime is the crime of the collectivity, but not the crime of any single individual.

There are many questions to be raised about all those issues. If I am not mistaken, (post)modern discourse on ethics will center mainly around these issues.

What is the scope of the prospective individual responsibility? For whom is a modern person responsible? Who is in "charge"? Kant would answer with the categorical imperative: the moral law is humankind in us, which means that we are responsible for all human beings who ever lived, who are now living, and who are going to live in our world. Levinas would answer: we are responsible for the Other who looks at us, who faces us, to all Others who raise claims on us (God included?). But if we are responsible for everyone we cannot assume *active* responsibility. Active responsibility can be taken only for men and women who are within the reach of our *action radius*, for whom, and against whom, we can do something directly. Is this enough? Or is it too much? Or possibly something other then closeness/remoteness needs to decide matters of responsibility? Perhaps the need of the other is better to decide? Or does everyone decide for whom one carries responsibility and for whom none? Is there a quantity in taking responsibility? To what extent are we duty bound to take responsibility for ourselves? And what if responsibility taken for ourselves collides with the responsibility taken for the others? And what are the criteria for taking responsibility?

Even more and more variegated questions are raised about the responsibility of "collective crimes." What kind of collective action can be called a crime? If there is no responsibility, can there be a crime? How can one call capitalism a "crime"? Or, how can we say that Europeans committed "crimes" against colonized men and women? What was their crime? Can one say that what they have done was done by necessity – or by choice? Was there a choice? Where is there a choice? Is there anything like "historical necessity" which might exempt us from responsibility? Are crimes collectively committed the crimes of the collectivity? Are all Germans criminals because Germans committed the Holocaust? Are all members of all communist parties criminals because communist parties send people to the Gulag to die? And is it true that if there is a collective crime, no one is responsible for it? Or are there different levels of free choice and thus different levels of responsibility? Or is freedom not quantifiable? But, if it is not quantifiable, everyone who has participated in a collective crime is equally responsible for this crime. Is this right? Is this a just moral judgment – and a just political judgment? Can repentance or confession of guilt still count as a mitigating circumstance? Yet who will give the absolution if God is dead? Is there any punishment other than the legal? Is it right that one can answer for collective crimes only before a court of justice? Can the nonlegal be moral? For example, can retroactive legislation still be an act of morality, or not? Who is the judge in such a case? Who or what authorizes judgment?

Is there a collective, prospective responsibility? Who (which collective entities) carries responsibility for the fate of the human race? For the survival of modernity? For nature? For a (relative) peace and a (relative) security? For political freedom? Can one group (nation or alliance) carry responsibility for the others, for all others – and for which others, in what relation and to what extent?

What is the difference between political and ethical responsibility? Does the Weberian "ethics of responsibility" still make sense? Can we judge political acts on the ground of their consequences? What consequences? Consequences for whom? Short-term or long-term consequences? What about unforeseeable consequences (the possibility of which has certainly not decreased in our postmodern world)?

I have come up with only one answer. And this is also just a general answer which leaves many of the concrete questions open. I have suggested that it is good if faith is vested in ends which are not morally absurd, and it is better if faith is not vested in ends which seem to be – for us, now – pragmatically absurd.

This means that far more questions are raised than answered.

But (post)moderns raise more questions than they answer, but not because they are cowards. It is easier to answer questions than to leave them open.

Postscript: perhaps I have answered too many questions – more than I should have. If this is so, please re-translate my answers into so many new questions.

Notes

Preface

1 I discussed the status of social sciences in my paper "Hermeneutics of Social Sciences," in Agnes Heller, *Can Modernity Survive?* (Berkeley: University of California Press, 1990).

2 Agnes Heller, *A Theory of History* (Boston: Routledge & Kegan Paul, 1982).

3 In Hungarian, Ferenc Fehér and Agnes Heller, *A modernitás ingája*, (T. Twins, 1993) and in Spanish, Agnes Heller and Ferenc Fehér, *El Pendulo de la Modernidas Peninsula* (Barcelona, 1994).

4 Otto Hevizi distinguished between four kinds of choosing a foundation in his study on "relative supposition" (in manuscript). He exemplified with the four case types of Kant, Nietzsche, the ironist (Kierkegaard, young Lukács, or Rorty), and Wittgenstein.

1 Modernity from a Postmodern Perspective

1 It is not necessary to offer a nominal definition, although it is not excluded.

2 Heidegger once said about reflection, "Rückbeugung auf sich selbst" (Gesamtausgabe, 79 Band, p. 138). It is roughly in this sense that I speak of "reflected postmodernity."

3 I use the term "family" here in Wittgenstein's sense.

4 Regarding the stages of historical consciousness, see my book, *A Theory of History* (Boston: Routledge & Kegan Paul, 1982).

5 The question of personal identity formation cannot be discussed here, nor can the main constituents of identity (memory, narratives, the regard of the other, etc.), the question of multiple identities, or the issue of the divided self.

6 Of course, the question "Where are we going?" does not necessarily refer to a mythological, collective future-orientation, as it does incidentally in the Tahiti case.

7 Actually, they are like Hegel's "Gestalten der Welt" in his *Phenomenology of Spirit*, trans. A. V. Miller (Oxford: Oxford University Press, 1977). I do not distinguish between "Gestalten des Bewusstseins," "Gestalten des Selbstbewusstseins," and "Gestalten der Welt" because I do not want to

attempt a new version of the grand narrative. Although, I confess, Foucault was right. That is, it is difficult to abandon Hegel, and some kind of a grand narrative cannot be avoided. However, it can be treated as typology, as a booster for inculcation, and perhaps it can be treated ironically as well.

8   "Reflected postmodernity" is neither a sect nor a school. Finally, all who share our world have a share in the postmodern condition. When thinkers such as Habermas, who can still be regarded as high modernists in one respect, speak about the inscrutability and intransparency of the modern world, he engages in a dialogue of reflected postmodernity in my sense of the term, although they may strongly protest against such a description.

9   See György Lukács, *Soul and Form*, trans. Anna Bostock (Cambridge: MIT Press, 1974). In particular, the first preface is laden with a kind of postmodern atmosphere. I already mentioned that even Max Weber can be understood as an early swallow of the postmodern perspective. It is true that he can also be understood as a high modernist. In his next famous book, *The Theory of the Novel*, trans. Anna Bastock (Cambridge, MA: MIT Press, 1971), Lukács actually turned entirely toward high modernism. Regarding this development, see Paul de Man's study on the Theory of the Novel.

10 And again, in *The Postmodern Heidegger* (Budapest: Századuég, 1994), Mihaly Vajda claims the Heidegger after the *Kehre* for the postmoderns, and not without justification. This is not the only place Vajda makes this claim. It is true that Heidegger can also be regarded as a representative of "high modernism," particularly in his earlier period, in *Sein und Zeit*.

11 The change in the self-understanding of natural sciences due to the philosophy of science belongs to this story. Kuhn's conception of the scientific paradigm changes was a great blow to the high and mighty modernist and unilinear progressivist historical consciousness of positivism.

12 The works of Herbert Spencer, the typical progressivist of this kind, could be found not only in the libraries of the British, but of the "cultivated" European middle classes. Spencer *brevaria* were even more widely read.

13 This was also the position of Hegel, in both his *Phenomenology of Spirit* and his *Science of Logic*.

14 Leibniz developed the thought about the identity of the incomparable ones, the self-sameness of *ipseity*. His wisdom that only phenomena can be compared (never essences, substances, or monads), that the whole cannot be known from any of the perspectives (except the perspective of God), is not such a far cry from postmodern imagination.

15 Leibniz said that the truth of facts is contingent, because the facts described could have been otherwise. Yet, he establishes the truth of all contingent facts, insofar as God had a foreknowledge of everything that has happened, is happening, and is going to happen (contingently). Of course, the past, present, and the future tenses cannot do justice to God's eternal – in this case absolutely synchronic – knowledge.

16 I elaborated on the awareness of the cosmic and social contingency in my book, *A Philosophy of History in Fragments* (Oxford and Cambridge, MA: Basil Blackwell, 1993), in my discussion of Pascal in chapter 1.

17 Pascal writes in his *Pensées* that the modern man is squeezed between the Zero and the Infinite. Blaise Pascal, *Pensées*, trans. A. J. Krail Sheimer (Penguin Classics, 1995).

18 I borrow the expression "institutions imaginaires" from Cornelius Castoriadis. *The Imaginary Institutions of Society* (Cambridge: Polity Press, 1987).

19 At this time Hegel became a "dead dog," to use Marx's expression, precisely because he proposed that we settle in the present.

20 In the 18th century, revolution could have still been understood in its original meaning (revolving), and in the postmodern imagination this ancient interpretation, which is lost in the 19th century, is to return. It is true that Nietzsche's myth of the eternal recurrence of the same can also be interpreted as a postmodern version of the interpretation of revolution. In my mind this is a too strong, although not an impossible, interpretation. At any rate, Nietzsche's personal myth was atypical in the second half of the 19th century.

21 The idea of infinite progression (of human society and the human species) on the one hand, and infinite regression in scientific knowledge on the other, is fully elaborated by Kant. Although Kant emphasizes that we do not know whether this progression toward the better will happen, he still emphasizes that we had better presuppose it (for example, in order not to flatter the tyrant, as he expresses himself in a famous footnote to his work, "The Perpetual Peace"). Although Kant does not speak of a pivotal role of technology, he speaks about the progression in the culture of skills. Kant was actually claimed as a major ally by both camps, by the liberal progressivists, as well as certain socialists (e.g., Otto Bauer and other Austro-Marxists). The latter emphasized that Kant could at least presuppose (that is, he did not exclude) the possibility that "nature" develops toward "freedom," toward an "ethical state" in his book, *Religion within the Boundaries of Mere Reason*, trans. Allen W. Wood (Cambridge: Cambridge University Press, 1999).

22 This hidden teleology brought together the two otherwise irreconcilable conceptions: the future is open and free, yet it is certain, at least as far as its essence is concerned. György Markus, in his book *Marxism and "Anthropology"* (Assen: Van Gorcum, 1978), deciphered this hidden teleology in Marx's *Paris Manuscripts*. It was because of this hidden teleology that socialist conceptions, mainly the chief Marxian one, had often been unmasked as the secularized version of Jewish Messianism, Christian Millenarian creeds, and similar religious visions. (The latter is particularly emphasized by Mannheim in his *Ideology and Utopia* as a typical form of utopia. Carl Schmitt, *Political Theology* (Cambridge, MA: MIT Press, 1985), develops similar ideas about the political categories of liberalism. Hans Blumenberg, *Work on Myths* (Cambridge, MA: MIT Press, 1985), rejects this conception and points to the unmistakably modern features of the political categories of the 19th century. I would agree with Blumenberg, with one *proviso*. The stages of historical consciousness expressed by the liberal as much as the Marxian/socialist versions of the faith in "progression" are manifestations of the stage of historical consciousness which I termed "reflected universality." Since the Jewish/Christian consciousness is

(in my story at least) the consciousness of unreflected universality, there is a similarity between them; namely, their universality, which expands over all three dimensions of history, secular or sacred. The future is open and yet overdetermined, and the same for the whole human race (although not the same for all persons). But the similarity of certain structural elements within the two "universalistic" stages of historical consciousness, and the undeniable fact that reflected universality could employ as its tradition certain versions of unreflected universality even if it developed hostility toward the religious tradition from which it grew and with which it needed to compete, is not reason enough to treat modern conceptions simply as versions of a secularized theology.

23 The Marxian metaphor (in *Capital* I) of the pregnancy of capitalism, which brings the future into the world in pains of delivery (this is meant to be the revolution), where those pains of delivery might be alleviated by the action of the midwife – the revolutionary proletariat – is also a story of legitimation.

24 I refer to *Kairos* (the proper time for ...) as a Greek idea because it played a central role in Greek thinking. See Cornelius Castoriadis, *The Imaginary Institutions of Society* (Cambridge: Polity Press, 1987). As I learned from Gyula Rugasi's essay, "The Restoration of the Church" (Vilagossag, 1966, 12) p. 53, the Hebrew word *et* has the same shade of meaning as the Greek word *Kairos*.

25 George Sorel, in his book *On Violence* (Glencoe, IL: Free Press, 1950), prophetically described this combination before it became the structural frame of the ideologies of the Bolshevik and Nazi parties. He called the concoction a myth (the myth of the general strike).

26 The reason why I speak of moral transgression is clear. By ontological transgression I mean the willful violation of nature (creating an entirely new nature *à la* Stalin, or new human races *à la* Hitler). By metaphysical transgression I mean the resolve to wipe out the biblical God from the memory of men, to create new gods.

27 It makes no sense to enter the circle. Obviously, the detection of the dramatic increase in pollution accelerated the change in historical consciousness, as the change of historical consciousness created the sensitivity for ecological problems (and particularly for the premonition of ecological disasters). The great apocalyptic visions of the "end of life" on Earth are, however, the follow-up to the revolutionary model formulated in a negative way, such as "Here is the time, now is the time to prevent life from dying out on our planet. Today we can still do it. Tomorrow it will be late."

28 It has become fashionable in the contemporary dialogue (also inspired by the excellent works of Hans Jonas) to propose taking responsibility of the far and yet unknown future in matters that concern life (ecology). As I said before, I detect here the traces of the old grand narrative of decadence, this time merging in alliance with the preceding revolutionary combination of *Kairos* cum Apocalypse. Since all kinds of thinking and consciousness are coexisting

in our present, this concept of responsibility can also become widespread. In my mind, however, it is a fairly irresponsible concept of responsibility. This is because, just as in old times, our contemporaries – that is, our Togetherness – is asked to sacrifice itself on the altar of our great-grandchildren, the conditions of life of which we are entirely ignorant, and the wishes of which cannot even be extrapolated from our present observations.

29   We shall see in the following chapter that Hegel makes his story much stronger.

30   This is so in all cases. An actual child has a greater claim on a parent than a possible child.

31   For example, I can wish to live in the ancient *polis*, but this is an emotional nostalgia. I can dream of living in the 22nd century, but this is an empty image. I cannot take responsibility for Socrates, or for the men and women of the 22nd century.

32   Regarding the transformation of a contingent age into destiny in the life of a denizen of the age, see my book, *A Philosophy of Morals* (Oxford and Cambridge, MA: Basil Blackwell, 1990).

33   Jacques Derrida distinguishes between "Messianic" and "Messianistic" in his book, *Spectres de Marx* (Paris: Galilee, 1993). I accept this distinction. At the same time, Derrida makes the attempt to name the occupant of the chair "radical democracy." (He does the same in his book *The Politics of Friendship*.) As is obvious from my train of thought, I take a stand against all kinds of naming.

34   The expression stems from Walter Benjamin, to whom I owe my conception of weak Messianistic force.

35   Aristotle, *Politics*, in *The Basic Works of Aristotle*, trans. Richard McKeon (New York: Random House, 1941), pp. 1127–324.

36   See Miguel Vatter, "Machiavelli and the republican freedom," in manuscript.

37   Nietzsche was, in fact, right when he emphasized the organic relationship between the Jewish "slave revolt" and the emergence of the idea of modern democracies.

38   If I wrote a "history of the ideas," I would need to point out the essential differences between those autobiographies of Europe. Before the times of the Enlightenment, freedom was conceived almost entirely politically and ethically. It was identified with political institutions, personal independence, liberties, and so forth. Moreover, freedom, on the one hand, and knowledge, civilization, and cultivation, on the other hand, were not connected, or if they were they were rather in contrast. That industry makes slaves of all of us was the general creed of economic romanticism. As is well known, in Rousseau the development of civilization is hostile to equality, morality, and political independence. In Condorcet, who was perhaps already the first progressivist, knowledge and freedom develop simultaneously, although they always have the potential of colliding. It is only in the modern world that they will be reconciled. That the development of civilization, technology, and industry is one of the conditions of the freedom of the moderns is a

new idea in the 19th century, but it soon gathers momentum, to become deeply problematic again in our own age.

39   I will return to the question, "How did freedom become the foundation of the modern world?" in the chapter on the dynamics of modernity. I mentioned European autobiography, yet it will soon turn out that modernity, although born in Europe, quickly became global, and that freedom as the foundation of modernity is also global.

40   The German language has the advantage of using related expressions for "ground" and "abyss," *Grund* and *Abgrund*, respectively. Hegel, in his *Science of Logic*, refers to the self-removing of a ground as "zu Grunde gehen." The expression has a double meaning: to go into the ground (where the ground is heterogeneous in comparison to the former ground, and contains the former in its contrariety), and to be destroyed. In Hegel's logic there is always a safety net. Heidegger also plays on the relation between *Grund* and *Abgrund*, although he does not use Hegel's safety net.

41   I will discuss the deconstruction of the pre-modern "natural artifice" in the chapters dealing with the dynamics of modernity and the modern social arrangement.

42   There is a version of Heidegger's metaphysics saga (and its interpretation) which establishes a relation (almost a causal relation) between metaphysical thinking (subject/object thinking), on the one hand, and modernity, particularly modern technological thinking, on the other hand. Without denying the connection, I would like to point out the opposite tendency: modernity does not tolerate metaphysics in the sense developed from Plato through German idealism. When the common world of the moderns is no longer firmly founded, philosophy cannot be firmly grounded either.

43   Aristotle, *Metaphysics* in *The Basic Works of Aristotle*, ed. Richard Mac-Keon (New York: Random House, 1941), Book Gamma.

44   The discussion of the structural requirements of, claims of, and limits to metaphysics, is beyond the grasp of the present topic.

45   A transcendental argument is already reflection. Not all metaphysical constructs are reflective, however. For example, Plato's metaphysics is at times not reflective.

46   Metaphysical grounding becomes theology, of course. After all, the existence of God is also to be proven. Finally, it is proven (in all kinds of arguments) with and through itself. The ingenious gambit of Spinoza, beginning his *Ethics* with *causa sui*, makes this clear.

47   In philosophy as in metaphysics, the higher (first or second) world has as much a de-legitimating as a legitimating function. This issue will be addressed, in the chapter on the dynamics of modernity.

48   This is also a transcendental argument, yet without stating that there is a world. It is a truncated transcendental argument, a modern one.

49   I will discuss the question of whether there can be two worlds after the deconstruction of "the natural edifice" (artifice) and of metaphysics, in the chapter on "culture."

50 That is, it reflects the empirical humankind as the sum total of all cultures with which we share the globe, as cultures which are empirically coeval with one another. I discussed this question in my book, *Beyond Justice* (Oxford and New York: Basil Blackwell, 1987).

51 All the Kantian antinomies are paradoxes; either the paradoxes of truth (reason, knowledge) or the paradoxes of freedom. The resolution of the antinomies is possible (within the Kantian system) through the absolute division (the onto/metaphysical division) between two worlds: the world of freedom (the normative world) and the world of nature (the empirical world). The dual ontology became unable to maintain in post-metaphysical philosophical reflection. However, if there is no absolute abyss between Freedom and Nature, the abyss appears somewhere else – in the foundation itself.

52 This is the "*Mache*" Heidegger used to speak about.

53 Perhaps it does not even understand. Heidegger expressed this far better than I can. He wrote in the V. Freiburg lecture (op. cit., p. 175), "*Wir bleiben auf dieser Erde im Verhaltnismässigen angesiedelt.* Jemand ... könnte dem entgegen: Dann ist eben das Verhaltnismässige das Absolute. Richtig. Doch bleibt die Frage, ob wir im Denken mit blossen Richtigkeiten auskommen und mit ihrer Hilfe je sagen konnen, was dies denn heisst: absolut." Stressed by Heidegger. A.H.

54 By "historical" truth I mean, again, *geschichlich*, not *historisch*. That Julius Caesar was killed on the Capitolium is not a *geschichtliche* but *historische Wahrheit* (truth). No one is involved in this truth. Only as long as one is involved in a truth does the truth become historical in the sense of *geschichtlich*. Statements such as "the cat is on the mat" are banal true statements (if the cat is on the mat).

55 By "approximation" he does not have in mind approximative knowledge, although one also "leaps" in the case of approximative knowledge. He meant that one should conduct a life in approximation. Again, to quote Heidegger, "Wir bleiben auf dieser Erde im Verhaltnismassigen angesiedelt."

56 Kierkegaard added that "my truth" cannot be replaced with "our truth," for I cannot take responsibility in the name of others. This move avoids the danger of fundamentalism.

2 The Challenge of the Heritage

1 The most grandiose, all-encompassing theories of modernity were developed in Germany, where modernity was in a way underdeveloped. By choosing these three authors as the representative theorists of modernity, I have confirmed Marx's observation that the Germans accomplished in philosophy what the French did in politics. In discussing the constituents, logic, and additional singular aspects of modernity, I will of course return to British and French philosophy, whereas among the most representative contemporary

moderns, Germans (with the exception of Heidegger) will no longer occupy a special position.

2 Centuries do not begin on the even 100 mark. Actually, the 19th century began after the battle of Waterloo in 1815.

3 In Hegel's mind, destruction is unsuccessful deconstruction also in matters of politics. See the chapter on Absolute Freedom (the Jacobin terror) and its collapse in the *Phenomenology of Spirit*.

4 In this respect, Nietzsche, in his *On the Genealogy of Morals*, trans. Walter Kaufmann (New York: Vintage Books, 1969), did something very similar to Hegel in his *Philosophy of History*, trans. J. Sibree (Chicago: University of Chicago Press, 1952).

5 I will soon return to this question.

6 The meaning of these statements will be deciphered in the chapter on culture.

7 All the previous references were to the preface of the *Philosophy of Right*.

8 "Reason in history," Introduction to *Lectures on the Philosophy of History*.

9 See the Introduction to my book, *A Philosophy of History in Fragments* (Oxford and Cambridge, MA: Basil Blackwell, 1993).

10 See G. W. F. Hegel, *Philosophy of Right*, trans. T. M. Knox (Oxford: Oxford University Press, 1952).

11 In his discussion of Enlightenment (in the *Phenomenology of Spirit*), Hegel recounts the story of switching from one metaphysical language (that of religion) to another, to the "metaphysics of the matter" (materialism). Both metaphysics are described as being essentially the same, on the ground that they both employ absolute presuppositions.

12 This was not so (according to Hegel) in the ancient world of *Sittlichkeit*, the Greek city–state. The individual had no room for self-development, and there were not three ethical powers, but only two: the laws of the city and the divine laws, the world of men and of women. There was no mediation. This is said to be the reason for the (self-)destruction of the ancient world.

13 Nation as community or as pseudo-community has not played an important role in Hegel's conception of modernity. Maybe now, in the world of more and more multi-ethnic and multinational states and alliances of states, this absence is not perceived as a great deficit.

14 Nowadays, after the neo-Kantians and Nietzsche, one speaks of values instead of ethical powers. Yet, I prefer to employ Hegel's terminology.

15 Hegel disliked the word "virtue." In his mind, it was outdated. He said in a remark in the *Philosophy of Right* that today only the French are virtuous.

16 This statement was one of the accusations raised against the "revisionism" of Eduard Bernstein. Contrary to Marx's statement that the "proletar" has no family, Bernstein – supported with well-interpreted statistics – argued that the situation changed in the second half of the 19th century. (Perhaps, in our present day it is about to change once again.)

17 The Jacobin dictatorship lacked the proper institutions of mediation. This is a good description. But the possibility of a well-entrenched modern world without mediation, without leaving enough elbow room for the individual

and the particular, has not entered Hegel's mind. It could have entered, perhaps, but Hegel was not interested in this possibility. This is – among other things – what his slogan about "the end of history" means. That many things can happen and change after the end of history was not excluded by Hegel. But that something entirely new can enter the stage within modernity, in the daylight of modernity, this was beyond his imagination. It is no wonder that this possibly went beyond almost everyone's imagination. But history never ends, not even in a Hegelian interpretation – because there are always things happening within our world, and not after it, which go beyond our (mostly bad) imagination.

18 This thought was expressed by Mihaly Vajda in his book *Nem az Orokke-valosagnak* (No(t) for Eternity) (Budapest: Osiris, 1997).

19 This is why I suggested in several of my papers that Kant's moral philosophy serves as a good crutch for a modern person in the situation of moral decision, whereas Hegel's philosophy is, at this point, of no great help.

20 I will arrive at the discussion of Hegel's conception of morality in his *Phenomenology* in the next chapter.

21 I disagree with Jacobson (*Hegel's Philosophy of Right*, Cardozo School of Law, 1992), in whose interpretation Hegel does not assign duties to rights. Jacobson's position is typical of a kind of American liberal postmodernism, particularly in its multiculturalist version. The interpretation is making a case against the relevance of Hegel's concept of the ethical powers.

22 Hegel criticizes the Kantian definition of marriage as a contract from this point of view.

23 As Nietzsche said in the *Twilight of the Idols*, if one abolishes the "true" world of metaphysics, one also abolishes the appearance. In the new metaphysics the true world was not abolished but relocated; thus, the appearance as "distortion" was not abolished either. Friedrich Nietzsche, *Twilight of the Idols or How to Philosophize with a Hammer*, ed. Duncan Large (Oxford: Oxford University Press, 1998).

24 Marx said (in *Capital* I) that if essence and appearance coalesced, one would not need science. This description is alien from the self-description of natural sciences; rather it fits metaphysics. Science is, in Marx's view, the only branch of mental/spiritualactivity which is not ideological and does not belong to the superstructure.

25 For example, Freud, *The New Introductory Lectures on Psychoanalysis*, trans. James Strachey (New York and London: W. W. Norton, 1965).

26 See Sigmund Freud, *Introductory Lectures on Psychoanalysis: A Course of Twenty-Eight Lectures Delivered at the University of Vienna* (London: Allen & Unwin, 1922).

27 This is how the eternal recurrence of the same and the will to power are presented.

28 The conception of enfolding/unfolding is of theological origin, employed by Meister Eckhardt, Cusa, and Hegel.

29 The phenomenological description of the main constituents of the generic essence as of *Dasein* is not entirely contingent, but includes contingent

elements in Marx as well as the later Heidegger. Marx did not acknowledge this aspect of contingency – nor did Heidegger.

30 For the discussion of the constituents of the human essence in Marx, I recommend György Markus, *Marxism and "Anthropology,"* as still the best interpretation of the project.

31 Subject/object philosophy always puts a premium on creativity, but it does not lead with any necessity to the paradigm of work, and even less to the paradigm of production. I differentiated between those two paradigms, also in Marx, in my "The paradigm of work, the paradigm of production" (in Ferenc Fehér and Agnes Heller, *Grandeur and Twilight of Radical Universalism* (New Brunswick: Transaction Publishers, 1991). In the same volume, the reader can also find my other contributions to the Marxian/post-Marxian understanding of Marx.

32 This was later termed (not by Marx) "historical materialism."

33 To avoid misunderstanding, I am not hostile to metaphysics. I criticize the kind of metaphysics that claims to be something other than what it verily is. That traditional natural sciences also work with metaphysical presuppositions is beyond doubt. Leibniz said about Newton: bad metaphysics, bad physics. By stressing that in Marx's case the fundamental standpoint (metaphysics) and "physics" (science) cannot be separated from one another, I repeat only what Marx said about himself. His economy, so he emphasized, is true and not just scientific like that of Ricardo, because he took the standpoint of the proletariat. That is, the perspective he took is the main constituent of the truth of his position. This perspective is not a paradigm because it is not presented as such, but as the world-historical truth and as the scientific foundation of true predictions of the future. This is a strongly and unconsciously metaphysical claim.

34 The extent to which the so-called empirical observations of the everyday attitude are metaphysical is first discussed in Hegel's *Phenomenology*.

35 Marx uses this expression in *Capital* I.

36 See, among others, Karl Marx, *Critique of the Gotha Programme* (International Publishers, 1938). Here Marx speaks of communism as the historical period in which nature will produce more than needs waiting for satisfaction; that is, as the age of absolute (total) abundance.

37 In *The Paris Commune* (New York: New York Labor News Company, 1945), Marx says that death is the victory of the species over the individual.

38 *Paris Manuscripts*.

39 This is an interpretation/application of Vico's famous saying, *verum and factum convenuntur* (*factum* in the sense of *facere*). See Giambattista Vico, *The New Science of Giambattista Vico*, trans. Thomas Bergin (Ithaca, NY: Cornell University Press, 1984).

40 There is an exception here that was expressed by Marx in *Capital*, vol. III (unpublished in Marx's lifetime); namely, that in communism the sphere of production will remain the sphere of necessity on the ground of which freedom will flourish.

41 For example, one cannot write great epic poetry like that of Homer in the modern world. Karl Marx, *Grundrisse*, ed. David McLellan (London: Macmillan, 1971), Preface.

42 *Grundrisse.*

43 Here, the proletariat plays the role of the elected people. This aspect of Marx's philosophy cannot be discussed in my limited framework.

44 For details, see Heller, "Marx and Modernity," in Fehér and Heller, *Grandeur and Twilight*, op. cit., pp. 101–17.

45 Certainly, no world revolution originated from the universalization of modernity. A description can be confirmed even if a prediction based on it is proven wrong.

46 In the first volume of *Capital*, Marx dedicated a whole chapter to the description of how rationalization had become one of the major productive forces in capitalism.

47 This is just like the later attitude of Weber.

48 This is what Hegel knew when he added the class of "bureaucracy" – that is, of the civil servants – to the functionally constituted classes in his model of modern stratification.

49 Lukács formed a whole philosophical theory based on these insights in his *History of Class Consciousness*. György Lukács, *History of Class Consciousness*, trans. Rodney Livingstone (Cambridge: MIT Press, 1971).

50 See the chapter "Fetishism of commodities," in *Capital* I.

51 See the discussion of the spectres in Marx by Derrida in *Spectres of Marx*.

52 Weber believed, obviously, that the times of innovative philosophy are over. Although he was strongly influenced by Nietzsche, he quoted him as far as I know only once, in 1920(!). He was convinced that, as far as philosophy is concerned, he was just a modest recipient of Rickert's neo-Kantianism. Yet he was a philosopher, and a far superior one to Rickert, whom he obviously admired and whose opinions he accepted. For example, he accepted Rickert's rejection of Lukács's habilitation request on the ground that Lukács authored only essays and no grand systematic works. In my opinion, the best works of Max Weber are also theoretical essays, of course, essays written in the full control of the field and in the spirit of the most solid scholarship.

53 Weber's concept of the relationship of science and evaluation cannot be discussed in this modest context.

54 For example, Weber speaks of capitalism in ancient Rome, which disappeared during the time of the Empire and returned only at the dawn of the modern age.

55 One can understand him as a postmodern thinker, yet one can also understand him as a high modernist. This depends on the perspective of the interpreter.

56 In the fashionable battle waged against "logocentrism," although justified, some fail to distinguish between reason and reason.

57 In German idealism the differentiation between *Verstand* and *Vernunft* took the place of the traditional differentiation between "ratio" and "intellect."

58 Weber's differentiation between value rationality and purposive rationality was later variegated, modified, and further differentiated in the Apel/Habermas school, as instrumental reason, pragmatic reason, practical reason, theoretical reason, and the like.

59 Weber was aware that all actions are also emotionally motivated. Yet, one cannot understand actions typically if one relies on their emotional motivations, which are personal and idiosyncratic, rather than social. One can predict and understand actions (socially) only from their rational motivations, and there are such in all kinds of actions, be they as emotional as they may.

60 Many of his interpreters, however, did.

61 Marx described the rationalized industrial work in factories in very similar terms. The rationality of the worker's work is truncated because he does not set the goal, nor does he choose the means to realize it. Marx understands truncated rationality in terms of "alienation."

62 The economic model of minimum input, maximum output is the prototype of rationalization, yet in Weber's mind it is not therefore also the cause of the rationalization of the legal system and other institutions.

63 Weber also detects the presence of charisma in democracies. But a democratically elected politician, as charismatic as he might be, is not legitimated by his charisma but by law.

64 Among others, in *Aesthetics I* (On natural beauty, last section).

65 It is not difficult to detect an ambiguity here. Weber is strongly committed to the German idea of state (far more than Hegel ever was, with his Napoleonic sympathies), but his sense of historical realism suggested that this is not what the future of the present has in store for us. It is interesting to re-read from this perspective Weber's magisterial lecture on *Politics as a Vocation*.

66 In one place, Weber also adds erotics to the value-spheres.

67 It was due to a major misunderstanding that Habermas added a moral sphere to the Weberian value-spheres.

68 Kierkegaard became well received in Germany around this time. I know from Lukács' personal communication that Kierkegaard's concept of existential choice was widely discussed in the Weber circle.

69 This can be also understood autobiographically. Weber himself stood before the choice between politics and science, and he chose science. He was not tempted to choose religion because, according to his own description, he was religiously "unmusical."

70 What is missing is Weber's lesson of our century. The inherent rules and norms of a value-sphere sometimes need to be put under critical scrutiny from the perspective of other value-spheres. This change of perspectives does not necessarily make one trespass over the borders. For example, some rules of the economic spheres can be criticized from the standpoint of the political, legal, or scientific spheres without engaging in an illegitimate intrusion into the territory of the economic sphere.

71 Weber wrote a lengthy study on the rationalization of music. About this, see Ferenc Fehér, "Weber and the rationalization of music," in Fehér and Heller, *Grandeur*, op. cit., pp. 351–67.

3 The Two Constituents of Modernity I

1 I have offered a brief summary of my conception of the dynamics in modernity in the study written with Ferenc Fehér, *A Modernitás Ingája* (in English, *The Pendulum of Modernity*; Budapest: T/Twins, 1993). See also Agnes Heller, "Undialektische Dialektik. Der Stand der Aufklärung," Loccum lectures, in manuscript.

2 This is true only about those regions of the globe (first and foremost Europe) where the modern social arrangement was not implanted by external forces; for example, colonizing armies or the pressures of the world economy.

3 This issue has already been tangentially discussed in chapter 1.

4 It is normally believed that Aristophanes, in his comedy, *The Clouds*, was "unjust" to Socrates and did not understand his point. I think that Aristophanes understood Socrates' point only too well. The comic exaggeration hit home. The issue at stake is whether Socrates leaves tradition in its place or, rather, destroys traditional morality. Yet Socrates did indeed destroy traditional morality. In a Socratic dialogue one could, indeed, not swear to Zeus as the maker of clouds. If there were no other witness to this, Plato would still be a good one. After all, he says – in the name of Socrates – that the common men abused gods because they believed that Zeus made clouds, thunder, and rain. Obviously, so Plato says, he does not make such things. The novel (and almost Judaic) concept of "god" in Plato does not resemble the Zeus of Homer. Yet the ethics, the ethical life of Athens, relied on the old myths and beliefs about the old gods. If someone destroyed those beliefs and ridiculed them, he destroyed the gods as people believed them to be.

5 Hegel noticed that Plato paid a high price for taming the dynamics of modernity, thus making dialectics fit into a rigid, restored tradition. Plato, he said, was conscious that a deeper principle than that of the traditional ethical reality is about to break into life, yet "as something corruptive." To combat it, he got help from the thing he had to combat. "By that means he thought to master this corruptive invader, and thereby he did fatal injury to the deeper impulse which underlay it, namely free, infinite, personality." See G. W. F. Hegel, *Philosophy of Right*, trans. T. M. Knox (Chicago: University of Chicago Press, 1952), Preface.

6 Hegel's most conclusive and most beautiful discussion of the dynamics of modernity can be found in the *Phenomenology of Spirit* chapter on "Morality." Hegel here calls the power of negation "the evil." (As it happens, in Goethe's *Faust* Mephistopheles represents the forces of the modern world and is, after all, the devil himself.) In all the previous configurations of the world, negation (the evil) destroyed the world. But this is no longer the case

in modernity, in the world of "morality" where the powers that negate (evil) can perhaps meet resistance. Yet, if the resistance is absolute, then the powers of the present become the powers of negation, of evil ("the hardened heart"). The power of evil realizes that he is destructive and asks for forgiveness. The old powers forgive – which means that they *find a common language* – and through the use of this common language evil disappears. That is, it ceases to be evil, it becomes absorbed by the world, or it absorbs the world. This is the dialectical unification of the powers of assertion and negation in a new assertion. And this dialectical process goes on and on – the evil is always absorbed and ceases to be an evil. Dialectics is not destructive; it is not "negative" but positive – destruction becomes construction.

7   Although modernity as such – and in its optimal political versions, such as liberal democracy – thrives on negation, many concrete versions of the modern social arrangement can be destroyed by it. And the issue remains open: Who is the one allowed or required to negate? Everyone? Someone? Perhaps only the dictators?

8   The reader may recall the brief discussion of dynamic justice in chapter 1.

9   I accept Rawls' distinction between the concept of justice and conception of justice. I have elaborated the distinction between static and dynamic justice in my book *Beyond Justice* (Cambridge, MA: Basil Blackwell, 1991).

10 See the *Phenomenology of Spirit* chapter entitled "The Enlightenment." See G. W. F. Hegel, the *Phenomenology of Spirit*, trans. A. V. Miller (Oxford: Oxford University Press, 1977).

11 Marx's radicalism allows him to disclose the "secret."

12 Both the Weberian concept of universality of rationalization and the Heideggerian concept of *Ge-stell* describe the imaginary institutions of rationalistic enlightenment. I will soon return to this question.

13 Goethe's poem, the "Zauberlehling," is about the magician's apprentice who lets out the spirit from the bottle and cannot control it any more. The ugly enlightenment is the spirit who, once let out of the bottle, can no longer be controlled and therefore becomes destructive.

14 The destructive character of enlightenment, particularly that of civilization was noticed prior to the German Romanticism by Rousseau, in his first (and also second) Discourse. In his remarks on Rousseau ("Mutmasslicher Anfang der Menschengeschichte") Kant slipped out from the difficulties in his usual way, in the distinction between the empirical/natural on the one hand (the ugly face) and the transcendental, noumenal freedom on the other hand (the beautiful face).

15 The word "end" figures here in a double meaning, just as in Heidegger's "the end of philosophy." It means that something comes to an end, and that it is likewise fulfilled, consummated, and accomplished.

16 How the dynamics of modernity lives in and from the cultural discourse, will be discussed in the chapter on culture.

17 Many fundamentalist movements borrow their fundaments from traditions, particularly religious traditions. But these are just postmodern "quotations,"

for they are freely chosen as a prevention from, or the answers to, the modernist ghost.

18 Fundamentalism is an "ism" because it does not provide a fundament. Men and women, after all, are incapable of devising and politically masterminding a fundament. Real fundaments – fundaments that are destroyed only through a nihilistic discourse – are traditional, and they legitimate the forms of domination by tradition. The tradition cannot be something which is just pulled out from a drawer for streamlined use: fundamentalist Islam is closer to Bolshevism and Fascism (Mussolinism) than to a religion.

19 I apply a Hegelian concept here: the determinate negation raises the discourse to a higher level.

20 This is the case when the pendulum of modernity swings between two extremes.

21 I do not invent the allegory when I speak of diagnoses and symptoms. For Nietzsche, nihilism was a kind of sickness. Nihilists are, in his mind, hostile to life.

22 In "Modernity's pendulum" I mention two cases of the emergence of the dynamics of modernity prior to our modern enlightenment: first, the Greek enlightenment, and second, Roman enlightenment at the end of the Republic. Yet in those cases the dynamics of modernity could not perform its work as a midwife. It could only destroy the traditional social arrangements, without being helpful in the birth of the new. Between those events of self-triggered dynamics, new worlds in fact may appear, yet they are also entirely "pre-modern," albeit different from the ones which have been destroyed. It is, of course, a rude generalization to speak about all pre-modern social arrangements in unison and without differentiation, yet this is the essential part of my present story. For the story's question is whether or not the dynamics of modernity always triggers the emergence of the modern social arrangement. For Nietzsche, the dynamics of modernity, enlightenment, is a solo dancer, for it performs the play on its own. This is not because Nietzsche does not detect the relationship between the nihilistic discourse on the one hand and modernity on the other hand, but because of his absolutely negative attitude toward modernity as a social arrangement. I would not say this attitude is toward modernity in general, for he is delighted by many modern things, particularly art and a few other branches of *Kultur*. Yet the social arrangement of modernity is based on the thought of equality and freedom of all, and Nietzsche rejects both the idea of equality and the value of freedom of all. This is why his story sounds so curious, although it is very logically told from his own perspective.

23 In history, there are always exceptions. One cannot make generalized statements without provisos, such as "for the most part."

24 See the next chapter, which discusses this issue in some detail.

25 This is the abbreviated and very simplified story of *The Genealogy of Morals*, trans. Walter Kaufmann (New York: Vintage, 1969).

26 It is true that Nietzsche does not use his own conception in the way I suggested it. In his mind, it was the denial of life, asceticism, which embodied nihilism and kept it alive. The ascetic priest is the Christian nihilist, not the heretic.

27 He sometimes speaks almost exclusively from the point of view of morality. He wants to unmask the hypocracy and decadent character of Christian morality. At other times, his story has rather a political edge. It is telling to compare the very miniscule differences between Nietzsche's discussion of nihilism (Christian and modern) in *Beyond Good and Evil*, trans. Walter Kaufmann (New York: Vintage, 1966) and in his *Genealogy of Morals*, trans. Walter Kaufmann (New York: Vintage, 1969).

28 See the *Genealogy of Morals*, op. cit.

29 The reader could notice that fundamentalism also figures in my story as a version of nihilism, and that I have proposed to speak of nihilistic enlightenment when nihilistic discourse is negated by an absolutist credo. Seen from this aspect, Plato, in Nietzsche's rendering, could really fit the bill. Yet neither Aristotle nor Aquinas could.

30 This is not said in the spirit of Adorno and Horkheimer's *The Dialectic of Enlightenment* (New York: Herder & Herder, 1972). The resolve to face the paradoxes as paradoxes offers an entirely different position to enlightenment than does negative dialectics. Undialectical dialectics is as little negative as it is Hegelian.

4   The Two Constituents of Modernity II

1 Aristotle, who knew only one social arrangement but with many internal variants, uses the term "distributive justice." Aristotle, *Nicomachian Ethics*, Book 5 in *Basic Works of Aristotle*, ed. Richard MacKeon (New York: Random Hose, 1941). Marx speaks of the "social division of labor," and this terminology was taken over with substantial modifications by Durkheim (*Division of Labour in Society*), who distinguished between two main kinds of social division of labor. I prefer Luhmann's expression because of its neutrality.

2 Small groups are exceptions. Perhaps, the third possibility exists in the tribes of a few dozen people.

3 In a good utopia, as in Marx's *Grundrisse*, there is neither social hierarchy nor division of functions. In a bad utopia, as in Marx's *Capital* III, the division of functions remains in force.

4 One can still keep them as regulative, theoretical, or practical ideas.

5 All of these could also be supported by empirical historical evidence, but even to provide examples is beyond the ambition of this study and requires a different genre. For example, the nihilistic tendency in British discourse at the beginning of the century was far from being destructive, because the might of the tradition (and the class that carried this tradition) was

overwhelming. The *volte face* is innocuous if it is restricted to economy or social policy (for example, in the pendulum movement between free market liberalism and Keynesian/social-democratic restrictions). If, however, the pendulum movement encompasses the political institutions and the totality of forms of life, as in the switches between democracy/totalitarianism and liberalism/fundamentalism, the turn is dangerous. Of course, the rejuvenation of the dynamics of modernity also plays a decisive role in the opposite direction (e.g., totalitarianism/democracy), but whether these dynamics are relatively free does not depend on the internal logic of the dynamic themselves. For example, in the last few decades of the Soviet regime there was a limited possibility for the dynamics of modernity to appear in Hungary, whereas it was almost entirely restricted in Czechoslovakia. The regime change, however, happened in both states practically simultaneously, for it has not come about essentially through the internal logic of modernity's dynamic, but has benefited mainly from the change in the external conditions.

6   "Pre-modern" should be read as the shorthand reference to the fundamental structure of all social arrangements prior to the modern. I am aware of the awkwardness of the term: it suggests, wittingly or unwittingly, that somehow the modern arrangement is the point of reference to which all previous social arrangements need to be compared. This is not my conviction. Yet I do not write history, but present rough ideal types. The difference between the pre-modern and the modern social arrangement will be elaborated later in this chapter, but in a too sketchy manner.

7   See Ferenc Fehér and Agnes Heller, *Biopolitics* (Brookfield, VT: Avebury, 1994).

8   Quantification and quantifiability of social relations, ambitions, and essences is a modern phenomenon. Weber's thesis of "rationalization" interprets one aspect of this quantifying trend. Later, Heidegger will speak of *Messbarkeit* as one central feature of *Machenschaft*. Quantifiability belongs to the technological imagination. In the next chapter, the question will be discussed separately.

9   For more than two millennia, political theory has always contrasted Athens and Sparta.

10 In times of Jewish enlightenment and assimilation, the view was generally held that the traditional Hasidic ways of life are entirely incompatible with the modern social arrangement. But it has turned out in absolutely modern countries, such as the United States and Israel, that the Hasidic way of life can be compatible with the modern social arrangement. It only limits the dynamics of modernity in certain, circumscribed areas (religion, ethics), yet not in other eras (e.g., technology).

11 I will return to the question of the death of God in the chapter on politics and the chapter on culture.

12 The rapid development of the modern social arrangement in Japan was sometimes attributed not to the presence, but to the absence, of democratic traditions.

13 It has often been pointed out that the rapid economic development and modernization in Southeast Asia was partly due to autocratic governments.

14 They also forget that the economy of this country is part of the circuit of the global economy, and that it lives on its oil resources.

15 This was also the case in ancient histories. One needed civil wars, internal uncertainties, and destructive discourse to make a movement, or at least a strong ideology, out of "returning to the origins"; for example, to the founding fathers. Machiavelli was the first to discover this. It is in the republican moment of freedom that the thought to return to the beginning occurs. This happens in republican constitutions. The story is told from the vantage point of an already modern, or at least modernistic, historicism. See Arendt; also Vatter, op. cit.

16 I must repeat that this means neither progression nor regression in comparison with the pre-modern social arrangements, which are as different in their concrete manifestations and empirical forms as modern social arrangements are and can be.

17 In the second half of the 20th century, mass media became a competitor of economy. The modern forms of life were disseminated by film, television, and advertisement. As a result, the attitude adequate to modern capitalist economy appears almost simultaneously with the economy itself. This was not the case in the 19th century. There it was only capitalism that spearheaded the modern transformation. Colonization was the representative way of expansions. The series "Dallas" can easily perform the work of battleships.

18 It is not by chance that I mentioned Germany and Central–Eastern Europe. In fact, totalitarian regimes, in their undemocratic radicalism, have wiped out the elements of pre-modern ways of life here more totally than democracies or autocracies. One can come across far more "pre-modern" elements in Spain than in Hungary.

19 Of course, only under the condition that modernity survives at least the next century.

20 *A priori* here means in principle (and not just contingently) prior to experience.

21 They cannot entirely dovetail. There remains a tension at the seam of not entirely successful dovetailing. Yet, if there is no dovetailing at all, the person will be unfit to survive. I wrote about this issue in detail in *General Ethics*, the first chapter, "The human condition" (Oxford and New York: Blackwell, 1987), and *An Ethics of Personality*, part II, dialogue 3 (Cambridge: Blackwell, 1996).

22 Although he, too, had second thoughts about it. This is understandable, because he himself was born after the finest days of Greek enlightenment and knew that some sophists were teaching the opposite, namely that no one is "by nature" the master of a slave.

23 To refer back to Nietzsche: Judaism and Christianity introduced certain confusions into this simple configuration, in emphasizing that men are

equal before God. But this confusion was not enough to shake the pre-modern social arrangement's social hierarchy, and the relationship between the hierarchical position on the one hand, and the function on the other hand (the "totality" of the function included) has for a long time remained in force.

24   This is evident, for this is the human condition (*Dasein*).

25   To express myself with traditional philosophical categories, the genetic a priori is the unity of the universal and the individual. Every newborn who is thrown into the world is a member of the human species and shares the constituents of the human condition. And every single person is an inimit-able, unrepeatable singularity, a uniqueness, a *to de ti*, an individual sub-stance, nothing but himself/herself, whereas particularity or difference rests in the social *a priori*. There is no "universalistic" social *a priori*, as there is no entirely idiosyncratic social *a priori*. In the modern world there are universal values and globalized institutions. But even the cultural networks where the universalized values play the greatest role are concrete cases of *hic at nunc*, where the actual network of concreteness presents itself in language, in the use of man-made objects, communication, and system of customs. Dovetailing can also be rendered as "mediation," the generic *a priori* (uni-versal and individual) needs to receive mediation in and through the concrete social networks via experience, interaction, and first and foremost via language, body language (gesture language included). It is an abstraction that the individual thrown into the world is faced by "the Other" as a single entity. The Other who looks at the newborn (the mother, siblings, father, nanny, and so on) appears as a mediator of expectations, of approval and disapproval, and of acceptance.

26   Lukács writes, "From contingency to necessity, this is the road of all proble-matic individuals." See György Lukács, *Soul and Form*, trans. Anna Bostock (Cambridge, MA: MIT Press, 1974).

27   I speak here about social contingency alone, and not about cosmic contin-gency. The experience of cosmic contingency historically precedes the gen-eral experience of social contingency. One is aware of social contingency if one asks "What am I thrown into?" and one is aware of one's cosmic contingency if one asks of "Who is the one that throws?" If both questions are asked – which happens for those who live under the empty sky after "the death of God" – the two contingency experiences merge.

28   It is to this description of normal objects that the accident of birth still determines the framework of further life. Poor children have limited chances, and there is a great probability that they will remain poor. But these empirical objections do not influence the model of the modern social arrangement. In both cases (the pre-modern and the modern) it is the ideal type that matters. The ideal type is not the philosopher's theoretical fancy; it is the dominating imaginary institution itself. For example, I can now ask a ten-year-old girl on the Fidsi Islands (as I did), "What are you going to do as a grown up?" and she will answer (as she did), "I will be a doctor, a pilot, a

hotel owner, an Olympic champion and so on." Three hundred years ago, even in the midst of Europe, one could not really ask the question, because the answer was obvious: a girl could not have any *telos* in her life other than to marry and to have children. Even in 19th-century England, girls had no other alternatives except to work as whores. (At that time there was no possibility in the Church of England to become a nun.) What exists in imagination, what guides imagination, actually exists. Everything else (to use Hegel's vocabulary) is possibly reality – important and hard reality – but it is not actuality.

29 Someone may be a director of a hospital but before or after was only a simple doctor: once a worker, later a capitalist, once a housewife, later an actress or a businesswoman. But those functions are not presupposed as identical to their beings; they do not represent this being – while, for example, a lord represented the lordship whether he was hunting, marrying, waging wars, or sleeping.

30 Here I ask readers to return to chapter 1.

31 This is why Hegel did not like the expression. He said that "all men are born free" is just the negation of the sentence "some men are born free." But, essentially, he too remained loyal to this basic sentence.

32 Aristotle, *Politics* in *Basic Works of Aristotle*, ed. Richard MacKeon (New York: Random House, 1941).

33 Drafting a constitution is described in terms of *technē* by Aristotle.

34 René Descartes, *Discourse On Method* in *The Philosophical Writings of Descartes*, trans. J. Cottingham, R. Stoothoff and D. Murdoch, vol. I (Cambridge: Cambridge University Press, 1985) and Rousseau, *Discourse on The Origins of Inequality Among Men*, trans. Donald Cress (Indianapolis: Hackett, 1992).

35 "Actuality" in Hegel.

36 The most typical case of discrepancy between norm and actuality is that of moral character.

37 In the previous chapter, I tried to show that Hegel describes a model for the essence of modernity in this understanding, whereas Marx insists that the discrepancy is not just a necessary constituent of capitalism, but is also increasing, whatever we are doing. Thus, in his mind one has to destroy capitalism and thereby destroy the discrepancy. A communist society is a society without a discrepancy, without dynamic justice, without justice in general. See A. Heller, "Marx and justice," in *Grandeur*, op. cit., pp. 177–93.

38 Habermas, as is well known, differentiates between three kinds of rationality: instrumental, pragmatic, and communicative. On the one hand, he complains about the colonization of the lifeworld, which is more and more controlled by rationalized institutions. On the other hand, he places a premium on the rationalization of the same lifeworld, meaning thereby its increasing openness to communicative rationality. In the second case, he wants to close the distance and approximate; in the first case, he would prefer a distance and less approximation.

39 Fourier interpreted the equality of opportunity in an essentialist/substantive understanding. For example, old women have to have an equal opportunity for a sex life. This is why it is an obligation for young men to provide such services for them. See Charles Fourier, *The Utopian Vision of Charles Fourier: selected texts on work, love, and passionate attraction*, trans. J. Beecher and R. Bienvenu (Columbia: University of Missouri Press, 1983).

40 I have to repeat that equal opportunity as the essence of the modern arrangement requires the dynamics of modernity, which is about to close the "gap" that cannot be closed.

41 The most significant productions in the literature of liberal American political philosophy (Rawls, Dworkin, Nozick) recommend or legitimize the kinds of distribution that can make up for initial inequalities.

42 This is for no other reason than an "anthropological" one. The genetic code placed in our envelopes cannot be changed by social condition or circumstance, whether or not the generic *a priori* fits into the modern social *a priori*. True, there are greater varieties of life-forms now than ever before, and it seems as if the dovetailing of the two *a prioris* would now also be easier to manage. Yet, this is an illusion. All forms of life, in fact, are modern, and even if no modern forms of life are also offered for single individuals, the form of life itself could be a handicap. It is difficult to swim against the tide. In my book *Beyond Justice*, I recommended a way of swimming against the tide. It is not entirely impossible.

43 I have distinguished between three logics in modernity since the writing of my book *A Theory of History*. But I identified the three logics in different manners. I made the distinction between the three logics in modernity in general, and in Western modernity in particular. There are shifts in the shades of my proposition, yet they are not essential differences.

5 The Three Logics of Modernity I

1 Maybe Herbert Marcuse was the first who, in his theory of "repressive tolerance" [Herbert Marcuse, *One Dimensional Man* (Boston: Beacon Press, 1964)], developed the idea that since negation is totalized in modern societies and all negations are absorbed by the existing order, one has to take a position outside it in order to negate it effectively. Heidegger's concept of "enframing" suggests something very similar in a far deeper, philosophically more relevant, conceptualization. But Heidegger's Hölderlinian hope in poesy as the "saving power" (given that poesy stems from *poiesis* just as *techne* does) is a very weak philosophical suggestion, if it is a suggestion at all ("Origin of the Work of Art"). Only a new god can save us, says Heidegger in his last and posthumously published *Der Spiegel* interview – and this gloomy formulation suits the latest Heidegger's vision of modernity better (if I may use the word "vision" to describe the position of someone who would have disapproved of it strongly).

2 Here, one could employ the terminology of system/environment, as Luhmann does. But Luhmann speaks of a system development as a unilinear tendency toward the reduction of complexities: see Niklas Luhmann, *Social Systems*, trans. John Bednarz Jr., with Dirk Baecker (Stanford, CA: Stanford University Press, 1995). I do not accept even such a universal tendency.

3 If exemplification is important, then there are thousands of examples to support this point. For example, many volumes have been written about the industrialization of Great Britain and Germany. The time difference in the grand-scale industrialization of these two countries has substantially influenced the basic structure of their respective industries.

4 This was the case in totalitarian states/societies. The blocking of the dynamics on the level of civil society also crippled the technological development. To refer to a well-known example: for a while cybernetics, as the offspring of "bourgeois science" had been excommunicated. It is also an open secret that the Soviet type of social arrangement has slowed down technological development which it was supposed to further far beyond the capacities of capitalistic societies.

5 This was one reason why Marx could entertain the idea that the development of the forces of production is the independent variable of historical development. For if there are no alternative technologies, technology either develops in one direction or stops developing. There is no third possibility. Until this very moment there was none. This should not, however, serve as a prediction.

6 This is the main problem with the "end of history" thesis, particularly in Fukuyama's rendering. Since, as I tried to point out in the previous chapter, the modern social arrangement is compatible with autocratic or fundamentalist governments, there is no strong reason to believe that liberal democracy is the sole method of political domination in modernity.

7 It is at this point that I find Arendt's distinction between the three kinds of active life (action, work, and labor) relevant. One can interpret her understanding of modernity in the above terms in many different ways. I mention only two of them: firstly, that labor became the dominant kind of active life in contemporary modernity and there is no more space left for action; and secondly, that action can always be retrieved into the political sphere, but remains irrelevant in the social and the technological spheres. Cognition is in Arendt always associated with problem-solving, while thinking has a universal significance in the theoretical (speculative) attitude. See Hannah Arendt, *The Human Condition* (Garden City, NY: Doubleday, 1959).

8 I will return to this question in the first subsection.

9 It was not so in early modernity. Not even in the 19th century was the development of industrial technology dependent on scientific discoveries.

10 See Thomas Kuhn, *The Structure of Scientific Revolutions* (Chicago: University of Chicago Press, 1970).

11 See the next subsection.

12 See Immanuel Kant, *Critique of Pure Reason*, trans. Norman Kemp Smith (New York: St. Martin's Press, 1965).
13 Weber distinguished between three types of political actors: the bureaucrat, the politician, and the statesman. I would accept this distinction.
14 As far as I know, only the English language applies two different expressions to these different activities.
15 This is Arendt's example.
16 Social sciences are not cumulative. See "Hermeneutics of social sciences" in Heller, *Can Modernity Survive?* (Berkeley: University of California Press, 1990).
17 About the intransparency of the modern world see Heller, *Philosophy of History in Fragments* (Oxford and Cambridge, MA: Basil Blackwell, 1993), the chapter on "Absolute Spirit."
18 Heidegger, "The question concerning technology" in *Basic Writings* (New York: Harper and Row, 1977), pp. 283–319.
19 I do not repeat Heidegger's story, but sum up only its "essence."
20 Sometimes it *is* truth. Heidegger shifts his concept of truth several times after his so-called "turn." I cannot follow these shifts here.
21 "Thus when man, investigating, observing, pursues nature as an area of his conceiving, he has already claimed by a way of revealing that challenges him to approach nature as an object of research, until even the object disappears into the objectlessness of standing reserve" (p. 300).
22 op. cit., p. 301.
23 Heidegger: "Das Ge-Stell" M. Heidegger, *Bremer und Freiburger Vortrage Gesamtausgabe*, 78 Klosterman, 1994, p. 34.
24 Heidegger's reference to "Seinsgeschichte als Seinsgeschick" is not meant as an explanation but as nonexplanation. The event does not explain.
25 Only moderns "have," according to Heidegger a *Weltbild* (world picture) or *Weltanschauung* (world view). I think that world explanation belongs to the human condition, and is not identical with the modern world picture. I think, furthermore, that moderns are characterized by the fragmentation of a once unified and homogeneous world explanation, rather than by the opposite.
26 Leo Strauss on his part accuses modern authors (especially Max Weber) of making things worse, of contributing to the process of "enframing" (of course, he does not use this language). It is the dynamics of modernity and modern philosophy's participation in it that is to be blamed for fragmentation and for ethical/political degeneration. See Leo Strauss, *Liberalism, Ancient and Modern* (Ithaca, NY: Cornell University Press, 1989).
27 See chapter 2. Weber speaks about rationalization of religion as well as rationalization of music.
28 See Niklas Luhmann, *Social Systems*, trans. John Bednarz Jr., with Dirk Baecker (Stanford, CA: Stanford University Press, 1995).
29 This is why he speaks of "an autonomous" (read: democratic) society.

30 It is well known that democracy also belongs in Heidegger's story to man's state of being enframed. For him, only one logic of modernity exists. Political institutions (whether totalitarian or democratric) equally present this essence. Castoriadis, just as Heidegger or Luhmann, thinks in terms of one decisive characteristic, but for him democracy, as the great promise, is the decisive aspect of the modern world. However, he is not a progressivist; he would not use the term "logic."

31 See Jürgen Habermas' beautiful analysis in *Technik und Wissenschaft als "Ideologie"* (Frankfurt am Main, Germany: Suhrkamp, 1968).

32 *Ursprüngliches Denken* by Heidegger.

33 At the time of the anti-nuclear peace demonstrations in Germany, A. Rabinbach wrote wittily in his article in which he (in my mind rightly) criticized the demonstrator's bad conscience, that hundreds of thousands of "shepherds of Being" are demonstrating in the streets of Bonn. (Dissent.)

34 I have no competence to speak of the Greek associative understanding of the words of *technē* and *poiesis*. I speak only about the issue of how modern man poetically dwells on Earth or, rather, how they had dwelled poetically to understand it.

35 Foucault concentrates on the analysis of technology to establish and use power relations in civil life and science. He admits that in grand-scale politics another tendency does, or at least can, prevail. This is one of the possibilities in speaking of the "revolving door of reason," the beautiful expression in which Foucault describes one of the paradoxes of modernity, and to which I have already referred in chapter 1.

36 In my book, *Philosophy of History in Fragments* (Oxford and Cambridge, MA: Basil Blackwell, 1993), I use the term of the "prisonhouse of historicity."

37 I am speaking about hermeneutics not in a universal sense as the essence of the human condition (as Heidegger and Gadamer sometimes do), but in a historical sense.

38 In Nietzsche's *The Use and Abuse of History*, trans. Adrian Collins, 2nd revised edn (Indianapolis: Bobbs-Merrill, 1957), the kind of historiography which goes on accumulating data is juxtaposed to two different kinds of history telling. Neither of the two follows the technological model. Heidegger distinguishes between *Historie* and *Geschichte*, where the first stands for positivistic (cumulative, technological) history writing. Heidegger's *Geschichte* does not differ essentially from what I mean by historical imagination. It is only that I juxtapose this imagination to enframing and associate *poiesis* and interpretation first and foremost, but not exclusively, with the modern consciousness of historicity. See Martin Heidegger, *Being and Time*, trans. John Macquarrie and Edward Robinson (New York: Harper, 1962).

39 Religion as the dominating world explanation has not set the past free. There were firmly set limits to interpretation. The same is true about all myths as long as people believe in them.

40   I will again discuss the "age of universal hermeneutics" in the chapters on culture and civilization.

41   I discuss this issue in my book, Agnes Heller, *The Concept of the Beautiful*, in manuscript.

42   If they are received according to their essence. The ideological (e.g., nationalistic) use of history writing and of poetry is well known. This is, indeed, the practice one can describe as the instrumentalization of *poiesis*. Yet even this use or misuse is not entirely understandable merely according to the scheme of technological imagination.

43   It is said that Petrarca was the first to "discover" the beauty of nature while climbing to the peak of Mount Vernoux. But Petrarca's "climbing" also had an ethical significance; it was still shaped on the Platonian/Christian model of "ascension." The enlightenment's premium on the absence of interest, which is so strongly emphasized and philosophically underpinned in Kant's *Critique of Judgment* [trans. J. H. Bernard (New York: Hafner, 1951)], signals an entirely new attitude to nature, an attitude which we have not entirely lost.

44   Landscape painting is a modern kind of painting. Landscape, or things of nature portrayed without human presence, yet not for the purpose of decoration, is also modern. Lukács was right when he said that Cézanne's still lifes are "historical paintings." See György Lukács, *Probleme der Ästhetik* (Neuwield: Luchterhand, 1969) and *Heidelberger Ästhetik (1916–1918)* (Darmstadt: Luchterhand, 1975).

45   I will speak about the distribution of cultural goods in the chapter on culture.

46   See György Markus, "Hermeneutics of natural sciences," in *Language and Production: a critique of the paradigms* (Dordrecht and Boston: D. Reidel/ Hingham, MA: Kluwer Academic, 1986). Popper, who in many ways still stands in a positivist tradition, already says that in natural sciences, too, there are only interpreted facts. Kuhn's famous story of the change of paradigms in natural sciences [Thomas Kuhn, *The Structure of Scientific Revolutions*, 3rd edn. (Chicago: University of Chicago Press, 1996)] follows very much the patterns of our historical understanding and self-understanding. Koselleck gives interesting insights into the terminological interplay between understanding history and theories in natural sciences. [The term "revolution" is also a case in point. See Reinhart Koselleck, *Preussen zwischen Reform und Revolution* (Stuttgart: Klett, 1967).]

47   Karl Marx, *Capital*, vol. I, trans. Samuel Moore and Edward Aveling (New York: International Publishers, 1967).

48   The employment of atomic energy was a crucial "event" in technological development for both Heidegger and Arendt. Heidegger often speaks about the present as the "atomic age." This is not very convincing.

49   Hannah Arendt, *The Human Condition* (Garden City, NY: Doubleday, 1959).

50   Ibid.

51 One exception is the typewriter, but the typewriter certainly made far less impact on the change in imagination than the television or, in the era of the invention of the typewriter, the railway network.

52 Knowledge in the sense of "knowing about" precedes belief or faith. One cannot have faith in something or someone one that does not know anything about – not even its existence, concept, or idea.

53 Hegel knew this. Among other things, this is why he speaks about the "end of art" in a world in which art cannot serve as superhuman authority; that is, as a religion. And, as the final pages of his *Lectures on the Philosophy of Religion* suggest, he has entertained serious doubts as to whether philosophy is able to take over religion's role.

54 Hume was the first to formulate this in the manner that no "Ought" can be deduced from the "Is."

55 This kind of blind faith in scientific discoveries is a corroboration of science as a dominating world explanation, even if the scientific discovery is authentic in the sense that it was proven by the then available means. For, as I said, the spirit of science requires raising certain doubts even if the proof is there – for every proof can be disproven.

56 Scientists like to distinguish between real sciences and pseudo-sciences. The latter are regarded as cuckoos laying their eggs in the nest of true knowledge. Things are not that simple. Great scientific discoveries are frequently abused as "pseudo" sciences before being accepted. And even if certain "sciences" are regarded as "pseudo" continuously, it is sometimes not the spirit of science, but the institution of sciences, that excludes them. After all, it is not written in the stars in what concrete ways certain sciences will develop. Sometimes, when the institutions of science exclude alternative scientific explorations, the latter will be entirely marginalized and the possibility of developing sciences in its direction will be thwarted. This is, however, no proof of its being "unscientific." (This happens even though science returns to a formerly rejected proposal after a long time.) One needs to see that in a few branches of sciences (e.g., in medicine, which is fairly empirical) oriental knowledge can raise claim of its own "scientific character" and not without justification. For what justifies medicine is success. Every medical practice can be called true in a broader sense if it heals the patient. It is true, perhaps, in many cases even if the process which actually brings about healing is not known, or is described in a way which is unacceptable to modern Western sciences, and perhaps not acceptable at all. There are no fixed borders by which to determine where the real science begins and where pseudo-science ends. But both (if there is some kind of a border between the two) indeed contribute to science's function as a dominating ideology or world explanation. The Eastern methods of healing are not embraced because they are magic, nor exalted for their religious significance, but they are embraced because they claim to be as scientific as Western sciences. From my perspective, this is what counts. I would say that no proposition can be termed unscientific if the person who proposes something that does not fit a pattern

knows the current and alternative propositions and can argue either with or against and, therefore, recapitulate the arguments. If he or she can do this, he or she is certainly no dilettante, nor a dreamer, nor a magus. And this needs to be enough. From a postmodern perspective, the rigid and prejudiced politics of scientific excommunication became suspect. It seems obvious that as far as the inmates of contemporary scientific institutions are concerned, recommendations coming from outside institutions are sometimes treated the same way as heretics were treated by the Orthodox Church in the Middle Ages.

57   Foucault rarely mentions so-called hard sciences. The truth of hard sciences does not directly reach anyone but the scientists of the same or a similar field. Yet, one could add, truth is also produced in the discourse of hard sciences. At least, the Kuhnian conception of paradigms can also be interpreted in this way.

58   It is difficult to divide credulity from well-grounded belief or grounded intuition; but in concrete cases it is still possible and also recommended.

59   This was the case under the totalitarian pressure over science; e.g., when Lysenko's biology was declared the only true one. However, this truth was not produced in the discourse of the community of scientists.

60   Wittgenstein's language game theory can be interpreted in both ways. Every language game is relevant on its own. This would lend support to the Foucauldian technological description. Yet if all language games are also forms of life, this position would rather lend support to the Heideggerian concept of *aletheia*.

61   We owe the analysis of this development to Foucault. The scientific classification of man, the "scientific" analysis of human beings aiming at their control, leads to the establishment of the modern "science based and guided" madhouses, prisons, and institutions of education, and of sexual discourse. Foucault, as I mentioned, applies technological language to describe technological imagination. I will return to Foucault's description of modernity in the chapter on culture and civilization.

62   These are Foucault's favorite themes.

63   Foucault here suggests the contrary. In his mind, normalization in no way has the objective of limiting criminality but, rather, to reproduce the "criminal" or to reproduce the "deviant." This can be accepted, but this is not my point. Neither is the problem of science as dominating world explanation and its tensions. The inherent purpose of chemistry is to develop chemistry. The inherent purpose of psychology is *not* to make the smooth control of society possible, even if "normalization" serves this purpose. It makes a difference whether something (a discourse) achieves its inherent purpose or develops in this direction, or if something achieves a purpose which, to the contrary, inheres in another language game.

64   I think that it is obvious from this simple example, where "imitation of science" and the exercise of power through the ideology of science does not inhere in the language game itself. In psychology, medicine, education, even

in learning languages, and in acting or in film-making or advertising, science is used as ideology. (If not, it will be a disaster. One can perhaps still remember the scientifically recommended practice of "speed reading.") For it is not the logic of technology, but the logic of the market that is in control. (Or in another case, the logic of totalitarianism.) This is why the purpose does not inhere in the logic, and this is why entirely different, even opposite models can similarly claim to be proven by scientific means.

65 Alain Touraine, for example, has analyzed the French new left movement in 1968 in these terms: see Alain Touraine, *Critique of Modernity*, trans. D. Macey (Cambridge, MA: Basil Blackwell, 1995). The modernization of the French institutions required a drastic change in the methods of education. The mass movement has (wittingly or unwittingly) achieved this goal. The French society became restructured after 1968, responding first and foremost to the requirement of technological development. This development was no more in harmony with the technological and educational organization of French society, yet it was modelled on ancient "purposes." Not surprisingly, Foucault and others who were, like him, also influenced by the French 1968, were the first to ask questions about different force fields and their eventual tensions.

6 The Three Logics of Modernity II

1 See A. Heller, *Beyond Justice* (Cambridge, MA: Blackwell, 1991).
2 See F. Fehér and A. Heller, *A modernitás ingája* (in English, *The Pendulum of Modernity*; Budapest, 1994).
3 Hegel said that one learns only one thing from history; namely, that no people ever learned from history. This is a witty, yet perhaps too strong, remark. One sometimes overlearns from past histories or from the experiences of others in the present; at some other times one underlearns. It is difficult or, rather, irrelevant to speak of accumulation here. See, for details, A. Heller, *A Theory of History* (Oxford: Blackwell, 1992).
4 Karl Polanyi, in his book *The Great Transformation* (New York: Octagon, 1975), described how the self-regulating market functioned as the utopia of 19th-century liberalism, how it was increasingly necessary for the state to intervene and push back the development of the second logic in another direction. What is "more rational"? The relatively "free market" (and its idea) of yesterday, or the presumably not that free world market today? In his latest interview (January 1997) George Soros, one of the major figures of the international "casino capital," and one of the Americans with the highest yearly income, warned against the idea of an absolutely free market and recommended regulations, for the free market is, in his mind, not rational enough and does not offer the best possibilities for an "open society."
5 For example, is the utopia of a full "welfare state" more or less "rational" than the utopia of the completely "free market"? The problem lies in the

term "rational." The question of which one can be optimized better cannot be answered without answering the question "What is to be optimized." For example, great expenditure for education and high taxes – is this "basket" rational or not?

6 In my study "Everyday life, rationality of reason, rationality of intellect" in Agnes Heller, *The Power of Shame: A Rational Perspective* (London and Boston: Routledge & Kegan Paul, 1985), I distinguished in modernity between two major types of rationality.

7 This is why one cannot dissect purposive rationality from value-rationality.

8 Both Plato and Aristotle describe such contestations and changes within the ancient Greek city–states.

9 See F. Fehér, A. Heller, and G. Markus, *Dictatorship over Needs* (New York: St. Martin's Press, 1983).

10 Examples of arbitrary pendulum movement can be amply found in the history of the Soviet Union in the 1920s. The political power game between Buhkarin and Stalin, for example, decided the swing.

11 This is nothing new – only put into another theoretical context.

12 The market is obviously the overarching institution. Even Soviet-type societies could not manage their economies, not even at a very low level, without a market or a simulated market.

13 I will return to this question in chapters 8 and 14.

14 That modernity is characterized by the dissolution of "natural" or "organic" communities is one of the first accusations mounted against the modern social arrangement. The same can also be emphasized in a positive sense.

15 I may refer back to Hegel, who in the chapter on abstract law speaks of "the person" as the atom of the modern world.

16 Contract theories presuppose that singular persons enter the political contract. The spirit of modernity is, in this respect, properly expressed in the various models of the social contract.

17 Modernity's pendulum can also be observed first and foremost in the swings between the self-regulating market and the regulated market. As the market cannot be entirely self-regulating, it can also not be entirely regulated. The pendulum swings between the two extremes without reaching the extremes.

18 This is also Marx's remark.

19 Even after WWII in some countries (e.g., Spain, Italy, and so on), where the old qualitative values such as honor or grace, as well as the local family powers of influence, are preserved, human relations are not quantified in the same way they are in the USA. However, through "modernization" – for example, through the government of socialist parties – the tendency becomes accelerated.

20 Except in times of crisis, when the dynamics of modernity had already been practiced. See chapter 1.

21 For example, the relation between lords and serfs presented itself as the relation between Lord X and his own serfs.

22 Europeans were surprised when they noticed that American bosses and workers drink in the pub together instead of patronizing different clubs or societies. Or, the more monetarized family relations became, the less the woman was absolutely and personally dependent on her husband.

23 Kant's recommendation of distinguishing person and personality follows from his metaphysical ontology. The personality is the noumenal being, transcendental freedom, humankind in us. But this ontologico-metaphysical solution which I cannot accept does not need to prejudge against Kant's intitution. There is "something" in a man that is priceless, and even if this is not identical with "humankind in us," even if this is broader than morality, and even if one cannot define exactly what it is, one knows that it has no market price. That conscience cannot be marketed, because it is priceless, is a strong and frequently repeated statement, but unfortunately not very true unless one defines "conscience" in the Kantian manner, as the moral law or transcendental freedom.

24 I have already mentioned that modern man's world is broader than modern man's life (and can also be in some sense different). The world of modern man also permeates his life. Even if life would lead to total monetarization of human relations, this will not happen in a modern man's life, which is deeply permeated by his world.

25 In the recent past, the movements of 1968 represented a counter-trend to total monetarization.

26 For example, different needs are allocated to the first, second, and third sons of great titled families.

27 As Aristotle says, too much is an extreme; for example, the qualitative need for property is the need for medium property, because both extremes (property that is too large or no property at all) must be avoided.

28 For example, being an actor is below the dignity of the noble gentry. Seeking kingship means reaching beyond one's allocated needs and satisfiers (*hybris* in both cases).

29 There are exceptions; for example, in the Scandinavian type of welfare state.

30 Marx was right when he said that the miser who hoards gold is not characteristic of modern (capitalistic) production and consumption.

31 This was also observed by Marx. But in the time since his observation, this tendency has increased and its tempo has been accelerated.

32 I do not speak of economy. This is why I do not mention supply and demand. Nowadays economists speak about supply-side economics. Yet concrete issues cannot be discussed in the framework of general philosophical theories.

33 Much has been written on the costs of advertisement, be they monetary or spiritual. It has also become fashionable to blame advertisement for the novelization of imagination, for the shrinking of personal opportunities of choice, for the crippling of personal taste, particularly through the media.

34 It is well known that advertisements on commercial TV channels are targeted at specific viewers of specific programs. One commercial serves a way

of life for the viewers of "Dallas," and another commercial a way of life for the viewers of "Murder One."

35 This is provided that one can avoid legal consequences.

36 This is one reason why wealthy people bequeath money or valuable to galleries, museums, and universities. Wealth is perishable. No one remembers the names of those who are wealthy unless there are bequests, which preserve the name and protect it from mortality.

37 This is the case from Sismondi to Nietzsche. Sismondi says that modernity has made slaves of us all. Marx enumerates "universality" among the main constituents of the "generic essence" in his *Paris Manuscripts*. Professionalized knowledge is, in Nietzsche's mind, sterile Alexandrinism.

38 Hegel, *Phenomenology of Spirit*, trans. A. V. Miller (Oxford: Oxford University Press, 1977).

39 I will discuss this in chapter 8.

40 This is obvious if we compare the social–democratic model with a free market model, or if we consider the policies of affirmative action. In the latter case (particularly in America) the political institutions intervened in order to correct historical injustices. For this to happen, one needs to have a picture of historical justice or injustice and tell a new story about history, the genealogy of inequalities, and so on.

41 This takes the clearest form in the USA. However, in dictatorships the state is highly oppressive and "civil society" is characterized by solidarity.

42 Here, I employ Foucault's metaphor of the body being imprisoned by the soul. Michel Foucault, *Discipline and Punish*, trans. Alan Sheridan (New York: Vintage, 1979).

43 This was discovered by Hegel as well by Marx. Yet the existence of the "underclass" is not just the result of "exploitation," but of the modern social arrangement in general. It is inherent within the model.

44 Let me refer back to Heidegger's distinction between *Historie* and *Geschichte*.

45 Here I refer back to Kant's distinction between person and personality. Insofar as someone practices his skills, he acts as a person. Insofar as he distances himself from his own skill, relativizes his institution and his place in the hierarchy, becoming-being aware of finitude, transience, and what it entails, and seeks for meaning and truth other than the kind that is forged in "scientific" discourse, he is a personality, but not a purely moral one.

46 See Karl Mannheim, *Ideology and Utopia* (New York: Harcourt Brace, 1936).

47 I redefined the issue of objectivity in the social sciences in my study "Hermeneutics of social sciences," in *Can Modernity Survive?* op. cit.

48 This is the rewording Foucault uses in "Truth and power," p. 73, in Michel Foucault, *The Foucault Reader*, ed. Paul Rabinow (New York: Pantheon, 1984).

7 The Three Logics of Modernity III

1 The ancient (e.g., Greek) political structure was not regarded as a mere superstructure. (See Karl Marx, "Introduction to a critique of political economy," in Karl Marx and Friedrich Engels, *The German Ideology*, trans. C. J. Arthur (New York: International Publishers, 1972).

2 See Robert Nozick, *Anarchy, State and Utopia* (New York: Basic Books, 1974). Nozick polemicizes here against an alternative liberal option, that of Rawls' Theory of Justice. Although Rawls, also true to the liberal tradition, gives preference to the principles of liberty as against the principles of well-being (principles based on the pure and simple value of Life, which also requires a social state, the redistribution of goods and services) Rawls's state is not a minimal state, but the idealized version of the Rooseveltian USA. Nozick's utopia (where all utopias are realized) indeed requires a minimal state; that is, a state whose function is exhausted by warranting security and performing the function of retributive justice.

3 Stagnation is not necessarily economic in character. It can manifest itself in the loss of excitement, color, variety in life or lifestyles, boredom, the loss of the capacity to take initiatives, in the client relationship to the state, and many other things.

4 For example, contemporary technology requires higher skills. This alters the character of the unemployed population. There is an increase in the unemployed population that cannot be treated as "normal" even if unemployment benefits are enough to keep people on a level of a standard of living that is still acceptable in their cultural milieu. It has turned out that at the present time the German unemployment figures have surpassed the limits of tolerability. Something, then, must be done. But the question is, by whom? By the state.

5 For example, unemployment benefits, child support, housing concessions, and the like.

6 This is one of the reasons why Hannah Arendt insisted that the economic realm has nothing to do with politics, and that economic matters, even if treated by the state, are issues of problem-solving and not of political action, and need to be taken care of by scientists who are good at problem-solving.

7 It was important for Machiavelli that the Roman constitution was not forged by Romulus, but by his successor.

8 Many references are made to England, with its "unwritten" constitution deeply rooted in the tradition. Yet, even this unwritten constitution is somehow "written," for everyone knows what it contains. In addition, there have been many voices raised lately, even movements launched, in order that Britain now should become modern, and have at least a written Charter of Rights.

9 For example, this is what is now happening in Hungary.

10   Islamic fundamentalism has not lowered oil prices. At this level, the global economy rules supreme, as well as modern technology. Women's veils are fabricated in modern factories and sold on the market.

11   See the history of parliamentary democracy in England. Ronald Butt, *A History of Parliament* (London: Constable, 1989).

12   Ferenc Fehér, in his study "Dialogue between the Old and the New World" (in manuscript), points at the numerous misunderstandings of the two political cultures while they read one another. This misunderstanding stems from the difference in traditions and from analogical thinking (both understand the other from the background of their own tradition).

13   In this sense, Arendt was absolutely right. Politics is about action insofar as only actions are kept in long-term historical memory.

14   Even history writing was normally once concentrated around telling stories of political actions. It was only the Annales school and structuralism that put at the center of historiography the analysis of the functioning of institutions, including the institutions of everyday life. Yet this kind of historiography has not influenced living historical imagination; it has remained a delicacy for the experts.

15   Augustine described imagination as future-oriented memory and memory as past-oriented imagination.

16   I do not like to coin new mana-words, nor to employ Heidegger's philosophical neologisms. But here I could not resist using "worlding" (*welten*), for this is the only way to approximately say what I wanted; that is, letting a world be as it becomes.

17   So-called "world drama" turned out to be a disaster, or just a local story expanded to world historical dimensions, such as the second part of Goethe's *Faust*, Ibsen's *Peer Gynt*, or the Hungarian drama by Imre Madach, *The Tragedy of Man*.

18   The particularistic use of works of art is a general tendency in modernity, primarily in modern nationalism.

19   One can tell the stories of the Bible to the Jews as the stories (histories, myths, of the Jews). To "unmask them" as mere lies or works of fantasy is one of the most stupid moves of the Enlightenment. Yet if one claims "Judea and Samaria" for Israel on the account of biblical stories, this can be easily unmasked, not necessarily as the cover-up for "interests," for perhaps men who believe in it have no "material interest" to support their beliefs, but certainly as a wrongful claim to justice, truth, and rightness.

20   Here I mean the three modern ethical powers discussed by Hegel, such as the family, the institutions of civil society, and the state. (All of these can be associated with the people, the folk, the nation, the class, the ethnic groups, and so-called races and genders.)

21   It is impossible to sever all concrete ties with "reality." One cannot go on telling lies in a sequence of many sentences without also telling some truth.

22   This concept of reality does not annul the (Hegelian) distinction between actuality and reality.

23 Here it is not the collective memory that preserves such claims, but the inventive professional mind that formulates them. Such was the case, for example, with the myth of "Black Athena."

24 Alexis de Tocqueville, *Democracy in America* (New York: H. G. Langley, 1845).

25 Since I am not writing history here, I contrast only one type of the New World with one type of the Old. In Australia, for example, nationalism plays no significant role in history, nor does race. The national myth is almost entirely based on nature, on the mythologization of the landscape and of the space. Australians keep telling the following joke with gusto: "What is the difference between an Englishman and an Australian? For an Englishman two hundred miles is a distance; for an Australian two hundred years is history."

26 This is why the use of racial language distorts politics into biopolitics. See F. Fehér and A. Heller, *Biopolitics* (Brookfield, VT: Avery Press, 1994).

27 The major popular art form in America, the movie, has constantly presented the two myths (the Wild West and the court drama) from its early days until the present time. See also my paper "The non-tragic drama of American democracy," Agon (Berkeley: University of California Press, 1998).

28 The great tragedies center mostly around revenge or justice, while epic poetry normally portrays wars.

29 The crusades were "ideological" enough in my broader sense of the word, whereas the dynastic wars of the 17th century or the wars between 1815 and 1914 were fought under a very thin ideological "mask."

30 World wars are now replaced by local wars. One could vest some hope in "the end of wars" on the ground that in a modern democracy people do not like to fight. It was difficult to drag America into the major European wars. The Vietnam war ended in a pacifistic mood, and nowadays it is a slogan of some young Americans that "nothing is worth dying for." Wars are preferred only where technology is used, but not a single soldier dies. The hedonistic tendencies of modern democracy do not whet the appetite for wars. This, however, can change, as can all moods. For example, boredom, one of the frequently occurring moods, is a great incentive that can induce the adventure of war. But if one thinks in terms of the end of wars, one has to take account not just of the profits, but also of the losses. For example, a world government that prohibited wars would be a nightmarish kind of tyranny.

31 This "state form" is a hylomorphic expression inherited from Aristotelean metaphysics. Actually, I think that the matter/form relation works always as an analogy, the origin of which can be traced back to sculpture. Only in the case of sculpture does the matter/form relationship make full sense. If the state is the form, what is then the matter of this form? Is society the matter "formed" by the state? Or are the citizens the matter formed into the frame of the political institutions?

32 It makes sense also to speak of totalitarian democracy. How the rule of majority becomes tyrannical has been observed already by Tocqueville. The

pre-Bolshevik character of the Jacobin dictatorship was pointed out by Ferenc Fehér, in his book *The Frozen Revolution: An Essay on Jacobinism* (New York: Cambridge University Press, 1987).

33   This happens frequently; for example, in African states inhabited by several tribes. The majority tribe gets into government by free elections and thus legally oppresses the members of the minority tribes. The oppression can in a sense be called totalitarian, because all of the methods of modern totalitarianism are at the disposal of the government.

34   Totalitarian states normally also define themselves as dictatorships; for example, the "dictatorship of the proletariat."

35   This does not prevent totalitarian dictators from mobilizing historical consciousness and its myths, but they do it extremely selectively. The bulk of the tradition is normally rejected as cowardice, opportunistic, and unclean, since otherwise they could not make a case for the revolutionary character of their regimes.

36   See, for details, F. Fehér, A. Heller, and G. Markus, *Dictatorship over Needs* (New York: St. Martin's Press, 1983). In this book we described how a modern totalitarian society works, including its economy, system of powers, political structure, ethics, and ideology.

37   For this reason, and because of the unfinished totalization of society, Mussolini's fascist state cannot be called fully totalitarian. This is all the more interesting since Mussolini was the first to invent the word "totalitarianism," applying it to his own rule in a positive sense.

38   See, first and foremost, the brilliant analyses of Zygmunt Bauman, in *Modernity and the Holocaust* (Oxford: Polity Press, 1990).

39   Although one cannot have the first without the second, and vice versa.

40   This is significant even if the Nazi chiefs boasted of murdering the Jews or declared it to be meritorious. (See Himmler's speech on the occasion of the initiation of SS officers [Heinrich Himmler, *Geheimreden 1933 bis 1945 und andere Ansprachen* (Frankfurt am Main: Propylaen Verlag, 1974)].

41   Heidegger indeed identifies Nazism, Bolshevism, and modern democracy socio-ontologically. He does not identify them morally, for he does not take the moral point of view. There is an absolute moral difference between mass murder on the one hand and the technological/bureaucratic handling of political business (as an object) on the other hand.

42   The Gulag and Chernobyl are not just morally but also ontologically incomparable, for they are of entirely different significative magnitudes.

43   The examples are inexhaustible. Stalin allows his best generals to be killed before the war; Hitler uses the wagons that are badly needed on the Eastern front for transporting the Jews as fodder to the killing machines.

44   In this framework, I cannot even attempt to outline a theory of democracy, even less a history of this theory. In the modern discourse, democracy was first identified with ancient democracy. This is how, for example, Kant uses the word. The system of representation was regarded as republican (from the

Roman tradition) or liberal. The Greek model was not representative at the beginning. Later, particularly in the democracy theories of the 20th century, the Greek model became dominant. The political philosophers who give absolute priority to the Athenian political model reject the system of representation. So do, for example, Hannah Arendt and Cornelius Castoriadis. Arendt and Castoriadis, like many other mainly leftist authors, prefer the so-called direct democracy to representative democracy. Nowadays, when we speak of democracy we mean "liberal democracy" without making a strict distinction between liberalism and democracy.

45 This warrants in fact what is termed popular sovereignty; namely, that all powers originate in the "people." According to Hannah Arendt, the term "popular sovereignty" makes no sense in the United States, for the institution of the township was an agency of direct democracy or mixed democracy. In Tocqueville, however, one finds a different interpretation. Tocqueville includes the political activity in the townships in the category of popular sovereignty.

46 About the political role that the judiciary power plays in the American democracy, see Tocqueville. op. cit., chapter 6.

47 The question is raised of who the citizens are. For example, the slaves of America were not citizens. And even later, blacks and immigrants encountered serious barriers to achieving the status of citizenship. The blacks were frequently prevented from participating in the election even after they had been granted citizenship.

48 See Isaiah Berlin, *Four Essays on Liberty* (New York: Oxford University Press, 1970).

49 Tocqueville, op. cit., chapter 7.

50 As Hamlet says (Act I, Scene III), "Take each man's censure, but reserve thy judgment."

51 Human rights, just as much as the institution of representation, originate in the Christian tradition. There is, however, a difference between the concept of natural law and that of natural rights. See Leo Strauss, *Natural Right and History*, (Chicago: University of Chicago Press, 1953). One could say that the democratic aspect of the modern political body is "ancient," whereas the liberal tradition is "Christian" in its origins. But, all the same, this is not so simple.

52 We do not refer to the French 1790 as to a democracy. This was already Tocqueville's point.

53 The civil law mirrors this difference too. It is far more difficult to win a libel suit in the USA than in Great Britain, and what counts as defamation of character in the latter goes unpunished and is common practice in the former.

54 As has been pointed out many times, there are contradictions not only between liberal and democratic freedoms, but also between various liberal rights. One example is the possible collision between the right to hold property (and its interpretation) and coalition right, such as the right to

organize trade unions (and its interpretation). Historically, however, the contradictions between liberal rights can be eliminated, insofar as the different liberal rights can be interpreted so as to give a green light to the other. However, the tensions and collisions between democratic freedoms and liberal freedoms can finally be settled in the books of normative political philosophers alone.

55 Persons can also be legal persons, of course.

56 This is also taken for granted by the American theorists of democracy. This is why Rorty insists that liberal democracy does not call for legitimation. Freedom is self-legitimating. The possibility of a serious threat to liberties is not seriously considered.

57 Ferenc Fehér discusses in detail how Tocqueville discovered the centrality of equality in the American democracy. See F. Fehér: "The evergreen Tocqueville," *Thesis Eleven*, 42, 1995.

58 Op. cit.

59 According to Karl Polanyi in his book, *The Great Transformation* (New York: Octagon, 1975), the self-regulating market was the negative utopia of 19th-century liberalism. There has always been state intervention, but the kind and extent of the intervention has varied.

60 The "per capita income" is nowadays acceptable as a measure of the wealth of a nation, but is not applicable to the opportunity of single persons. (One needs more for the same opportunity, whereas the other needs less – for example, one is more clever or energetic than the other.)

61 Whether it is legitimate to call all the socio-economic rights rights is a frequently discussed issue. They are not absolute rights like liberties, and they are in themselves also conditional. For example, freedom of conscience is not granted under the conditions that ... but unemployment benefits are granted under certain conditions; for example, of unemployment, health care service, and so on. Sociopolitical rights are permissions insofar as they are due to people who belong to a certain social category (e.g., widows, single mothers), whereas liberties are unconditional, since they are not due to members of certain groups but to all citizens.

62 The Athenian institution of ostracism is a well-known example of this attitude.

63 Dworkin and other American liberal theorists suggest that talents are won on the natural lottery; they are not "merits" and this is why they do not deserve special consideration. This is a beautiful manifestation of *ressentiment*, although the theorist may be unaware if it.

64 Sometimes substantive egalitarianism is also extended to the economic domain. If everything that is not equal is undeserved, greater wealth or property belongs to them. Yet, as I said, the idea of equality is not expanded to all territories. For example, it has not really expanded to the economic domain in the United States.

65 Nietzsche used this French term first in this sense in his *On the Genealogy of Morals*, trans. Walter Kaufmann (New York: Vintage, 1969), part one.

66 A personal confession: ugly for me. I do not think that morality can be defined with the contrast of "high" and "low," but I think that a person's moral worth is greater if she is beyond envy and resentment.

67 Nowadays Europeans begin to follow in the footsteps of the American model. The crisis of European political institutions, which has developed in many states lately, mirrors this transformation.

68 How fast the pendulum can swing back from the extreme in this case has been described by Hannah Arendt in one of her letters addressed to Karl Jaspers. Arendt here tells how the Cold War and its witch-hunt ceased and disappeared as suddenly as it emerged. See Arendt and Jaspers, *Correspondence*, trans. Robert and Rita Kimber, eds. Lotte Kohler and Hans Saner (New York: Harcourt Brace Jovanovich, 1985).

69 As a counter-example: during Roosevelt's presidency, under very similar circumstances, the democratic interpretation of liberal rights became the policy of the New Deal. In Germany there was no New Deal. Not only, but also, because of this Adolf Hitler's Nazi party could get enough votes for the seizure of power and for the successive elimination of the democratic institutions. See this connection in detail in Mihaly Vajda, *A Fasimusrol* (Budapest: Osiris, 1993).

70 Rawls has never accepted the communitarian agenda, not even recently, when his position became defensive and weakened by the communitarian ethos. In practice, PC (political correctness) is a typical case of liberalism's defenselessness against the terror of an alleged majority. Of course, as always in similar cases, the majority is just "alleged." It is the majority of the loud crowd, of the activists, the men and women in the state of constant indignation.

71 Of course, there are no legal private armies, for illegal private armies can be found in many states; for example, where the Mafia is strong.

72 The American model is not general, yet it best shows the place of violence in the modern world.

73 It is precisely this task that the so-called minimal state has to perform. See Nozick, op. cit.

74 Governments that cannot ensure security will lose their legitimacy. This can be seen from the recent situation in the former Soviet states, particularly in Russia.

75 The right to hold arms is an important democratic right. In Athens, every citizen could keep his weapon at home. In the modern democracies only New World countries took over this tradition. In Australia, because of a terrible incident, this right had been limited with the consent of the population. In America, this is still a hot issue.

76 This is all the more so because the word that Weber uses, *Gewalt*, means both force and violence in English.

77 See the following chapter.

78 See Michel Foucault, *Discipline and Punish*, trans. Alan Sheridan (New York: Vintage, 1979).

79　The best known definition is presented by Carl Schmitt's, *The Concept of the Political*, where he identifies this concept with the friend/foe dichotomy. Hannah Arendt identified "the political" with action, avoiding the issue of decision. See my essay "The concept of the political" in Agnes Heller, *Can Modernity Survive?* (Berkeley: University of California Press, 1990).

80　See J. G. A. Pocock, *The Machiavellian Moment* (Princeton, NJ: Princeton University Press, 1979) and Miguel Vatter, "Machiavelli and the Republican Freedom" (unpublished manuscript).

81　I described the Hungarian Revolution of 1956 in this sense. See Agnes Heller, "The Great Republic," *Praxis International* (Oxford) 5:1, April 1985.

82　This is the idea of "republicanism" in the stories of Zoltan Szankay and his group of political theorists and activists in Bremen, Germany.

83　The political institutions of the modern world had always been criticized because of their lack of grandeur. The criticism is to the point, particularly if one compares democratic politics with the politics of aristocracy or of ancient democracy. But there are great exceptions. By the great exceptions I do not mean the so-called "heroic" historical age of the bourgeoisie from the French Revolution to Napoleon, but several recent political events.

8　Culture and Civilization I

1　Oswald Spengler, in his influential and controversial book, *The Decline of the West*, made a sharp distinction between culture and civilization. To summarize, he interpreted the histories of various cultures in the sense that as long as culture is at its highest civilization is underdeveloped, whereas the development of civilization brings about a cultural decay. According to his description, the modern world had already entered the period of cultural decay, and this was, indeed, accompanied by the progression of civilization. The distinction, although in a slightly different setting, is by far not new. See Oswald Spengler, *The Decline of the West*, trans. Charles Francis Atkinson (New York: A. A. Knopf, 1926–8). One need only recall Rousseau's first discourse or Nietzsche's sharp contrast between *Kultur* and *Bildung* – where *Bildung* stands for spiritual or scientific civilization. See Rousseau's "Discourse on the sciences and the arts," in Jean-Jacques Rousseau, *The Basic Political Writings*, trans. Donald Cress (Indianapolis: Hackett, 1987). See also Friedrich Nietzsche, *On the Genealogy of Morals*, trans. Walter Kaufman and R. J. Hollingdale (New York: Random House, 1967).

2　For Adorno, the culture industry and the market are blamed simultaneously. This follows from the albeit obscured yet still Marxian origin of the theory. For Nietzsche, democracy is the main culprit in this decay. In the wake of all new technological inventions, there is a subsequent wave of cultural criticism predicting that this technology will certainly kill culture. Nowadays, it is the Internet that is suspected to destroy the "Gutenberg galaxies," literacy, and everything that we have traditionally enumerated under the heading of "high

culture." Such predictions repeatedly make headway. The explanation perhaps goes back to Plato, who was afraid that literacy would take the place of
oral culture (and would destroy memory). This has never, ever, happened.
Education, for example, could never rely upon written texts. Books were
always orally mediated and discussed. When the so-called "book drama"
became fashionable, cultural critics believed that people would no longer
visit the theaters; this fear reoccured when the moving picture was invented.
When the television became widely used, one was sure (it seemed certain)
that now no one would go to the movies; when the record player appeared,
cultural critics predicted that concert halls would become empty, and so on.
None of these predictions came true. The proliferation of access to entertainment, scientific information, political information, or artistic delight does
not make the earlier channels unused or obsolete, because these appeal to
different needs. It is true that certain phenomena can become obsolete. For
example, there are no more newsreels in the movie theaters, as there were
once upon a time, before the era of television news; pornographic drawings
no longer draw business, since pornographic films have appeared on the
market.

3   Here I rely heavily on the work of György Markus and his philosophy of
culture. I refer mainly, although not only, to three papers by Markus from
recent years: one on the problems of culture in general, one on Hegel's
conception about the end of art, and one on the German philosophy of
culture about the turn of the century. However, I employ Markus's categories
quite freely and highly selectively, and thus I alone should be blamed for
the sketchy character and the idiosyncrasies of this section. To begin with, the
main difference between Markus's categories and my use of them is that he
distinguishes between two concepts of culture – the concept of high culture
and the "anthropological concept" – whereas I distinguish between three.

4   Later, I will exemplify this idea on the traditional model of cultural discourse: Kant's analysis of the judgment of taste in his *Critique of Judgment*.
See Immanuel Kant, *Critique of Judgment*, trans. Werner Pluhar (Indianapolis: Hackett, 1987).

5   It is interesting that according to Hegel's thesis on the end of art, the religion
of art is a matter of the past. The plastic marble and bronze statues of ancient
gods represented "the religion of beauty." Actually, although the statues
represented gods, classical Greece hardly considered artists to be "divine."
They did not even have such a word as "artist." *Poiesis*, or *technē*, were acts
of creation and creative skill, and regarded normally as belonging to humans.
Even when Aristotle elevates writers of tragedy together with philosophers
above the historians – for they portray things as they could have happened
and not just as they did happen – he does not show the slightest indication of
the tendency toward divinification of art. This became the mainstream idea
in Hegel's time. Yet, perhaps this was one reason why Hegel placed
the religion of art in the past. A real religion does not demand a "genius,"
but an apostle. And the artists were termed in Hegel's Encyclopedia,

"The masters of God." See G. W. F. Hegel, *The Encyclopaedia Logic*; Part I of the Encyclopaedia of philosophical sciences with the Zusätze (Indianapolis: Hackett, 1991).

It is true that there is an ambiguity in this formulation. It can be understood such that the artist is just a master under divine command (like an apostle), yet also in the sense that the artist creates gods (as statues). Yet even if one takes the second interpretation, the culture or the religion of art is never the culture of the artistic genius, but always of God. It seems as if Hegel regarded the divinification of his time as particularly phony.

6 Søren Kierkegaard makes this difference particularly clear in his essay, "The difference between the genius and the Apostle," in *The Present Age, and of the Difference Between a Genius and an Apostle*, trans. Alexander Dru (New York: Harper & Row, 1962).

7 Hannah Arendt, *Between Past and Future: Eight Exercises in Political Thought* (New York: Viking Press, 1968).

8 One could think about the coincidence that the concept of transcendence appears in the same period. The Greek tradition is metaphysical and does not know of transcendence, whereas the Oriental, and particularly the Jewish, culture is rooted in the image of transcendence. The last pagan philosophers did their best to insert the Jewish (then already also Christian) tradition into the Greek/metaphysical one. Plato himself (in one of the arguments in *Parmenides* at least) gave some food for such speculation. For example, in Plotinus, the One is beyond Being. That the One is beyond Being, i.e., that it cannot be encompassed as "the most perfect Being" in the *genus proximum* of Being, is an indication of the emergence of the idea of transcendence. See *The Collected Dialogues of Plato*, eds. Edith Hamilton and Huntington Cairns (Princeton University Press, 1961). See also Plotinus, *Enneads*, trans. Stephen Mackenna (Penguin Books: London, 1991).

9 This main tendency and its counter-tendency is beautifully discussed by Hans Jonas in the introduction to his book, *The Gnostic Religion: The Message of the Alien God and the Beginnings of Christianity* (Boston: Beacon Press, 1963).

10 The appreciation of high art belongs to culture, yet they are not of the same extension.

11 The alien was represented of course by the *elite* of Oriental people.

12 There are many other possibilities. Being possessed can also signal the capacity and the condition of entry.

13 It was Plato who spoke about the four kinds of frenzy in the *Phaedrus*. See *The Collected Dialogues of Plato*, ibid.

14 The great work of art is never entirely absorbed by "culture." This will become more obvious in modern times.

15 In cultures in which the dynamics of modernity have not made their appearance, the standards for works of art are stable. One has the impression (which is not quite accurate) that, for example, Egyptian art has not changed at all throughout centuries or even over millennia.

16 For the classical formulation of this issue, see David Hume, "Of the standard of taste," in *Of the Standard of Taste and Other Essays*, ed. John Lenz

(Indianapolis: Bobbs–Merrill, 1965). I have analyzed the question of the standard of taste from the perspective of the concept of the beautiful in Agnes Heller, *The Concept of the Beautiful*, Part II, in manuscript.

17 See *The Concept of the Beautiful*, Part II, op. cit.

18 See chapter 3 of this book.

19 Of course, this is with the exception of a paradigm change.

20 I mean culture according to its first concept, which I am still discussing.

21 Markus gives a more complex argument.

22 The (in)famous slogan of the students in many American universities, "Western culture has got to go," is the manifestation of *ressentiment* clad in the costume of solidarity and respect for difference. I shall return to this issue later. In recent times, one can also observe the opposite tendency, Harold Bloom, in his book; for example *The Western Canon* (New York: Harcourt Brace Jovanovich, 1994), makes a case for the reinforcement of such a canon. The question is not so much about the concrete works enumerated in the canon (since one can always replace most of them with various others), but about the existence of a canon itself. Just recently, in Cartagena, Colombia, I had the opportunity to cast a glance at the list of books that Colombians regarded as "necessary" reading (the canon of high culture). There were, of course, at least five times as many Spanish-language books included than one could expect from a similar canon in France or Hungary, yet there were at least 15 works included which, in my view, would be included in all lists of "necessary" reading everywhere in the "cultured" world.

23 This kind of resentment seems to be a new phenomenon of modern mass democracies. Yet the "elitist" Greek philosophers and dramatic writers (e.g., Plato or Aristophanes) reported very similar feelings of *ressentiment* in the ancient Athenian democracy. The history of the Roman Republic can also be similarly understood. Just as the politician needs to "flatter" the crowd (the story of Coriolanus), so the philosopher needs to flatter the illiterate, who resent refinement and taste, as in *Timon of Athens*. See William Shakespeare, *The Tragedy of Coriolanus*, ed. Tucker Brooke (New Haven: Yale University Press, 1924), and also William Shakespeare, *The Life of Timon of Athens*, ed. J. C. Maxwell (Cambridge, UK: Cambridge University Press, 1957).

24 One could object that the situation is similar in matters of true knowledge, particularly in philosophy. However, I do not think so. In philosophy, one is entitled to choose a foundation and build a philosophical quasi-system up on this hypothetical foundation. Although the ultimate principle (the *archē*, the foundation) cannot be argumentatively justified, the things built on it can be – if one understands that argumentation in a very broad way, including narratives and aphorisms. In contemporary sciences, there is something that one can call "results." For example, one can recognize the tree from the fruit that grows on it, through the cumulation of knowledge and in technology, so that others can continue what someone else has started. In judgments of taste (about works of art), one cannot construe a foundation

for taste that others should accept. The reception of a work of art is not a "result," for it can be entirely temporary, and it remains a matter of taste.

25 I discussed the first in chapter 2, and the second in chapter 5.

26 The social analysis is sketchy at this point. But it is not my task to go into detail, for I only want to offer a new approach to the concept of "high culture."

27 Still, my distinction between high and low art follows the logic of Kant's distinction between the beautiful and the agreeable.

28 This is not my use of the term.

29 Of course, all artists desire recipients, and modern artists want to make a living with their music or painting or novels. But they are still authors.

30 Nostalgia remains the offspring of historical imagination in mass culture too, whereas future-oriented imagination has become entirely technological. All utopias, whether positive or negative, are science fictions.

31 During times of great artistic outpourings in recent European history, it has been taken as self-evident that popular art has to feed high art. Goethe collected Serbian popular poetry, the Grimm brothers folk tales, and still, in the 20th century, Bartok used Hungarian folk music and, later, jazz for musical quotation. High art lived, among others, from "quotations" of popular art. Nowadays, high artworks quote instead artworks of bygone ages.

32 I do not want to propose that high culture (or the works of art that are retrospectively put into the cluster of high culture) needs folk culture as its source. One has to modernize histories in order to believe in this connection. In the 19th century, the widespread theory that there was no poet called Homer, but rather only a person who collected popular poesy and then became called "Homer," expressed the ideas and the experiences of the nineteenth century. This theory has since been disproven, but I doubt whether this present conviction, although philologically sound, is final.

33 The second concept of culture grew out of discussions in the cafés and salons of the 18th century. In the cafés, men, and in the salons, women, were the protagonists. They "organized" cultural discourse. See Jürgen Habermas, *The Structural Transformation of the Public Sphere: An Inquiry into a Category of Bourgeois Society*, trans. Thomas Burger with the assistance of Frederick Lawrence (Cambridge, MA: MIT Press, 1989), and Hannah Arendt, *Rahel Varnhagen: The Life of a Jewish Woman*, trans. Richard and Clara Winston (New York: Harcourt Brace Jovanovich, 1974).

34 As far as the content of their description is concerned, the first and the second concepts of culture frequently overlap. But they are still two emphatically different concepts of culture. High works of art *as such* are *not* included in "culture" in the second concept: only the *discussion about them* is. Thus, the second concept acknowledges the "secret" of the work of art which remains *external* to culture – being "transcendent," so to speak.

35 One could say that the Platonian dialogues are already models of such a conversation. But in fact this is true only of the early ones, written prior to

Plato's metaphysical turn. Yet the dialogues also show that certain modern kinds of cultural discussion took place in Athens prior to Plato's time.

36 That in certain places of the world the general dynamics of modernity has remained underdeveloped is partly due to the absence of the culture of conversation or of the general reflective discourse.

37 Such kinds of cultivated exchanges of opinions have maintained the sanity of many men and women in totalitarian states. The Party could expel the manifestation of diverging opinions from the press and from official institutions, but no totalitarian state could entirely prohibit the private exchanges of opinions about politically indifferent matters. Yet this is enough to maintain the practice of discourse, even if only on a restricted level.

38 Kant speaks about enthusiasm as a passion vested in freedom as its object. This concept of enthusiasm can be broadened to encompass cultural discussion.

39 Not everything termed "culture" belongs under the heading of the second concept of culture. For example, "sexual culture" belongs to the cluster that will be discussed under the heading of "civilization."

40 Public fiction is one of the major characteristics of cultural politics. Public fiction is defined as a discussion of politics as if each person was interested in an idea and in the well-being of people only, and not in his or her advancement and private passion. Everyone presumes that this, in fact, is not always the case, but it is still important to maintain the "fiction." Public fiction can also be maintained, within political institutions, in discussions that are aimed at decisions, although we do not count such discourses among the cases of cultural conversation. Yet whether the practice of cultivated political discussion is largely present or absent outside of official institutions is what contributes to the presence or the absence of the public fiction within institutional constraints as well.

41 This is generally the case, unless a person is overly sensitive. This can, of course, happen.

42 The *venue* of a discussion can also be the university, a theater, and so on, but only in offering space, opportunity, or other such conditions.

43 I have already indicated that the phenomena themselves are not necessarily different, even if the concept that encompasses them is. One can interpret high works of art as a famous art critique and still discuss the same works in the company of friends.

44 I have analyzed Kant's model of cultural conversation in great detail in my book *Philosophy of History in Fragments* (Cambridge, MA: Basil Blackwell, 1993), in the chapter entitled "Culture, or invitation to luncheon by Immanuel Kant."

45 Immanuel Kant, *Anthropology From a Pragmatic Point of View*, trans. Mary J. Gregor (The Hague: Martinus Nijhoff, 1974), par. 88.

46 The "real" world is the world of unsocial sociability. Men and women do all the wrong things to each other: they fight with one another, they purposely hurt each other – only in order to be loved and respected. The situation of

social sociability promises respect and inclination in social commerce where no one is hurt.

47   This is why *Bildung* is normally described as a case of nihilism in Nietzsche.

48   Markus, op. cit.

49   Decades can elapse between the first and second moves. The hierarchization of "culture" historically precedes the tentative equalization of cultures.

50   No such expression is applied in sociological/anthropological research of "subcultures." But they mostly follow the same pattern. Subcultures need to be understood on their own terms, whatever those terms are. The researcher has no right to superimpose his or her values on the group he or she researches. This norm is, in fact, phony; if one chooses a group of people as the object of a study, then the choice itself shows the interest of the researcher. In the case of participating in research, one rarely makes such phony claims. When one participates in the life of a people or a group of people, one is existentially and not just scientifically interested. Participation means practical entry. And in the case of practical entry, identification also goes in hand with taking sides or in taking, at least in part, the perspective of the group that one studies. Such a perspective is not neutral, and it often hierarchizes. Which is the "ethnos," and who will provide the yardstick, is not important in this case – at least not for the study of the anthropological concept of culture.

51   Markus also works out the paradoxical character of the anthropological concept in a very similar way. See Markus, op. cit.

52   I have compared the similarity between Kant's conception of judgment of taste and of *Gunst* with the model of general elections in my study, "Freedom and equality of Kant's *Critique of Judgment*" (in Hungarian translation, in *Eletkepes-e a modernitas*, Latin Betuk, 1997).

53   I discuss the phony logic in my book *Beyond Justice* (Cambridge, MA: Blackwell, 1990), chapters 1 and 2.

54   I have read a similar argument by Charles Taylor in his debate on multiculturalism. See Charles Taylor, *Multiculturalism and "The Politics of Recognition": An Essay*, edited and with commentary by Amy Gutmann (Princeton: Princeton University Press, 1992).

55   Ideal types are simplifications. In fact, in contemporary times, all of the three concepts of culture are applied, mostly without our being aware of their tensions. One needs to think them through philosophically, to recognize how and to what extent they limit or even exclude one another.

56   The relativization of European culture has always been one of the themes of the European romanticism.

57   Lately, Richard Rorty takes this position. He declares himself openly "ethnocentric" in the sense mentioned above.

58   Tribal wars break out frequently in African states because, after fair parliamentary elections, the legally elected government of the majority (tribe) excludes the members of the minority (tribe) from decision-making, does not grant their rights, and further limits their opportunity.

59 This kind of contextuality is explored by neo-pragmatists such as Richard Bernstein and Richard Rorty.

60 Such is the choice between the pro-life and the pro-choice position in the case of abortion, or when the question arises as to whether international organizations have the right to interfere in local wars where many thousands or more human lives are at stake, or whether Muslim girls should be allowed to wear veils in state-run schools.

61 Another question is that of identification: On what ground does a culture identify itself? Recently, in an unfortunate rebirth of race-thinking, it is frequently biologico-ethnic marks such as race and gender which are said to serve as indicators of identifications. Whenever marks of "race" (or gender) become significant in political identification, politics becomes "bio-politics" and will fall short of granting liberal rights and political liberties. About this question, see Ferenc Fehér and Agnes Heller, *Biopolitics* (Brookfield, VT: Avebury, 1994). A related issue is the conflict between self-representation and the representation by the other. If a group raises claims of exclusive self-representation, political liberty is, once again, curtailed. See Agnes Heller, "Representation and self-representation in modern politics," Paper presented in the conference on multiculturalism, Ashborn Center, Melbourne, in manuscript.

9 Culture and Civilization II

1 In exceptional times, the whole upper stratum was supposed to qualify for cultural wine-tasting. In the *Politics*, for example, Aristotle says that when all free citizens sitting in the theater are forming their judgment, the result in judgment will be fair, for the single judgments correct one another and their average will be "good." See Aristotle, *The Politics*, trans. Carnes Lord (Chicago: University of Chicago Press, 1984).

2 Intellectuals of the old "socialist" regimes in Central–Eastern Europe raised the same claims after the change in systems. They believed that one could abolish party dictatorship over culture, yet still preserve something of an ideology-free state patronage over culture to protect the quality of culture against market forces.

3 Zygmunt Bauman, *Legislators and Interpreters* (Oxford: Basil Blackwell, 1987).

4 I have discussed this issue in chapter 5.

5 The "turn" toward the reader has expressed this tendency well.

6 This was the case of Nietzsche, as the last of the avant-guardists.

7 Sándor Radnóti, in his book *Hamisitas (Forgery)*, associates this development with the emergence of postmodernism, particularly with the appearance of pastiche and quotation as legitimate artistic forms and styles. See Radnóti, *The Fake: Forgery and Its Place in Art* (Rowman & Littlefield, 1999).

8   These two, the text and its authority, can also be identified; for example, by the Jewish mystics who claimed that the whole *Torah* is but God's name.

9   See the previous chapter, especially the first concept of culture; i.e., "high culture."

10 For three decades, the celebration of the paradigm of language, in its many *variants*, was a cultural fashion in philosophy. Contrary to the outdated paradigm of consciousness, the language paradigm was seen as that which had finally "solved" the "insoluble" questions – this included the so-called question of intersubjectivity, among others. At this point, that fashion is over. Needless to say, no paradigm "solves" philosophical questions, for philosophy is not about problem-solving. Every paradigm produces paradoxes, albeit different ones.

11 It is interesting to follow Roland Barthes from his acceptance of a structuralist version of the paradigm of language to the abandonment of the same paradigm. See, for example, Roland Barthes, *A Lover's Discourse: Fragments (Fragments d'un Discours Amoureux)*, trans. Richard Howard (New York: Hill and Wang, 1978). See also Gergely Angyalosi's discussion of this in his book *Roland Barthes, a semleges profeta (Roland Barthes, the Neutral Prophet)* (Budapest: Osiris, 1996).

12 A decade ago, it was fashionable to speak about "the death of the author."

13 In this "multicultural" world, one is rarely socialized solely by one tradition; one has more than one "cultural identity," although these are still restricted in numbers.

14 Not all cultures move away from the consciousness of unreflected generality (see chapter 1). This consciousness does not entail, at least not necessarily, stories of people. There are people without history. Saul Friedlander tells us, in his book on the historical consciousness of the Jews, that this people, who were among the first to understand itself in and through histories, ceased to be conscious of its own history in the Diaspora. See Saul Friedlander, *The Jews in European History: Seven Lectures*, ed. Wolfgang Beck (Cincinnati: Hebrew Union College Press in association with the Leo Baeck Institute, New York, 1994). Jews had not told, or told only parsimoniously, their post-exile histories for almost two thousand years – as if time had stood still! It has indeed stood still in terms of salvation time, but not in terms of historical time. All peoples surrounding the Jews had their histories, whereas Jews remained distanced from their own. This did not change until the time of the Jewish Enlightenment, when Jews entered European history, then again during the history of the New World, and finally again with the establishment of the first secular settlement in Palestine.

15 It has only been recently that some have tried to create one. There is an ensemble, for example, that plays so-called "world music," composed from the popular music of very different people. The ensemble performs with great success everywhere.

16 In my study, "Why Hannah Arendt now?" (in Hungarian, *Az Idegen*, Mult es Jovo, 1997), I discussed the process in which novel and novel interpretanda feed academic discussions and conferences in philosophy. Discussions always need to center around a few interpretanda, because without this self-

limitation, participants could not even speak to one another, let alone have extended discussions. Yet very soon, a hermeneutical exhaustion sets in, a kind of satiation, and new interpretanda need to be put at the top of the agenda of courses, conferences, and the like.

17 The change in the curriculum in humanities shows this tendency. Without it, fashionable lobbies could not make their headway in the university curriculum. Now everything can be taught for which students are ready to pay, given that everything is something "to know."

18 See Friedrich Nietzsche, *Beyond Good and Evil*, trans. Walter Kaufmann (New York: Vintage, 1966).

19 I am speaking here about interpretations, but it is also possible to refer to the art world. It is not contingent which authors and works become "famous," or prescribed reading, or themes for conferences, and quoted many times; but it is entirely contingent which do not. There are at least ten times as many authors who are neither worse nor less interesting than those who have "made it," and yet they remain entirely unknown, and rarely published. It becomes important, for example, where one happens to be born. A man or woman who is born in Paris has a thousand times greater opportunity to become prescribed reading than a person born in Australia. Whom one knows, who is quoting someone, and who meets whom (by accident) are also important factors of selection. And, in addition, it is often the case that the world famous too, are dancing, symbolically, just for one summer. Nowadays Sartre, who was not long ago still at the top of the world, rarely gets into the list of prescribed reading. In my judgment, he did not deserve his grand fame then, nor does he deserve his low repute now.

10 Culture and Civilization III

1 Kant distinguishes between two kinds of culture: the culture of skills and the culture of morals. (Among others, also in Kant's *Critique of Judgment*, op. cit.) Culture, in Kant's mind, can be progressive (in contrast to morality) where there is no progress. Kant's concept of culture is discussed here within the framework of the concept of civilization.

2 I discussed this system of objectivation, which I termed "The system of objectivation in-itself," in my book *Everyday Life*, trans. G. L. Campbell (Boston: Routledge & Kegan Paul, 1974), and in my study "Everyday life, rationality of reason, rationality of intellect," in *The Power of Shame: A Rational Perspective* (Boston: Routledge & Kegan Paul, 1985).

3 Since I do not write history, I am simplifying. For example, I have left out tribal cultures entirely from this consideration.

4 Norbert Elias's book is still the classic text on this subject. See Norbert Elias, *The Civilising Process*, trans. Edmund Jephcott (NY: Urizen Books, 1978).

5 Nicolas of Cusa, *De Sapientia*.

6　About this issue, see Michel Foucault's *History of Sexuality*, vol. II (Michel Foucault, *History of Sexuality*, vol. II, trans. Robert Hurley, New York: Pantheon, 1978). There, Foucault discusses the regulation of sexuality in ancient Greece and juxtaposes it with the Christian regulation. The Greek regulation did not work through interdictions and command, nor was it based on obedience to norms. Rather, it succeeded through the imitation or, rather, the development of characters. Proper behavior was not imperative, but only advisable.

7　In Molière, one comes across many types who become ridiculous because they remain uncivilized. See, for example, Molière, *The Bourgeois Gentilhomme*, trans. Curtis Hidden Page (New York & London: G. P. Putnam's Sons, 1908).

8　Again, I refer to Molière. The young girls are ridiculous in this manner, for example, in Molière's *Les Precieuses Ridicules*.

9　E. Goffman, in his book, *Presentation of the Self in Everyday Life*, speaks normally about secondary everyday life – not about family, not even about primary school. See Erving Goffman, *Presentation of the Self in Everyday Life* (Garden City, NY: Doubleday, 1959).

10　Jean-Paul Sartre, *Being and Nothingness: An Essay in Phenomenological Ontology*, trans. Hazel E. Barnes (New York: Citadel Press, 1964).

11　I will speak about this development in chapter 12.

12　Even if the increase in population slows down, we can still expect a doubling of the Earth's population. The population density is now a great problem in many parts of our globe: in Africa, the Americas, and Asia. There are parts of the Earth which are not open for habitation, for various reasons that cannot be discussed here.

13　There is no link between the frequency of ideologically motivated war on the one hand, and the rules of civility on the other. In many republics of the Soviet Union, the rules of civility were not developed, whereas Germany and Japan were fairly civil, especially in the middle or upper classes. This civility, however, was not an obstacle in the way of totalitarian rebarbarization. In fact, Daniel Goldhagen introduces the problem of civility with the example of an officer who commanded the genocidal killing of Jews, but protested against a command that his soldiers should steal; apparently, not stealing as a matter of civility must be taken for granted as an essential ingredient of a German soldier. See Daniel Goldhagen, *Hitler's Willing Executioners: Ordinary Germans and the Holocaust* (New York: Vintage, 1996).

14　The best source about the civilizing process, and particularly about table manners, is still Norbert Elias, *The Civilizing Process*, op. cit.

15　Let me note here that Marx was absolutely convinced that "human nature" as internal nature could be "pushed back," and that its potential for "humanization" was inexhaustible.

16　This transformation begins with the *"noblesse de robe."* See also Lucien Goldmann, *The Hidden God*, trans. Philip Thrody (New York: Humanities Press, 1964).

17 See, among his other works, Jean-Jacques Rousseau, *La Nouvelle Heloise*, trans. and abridged by Judith H. McDowell (University Park, PA: Pennsylvania State University Press, 1968), and *Emile*, trans. Allan Bloom (New York: Basic Books, 1979).

18 For example, Jewish women such as Rahel Varnhagen or Dorothea Mendelssohn/Schlegel opened salons where they entertained the best society.

19 In what follows, all references to Foucault are to *Discipline and Punish*, op. cit.

20 For Foucault, oppression does not necessarily mean repression. In fact, he rejects the thesis of the repression of sexuality in modern times. See Michel Foucault, *History of Sexuality*, vol. I, op. cit.

21 The expression stems from *Discipline and Punish*, op. cit.

22 Actually, World War I was greeted enthusiastically in Europe because it offered "great freedom," i.e., liberation from "civilization." The civil discipline of the body was replaced by a war discipline, and many pressures were lifted. Soldiers could make "free love" with the women of the enemy; they could also rape them without meeting sanctions, and first and foremost they could kill. At the same time, women who were left alone, i.e., without husbands, could for the first time enter the workforce *en masse*, in occupations that had been closed to them earlier. They were liberated from the discipline of a "closed home," from the crippling of their sexuality, and the like. After World War I, the situation of women had changed definitively, although at first they had to return to their daily routines in their closed spaces.

23 I had to sit still, hands folded behind my back, during classes in the elementary school. During intermission we walked in the corridor in pairs, and were not allowed to talk to each other.

24 The mechanism of disciplining, as well as the space created for and by this mechanism, is brilliantly described in detail by Foucault. I refer again to his book *Discipline and Punish*, op. cit. In this framework, I cannot discuss this issue in its full merit.

25 The Darwinian theory of the "survival of the fittest" reinforced this disciplinary mechanism. Since the fittest is to survive, the goal of an institution is to create "the fittest" not in general, but the fittest-for-something. Disciplining of the mind and the soul seemed to be the royal path to creating the "fittest." Again, not only the body, but also the mind, happened to be imprisoned by the soul.

26 For example, the wearing of blue jeans is no more a matter of rebellion, as it was even a few decades ago. Rather, they have now become a kind of uniform; also fashionable are holes in jeans.

27 Katie Roiphe, *The Morning After: Sex, Fear, and Feminism on Campus* (Boston: Little, Brown, 1993).

28 The colonization of the life world, coined by Habermas, is a very telling expression. See Jürgen Habermas, *The Theory of Communicative Action*, vol. 1, *Reason and the Rationalization of Society*, trans. Thomas McCarthy

(Boston: Beacon Press, 1984), and *The Theory of Communicative Action*, vol. 2, *Lifeworld and System: A Critique of Functionalist Reason*, trans. Thomas McCarthy (Boston: Beacon Press, 1987).

29 See Agnes Heller, "Colonization of intimate life."

30 Obviously, my description is not value-free. Yet I should add that a person is normally in need of controlling his or her body/mind somehow; the control is oppressive, and yet also is the condition for preventing total chaos. For example, total promiscuity is total chaos, obviously leading to psychic disturbances to the same extent as the total repression of sexuality (although this cannot be measured).

31 This one can, however, do in many places. To honor the public place by wearing more festive dresses is out of fashion. To show off, however, is more in fashion than ever.

32 This is not said against psychoanalysis in general, but against psychoanalysis as a mass phenomenon. I will discuss Freud's impact on modern imagination in the next chapter.

33 In medieval and early modern Europe, the Christian image of soul/body/mind (*pneuma, soma, psychē*) was still maintained. True, popular belief preferred the more primitive concept of immortality and the duality of the immortal soul/mortal body. There was no "pluralism," only heresy. In a pluralistic universe such as the modern one, one needs to discover that we do not carry the same map "inside." To develop plural personalities, one needs to understand oneself by a custom, home-made map. Visiting the analyst just as one attends school results in a levelled, uniform method of self-understanding. The common schemas of understanding produce similar selves. One is afraid of cloning. Humans cannot be cloned biologically, for memory cannot be cloned. The social practices that level human self-understanding, and thereby homogenize the self, are methods of *human cloning*.

34 Even liberation does not follow the above libertarian politics. For example, gay liberation aims at the recognition of gay sex as a legitimate form of sex. One can say, "We are the ones who do not care what others are going to say. We do what we consider to be good to do, without hurting anyone."

35 The most representative book in this line is the work of Zygmunt Bauman.

36 As in Daniel Goldhagen's book, op. cit.

37 See the book by Saul Friedlander. Friedlander covers only the first six years of the Nazi regime. The combination of two imaginary institutions characterizes Nazism from the beginning. This, I repeat, does not contradict the relevance of the contingency theory. That some phenomena, or the emergence of some phenomena, cannot be explained in full does not mean that they are irrational. God cannot be explained, neither can be morality, but it would be both outrageous and ridiculous to say that those concepts are "irrational." Conversely, the irrational can sometimes be explained and understood.

38 Heidegger made a few interesting remarks about this connection in his lectures on Parmenides from 1942 to 1943, where he refers to Lenin's

program of electrification + Soviets – as the prototype of technological imagination. (He could have chosen similar examples from the Nazi vocabulary.) In fact, Lenin's slogan was the offspring of the unholy matrimony of both historical consciousness and technological imagination. These two were coupled (as an addition (+) in his program!). See Martin Heidegger, *Parmenides* (Frankfurt am Main: Klostermann, 1982).

39 The loss of these capacities is properly termed "brainwashing."

40 This is obviously different from the ancient distinction between *physis/ nomos* and *physis/thesis*, not just because the concept of *physis* is unlike the concept of nature (this has been pointed out by Heidegger), but also because the ancient Greek *nomos* or *thesis* is not the same as modern society. Even the Latin *societas* is not identical to modern society.

41 The story differs essentially from the biblical Genesis. Here, God offers man control over all living creatures; yet, immediately afterwards, he assigns man the task of caring (taking care) of all living things of nature (Genesis 1: 26–8). But man's fate there is final. Man earns his bread from the sweat of his brow, while woman bears her child in pain; yet both men and women are mortal. The idea that men's (society's) power over nature and creatures of nature is increasing – that there is a battle going on here – is completely alien to the text of the Bible and also to the Christian imagination. Francis Bacon speaks first about technology as the means of ascertaining man's control over nature. Technology is knowledge or, rather, knowledge is technological knowledge, and as such power (see Francis Bacon, *Novum Organum* (Chicago: Encyclopaedia Britannica, 1952). Bacon says that truth is the offspring of times. Truth (identified here with knowledge and with know-how) develops slowly, as do the conditions of our control of nature.

42 Interestingly, this fear can be found also in Kant, who is worried that, perhaps one day nature will "take back" everything that we have appropriated from it.

43 The appearance of new epidemics, such as AIDS, has made such formulations popular again.

44 In the drama of a Hungarian playwright from the nineteenth century, *The Tragedy of Man* by Imre Madach, mankind will die of hunger and cold when the Earth cools down. Malthus believed that mankind will lose the struggle through overpopulation; nowadays, ecologists warn us that this war is (for us) a no-win war.

45 See the discussion of Benjamin Franklin's diary in Max Weber's *Protestant Ethic and the Spirit of Capitalism*, trans. Talcott Parsons (New York: Scribner Press, 1958).

46 I am going to speak about time and space in the following chapters.

47 I do not mean just European philosophy.

48 Immanuel Kant, *Anthropology*, op. cit.

49 No one becomes angry at the weather if it is colder than expected. But one is indignant if the heating does not work properly. We are not angry at an aching tooth, but if a much advertised car proves to be no better than a

wreck, we are outraged. There is no such thing as a two-year warranty except in matters of technological civilization.

50 Perhaps the best known among them is Ferdinand Tönnies, *Community and Society*, trans. Charles P. Loomis (East Lansing: Michigan State University Press, 1957).

51 For details, see chapter 3.

52 It has frequently been said that awareness of their presence is not the same as the knowledge of their function. But it is an absurd exaggeration to believe that in pre-modern times people were also ignorant about the physical, the mechanisms of the things they used (boiling water, the wheel, their own hands and feet), although they could use them well and were (sometimes and in some instances) able to re-do or recreate them.

53 These are not necessarily also identical to technological revolutions. The discovery of the anti-pregnancy pill has changed the lives of women far more radically than the latest discoveries in nuclear physics.

54 This tendency has in fact ended. One could invent a few new household machines, but they will not radically change the picture unless a babysitting robot is manufactured – but this belongs to the territory of science fiction.

55 That the change of family structure is somehow bound to the socialization of certain household tasks was a frequently discussed issue in traditional socialism. Collective cooking and communal child care had to replace the individual household. In fact, the Israeli *kibbutzim* implemented this idea with some success. The idea eventually became less attractive for many reasons. One reason was that industrial civilizations and their carrier and distributor, the market, had successfully, although perhaps less humanely, executed the task that the ideologists only dreamt about.

56 This does not mean that technological civilization "determined" the latter. For, as has been pointed out many times, technological civilization also results from technological imagination, and technological imagination is dependent on many conditions. Still, the snake does not bite its own tail; it is as difficult to make a case for circularity as for linear progression.

57 Progression entails more replacement if the progressive movement is also a democratizing one, or if it includes the change in the dominating form of habitat. For example, the no longer inexpensive labor force must be replaced by household machines; these machines "serve" everyone. Or, the cold cellars of farmhouses must be replaced by refrigerators in the crowded cities, where people are in possession of a matchbox-sized apartment – squeezed between, below, and above many similar matchboxes in an apartment building.

58 It was a simplifying description, for the issue deserved a longer study.

59 I will return to the ethical issue in the next chapter. Yet the whole issue of technological civilization can hardly be theorized entirely without discussing some ethical elements.

60 This is only a brief and incomplete enumeration of the pro- and anti-technological civilization arguments.

61 Herbert Marcuse spoke of the "one dimensional man" in his famous book
    about 1968 leftist/romanticism. See Herbert Marcuse, *The One Dimen-
    sional Man* (Boston: Beacon Press, 1964).
62 This is roughly my definition of static justice in *Beyond Justice*. See Agnes
    Heller, *Beyond Justice* (New York: Basil Blackwell, 1987).
63 In Heller, *The Power of Shame*, "Everyday life, rationality of reason, ration-
    ality of intellect," op. cit.

11 Worldtime and Lifetime

1 I take this juxtaposition from the title of Blumenberg's book, *Lebenszeit und
   Weltzeit*, (Suhrkamp, 1986), and employ these terms in a similar fashion. He
   is also not entirely consistent in using these terms (with reference to phenomenology), but I do not mean this critically.
2 The reader cannot expect even here a provisionally all-round discussion
   of either time and history or space. I analyze only the major and most
   conspicuous changes that those concepts and experiences have undergone
   in modernity, and very briefly at that. About the change in the concept of
   time, see Agnes Heller, *Renaissance Man* (Boston: Routledge & Kegan
   Paul, 1978). About the detailed discussion of history, of historicity,
   see Agnes Heller, *A Theory of History* (Boston: Routledge & Kegan
   Paul, 1982).
3 See Martin Heidegger, "Der Begriff der Zeit," talk to Marburg Theologians,
   July 25, 1924.
4 Here Heidegger does Hegel injustice. Hegel's concept of time cannot be
   identified with the concept that he elaborates in his philosophy of nature.
   In the spirit of Hegel's own philosophy, such a determination is just *one*
   determination, while others are forthcoming. There is no complete "definition" of time. The reader can be reminded, for example, about the famous
   passage in Hegel's *Philosophy of Religion* where he speaks about the demise
   of the eternal truth in (our) time, where "time" stands for the truth of our
   "congregation" (*Gemeinde*). In addition, he also refers to an empirical time,
   which is the continuous future tense of historically contingent happenings.
   See G. W. F. Hegel, *Lectures on the Philosophy of Religion (Vorlesungen
   über die Philosophie der Religion)*, trans. R. F. Brown, P. C. Hodgson, and
   J. M. Stewart, with the assistance of J. P. Fitzer and H. S. Harris, vol. II
   (Berkeley: University of California Press, 1984).
5 See Hans Blumenberg, op. cit.
6 Aristotle, *Physics* and *Metaphysics* in *The Basic Works of Aristotle*, ed.
   Richard Mckeon (New York: Random House, 1941).
7 See, in detail, Rugasi Gyula, *Orok Romokon* (*On the Eternal Ruins*, Latin
   Betuk, 1996). Nietzsche reformulated the idea of the eternal recurrence of
   the same, but in a postmetaphysical manner.
8 See chapter 1.

9   Hegel would be ill at ease were he to realize how Jewish his philosophy of history has been!

10 Hans Blumenberg, op. cit. Blumenberg, in fact, quotes Hitler's alleged conversation with Bormann, in which he complains about the terrible pressure of time. Again, the Devil is under time pressure, not the Good. I have some doubts ...

11 Whether divine grace is granted by ways inscrutable to men, or whether grace is a kind of gift granted to the decent person by God, does not really modify the "pressure of time" in the life of the exister. One never knows!

12 The metaphor of the container stems from Hegel's critique of Newton.

13 Blumenberg, "Die Wahrheit – Tochter der Zeit?" *Lebenszeit*, op. cit., chapter VII.

14 The renewed fashion of astrology, however, suggests, that the image of *"fatum"* has not disappeared. *Fatum* is "objective" (one cannot change it, it is "written in the stars"), but it has kept its relation to the idea of personal providence. It is rooted in a metaphysical conception that relates to the single exister.

15 "In der Entdeckung des Zusammenhangs unter den Begriffen Sinn, Sein, Zeit und Geschichte ist Heideggers Philosophie Ausdruck der ersten Nachkriegswelt, ... Wenn der Begriff der Zeit in der Antwort auf die Frage nach dem Sinn vom Sein überhaupt vorkommen darf ... dann muss der Seinssinn selbst zeitempfindlich sein" (Blumenberg, op. cit., p. 93).

16 Martin Heidegger, *Being and Time*, trans. John Macquarrie and Edward Robinson (New York: Harper, 1962), par. 71.

17 See, or rather listen to, Vivaldi or Haydn.

18 Søren Kierkegaard, "How to become subjective," in *Concluding Unscientific Postscript to Philosophical Fragments*, trans. David F. Swenson (Princeton: Princeton University Press, 1944). The subjective thinker.

19 In his book of youth, *The Theory of the Novel*, Lukács discovered this new conception of "experienced time," which was "subjective time" in Flaubert. George Lukács, *The Theory of the Novel*, trans. Anna Bostock (Cambridge, MA: MIT Press, 1971).

20 See Alfred Schutz, *The Phenomenology of The Social World*, trans. George Walsh and Frederick Lehnert (Evanston: Northwestern University Press, 1967). I tried something similar in my book *Everyday Life*, op. cit.

21 Heidegger exemplifies this difference between the pre-WWI and post-WWI conceptions of *Lebenszeit* in his criticism of Dilthey's *Lebensphilosophie*. I agree with Heidegger's criticism as far as Dilthey is concerned.

22 I will turn to the discussion of the category of authenticity in the last chapter.

23 Gergely Angyalosi called my attention to the interesting fact that in *Remembrance of Things Past*, M. always remembers the "petite melodie," and not the piece of music.

24 Heidegger, *Being and Time*, op. cit., par. 71.

25 I mean this brief discussion as a shortcut. Heidegger changes his mind later, and Proust's novel was actually published in the 1920s.

26 Nietzsche's eternal recurrence of the same can be understood as a polemical device against the Judeo-Christian linear conception of history, and also against the positivist/progressivist secularized version of the same. But there is no strict division in Nietzsche between lifetime and worldtime. The eternal recurrence of the same can be interpreted in both ways.

27 This is Heidegger's expression.

28 The circular concept of time relativizes the earlier and the later only in relations of two cycles, not within the self-same cycle. And this is so in all cyclic activities, or even repetitive activities.

29 There are perhaps still a few exceptions; for example, the small Indian tribes of the Amazon.

30 I do not identify objective time with worldtime and with measured time.

31 I discussed this issue in detail in my book *A Theory of History*, op. cit.

32 I discussed lived history in detail in my book *A Philosophy of History in Fragments*, op. cit.

33 I will return to this experience in the last chapter.

34 This is mentioned in chapter 1.

12 Space, Place and Home

1 As Pascal said in his *Pensée*, men are squeezed between two infinites. Man is the Zero between the two infinites. This is the first experience of cosmic contingency. See, for details, Agnes Heller, *Philosophy of History in Fragments* (Cambridge, MA: Basil Blackwell, 1993).

2 Columbus believed that he had arrived in India when he reached America, because although he worked with the hypothesis of a round world, he believed that the globe was far smaller than it actually is. This is what I mean by the expansion of the human habitat.

3 Immanuel Kant, *Anthropology from a Pragmatic Point of View*, trans. Mary J. Gregor (The Hague: Nijhoff, 1974), op. cit.

4 It is indeed a galaxy, for it expands the world that one knows in very different directions. There are various constellations in this galaxy; all the traces left by the past are only available (if beyond our direct reach) through their orientation in the Gutenberg galaxies.

5 Some famous ancient cities also had a privileged position. Athens was the city of "culture" long after becoming politically insignificant. Rome was the center of a world, as was Alexandria. To be exiled to the provinces was suffered as a terrible fate at that time also. Babylon, as the symbol of darkness or evil, has an entirely different kind of prominence.

6 It is foolish, though very fashionable, to believe that a journey in the virtual space of the Internet can be substituted for a journey to actual places. The body is not just an appendage of the mind.

7 For example, a natural catastrophe or a political crisis.

8   In my study, "Where are we at home?" *Thesis Eleven*, Number 41, 1995, I
     discussed these issues in greater detail. I termed the world of the united
     tourist the world of absolute present time. My idea is that they do not inhabit
     a place, but a time. They share the present (without the third dimension of
     the past and the future of the present) as their home.

9   I will speak about the image and experience of the stranger shortly.

10   This pattern of communication is described by Garfinkel and by Goffmann.
     See Erving Goffmann, *Forms of Talk* (Philadelphia: University of Pennsylva-
     nia Press, 1981).

11   This is true only if the things that I communicate are on the same level. One
     needs to be cautious about communicating certain intimate things in the
     situation of closeness as well.

12   See Aristotle, *Poetics*, in *The Basic Works of Aristotle*, ed. Richard McKeon
     (New York: Random House, 1941).

13   In this sense, the Bible says that Adam knew (that is, recognized) Eve.

14   Plotinus, *Enneads*, trans. Stephen MacKenna (London: Penguin, 1991).

15   Freud's observation and interpretation that we long to go back into our
     mother's womb is just another interpretation of "homesickness."

16   I will speak about joy and happiness in the next chapter.

17   One of the most beautiful artistic expressions of this double meaning of
     homesickness can be found in the Lied-cycle, "Winterreise," by Schubert.

18   This was the phenomenon described by Kierkegaard in the "either/or" of the
     aesthetic stage. ("Marry, you will regret it; do not marry, you will regret it.
     Whether you marry or do not marry, you will regret both.") Every choice
     excludes possibilities. Depression, or melancholia, is also anxiety about the
     possibility of the final exclusion of possibilities. See Søren Kierkegaard,
     Either/Or, vol. I, trans. Howard V. and Edna H. Hong (Princeton, NJ:
     Princeton University Press, 1987).

19   I discuss the modern experience of transience in my book *The Concept of the
     Beautiful* (in manuscript), second part, in the subsection on Freud.

20   This is, among other things, why Max Weber said that we never die "satiated
     with life."

21   I have neglected the social manifestations of "being alien." It is fashionable
     to search for "roots." The universal tourism and homesickness can be easily
     combined, if one undertakes long journeys to strange places from where
     one's family departed 100 years ago or more, searching for one's roots.
     Americans of Polish or Jewish origin, for example, organize pilgrimages to
     Poland, the customs and language of which they do not understand, to
     search for their roots. They can arrive at a village, an entirely unfamiliar
     place about which they have been told that their great-grandfather had
     lived there. They look at the houses and fields, take pictures of the peasants,
     and return (home?) with the satisfaction that they finally had been "at
     home."

22   The fundamentalist movements want to glue the umbilical cord together,
     and so do many psychotherapists. They satisfy a need, a desire. These are

manifestations, as well as the nonpotent (or acute) remedies taken against the double homesickness.

23 I discussed "the problem of the body" in the case of Leibniz in my book on Leibniz's existential metaphysics. See Agnes Heller, *Leibniz Egzisztencialis Metafizikaja* (Budapest: Kossuthl, 1995).

24 It has already been discussed briefly in the chapter on culture.

25 I will return to this question shortly

26 There are also many understandings of what "material" means: money, goods, the well-being of the body, sensual satisfaction, and this-worldly happiness of any kind.

27 One could say that Freud abandoned the concept of "spirit" (*pneuma*) which became the third party in addition to the body (*soma*) and the soul (*psychē*) in the Christian tradition. Yet this was also the case in Gnosticism.

28 The Freudian interior topology could also be described as the secularization and reversal of the topology of the mystics. The mystics transplanted the map of the Neoplatonian and Gnostic hierarchy of the spheres into an internal hierarchy of the soul. The mystic begins his perfection in the lowest sphere of his soul, and from here he ascends to the top, to the mystical the extasis.

29 This is a Gnostic element. The Gnostics did not know evil as sin, but only as suffering. See Hans Jonas, *The Gnostic Religion* (Boston: Beacon Press, 1958–63). I will come back to mention certain Gnostic elements in Freud.

30 Sigmund Freud, *The Ego and the Id*, trans. Joan Riviere and ed. James Strachey (New York: W. W. Norton, 1960).

31 The first pair has already been relativized by Hegel.

32 Freud was neither overly pessimistic nor overly optimistic. He was not a romantic, and did not subscribe to the redemptive paradigm of Marx. Even if one believes in the healing power of psychoanalysis, only individual persons can be healed, here and there, and not the whole human race.

33 The Hungarian poet, Attitla Jozsef, wrote, "Itt a szenvedes belul, am ott kivul a magyarazat," which means roughly in English "inside here is the suffering – outside there the explanation." But if this is the case, the "outside" needs to be an entirely "corporeal" phenomenon, and the "inside" just a reaction, an answer, an adequate answer to the wrongs done on the outside. This is the rationalistic scenario. It remains the insoluble puzzle for all those who entertain the grand illusion summed up in this beautiful verse; how could a Hitler and a Stalin get free hand for murdering untold millions two centuries after the age of Enlightenment?! If the "evil inside" is just an invention, then what? Is the sickness "inside" rather the cause of the Evil outside? This sounds like a most "normal" answer. But, as a result of this "normal" answer those who do evil and are evil get away with it, at least "from the inside." There is no repentance in the modern age. One identifies oneself with one's own wrongdoings as long as this is the "trend," and one distances oneself from the same deeds if a new trend is on. But this distance is not moral but spatial. No one takes responsibility. Although all modern

persons are strangers on Earth in an existential/ontological sense, and having a "home" becomes more conditional and abstract than ever, there is no less scapegoating, no less an outburst of anger against the stranger, the alien, as before. Psychologically, this is understandable. Two certainties contradict one another – and two uncertainties contradicting one another can result in very similar attitudes and acts. It is foolish to wish that one did not have prejudices, because there is always a difference between autorepresentation and representation by the other. Still, one can wish that prejudices should not result in acts of hate. Regarding this topic, see my papers, "On prejudice," "Autorepresentation and representation by the other," "Once again on bio-politics," "Multiculturalism," and "The stranger," contained in the volume *The Stranger/Az idegen* (Budapest: Mult es Jovo, 1997) and, with Ferenc Fehér, *Biopolitics* (Brookfield, VT: Avebury, 1994).

13   Law, Ethos, and Ethics

1   In his last works, he modified his conception.
2   Alisdair MacIntyre, *After Virtue* (Notre Dame: University of Notre Dame Press, 1984).
3   See Alasdair MacIntyre, *Whose Justice? Which Rationality?* (Notre Dame: University of Notre Dame Press, 1988).
4   I have also expressed my skepticism about the mere procedural idea of discourse (see chapters 7 and 8). Yet, perhaps procedural/discourse ethics is not the sole alternative to an Aristotelian/Thomist teleological moral of perfection.
5   I still want to remain faithful to the style of this book, to make reference to concrete books and authors – with a few exceptions – only in the footnotes, because I do not want not to interrupt the chain of thought, and I wish to keep the book relatively short.
6   I wrote a chapter on the legitimation of Soviet-type societies in the book by Ferenc Fehér, Agnes Heller, and György Markus, *Dictatorship over Needs* (New York: St. Martin's Press, 1983), where I tried to show that the Soviet communist state went through a process of change in legitimation from charisma to tradition, yet it was never legitimated by law.
7   Where there are "state churches," churches with a privileged status, legitimation by law does not live up to its own idea.
8   The propositions of Hobbes, Locke, Rousseau, and Kant (not to mention the issue of "tacit consent" in Hume) are entirely different, yet all agree that the law or the legal order is based on some initial agreement or consecutive agreement, and that it is secular, positive and rational.
9   Whether the law is, in fact, always or even mostly indifferent in matters of faith and truths is an other, empirical question. The norm is in all probability never entirely fulfilled. Nowadays, however, even the principle of indifference is queried, and not just in matters of religion, but also in matters of

ethnic conflicts. I think that the principle should be maintained, even in the awareness that it does not fully work empirically. But to abandon the principle would, in my mind, breed havoc.

10 Montesquieu in his *The Spirit of the Laws* mentions a few examples, among them homosexuality. See Charles de Secondat Montesquieu, *The Spirit of the Laws*, trans. and ed. Anne Cohler, Basia Miller, Harold Stone (Cambridge, UK: Cambridge University Press, 1989).

11 Whether the maintenance of the social minimum – that is, to secure the socio-economic rights – belongs to the function of the state is a disputed question. I vote with those who say that the conditions of survival on the minimum civilized level needs to be granted to everyone in a state, for this belongs to the state's function of providing security (yet not to its function to provide the conditions of freedom). However, György Markus, in his essay on freedom and on the paradoxes of freedom in politics, believes that to grant social security of a kind is a matter of providing freedom because they belong to the constitutions of being able to act in freedom. (See György Markus, *Meg egyszer a szabadsagrol: realiak es illuziok*, in manuscript.)

12 The distinction between honor and virtue (in this sense) stems from Montesquieu, op. cit.

13 This argument is also presented in Tolstoy's novel, *The Resurrection*. See Leo Tolstoy, *The Resurrection*, trans. Louise Maude (Oxford: Oxford University Press, 1994).

14 As far as I know, among contemporary philosophers only Derrida has reflected upon this antinomic character of the situation to pass a judgment on the ground of the law. Derrida says that in each and every singular judgment the judge is the one who (re)originates the law. Derrida speaks about the "mystical" origination of the law. The case of the legal laws here also exemplifies the validity and validation of the law.

15 In fact, MacIntyre's argument against liberal discourse and its formalism is also an argument on behalf of this cluster.

16 See in detail Agnes Heller, *Beyond Justice* (Cambridge, MA: Blackwell, 1990).

17 Of course, I am the last to deny that one can make an argument for everything and the opposite of everything. One can say that if one is concerned with justice, this concern makes justice for oneself a matter of self-interest. The concept of self-interest can be explained so that it includes all selfless actions, for selfless men and women love to do selfless things; and since they love it, to act selflessly is in their self-interest. Kant has considered all of this, and this is why he cut the story short and in his Categorical Imperative prohibited not just the intrusion of interest but also the intrusion of any kind of sentiment or emotion into the pure moral motivation. For this beautiful philosophical radicalism, one needs to pay a price (the price of metaphysics). As I have already mentioned, and will do so briefly once again, contemporary philosophers are very reluctant to pay this price.

18 This was expressed by Hegel in the way that it is real but not actual; it is "merely" positive, reality without spirit, because the "spirit of the law" is always the citizenry which legitimizes this law.

19 One reason why the term "values" was dropped like a hot potato was its frequent employment by Nietzsche. The whole postwar Frankfurt school preferred to speak of norms and not of values.

20 The subtitle of his planned magnum opus "The will to power," would have been "Revaluation of all values" – a plan that he later abandoned.

21 See Max Ferdinand Scheler, *Formalism in Ethics and Non-formal Ethics of Values*, trans. Manfred Frings and Roger Funk (Evanston, IL: Northwestern University Press, 1973).

22 In an early essay, I tried to make sense of the concept of moral value in a Marxian framework. (See Agnes Heller, "Towards a Marxist theory of value.") Already at that time, my main concern was to detach the concept of value from that of interest, whether personal or collective.

23 Kant's solution is to form the concept of moral good constituted by the moral law itself and keep for it the supreme place. But where goods (substantive goods) are concerned, he had to reintroduce a teleological structure without keeping a hierarchical structure. Teleology is, then, a regulative theoretical idea of reason or, later, it becomes the organizing principle located in the faculty of teleological judgment.

24 I will turn shortly to the discussion of the fate of the concept of happiness also.

25 Multiculturalism is also the result of the contestation of justice. Multiculturalism is the state of affairs where different hierarchies of values coexist in the self-same social world (nation, society, state).

26 The period in which the practice of levelling value hierarchies of different ways of life was still exceptional. Assimilation to certain value hierarchies and ways of life was a matter of self-interest, the condition of comfortable life, perhaps even of acceptance. This was the case, for example, of the Jewish assimilation. Heine said that by having been baptized, he bought himself the entry ticket into German society.

27 As is well known, for Nietzsche the switch from the distinction good/bad to the distinction good/evil indicates a total reversal of the value system resulting from the slave revolt of the Judeo-Christian world. Returning to the good/bad distinction would mean a re-valuation of all values and, as such, a new radical turn in the contemporary value hierarchy, this time in favor of anti-nihilism. See, among others, Friedrich Nietzsche, *Beyond Good and Evil*, trans. Walter Kaufmann (New York: Vintage, 1966) and *The Genealogy of Morals*, trans. Walter Kaufmann (New York: Vintage, 1969).

28 The discussion of this issue belongs to the competence of cultural criticism.

29 True, the tradition also knows about conflicts of goods. For a Christian monk, asceticism stands higher in the order of goods than holy matrimony. But matrimony does not cease to be holy, an end that men and women should covet.

30 And also in an Epicurean tradition. Anatole France says, for example, that
    love is a virtue, and he means erotic/sensual love.
31 See Jacques Derrida, *The Politics of Friendship*, trans. George Collins (Lon-
    don: Verso, 1997).
32 See the discussion of work ethics on the example of Benjamin Franklin's
    autobiography in Max Weber, *The Protestant Ethic and the Spirit of Capit-
    alism*, trans. Talcott Parsons (London: HarperCollins, 1991), op. cit.
33 Work is certainly a value as an accomplishment, as an effort, as something
    deserving renumeration. The idea of justice "to each according to their
    work" remains valid.
34 Even to see a doctor, or to send someone else to the doctor, may sometimes
    require courage. Every value-related leap in life is also a matter of courage:
    to enter a love relationship, to marry, to choose a profession, to think a new
    thought.
35 Conscious sacrifice of life is not required, although it can be taken also (or
    otherwise freely granted). Many human rights activists have been killed, for
    example, also recently in Columbia.
36 One can risk many things: one's job, marriage, even one's reputation.
37 Indirectly, this may happen. If one puts one's job at risk, one also puts one's
    family's income at risk. If one puts one's reputation at risk, one may put the
    reputation of one's closest friends at risk as well.
38 Hegel speaks here of "hardened heart" in his *Phenomenology*, Chapter
    "Morality" op. cit. See G. W. F. Hegel, *Phenomenology of Spirit*, trans. A.
    V. Miller (Oxford: Oxford University Press, 1977).
39 Several American films, particularly those directed by John Ford, portray
    the display of civic courage in such circumstances. The American court
    drama also likes to portray the display of civic courage. See "Twelve Angry
    Men."
40 Romanticism developed a contempt against this tendency. Balzac said that in
    a bourgeois world the few great vices are exchanged for many petty vices,
    whereas the few great virtues are exchanged for many petty virtues. The
    description may be correct, yet the "petty virtues" are sometimes not so
    petty, and since these are the virtues of modern times, they need to be
    cherished. And, after all, who has the authority to compare courage with
    courage? One could even say that to suffer from the loss of one's career
    throughout a long working life is more difficult to endure than facing a
    sudden violent death.
41 Lukács loved to quote Browning's verse "I go to prove my soul" to char-
    acterize the bravado of the heroes of Dostoevsky. Such a bravado can also be
    immoral, as we know from the case of Raskolnikov or Ivan Karamasov.
42 Being regulated by values means, in Weber's terms, acting in a value-rational
    manner, yet not in a purposive-rational manner. Courage is not a means to
    an end.
43 This is so in all worlds where the dynamics of modernity made its appear-
    ance. But I discuss here modernity alone, because, as I have proposed, the

concept of the teleologically organized chain of "goods" describes all pre-modern arrangements better than the concept of value.

44 This is the point made by Weber.

45 I have made the distinction between norms and rules – moreover, between concrete and abstract norms – in many places. I have also discussed the process of the abstraction/universalization of norms in modernity. See Agnes Heller, *Radical Philosophy, The Power of Shame* (London: Routledge and Kegan Paul, 1985), *Beyond Justice* (Cambridge, MA: Basil Blackwell, 1990), *An Ethics of Personality* (Cambridge, MA: Basil Blackwell, 1996), *Philosophy of Morals* (Oxford, UK: Basil Blackwell, 1990), and *The Concept of the Beautiful* (in manuscript).

46 The difference between maxims and imperatives is beautifully discussed by Kant in his *Groundwork to the Metaphysics of Morals*, trans. H. J. Pato (New York: Harper and Row, 1964) and in his *Critique of Practical Reason*, trans. Mary Gregor (Cambridge, UK: Cambridge University Press, 1997).

47 In the chapters on culture and civilization.

48 I discussed borderline situations as well as moral conflicts in my book *Philosophy of Morals*. See Agnes Heller, *Philosophy of Morals* (Oxford Blackwell, 1990). If there were no virtues other than being law-abiding, no single person would stand the test of a borderline situation. But some do.

49 Modern philosophy cannot make a case for moral sense. There is neither an empirical nor a logical way to argue for its very existence/presence. Yet since moral argumentation has its limits, and it is – in spite of this limit – not in vain to argue morally, one must or at least can presuppose as a *supposition relativa* in Kant's terms (Hevizi, Holmi, July 1997) the preexistence of "moral sense" or "the logic of the heart."

50 *Gunst* in German. Kant speaks about *Gunst* (favoring) in case of the judgment of taste: if I say this rose is beautiful, I favor the rose. See Immanuel Kant, *Critique of Judgment*, trans. J. H. Bernard (New York: Hafner, 1951), op. cit.

51 Freedom here means political freedom. There is no question of having political freedom without the exercise of power. The question is, rather, whether maximum political freedom can work together with the maximum protection of the citizen against violence and chaos.

52 One can recall here Marx, who praised capitalism for the same reason in the *Communist Manifesto*.

53 I use here the term "anomie" in Durkheim's interpretation.

54 In his beautiful book, *Passion and Interest*, O. Hirschmann discusses how interest-motivation was first regarded as the best remedy against unruly passions; that is, more as an ethical bonus than as an ethical deficit.

55 John Carroll calls this "remissive" culture. See John Carroll, *Puritan, Paranoid, Remissive: a sociology of modern culture* (London: Routledge & Kegan Paul, 1977).

14 Happiness, Perfection, Authenticity

1 Concerning the questions that I touch upon here only briefly, the reader can find my conceptions in *A Philosophy of Morals* (Oxford: Basil Blackwell, 1990) and *An Ethics of Personality* (Cambridge, MA: Basil Blackwell, 1996), op. cit.

2 I speak of "high civilizations" in the case of hierarchically structured integrations (from city to empire) with literacy, where works of literature, philosophy (wisdom), and religion formulated and provided one or more ethics of perfection and happiness, such as the Chinese, the European, the ancient Mediterranean, the Indian, the Japanese, and a few others.

3 Although Aristotle criticizes hedonism, he remarks that the hedonist philosopher (Aristippos?) is unlike his teaching, because he is a perfect gentleman.

4 This is actually the simile of Plotinus in his *Enneads*. See Plotinus, *Enneads*, trans. Stephen MacKenna (London: Penguin, 1991).

5 For Descartes, the conditions are not necessary conditions. If one is only ethical, this suffices for being happy. See Descartes' letter to Princess Elisabeth in René Descartes, *Philosophical Letters*, trans. and ed. Anthony Kenny (Minneapolis, University of Minnesota Press, 1970).

6 Kant actually says that the man who follows the Moral Law is melancholic.

7 See Kant, *Religion within the Boundaries of Mere Reason*, trans. Allen Wood (Cambridge: Cambridge University Press, 1999).

8 Hegel attributes the constitution of subjectivity of the so-called "internal rooms" to Lutheranism, and rightly so, although the practice of the confession already contributed to the emergence of subjectivity. Regarding the latter, see Jacques LeGoff, *History and Memory (European Perspectives)*, trans. Steven Rendall (New York: Columbia University Press, 1996).

9 See Ludwig Wittgenstein, *Tractatus Logico-Philosophicus* trans. C. K. Ogden (London and New York: Routledge, 1922) and Wittgenstein, *Notebooks 1914–1916*, 2nd edn., eds. G. H. Wright and G. E. M. Anscombe, trans. G. E. M. Anscombe (Chicago: University of Chicago Press, 1961).

10 Nietzsche, of course, identified the immoral moralists with the persons who say "yes" to life in the above understanding.

11 I discuss the story of Faust from the standpoint of the happy moment in my book *The Concept of the Beautiful* (in manuscript).

12 It is rarely pointed out that modern subjectivity places a great weight on the person. Traditional ceremonies and customs might alleviate the difficulty of coping with the confusion of emotional occurences on our own. This is the position of Arnold Gehlen in his book on institutions, *Man, his Nature and Place in the World* (New York: Columbia University Press, 1988), but I doubt whether modernity can offer this avenue for unburdening under normal circumstances. Totalitarian parties of fundamentalist movements do offer some psychological help, but this remedy against headaches kills the patient too, namely the – even shallow – personality of the sufferer.

13 When Hume said that reason ought to be the slave of passion, he did not abandon the teleological model, but reversed it in a pre-Nietzschean fashion. He did not identify the source of teleological constitution (freedom of personality) with reason and adequate knowledge.

14 I do not mean "existentialism," for I do not mean any "ism" here. Every philosophy is a philosophy of existence, in which ethical/moral questions and the possibilities of modern personalities are raised from the perspective of the exister and the "existing thinker." These are the philosophers who are passionately interested in existence.

15 Freud, for example, offered an essentialist map of the human "interior."

16 Friedrich Nietzsche, *Ecce Homo*, trans. Walter Kaufmann (New York: Vintage, 1989).

17 I use this term in Heidegger's understanding of *Geschick*.

18 I have discussed the existential choice and all its variants in several of my books, particularly in *Philosophy of Morals*, *Ethics of Personality*, op. cit. I cannot here give even a brief summary of the main points that I have made in those books.

19 To return to an earlier thought, the most general/universal virtues are courage and justice, the most beautiful is gratitude, and the most sublime is authenticity. The concept of the sublime refers to something "high," and this association is maintained here. Sublimity also indicates the rarity of the phenomenon. Perhaps there are not so many people who have chosen themselves, and authenticity is not the matter of quantity, whereas courage and justice is. There is not enough if there is only one courageous or just person in a modern world, but it is *enough* if there is only one person who has fully lived up to his or her existential choice, who was exclusively pulled by his or her own destiny.

20 This is the model that was first worked out by Kant when he said that no one knows whether anyone at any time has entirely subjected all of his or her maxims to the approval of the Categorical Imperative. Kierkegaard added that since the internal does not appear, we do not know which common man is "the knight of faith." See Immanuel Kant, *Critique of Practical Judgment*, trans. Mary Gregor (Cambridge, UK: Cambridge University Press, 1997) and Søren Kierkegaard, *Fear and Trembling*, trans. Howard V. and Edna H. Hong (Princeton, NJ: Princeton University Press, 1983).

21 In his book *Between Facts and Norms*, trans. William Rehg (Cambridge, MA: MIT Press, 1996), Habermas makes a distinction between ethical, legal, and moral discourses.

22 I have borrowed this expression from Hegel and Kierkegaard.

23 Nonviolent acts can still be exercises of power.

24 I do not discuss argumentation in the sciences here, particularly not in the natural or hard sciences.

25 The surface is, however, not just a mask. One must take it seriously; one must prepare a powerful argument, even if something else decides.

26 I already discussed argumentation in the chapter on the three concepts of culture, and in the chapter on civilization. Here I do it from a different perspective.

27 One cannot prove with arguments to a child that to torture a cat is wrong, because he or she will be able to counter-argue. In ancient times, one did not argue. One said, "Obey God's command" or "Just do what I say; follow my command." But in our age one needs to argue, and this is not done in vain. For even if the argument can be countered by new arguments, there can be a stage where the boy or girl will give up because the logic of the heart (faith) will encourage him to do so.

28 This is the point that I accept from the philosophy of Apel and Habermas.

29 Of course, modern men can also believe in the absurd. But they will not then prove it by rational arguments.

30 One always reasons about means occasionally or regularly.

31 I do not mean thereby that we cannot carry responsibility for arguing in this way or that way. Sometimes we do. We are also co-responsible in advising someone.

Selected Bibliography

Adorno, Theodor and Max Horkheimer, *Dialectic of Enlightenment* (New York: Herder & Herder, 1972).

Angyalosi, Gergely, *Roland Barthes, a semleges profeta/Roland Barthes, the Neutral Prophet* (Budapest: Osiris, 1996).

Arendt, Hannah, *Between Past and Future: Eight Exercises in Political Thought* (New York: Viking Press, 1968).

——, *Rahel Varnhagen: The Life of a Jewish Woman*, trans. Richard and Clara Winston (New York: Harcourt Brace Jovanovich, 1974).

Aristotle, *The Basic Works of Aristotle*, ed. Richard McKeon (New York: Random House, 1941).

——, *Metaphysics*, trans. Hippocrates G. Apostle (Grinnell, IA: Peripatetic Press, 1979).

——, *Physics*, trans. Hippocrates G. Apostle (Grinnell, IA: Peripatetic Press, 1980).

——, *The Politics*, trans. Carnes Lord (Chicago: University of Chicago Press, 1984).

Bacon, Francis, *Novum Organum* (Chicago: Encyclopaedia Britannica, 1952).

Barthes, Roland, *A Lover's Discourse: Fragments (Fragments d'un Discours Amoureaux)*, trans. Richard Howard (New York: Hill and Wang, 1978).

Baumann, Zygmunt, *Legislators and Interpreters* (Oxford: Blackwell, 1987).

——, *Modernity and the Holocaust* (Oxford: Polity Press, 1990).

Beilharz, Peter, Gillian Robinson, and John Rundell (eds.), *Between Totalitarianism and Postmodernity* (Cambridge, MA: MIT Press, 1992).

Berlin, Isaiah, *Four Essays on Liberty* (New York: Oxford University Press, 1970).

Bernstein, Richard J., *Philosophical Profiles* (Philadelphia: University of Pennsylvania Press, 1986).

Bloom, Harold, *The Western Canon* (New York: Harcourt Brace Jovanovich, 1994).

Blumenberg, Hans, *Work on Myths* (Cambridge, MA: MIT Press, 1985).

Castoriadis, Cornelius, *The Imaginary Institutions of Society* (Cambridge: Polity Press, 1987).

Carroll, John, *Puritan, Paranoid, Remissive: a sociology of modern culture* (London: Routledge & Kegan Paul, 1977).

Descartes, René, *Philosophical Letters*, trans. and ed. Anthony Kenny (Minneapolis: University of Minnesota Press, 1970).

——, *The Philosophical Writings of Descartes*, trans. J. Cottingham, R. Stoothoff, and D. Murdoch, vol. 2 (Cambridge: Cambridge University Press, 1985).

Derrida, Jacques, *The Politics of Friendship*, trans. George Collins (London: Verso, 1997).

——, *Specters of Marx*, trans. Peggy Kamuf (New York: Routledge, 1994).

Elias, Norbert, *The Civilising Process*, trans. Edmund Jephcott (New York: Urizen Books, 1978).

Fehér, Ferenc, "The evergreen Tocqueville," *Thesis Eleven*, 42 (1995).

——, *The Frozen Revolution* (New York: Cambridge University Press, 1987).

Fehér, Ferenc and Agnes Heller, *Biopolitics* (Brookfield, VT: Avebury, 1994).

——, *Grandeur and Twilight of Radical Universalism* (New Brunswick: Transaction Publishers, 1991).

——, *The Pendulum of Modernity* (Budapest: Osiris, 1994).

——, *The Postmodern Political Condition* (Oxford: Polity Press, 1988).

Fehér, Ferenc, Agnes Heller, and György Markus, *Dictatorship Over Needs* (New York: St. Martin's Press, 1983).

Finkielkraut, Alain, *The Defeat of the Mind* (New York: Columbia University Press, 1995).

Friedlander, Saul, *The Jews in European History: Seven Lectures*, ed. Wolfgang Beck (Cincinnati: Hebrew Union College Press, in association with the Leo Baeck Institute, New York, 1994).

Foucault, Michel, *Discipline and Punish*, trans. Alan Sheridan (New York: Vintage, 1979).

——, *History of Sexuality*, 2 vols, trans. Robert Hurley (New York: Pantheon, 1978).

Freud, Sigmund, *The Ego and the Id*, trans. Joan Riviere and ed. James Strachey (New York: W. W. Norton, 1965).

——, *The New Introductory Lectures on Psychoanalysis*, trans. James Strachey (New York and London: W. W. Norton, 1965).

Gehlen, Arnold, *Man, his Nature and Place in the World* (New York: Columbia University Press, 1988).

Giddens, Anthony, *The Consequences of Modernity* (Oxford: Polity Press, 1990).

Goffman, Erving, *Forms of Talk* (Philadelphia: University of Pennsylvania Press, 1981).

——, *Presentation of the Self in Everyday Life* (Garden City, NY: Doubleday, 1959).

Goldhagen, Daniel, *Hitler's Willing Executions: Ordinary Germans and the Holocaust* (New York: Humanities Press, 1964).

Goldmann, Lucien, *The Hidden God*, trans. Philip Thrody (New York: Humanities Press, 1964).

Habermas, Jürgen, *Between Facts and Norms*, trans. William Rehg (Cambridge, MA: MIT Press, 1996).

Habermas, Jürgen, *The Philosophical Discourse of Modernity* (Cambridge, MA: MIT Press, 1987).

——, *The Structural Transformation of the Public Sphere: An Inquiry into a Category of Bourgeois Society*, trans. Thomas Burger, with the assistance of Frederick Laurence (Cambridge, MA: MIT Press, 1989).

——, *The Theory of Communicative Action*, 2 vols, trans. Thomas McCarthy (Boston: Beacon Press, 1984–7).

Hegel, G. W. F., *Encyclopaedia of Logic* (Indianapolis: Hackett, 1991).

——, *Lectures on the Philosophy of Religion*, vol. 2, trans. R. F. Brown, P. C. Hodgson, and J. M. Steward, with the assistance of J. P. Fitzer and H. S. Harris (Berkeley: University of California Press, 1984).

——, *Phenomenology of Spirit*, trans. A. V. Miller (Oxford: Oxford University Press, 1977).

——, *Philosophy of History*, trans. J. Sibree (Chicago: University of Chicago Press, 1952).

——, *Philosophy of Right*, trans. T. M. Knox (Chicago: University of Chicago Press, 1952).

Heidegger, Martin, *Basic Writings* (New York: Harper & Row, 1977).

——, *Being and Time*, trans. John Macquarrie and Edward Robinson (New York: Harper, 1962).

——, "Das Ge-Stell," *Bremer und Freiburger Vortrage Gesamtausgabe*. 78 Klostermann, 1994, p. 34.

——, *Parmenides* (Frankfurt am Main: Klostermann, 1982).

Heller, Agnes, *Beyond Justice* (Oxford and Cambridge, MA: Blackwell, 1987).

——, *Can Modernity Survive?* (Berkeley: University of California Press, 1990).

——, *An Ethics of Personality* (Cambridge, MA: Blackwell, 1996).

——, *Everyday Life*, trans. G. L. Campbell (Boston: Routledge & Kegan Paul, 1974).

——, "Freedom and equality of Kant's *Critique of Judgment*," in *Eletkepes-e a modernitas* (Latin Betuk, 1997; in Hungarian).

——, "The Great Republic," *Praxis International* (Oxford) 5:1, April 1985.

——, "The human condition," in *General Ethics* (Oxford and Cambridge, MA: Blackwell, 1993).

——, *Leibniz egzisztencialis metafizikaja* (Budapest: Kossuthl, 1995).

——, *A Philosophy of History in Fragments* (Oxford and Cambridge, MA: Blackwell, 1993).

——, *A Philosophy of Morals* (Oxford and Cambridge, MA: Blackwell, 1990).

——, *The Power of Shame: A Rational Perspective* (Boston: Routledge & Kegan Paul, 1985).

——, *Radical Philosophy* (London: Routledge & Kegan Paul, 1985).

——, *Renaissance Man* (Boston: Routledge & Kegan Paul, 1978).

——, *The Stranger/Az idegen* (Budapest: Mult es Jovo, 1997).

——, *A Theory of History* (Boston: Routledge & Kegan Paul, 1982).

——, "Where are we at home?" *Thesis Eleven*, no. 41 (1995).

Heller, Agnes, "Why Hannah Arendt now?" in *The Stranger/Az idegen* (Budapest: Mult es Jovo, 1997).

Jay, Martin, *Force Field* (New York: Routledge, 1993).

Jonas, Hans, *The Gnostic Religion: The Message of the Alien God and the Beginnings of Christianity* (Boston: Beacon Press, 1963).

Kant, Immanuel, *Anthropology From a Pragmatic Point of View*, trans. Mary J. Gregor (The Hague: Martinus Nijhoff, 1974).

———, *Critique of Judgment*, trans. J. H. Bernard (New York: Hafner, 1951).

———, *Critique of Practical Reason*, trans. Mary Gregor (Cambridge: Cambridge University Press, 1997).

———, *Groundwork to the Metaphysics of Morals*, trans. H. J. Paton (New York: Harper & Row, 1964).

———, *Religion Within the Limits of Reason Alone* (LaSalle, IL: Open Court Publishing, 1960).

Kierkegaard, Søren, *Concluding Unscientific Postscript to Philosophical Fragments*, trans. Howard V. and Edna H. Hong (Princeton, NJ: Princeton University Press, 1992).

———, *Either/Or*, vol. 1, trans. Howard V. and Edna H. Hong (Princeton, NJ: Princeton University Press, 1987).

———, *Fear and Trembling*, trans. Howard V. and Edna H. Hong (Princeton, NJ: Princeton University Press, 1983).

———, *The Present Age, and Of the Difference Between a Genius and an Apostle*, trans. Alexander Dru (New York: Harper & Row, 1962).

Luhmann, Niklas, *Social Systems*, trans. John Bednarz, Jr., with Dirk Baecker (Stanford, CA: Stanford University Press, 1995).

Lukács, György, *History of Class Consciousness*, trans. Rodney Livingstone (Cambridge, MA: MIT Press, 1971).

———, *Soul and Form*, trans. Anna Bostock (Cambridge, MA: MIT Press, 1974).

———, *The Theory of the Novel*, trans. Anna Bostock (Cambridge. MA: MIT Press, 1971).

Lyotard, Jean François, *The Postmodern Condition* (Minneapolis: University of Minnesota Press, 1984).

MacIntyre, Alisdair, *After Virtue* (Notre Dame: University of Notre Dame Press, 1984).

———, *Whose Justice? Which Rationality?* (Notre Dame: University of Notre Dame Press, 1988).

Marcuse, Herbert, *One Dimensional Man* (Boston: Beacon Press, 1964).

Markus, György, *Language and Production: a critique of paradigms* (Dordrecht and Boston: D. Reidel/Hingham, MA: Kluwer Academic, 1986).

———, *Marxism and "Anthropology"* (Assen: Van Gorcum, 1978).

Marx, Karl, *Critique of the Gotha Programme* (International Publishers, 1938).

———, *Grundrisse*, ed. David McLellan (London: Macmillan, 1971).

———, "Introduction to a critique of political economy," in Karl Marx and Friedrich Engels, *The German Ideology*, trans. C. J. Arthur (New York: International Publishers, 1972).

Marx, Karl, *The Paris Commune* (New York: New York Labor News Company, 1945).

Molière, *The Bourgeois Gentilhomme*, trans. Curtis Hidden Page (New York & London: G. P. Putnam's Sons, 1908).

Montesquieu, Charles de Secondat, *The Spirit of the Laws*, trans. and ed. Anne Cohler, Basia Miller, and Harold Stone (Cambridge: Cambridge University Press, 1989).

Nietzsche, Friedrich, *Beyond Good and Evil*, trans. Walter Kaufmann (New York: Vintage, 1989).

——, *Ecce Homo*, trans. Walter Kaufmann (New York: Vintage, 1989).

——, *On the Genealogy of Morals*, trans. Walter Kaufmann (New York: Vintage, 1969).

Plato, *The Collected Dialogues of Plato*, ed. Edith Hamilton and Huntington Cairns (Princeton, NJ: Princeton University Press, 1961).

Plotinus, *Enneads*, trans. Stephen MacKenna (London: Penguin, 1991).

Pocock, J. G. A., *The Machiavellian Moment* (Princeton, NJ: Princeton University Press, 1979).

Roiphe, Katie, *The Morning After: Sex, Fear, and Feminism on Campus* (Boston: Little, Brown, 1993).

Rousseau, Jean-Jacques, *The Basic Political Writings*, trans. Donald Cress (Indianapolis: Hackett, 1987).

——, *Emile*, trans. Allen Bloom (New York: Basic Books, 1979).

——, *La Nouvelle Heloise*, trans. and abridged Judith H. McDowell (University Park: Pennsylvania State University Press, 1968).

Rugasi, Gyula, *Orok Romokon (On the Eternal Ruins)* (Latin Betuk, 1996).

——, "The restoration of the church," *Vilagossag*, 12 (1996), 53.

Sartre, Jean-Paul, *Being and Nothingness: An Essay in Phenomenological Ontology*, trans. Hazel E. Barnes (New York: Citadel, 1964).

Scheler, Max Ferdinand, *Formalism in Ethics and Non-formal Ethics of Values*, trans. Manfred Frings and Roger Funk (Evanston, IL: Northwestern University Press, 1973).

Schmitt, Carl, *Political Theology* (Cambridge, MA: MIT Press, 1985).

Schutz, Alfred, *The Phenomenology of the Social World*, trans. George Walsh and Frederick Lehnert (Evanston, IL: Northwestern University Press, 1967).

Shakespeare, William, *The Life of Timon of Athens*, ed. J. C. Maxwell (Cambridge: Cambridge University Press, 1957).

——, *The Tragedy of Coriolanus*, ed. Tucker Brooke (New Haven: Yale University Press, 1924).

Sorel, George, *On Violence* (Glencoe, IL: Free Press, 1950).

Spengler, Oswald, *The Decline of the West*, trans. Charles Francis Atkinson (New York: A. A. Knopf, 1926–8).

Strauss, Leo, *Liberalism, Ancient and Modern* (Ithaca, NY: Cornell University Press, 1989).

Taylor, Charles, *Multiculturalism and "The Politics of Recognition": An Essay*, ed. with commentary by Amy Gutman (Princeton, NJ: Princeton University Press, 1992).

Tönnies, Ferdinand, *Community and Society*, trans. Charles P. Loomis (East Lansing: Michigan State University Press, 1957).

Tolstoy, Leo, *The Resurrection*, trans. Louise Mande (Oxford: Oxford University Press, 1994).

Touraine, Alain, *Critique of Modernity*, trans. D. Macey (Cambridge: Blackwell, 1995).

Vajda, Mihaly, *A Fasimusrol* (Budapest: Osiris, 1993).

———, *Nem az Orokkevalosagnak (No[t] for Eternity)* (Budapest: Osiris, 1997).

———, *The Postmodern Heidegger* (Budapest: Szazedueg, 1994).

Vattimo, Gianni, *The Transparent Society* (Oxford: Polity Press, 1988).

Weber, Max, *Protestant Ethic and the Spirit of Capitalism*, trans. Talcott Parsons (London: HarperCollins Academic, 1991).

Wellmer, Albrecht, *The Persistence of Modernity* (Oxford: Polity Press, 1991).

Wittgenstein, Ludwig, *Notebooks 1914–1916*, 2nd edn., ed. G. H. Wright and G. E. M. Anscombe, trans. G. E. M. Anscombe (Chicago: University of Chicago Press, 1961).

———, *Tractatus Logico-Philosophicus*, trans. C. K. Ogden (London and New York: Routledge, 1922).

Index